NOT BY PAUL ALONE

Not By Paul Alone

The Formation of the Catholic Epistle Collection and the Christian Canon

David R. Nienhuis

BAYLOR UNIVERSITY PRESS

Cover design by Donna Haberstaat

Library of Congress Cataloging-in-Publication Data

Nienhuis, David R., 1968-
  Not by Paul alone : the formation of the catholic epistle collection and the Christian canon / David R. Nienhuis.
     p. cm.
  Includes bibliographical references and index.
  ISBN 978-1-932792-71-3 (cloth/hardcover : alk. paper)
  1. Bible. N.T. James--Criticism, interpretation, etc. 2. Bible--Canon. I. Title.

  BS2785.52.N54 2007
  227'.9106--dc22
                                    2006039309

For Teresa

A faithful friend is a sturdy shelter; he that has found one has found a treasure.
Sirach 6:14

CONTENTS

FOREWORD

The so-called "Catholic Epistles"—James, 1 and 2 Peter, 1, 2 and 3 John, and Jude—are usually studied in isolation from each other. Of course, obvious points of contact are duly noted and discussed. 2 Peter is intended as a sequel to 1 Peter and is probably dependent on Jude; 2 and 3 John serve as appendices to 1 John; and there are striking parallels between the three major letters in the collection (James, 1 Peter, 1 John), parallels commonly explained by appeal to shared parenetic tradition. Otherwise, the individual letters are normally interpreted without reference either to each other or to the later canonical process of forming them into a single collection. Fourth-century canonizers created the canonical collection out of texts that simply happened to be in circulation within the catholic church: or so it is assumed. On this model, the coherence thus imposed on these texts is artificial and secondary, and the interpretative task is to restore to each text its original independence and autonomy. We do not need to interpret James in the light of 1 Peter any more than we should interpret Matthew in the light of John; the various canonical collections are of little or no interpretative significance.

This anticanonical model is presupposed by scholars who otherwise differ considerably in their estimate of the individual texts. It unites those who believe that the letter of James was indeed written by the brother of the Lord, perhaps in Jerusalem in the early 40s C.E., and those who hold it to be a late first-century pseudepigraph. Whatever their other differences, it does not occur to either party to dissent from the consensus that James should be read on its own terms, without reference to its later canonical context.

In the present book, David Nienhuis argues persuasively that this taken-for-granted model is seriously deficient on both historical and literary grounds. Nienhuis proposes a paradigm shift in which the distinction between the "original" author and the "later" canonizer is abolished at a stroke. The Catholic Epistles collection is actually the work of the mid- or late second-century author of the letter of James, who seeks to forge a single collection dominated by the venerable figures of the "pillar" apostles, James, Peter and John—a collection which would serve as a canonical counterbalance to the Pauline dominance whose dangers had been exposed by Marcionism. Two crucial arguments are presented for the late dating, one negative and the other positive. First, there is no clear reference to the letter of James prior to Origen, writing in the first half of the third century. In other words, there is no external evidence that the letter existed prior to the mid- or late second century (chapter 1). Second, the "implied author" of the letter of James has significant traits in common with the James-image of other second- or third-century texts (chapter 2). The thesis about the intended canonical role is developed by way of a study of intertextual relationships between James, 1 Peter, 1 John, and the letter to the Romans (chapter 3). Among other things, wholly new light is shed on the vexed Paul-and-James issue.

Late datings of New Testament texts are often regarded as unacceptably "radical" by those for whom a first-century dating seems to be an indispensable prerequisite for authentic canonical status. If Nienhuis's hypothesis is "radical," however, it is also profoundly "catholic"—in the sense that it insists that the production of the New Testament texts cannot ultimately be detached from their reception as authoritative within the community of faith. This book makes a brilliant and original and (to my mind) convincing contribution to the current attempt to rethink the relationship between text and community, Scripture, and church.

This work first saw the light of day as a doctoral thesis submitted to the University of Aberdeen in the summer of 2004. As supervisor of this thesis, I would like to put it on record that its starting-point was an interest in intertextual relationships within the Catholic Epistles collection (chapter 3), which long predated the development of the historical hypothesis (chapters 1–2). There was even an initial prejudice against the assumption that literary relationships were susceptible to historical explanations. If the historical hypothesis eventually took over the entire project, this was because it proved so unexpectedly cogent and illuminating —both to its author and to his supervisor. This was genuinely a piece of research, and the outcome was neither foreseen nor foreseeable at the outset.

It is a pleasure and an honor to introduce David Nienhuis's exceptional work in its published form. I look forward to the debate that it is sure to generate.

Francis Watson
University of Aberdeen
August 2006

Acknowledgments

Writing acknowledgments for one's very first book is an emotionally overwhelming task. How do I rightly give thanks for the complex web of supportive mentors, friends, and family who have held me up over the years during which this project developed from an amorphous idea, to a Ph.D. dissertation, and now to this book?

I suppose it makes the most sense for me to begin by thanking Professor Francis Watson of the University of Aberdeen, who supervised my Ph.D. thesis. This book is really just a lightly revised version of the work I completed under his tutelage. Were it not for his insightful critique, endless creativity, and constant encouragement, I would not have had the courage to pursue the line of research presented here. Francis is producing some of the most important studies in biblical scholarship today, and I count it a great privilege to have had the opportunity to work under his direction.

Numerous others played central roles in getting me to the point of writing the dissertation in the first place. I must begin by mentioning my undergraduate academic mentor and friend, Dr. Les Steele of Seattle Pacific University, who was the first to inspire in me a love of theological learning. Les took me under his wing my freshman year of college and has since gone on to play an instrumental role in helping me to realize my vocation as a professor, initially by affording me my first teaching opportunity, and then by helping to orchestrate the pursuit of doctoral studies that eventually led to the writing of this book. I will be forever grateful for the influence he has had on my life.

Dr. Rob Wall was my first biblical studies professor, and anyone who reads this book will realize that I am standing partly on his shoulders. It was he who first introduced me to canonical approaches to Scripture, and his personal and professional support in the years since has been a great blessing to me. Along with Rob I want to thank all of my wonderful colleagues in the School of Theology at Seattle Pacific University, especially Drs. Bob Drovdahl and Rick Steele whose support and friendship has been unfailing.

A number of readers provided helpful comments along the way. Special thanks go to Dr. Pete Williams of the University of Aberdeen and Professor Judith Lieu of Kings College, London, whose recommended revisions for the Ph.D. dissertation went a long way to help sharpen and clarify my argument. I also want to thank Dr. Carey Newman of Baylor University Press for showing early interest in my research and for working so charitably with me in the publication of this book. My longtime friend Shawn Thomas has been a great conversation partner over the final editing process, and his willingness to read, correct, and comment on the manuscript is hugely appreciated. Also, I want to be sure to include a word of thanks to my brother Bill Nienhuis and his colleagues at Logos Bible Software, whose superb electronic study resources have long been an immense help in my analysis of the biblical text.

A final word of thanks goes to all the loving friends and family members who endure my many shortcomings with patience and grace. Chief among them is my best friend and companion, Teresa Osborn, to whom this book is dedicated. You are a sturdy shelter, Teresa, and I will thank God always for your presence in my life.

No peevish winter wind shall chill
No sullen tropic sun shall wither
The roses in the rose-garden which is ours and ours only[*]

---

[*] T. S. Eliot, "Dedication to My Wife," in *Collected Poems, 1909–1962* (New York: Harcourt, 1963), 221.

Abbreviations

1. Ancient Texts

Abr.	Philo, *De Abrahamo* (*On Abraham*)
Act Paul	*Acts of Paul*
Ad. Aut.	Theophilus of Antioch, *Ad Autolycum* (*To Autolycus*)
Adum.	Clement of Alexandria, *Adumbrationes in epistolas catholicas* (*Comments on the Catholic Epistles*, Cassiodorus)
Adv. Haer.	Irenaeus, *Adversus haereses* (*Against Heresies*)
Adv. Jud.	Tertullian, *Adversus Judaeos* (*Against the Jews*)
Adv. Marc.	Tertullian, *Adversus Marcionem* (*Against Marcion*)
Adv. Prax.	Tertullian, *Adversus Praxean* (*Against Praxeas*)
Ant.	Josephus, *The Antiquities of the Jews*
1–2 Apoc.	*1–2 Apocalypse of James*
Apoc. Abr.	*Apocalypse of Abraham*
Apoc. Pet.	*Apocalypse of Peter*
Apocr.	*Apocryphon of James*
As. Mos.	*Assumption of Moses*
2 Bar.	*2 Baruch*
b. San.	*Sanhedrin*
Barn.	*Letter of Barnabas*
Carm.	Gregory of Nazianzus, *Carmina*
Carn.	Tertullian, *De carne Christi* (*On the Flesh of Christ*)

catech.	Cyril of Jerusalem, "Catecheses"
Cels.	Origen, *Contra Celsus*
Cher.	Philo, *De cheribum* (*On the Cheribum*)
1 Clem.	*First Letter of Clement*
Comm. Jo.	Origen, *Commentary on John*
Comm. Matt.	Origen, *Commentary on Matthew*
Comm. Rom.	Origen, *Commentary on Romans*
Conf.	Philo, *De confusione linguarum* (*On the Confusion of Tongues*)
Deus.	Philo, *Quod deus sit immutabilis* (*That God is Unchangeable*)
Dial.	Justin, *Dialogus cum Tryphone* (*Dialogue with Trypho*)
Dom. or.	Cyprian, *De Dominica oratione* (*On the Lord's Prayer*)
Eleem.	Cyprian, *De opera et eleemosynis* (*On Works and Almsgiving*)
1 En.	*1 Enoch*
Ep.	*Epistula*
1–2 Esdr.	*1–2 Esdras*
Exhort.	Cyprian, *De Exhortatio Martyrium* (*Exhortation to Martyrdom*)
Fid. op.	Augustine, *De Fide et Operibus* (*On Faith and Works*)
Fort.	Cyprian, *Ad Fortunatum* (*To Fortunatus: Exhortation to Martyrdom*)
Fr. Luc.	Origen, *Fragments on Luke*
Gen. R.	*Genesis Rabba*
Gos. Heb.	*Gospel of the Hebrews*
Gos. Thom.	*Gospel of Thomas*
Hab. Virg.	Cyprian, *De habitu virginum* (*On the Dress of Virgins*)
Haer.	Hippolytus, *Refutio omnium haeresium* (*Refutation of All Heresies*)
Herm.	*Shepherd of Hermas*
Herm. Mand.	*Shepherd of Hermas, Mandate(s)*
Herm. Sim.	*Shepherd of Hermas, Similitude(s)*
Herm. Vis.	*Shepherd of hermas, Vision(s)*
Hist. Eccl.	Eusebius, *Historia Ecclesiastica* (*Ecclesiastical History*)
Hom. Exod.	Origen, *Homiliae in Exodum*
Hom. Jer.	Origen, *Homiliae in Jeremiam*
Hom. Josh.	Origen, *Homiliae in Joshuam*
Hom. Lev.	Origen, *Homiliae in Leviticum*
Hom. Num.	Origen, *Homiliae in Numeros*
Hyp.	Clement of Alexandria, *Hypotyposeis* (*Outlines*)
Ieiun.	Tertullian, *De Ieiuniis* (*On Fasting*)
Ign. *Eph.*	Ignatius, *To the Ephesians*
Ign. *Magn.*	Ignatius, *To the Magnesians*
Ign. *Pol.*	Ignatius, *To Polycarp*
Ign. *Rom.*	Ignatius, *To the Romans*
Ign. *Phld.*	Ignatius, *To the Philadelphians*
Ign. *Smyrn.*	Ignatius, *To the Smyrnaeans*
Ign. *Trall.*	Ignatius, *To the Trallians*

Jdt	Judith
Jub.	*Jubilees*
Life	Josephus, *The Life of Josephus*
1–4 Macc	1–4 Maccabees
m. Kidd	*Mishna Kiddushin*
Mart. Pol.	*Martydom of Polycarp*
Mort.	Cyprian, *De Mortalis* (*On Mortality*)
Mut.	Philo, *De mutatione nominum* (*On the Change of Names*)
Odes Sol.	*Odes of Solomon*
Paed.	Clement of Alexandria, *Paedagogus*
Pan.	Epiphanius, *Panarion* (*Adversus haereses*) (*Refutation of All Heresies*)
Pat.	Cyprian, *De bono patientiae* (*The Advantage of Patience*)
Praescr.	Tertullian, *De praescriptione haereticorum* (*Prescription against Heretics*)
Princ.	Origen, *De Principiis* (*On First Principles*)
Prob.	Philo, *Quod omnis probus liber sit* (*That Every Good Person is Free*)
Prot. Jas.	*Protevangelium of James*
Pss. Sol.	*Psalms of Solomon*
Pud.	Tertullian, *De Pudicia* (*On Modesty*)
Quis. div.	Clement of Alexandria, *Quis dives salvetur?* (*Salvation of the Rich*)
Scorp.	Tertullian, *Scorpiace* (*Antidote for the Scorpion's Sting*)
Sel. Deut.	Origen, *Selecta in Deuteronomium*
Sel. Ps.	Origen, *Selecta in Psalmos*
Sent.	Cyprian, *Sententiae LXXXVII episcoporum*
Sib. Or.	*Sibylline Oracles*
Sir	Sirach
Sobr.	Philo, *De sobrietate* (*On Sobriety*)
Strom.	Clement of Alexandria, *Stromata* (*Miscellanies*)
Symb.	Rufinus, *Commentarius in symbolum apostolorum* (*Commentary on the Apostles' Creed*)
T. Abr.	*Testament of Abraham*
T. Mos.	*Testament of Moses*
T. Naph	*Testament of Naphtali*
Test.	Cyprian, *Ad Quirinum testimonia adversus Judaeos* (*To Quirinus: Testimonies against the Jews*)
Tob.	*Tobit*
Unit. eccl.	Cyprian, *De catholicae ecclesiae unitate* (*The Unity of the Catholic Church*)
Vir. ill.	Jerome, *Liber de viris illustribus* (*Lives of Illustrious Men*)
Wis	Wisdom of Solomon
Zel. liv.	Cyprian, *De zelo et livore* (*On Jealousy and Envy*)

2. Modern Commentaries, Periodicals, Reference Works, and Serials

ABC	Anchor Bible Commentary
ABD	*Anchor Bible Dictionary*
ABRL	Anchor Bible Reference Library
ACW	Ancient Christian Writers
AJT	*American Journal of Theology*
AnBib	Analecta biblica
ANF	*Ante-Nicene Fathers*
ANRW	*Aufstieg und Niedergang der römischen Welt*
ANTF	Arbeiten zur neutestamentlichen Textforschung
APQ	*American Philosophical Quarterly*
BCNH	*Bibliothèque Copte de Nag Hammadi*
BDAG	Bauer, W., F. W. Danker, F. Arndt, and F. W. Gingrich, *Greek-English Lexicon of the New Testament and Other Early Christian Literature*. 3rd ed. Chicago, 1999.
BETL	Bibliotheca ephemeridum theologicarum lovaniensium
BibInt	*Biblical Interpretation*
BibSac	*Biblia Sacra*
BJRL	*Bulletin of John Rylands University Library of Manchester*
BNTC	Black's New Testament Commentary
BRev	*Bible Review*
BWANT	Beiträge zur Wissenschaft vom Alten und Neuen Testament
CBC	Cambridge Bible Commentary
CBQ	*Catholic Biblical Quarterly*
CCSL	Corpus Christianorum Series latina
CE	Catholic Epistle
CH	*Church History*
CSCO	Corpus scriptorum christianorum orientalium
CSEL	Corpus scriptorum ecclesiasticorum latinorum
CurTM	*Currents in Theology and Mission*
DLNT	*Dictionary of the Later New Testament and its Developments*
ETL	*Ephemerides theologicae louvanienses*
EvQ	*Evangelical Quarterly*
ExAud	*Ex Auditu*
Exp	*Expositor*
ExpTim	*Expository Times*
FB	Forschung zur Bibel
FC	Fathers of the Church
FRLANT	Forschungen zur Religion und Literatur des Alten und Neuen Testaments
GCS	Die griechischen christlichen Schriftsteller der ersten Jahrhunderte

GCSNF	Die griechischen christlichen Schriftsteller der ersten Jahrhun derte Neue Folge
HNT	Handbuch zum Neuen Testament
HTR	*Harvard Theological Review*
IBS	*Irish Biblical Studies*
ICC	International Critical Commentary
JBL	*Journal of Biblical Literature*
JETS	*Journal of the Evangelical Theological Society*
JR	*Journal of Religion*
JSNTSup	Journal for the Study of the New Testament Supplement Series
JTS	*Journal of Theological Studies*
LCC	Library of Christian Classics
LCL	Loeb Classical Library
LSJ	Liddell, H. G., R. Scott, H. S. Jones, *A Greek-English Lexicon*, 9th ed. with revised supplement Oxford, 1996.
MNTC	Moffatt New Testament Commentary
NCBC	New Century Bible Commentary
Neot	*Neotestamentica*
NHS	Nag Hammadi Studies
NIB	*The New Interpreter's Bible*
NIBCNT	New International Biblical Commentary on the New Testament
NICNT	New International Commentary on the New Testament
NIGTC	New International Greek Testament Commentary
NovT	*Novum Testamentum*
NovTSup	Novum Testamentum Supplements
NPNF[1]	*Nicene Post-Nicene Fathers,* Series 1
NPNF[2]	*Nicene Post-Nicene Fathers,* Series 2
NT	New Testament
NTD	Das Neue Testament Deutsch
NTS	*New Testament Studies*
OED	*The Oxford English Dictionary*
OT	Old Testament
PBR	*Patristic and Byzantine Review*
PG	J. Migne, ed., *Patrologia Graeca*
PL	J. Migne, ed., *Patrologia Latina*
PNTC	*Pillar New Testament Commentary*
PTS	Patristische Texte und Studien
RB	*Review Biblique*
SB	Sources bibliques
SBLSBS	Society of Biblical Literature Sources for Biblical Study
SC	Sources chrétiennes
SE	*Studia Evangelica*
SecCent	*Second Century*

SJT	*Scottish Journal of Theology*
SNTSMS	Society for New Testament Studies Monograph Series
SNTSU	Studien zum Neuen Testament und seiner Umwelt
SP	Sacra Pagina
StudBib	Studia Biblica
TDNT	*Theological Dictionary of the New Testament*
TLZ	*Theologische Literaturzeitung*
TU	Texte und Untersuchungen
TynBul	*Tyndale Bulletin*
VC	*Vigiliae Christianae*
VL	*Vetus Latina*
WBC	Word Biblical Commentary
WUNT	Wissenschaftliche Untersuchungen zum Neuen Testament
ZNW	*Zeitschrift für die neutestamentliche Wissenschaft*

INTRODUCTION

Sometime in or around the year 413, Augustine of Hippo wrote a treatise entitled *De fide et operibus* in which he articulated one of the earliest reckonings of the logic behind the final form of the NT apostolic letter collection (CSEL 41.33–97).[1] The work addresses contemporary errors associated with a misunderstanding of the relationship between faith and works in the Christian life: the first identified is the tendency of certain groups to justify the sin of schism in their zeal for the moral purity of the community; the second is the tendency for the church to teach only "faith" (by which he means "doctrine") before baptism with the understanding that "works" could be learned thereafter; and the third is the widespread belief that baptized Christians who persisted in sinful habits would nevertheless be saved—"albeit through fire"—in the assumption that it was possible to have a saving faith without the corresponding evidence of a transformed life.

[1] Patristic sources are noted at two levels in this book. For general references, I provide the abbreviated traditional title of the work, followed by the conventional citation numbers, followed by a parenthetical reference to the volume and page number in the critical edition used. When footnoting quotations of texts, I provide the traditional title and citation numbers, followed by a parenthetical reference, which includes the volume and page number of the critical edition as well as the source for the English translation if one was used. In such cases the initial citation will include the name of the translator as well as the book title or series abbreviation, with subsequent citations listing only the series abbreviation or the translator's surname. The reader is asked to consult the extended bibliography of texts and translations found at the end of the book for further information on the resources used in this study. English translations of biblical texts throughout tthis book are drawn from various sources at the discretion of the author.

1

This third error was in Augustine's mind "the most dangerous" (*Fide.* 49 [CSEL 41.9]) and was perpetuated by a "perplexing problem in the writings of the Apostle Paul" (*Fide.* 27 [CSEL 41.69; Ligouri, FC 27.254]).

> Therefore, let us now see what must be torn away from the hearts of the God-fearing to prevent the loss of salvation through a treacherously false security, if, under the illusion that faith alone is sufficient for salvation, they neglect to live a good life and fail by good works to persevere in the way that leads to God. Even in the days of the Apostles certain somewhat obscure statements [*subobscurae sententiae*] of the Apostle Paul were misunderstood,[2] and some thought he was saying this: 'Let us now do evil that good may come from it' [Rom 3:8] because he said: 'Now the law intervened that the offense might abound. But where the offense has abounded, grace has abounded yet more' [Rom 5:20]. . . . Since this problem is by no means new and had already arisen at the time of the Apostles, other apostolic letters of Peter, John, James and Jude are deliberately aimed against the argument I have been refuting and firmly uphold the doctrine that faith does not avail without good works [*fidem sine operibus non prodesse*]. (*Fide.* 21 [CSEL 41.61–62; FC 27.246–48])

Ending as it does with an allusion to the faith and works discussion of James 2, the essay proceeds by way of an intertextual reading of the apostolic letters, balancing passages from Paul with those of James, Peter, John, and Jude in order to arrive at a wholly apostolic understanding of faith and works, one that is properly informed by the entire apostolic witness and not by Paul alone. Augustine's primary Pauline text was Galatians 5:6, which insists on the priority of "faith working through love." It is repeated ten times, woven together with at least twenty-nine references to passages in James, 1–2 Peter, 1–3 John, and Jude. Peter "urged his readers to holiness in living and character" (*Fide.* 22 [CSEL 41.62; FC 27.248]), says Augustine, while "James was so severely annoyed with those who held that faith without works avails to salvation that he compared them to evil spirits" (*Fide.* 23 [CSEL 41.64.6–10; FC 27.249]). As for those Pauline passages that suggest one can be saved without a change of life, "another interpretation assuredly must be sought for them, and these expressions of the Apostle Paul must be counted among the passages in his writings which Peter says are difficult to understand and which men must not distort to their own destruction" (*Fide.* 26 [CSEL 41.68.18–22; FC 27.253]; cf. 2 Pet 3:16).

Though Augustine was apparently of a rather confident opinion regarding the coherence and orienting purpose of the non-Pauline letter collection traditionally known as the Catholic Epistles (hereafter "CE"), contemporary biblical scholarship appears to be far less sure. Indeed, the modern scholarly privileging of historical origins as the locus of textual meaning has led to the insistence that the subsequent collection of texts has little to no hermeneutical value. Since the rise of the Tübingen School, the standard historical-critical account has assumed that the ecclesial

---

[2] Given the appeal to 2 Peter 3:16-17 that follows later in the argument, it seems likely that Augustine is alluding to that passage in this context.

construction of the biblical canon tore these texts from their original context and redacted them to produce an artificial unity, one designed to mask the more unstable, conflictual diversity of the earliest Christian church. Over a century ago, Franz Overbeck offered a classic statement in regard to the effect this construction had on the interpretation of biblical texts:

> It is in the nature of all canonization to make its objects unknowable, and one can also say of all the writings of our New Testament that at the moment of their canonization they ceased to be understood. They have been transposed into the higher sphere of an eternal norm for the church, not without a dense veil having been spread over their origin, their original relationships and their original meaning.[3]

Canonization placed a veil over the "original" (and therefore "actual") meaning of the individual writings. Such attitudes regarding the distorting effect of canonization are far from outdated. More recently, Gerd Luedemann asserted,

> A canonical understanding and a historical understanding are mutually exclusive. . . . I can only regard "canonical criticism" without previous historical reconstruction as an error, since its representatives do not respect the authors of the original biblical documents sufficiently.[4]

According to this reckoning, Augustine's understanding of the function of the CE is erroneous, since it was offered without previous historical reconstruction; it was based simply on an assumption generated from the intertextual relations of the canonical letters themselves. In order to "respect the authors of the original biblical documents sufficiently," however, modern historical critical methodologies have insisted that the canon be deconstructed, its texts analyzed "on their own terms" according to "their own historical context" (that is, the one constructed according to the modern historical predilections of the trained scholar). Only in this way can the obstructing canonical veil be torn in two; only in this way can the reader gain unfettered access to the hidden truths residing therein. For those who continue to read the text in its final canonical context, however, the veil remains, lying over their hearts and hardening their minds, since they are inordinately committed to a text that has been distorted by ecclesial deceit.

Yet even in this rather "anti-canonical" state of affairs, the Gospel and Pauline collections were able to retain a basic level of cohesiveness to the scholarly eye, for critics could examine them according to a developmental scheme amenable to the precepts of modern historical-critical analysis. The CE collection, however, collapsed under the weight of historical criticism. Though some commentators have maintained the traditional title and contents,[5] the majority has chosen to redraw

[3] F. Overbeck, *Zur Geschichte des Kanons* (Chemnitz, 1880), 80; qtd. G. Luedemann, *Heretics: The Other Side of Christianity* (London: SCM Press, 1996), 270 n. 298.
[4] Luedemann, *Heretics*, 80 and 270 n. 297.
[5] German scholarship is occasionally more inclined in this direction: Cf., e.g., H. Windisch, *Die katholischen Briefe*, ed. H. Preisker (HNT 15; Tübingen: Mohr, 1951); and

its canonical boundaries because the collection is seen to lack the kind of robust, organizational center that would provide a sense of binding unity along historical, authorial, or generic lines. Thus, its contents are typically reassigned: 1–3 John are nearly always torn away to be read as appendages of the gospel (and occasionally the apocalypse) under the heading, "Johannine Writings"; 2 Peter is severed from 1 Peter to be read as "2 Jude" because of the clear literary relationship they share; and James and 1 Peter are considered against a Pauline backdrop, James as a response to, and 1 Peter as a development of the trajectory of early Christianity to which that canonical collection bears witness.

Recent introductory texts and multi-book commentaries appear to be particularly at a loss when it comes to the proper categorization of these letters. Among the latter, the most common format links James, 1–2 Peter and Jude,[6] though sometimes Hebrews and Revelation are also included.[7] NT introductory texts generally include chapters dealing with "the synoptic gospels," "the Pauline letters," and "the Johannine writings"; but from there one may find a chapter entitled "the General Epistles" including sections on Hebrews, 1 Peter, 2 Peter–Jude, and James,[8] or a chapter named "The Other New Testament Writings" including Hebrews, 1 Peter, James, Jude–2 Peter, and Revelation.[9] *The Cambridge Companion to Biblical Interpretation*, by contrast, includes a chapter called "The Non-Pauline Letters" that takes in Hebrews, the Pastoral Epistles, James, Jude–2 Peter, and 1 Peter.[10] Another introductory textbook lists 1 Peter, James, Jude, and 2 Peter as "Catholic Epistles" (despite the exclusion of the Johannine letters), and places these alongside Hebrews and the Deutero-Paulines in a chapter entitled "The Pseudepigraphical Letters."[11] Compared to the Gospel and Pauline collections, mainstream contemporary scholarship apparently finds it difficult to think of these seven letters as much more than an amorphous grouping of "other writings" with a limited sense of internal coherence.

This book argues otherwise. It is my contention that the final form of the CE collection was the result of intentional design on the part of the canonizing com-

H. Balz and W. Schrage, *Die katholischen Briefe* (NTD 10; Göttingen: Vandenhoek & Ruprecht, 1973).

[6] E.g., A. Chester and R. Martin's contribution to the *New Testament Theology* series (Cambridge: Cambridge University Press, 1994); P. Perkins's commentary in the Interpretation series (Louisville: John Knox, 1995), and the older Anchor commentary by B. Reicke (ABC 37; New York: Doubleday, 1964).

[7] E.g., *NIB* 12 (Nashville: Abingdon, 1998); L. Donelson, *From Hebrews to Revelation* (Louisville: Westminster John Knox, 2001), and G. Krodel's edited collection in the *Proclamation* series (Minneapolis: Fortress, 1995).

[8] L. T. Johnson, *The Writings of the New Testament: An Interpretation* (Philadelphia: Fortress, 1986), 409–63.

[9] R. Brown, *An Introduction to the New Testament* (ABRL; New York: Doubleday, 1997), 681–813.

[10] F. Young, "The Non-Pauline Epistles," in *The Cambridge Companion to Biblical Interpretation*, ed. John Barton (Cambridge: Cambridge University Press, 1998), 290–304.

[11] G. Theissen, *The New Testament* (London: T&T Clark, 2003), 125–43.

munity in the hopes that it might perform a particular canonical function, one quite close to that which was promoted by Augustine in the early fifth century. While this sort of argument has been made by others before me,[12] I will push the premise further to make the case that one of the letters in the collection—the letter of James—was actually *composed* with this particular canonical function in mind. That is to say, this book proposes that the letter of James was written with the nascent apostolic letter collection in view, in order that it might forge together a discrete collection of non-Pauline letters, one shaped according to a particular *logic* of apostolic authority (that is, "not by Paul alone") in order to perform a particular *function* in the larger Christian canon (the correction of Paulinist misreadings of the whole apostolic message).

The presentation of such an unusual hypothesis requires a good deal of unpacking, so the reader's patience is asked for as I attempt to carefully explain the basis for the argument of this book.

Canonical Approaches to the Catholic Epistle Collection

In response to the kind of historical-criticism that denigrated the church's canonical process and trivialized the hermeneutical significance of the final form of the canon, the latter third of the twentieth century saw the rise of various "canonical approaches" to Scripture. A number of helpful surveys of these approaches are available elsewhere,[13] so I will not spend significant time reviewing its various practices and practitioners; for our purposes it is enough to briefly describe the two dominant trends that have emerged in order to demonstrate where and how my own approach both builds on and seeks to extend the work of others.

Studies in the notion and definition of canon[14] often note that the Greek kan-wvn meant both "authoritative rule" and "fixed list" in ancient usage. The former is seen to denote an earlier, more fluid understanding of the term associated with a community's constantly negotiated "rule of faith," a set of communal assumptions and beliefs deriving from textual and non-textual authorities alike. The latter usage points to a later more standardized understanding of authority as it was embodied in a community's "fixed list" of authoritative *texts*. Gerald Sheppard employs the

---

[12] Principally Robert W. Wall, as the following overview of canonical approaches to the CE will demonstrate.

[13] See esp. G. T. Sheppard, "Canonical Criticism," in *ABD* 1.861–66, and "Canon," in *Encyclopedia of Religion*, 3.62–69. For a recent assessment of the state of critical issues surrounding the canonical approach to Scripture, see L. M. McDonald and J. A. Sanders, eds., *The Canon Debate: On the Origins and Formation of the Bible* (Peabody, Mass.: Hendrickson, 2002).

[14] See B. Metzger. *The Canon of the New Testament: Its Origin, Development, and Significance* (Oxford: Clarendon, 1987), 289–93; L. M. McDonald, *The Formation of the Christian Biblical Canon*, rev. ed. (Peabody, Mass.: Hendrickson, 1995), 1–21; and E. Ulrich, "The Notion and Definition of Canon," in *Canon Debate*, 21–35.

terms "canon 1" and "canon 2" to describe these differing ancient usages.[15] For early Christians, canon 1 was a composite authoritative voice which constituted the informally agreed-upon standard held by a particular community of believers. Under this earlier scheme, the community's "Scriptures" (that is, religiously authoritative texts) might rightly be called "canonical" because of their function as an authoritative component of the larger rule of faith. They would not constitute a "canon" however, for that suggests the kind of closed, "fixed lists" of authoritative texts which are widely agreed to have been a later phenomenon (canon 2). Thus, analyses of early Christian appeals to proto-NT texts suggest that the four-fold gospel, a collection of Paul's letters, 1 Peter and 1 John functioned *canonically* for many Christians by the end of the second century (canon 1) even though a closed *canon* (canon 2) does not appear to have been established until the fifth century.[16]

These two ancient understandings of κανών have informed two different (though not mutually exclusive) canonical methodologies: some scholars are more oriented toward the hermeneutical implications of the final literary *shape* of the canon (canon 2), while others are centered on an examination of the historical process of *shaping* that resulted in the form ultimately canonized (canon 1). These two options are rarely found in pure form, of course, and are probably best understood as points along a continuum of canonical interests. Nevertheless, the two founding advocates of canonical methodologies, Brevard Childs and James Sanders, can be seen to represent these two orienting interests.[17] According to Childs,[18] the final form of the canon is hermeneutically determinative insofar as it represents the normative fixation of the early Christian community's rule of faith. In this final redactional act, the canonizing community assembled its authoritative literature in a dialectically evocative and creative relationship, editing and arranging originally disparate materials in order to accent particular themes and forge meaningful intertextual connections. This arrangement provides a final literary "shape" which communicates the theological commitments of the originating community and places controls on contemporary readings of the Bible's constituent parts.

---

[15] "Canon," in *Encyclopedia of Religion*, 3.62–69.

[16] For a helpful examination of these options as they have been (mis-)applied to an understanding of canon history, see J. Barton's essay "The Origins of the Canon: An Imaginary Problem?" in his book *Holy Writings, Sacred Text: The Canon in Early Christianity* (Louisville: Westminster John Knox, 1997), 1–34.

[17] Here I am indebted to F. Spina's fine essay "Canonical Criticism: Childs Versus Sanders," in *Interpreting God's Word for Today: An Inquiry into Hermeneutics from a Biblical Theological Perspective*, ed. W. McCown and J. E. Massey (Anderson, Ind.: Warner Press, 1982), 165–94.

[18] See esp. Brevard Childs, *Introduction to the Old Testament as Scripture* (Philadelphia: Fortress, 1979); idem., *The New Testament as Canon: An Introduction* (Valley Forge, Pa.: Trinity Press International, 1985); and idem., *A Biblical Theology of the Old and New Testaments* (Minneapolis: Fortress 1993).

In contrast to Childs's more overtly literary approach, Sanders[19] does not privilege the final canonical product as the locus of interpretive control. Instead, he is interested in how an appreciation for the canonical process itself might shape contemporary hermeneutics. According to Sanders, one cannot rightly understand the significance of the final *shape* of the canon without apprehending how and why it was that the canonical *shaping* occurred as it did. The real hermeneutical payoff is not found in a synchronic literary analysis of the static biblical product (canon 2), but in a more diachronic understanding of the dynamic process by which faithful authors and interpreters adopted and adapted authoritative traditions for their contemporary faith communities (canon 1). An appreciation of the historical process, then, provides a guide for contemporary biblical interpreters as they seek to adapt the biblical traditions to their own communities of faith.

As already noted, these are not mutually exclusive postures, and many scholars interested in approaching the Bible as canon now find themselves working somewhere along the continuum between the two. In what follows, I seek to frame my own work within the larger conceptual categories just presented. What have other scholars argued about the canonical *shape* of the CE collection, and what has already been said about the process of its *shaping*?

The Shape of the Catholic Epistle Collection: Evidence of Design in the Final Form

Others have already isolated several features of the final form of the CE collection that bear the strong impression of design. Two are widely noted: first, the sequence "James–Peter–John" does not make sense according to stichoi length[20] and appears designed to echo Paul's listing of the "Pillars" of the Jerusalem church in Galatians 2:9.[21] Second, since the collection begins with a letter from "James, a servant of God and the Lord Jesus Christ," and ends with one from "Jude, a servant of Jesus Christ and brother of James," one might easily conclude that the collection as a whole is delivered in the "embrace" of letters from Jesus' brothers according to the flesh.[22] From there it is not too great a stretch to posit that the outward shape of

[19] See esp. James Sanders, *Torah and Canon* (Philadelphia: Fortress, 1972); idem., "Adaptable for Life: the Nature and Function of Canon," in *Magnolia Dei—The Mighty Acts of God: Essays on the Bible and Archaeology in Memory of G. Ernst Wright*, ed. F. M. J. Cross, et al. (Garden City: Doubleday, 1976), 531–60; and idem., *Canon and Community: A Guide to Canonical Criticism* (Philadelphia: Fortress, 1984).

[20] According to Metzger (*Canon*, 299), 1 John is longest at 269 stichoi, followed by James with 247 and 1 Peter with 237. Adding 2–3 John and 2 Peter to their respective authors puts Peter at 403 and John at 332.

[21] Cf., e.g., D. Luhrman, "Gal. 2:9 und die katholischen Briefe," *ZNW* 72 (1981): 65–87.

[22] E.g., J. Painter, *1, 2, and 3 John* (SP 18; Collegeville, Minn: Liturgical Press, 2002), xiii, 33–34.

the collection was intended to signify the letter group as a literary witness to the Jerusalem apostolate.[23]

But does such a realization bear any substantial hermeneutical significance?[24] No one has done more to answer that question affirmatively than Robert W. Wall. In a series of articles he has built the case that the final redaction of the CE collection bears a number of features designed to guide the interpreter toward a faithful reading of the entire apostolic canonical witness.[25] According to Wall, the placement of the Acts of the Apostles between the gospel and letter collections has the canonical effect of supplying readers with an "authorized" narrative context within which the letters might be rightly interpreted. Acts provides individual narrative "portraits" of the early Christian leadership and their harmonious collaboration, which combine to endow the reader with a particular strategy for framing the unity and diversity of their associated letters. By elevating the Lukan representations of the apostles in Acts, and drawing out points of correspondence in their attendant letters, Wall concludes,

> a principle concern of the *second* collection of epistles is to bring balance to a *Tendenz* toward religious syncretism by which the pressures of the surrounding pagan culture may distort if not then subvert the church's substantially Jewish theological and cultural legacy . . . a prior reading of Acts alerts the reader of the CE that an increasingly Gentile church (= Pauline) must consider its religious and public purity as God's people according to the redemptive calculus of their Jewish canonical heritage (Scriptures, practices, prophetic exemplars, etc.).[26]

The theo-logic of the Lukan narrative background is most powerfully underscored in the letter of James, an epistle from the chief representative of the early Jewish mission, which introduces the CE collection with the strident insistence that "one is justified by works and not by faith alone" (2:24). Wall invests particular importance in James 2:22, which insists that Father Abraham's "faith was active

[23] E.g., Metzger, *Canon*, 296–300.
[24] Childs himself doesn't think so: "[T]he term [Catholic Epistles] remains a useful one to designate a collection of New Testament writings which is distinct from the Gospels and the Pauline corpus. It is neither a precise canonical nor a modern genre classification. Its usage has no great theological significance other than to reflect the church's growing concern that the New Testament letters be understood as universal, even when, in their original form, they often carry a specific addressee (cf. II or III John)" (*New Testament as Canon*, 495).
[25] See four essays by Robert Wall in particular: "The Problem of the Multiple Letter Canon of the New Testament" and "Ecumenicity and Ecclesiology: The Promise of the Multiple Letter Canon of the New Testament," in *The New Testament as Canon: A Reader in Canonical Criticism*, ed. E. E. Lemcio and Robert W. Wall (JSNTS 76; Sheffield: Sheffield Academic, 1992), 161–207; "Introduction to Epistolary Literature" in *NIB* 10 (Nashville: Abingdon, 2002), 369–91; and "A Unifying Theology of the Catholic Epistles: A Canonical Approach," in *The Catholic Epistles and the Tradition*, ed. J. Schlosser (BETL 176; Leuven: Peeters, 2004), 43–71.
[26] "Unifying Theology," 59.

along with his works, and faith was completed by works" (2:22). This becomes the "controlling text" that "both captures the moral inclination of the entire CE collection and sounds a cautionary note that any reductionistic reading of the Pauline corpus may well denigrate into a *sola fideism*."[27]

While he includes some supporting comments on the historical process that led to this remarkably robust final shape, Wall's concerns are ultimately more literary than historical. He does attempt to draw the two together, however, by suggesting that the letter corpus reached its final form not principally because of external concerns (that is, those of nascent Catholicism) but because of an internal "aesthetic principle."[28] That is, the final canonical redaction was the one that gained purchase among faithful readers and auditors, and that acceptance was enabled by the literary and theological value of its particular shape over other available formats. Surely a key feature of this aesthetic recognition must have included the fact that the final redaction includes *seven* letters, which brings to mind the patristic emphasis on the symbolic significance of seven-letter collections. Paul, it was reasoned, wrote to seven churches (Rome, Corinth, Galatia, Ephesus, Philippi, Colossae, and Thessalonica) and three individuals (Timothy, Titus, and Philemon); since the Apocalypse of John also includes seven letters to seven churches (Rev 2–3), it was assumed that the presence of *seven* letters symbolized the wholeness or completeness of a collection. As the author of the Muratorian fragment famously noted,

> . . . since the blessed apostle Paul himself, following the example of his predecessor John, writes by name to only seven churches . . . it is clearly recognizable that there is one church spread throughout the whole extent of the earth. For John also in the Apocalypse, though he writes to seven churches, nevertheless speaks to all.[29]

Seven-ness is connected not only to the universality of the church spread across the earth, but also its essential unity. Similarly, Cyprian of Carthage (d. 258), in his exhortation to martyrdom written to Fortunatus, writes about the seven martyred Maccabbean brothers and extols the number seven as a "sacrament of perfect fulfillment" [*sacramentum perfectae consummationis*] (*Fort.* 11.90 [CCSL 3.205]). After illustrating this by appeal to most every instance of the number in the Jewish Scriptures, he turns to the apostolic writings:

> And the Apostle Paul, who is mindful of this lawful and certain number, writes to seven churches. And in the Apocalypse the Lord directs His divine mandates and heavenly precepts to the seven churches and their angels. The number is now found here in the brothers, that a lawful consummation [*consummatio legitima*] may be fulfilled. With the seven children is clearly joined the mother also, their origin and

---

[27] "Unifying Theology," 48.
[28] "Unifying Theology," 47; see also Robert Wall, "The Function of the Pastoral Epistles within the Pauline Canon of the New Testament: A Canonical Approach," in *The Pauline Canon*, ed. S. E. Porter (Leiden: Brill, 2004), 35–36.
[29] Muratorian Fragment, 47–60 (Eng. trans. Metzger, *Canon*, 306–7).

root, who later bore seven churches, herself the first and only one founded by the Lord's voice upon a rock.[30]

In both of these writers, seven-ness is equated with wholeness and completion or consummation and applied specifically to the essential unity, primacy and universality of the one true church. Comments very similar to these are also found in the writings of Victorinus of Pettau (d. 304; *Commentary on Revelation* 1.7 [CSEL 49.27.7]), Amphilochius of Iconium (d. ca. 396; *Iambi ad seleucum*, vv. 289–31 [PTS 9.38.300]), and Jerome (*Ep.* 53.9 [J. LaBourt, 3.22]).

With this notion of "wholeness," "completion," and "consummation" in mind, there may be more significance to the title placed on the final form of the collection than the explanation generally offered. Most agree that the Greek-speaking church called these letters "catholic" (καθολική, derived from the adverbial καθόλου, "in general" or "universal") because, in contrast to Paul's letters to particular churches and individuals, these bear a "general" or "universal" address.[31] This explanation finds its clearest ancient corroboration in the words of the sixth-century theologian Leontius of Byzantium, who says of the letters in the group, "They are called Catholic because they were not written to one group, as those of Paul, but generally to everyone."[32] As is widely noted, however, this is not an entirely accurate designation of their genre, for only 2 Peter and Jude are truly addressed generally. Though James' address "to the twelve tribes in the dispersion" is often rendered figuratively universal, 1 Peter and 2–3 John each address specific churches and individuals, and 1 John bears no address at all. Is it possible that there is more to the title "Catholic" than previously assumed?

Though we do not find the word clearly applied to our collection of letters until Eusebius does so in the early fourth century, the word gained ecclesial significance through the second century, first as an adjective meaning "universal," and eventually as a title for the Christian church.[33] Its first appearance in this vein is

[30] *Fort.* 11.101–8 (CCSL 3.205–6; Deferrari, FC 36.334–35); see also *Quir.* 1.20.22–33 (CCSL 3.20–21).
[31] See the citation list in G. W. H. Lampe, *A Patristic Greek Lexicon* (Oxford: Clarendon, 1961), 690.
[32] καθολικαὶ δὲ ἐκλήθησαν ἐπειδὴ οὐ πρὸς ἓν ἔθνος ἐγράφησαν ὡς αἱ τοῦ Παύλου, ἀλλὰ καθόλου πρὸς πάντα (*De Sectis Act* 2; PG 86.1199ff.).
[33] For more thorough accountings of patristic use of the term, see R. P. Moroziuk, "The Meaning of ΚΑΘΟΛΙΚΟΣ in the Greek Fathers and Its Implications for Ecclesiology and Ecumenism," *PBR* 4 (1985): 90–104; J. B. Lightfoot's discussion in his *Apostolic Fathers* (2.1.413–15; 2.2.310–12; Grand Rapids: Baker, 1981); and Lampe, 690–91. It is often difficult to tell exactly when a church father is using the word simply as an adjective, and when as a title, though it is safe to say that the further one progresses toward the third century, the more likely it is that the two uses have merged into one. In this book we will use the lowercase "catholic" when it may be the case that the writer simply means "universal" (as in Ignatius, or in Origen's unclear use of the term to describe certain letters). We will use the uppercase when we are speaking of the "Catholic" tradition or of a letter that is clearly titled

found in the letter of Ignatius of Antioch to the church in Smyrna (ca. 110). After denouncing those who "spout false opinions about the gracious gift of Jesus Christ that has come to us," he concludes:

[F]lee divisions as the beginning of evils. All of you should follow the bishop as Jesus Christ follows the Father. . . . Let the congregation be wherever the bishop is; just as wherever Jesus Christ is, there also is the universal church [ἡ καθολικὴ ἐκκλησία].³⁴

Here a parallel is drawn between the unity of the Father and the Son and the social and theological unity of the faithful church of Christ as authenticated by the presence of the authoritative bishop. The term *catholic* in this usage is therefore linked with the idea of the essential unity of the church; it is characterized not simply by *universality*, but also by *wholeness* in opposition to *division*.³⁵ The term appears again soon after this in the *Martyrdom of Polycarp* (ca. 155), where again it has primarily to do with the undivided unity of the church (*Mart. Pol.* 8.1; 16.2; 19.2 [Ehrman, LCL 24.376, 390, 394]). By the end of the second century, Clement of Alexandria says:

It is evident that these later heresies and those which are still more recent are spurious innovations on the oldest and truest Church. From what has been said I think it has been made plain that unity is a characteristic of the true, the really ancient Church, into which those that are righteous according to the divine purpose are enrolled. For God being one and the Lord being one, that also which is supremely honored is the object of praise, because it stands alone, being a copy of the one First Principle: at any rate the one Church, which they strive to break up into many sects, is bound up with the principle of Unity. We say, then, that the ancient and Catholic Church [τὴν ἀρχαίαν καὶ καθολικὴν ἐκκλησίαν] stands alone in essence and idea and principle and preeminence.³⁶

"Catholic." As for the word "church," I have followed the direction of the *SBL Handbook of Style*, ed. P. H. Alexander et al. (Peabody, Mass.: Hendrickson, 1999), only presenting the word in uppercase when referring to the title of an institution (e.g., the "Catholic Church" or the "Orthodox Church"). Where quoted sources break this rule, the style of the source text is allowed to stand.

³⁴ Ign. *Smyrn.* 6.2; 7.2; 8.2 (Ehrman, LCL 24.303–5). The Holmes edition (*The Apostolic Fathers: Greek Texts and English Translations* [Grand Rapids: Baker, 1999], 191) translates "catholic" here, but it seems more likely that Lightfoot and Ehrman's choice of "universal" is more accurate in Ignatius's case.

³⁵ See E. Ferguson, "Catholic Church," *Encyclopedia of Early Christianity*, 2nd ed. (New York: Garland, 1998), 226.

³⁶ *Strom.* 7.17.107 (SC 428.316–24); Chadwick and Oulton, LCC 2.162–63. Despite the translator's use of the uppercase in this instance, it may be argued that Clement simply means "universal" here, though again, it is likely that the adjective is functioning as a kind of title by this time. In like manner Irenaeus of Lyon described the churches aligned with Rome as belonging to "the tradition derived from the apostles, of the very great, the very *ancient and universally known* [*omnibus cognita*] church founded and organized at Rome" (3.3.1–2; SC 211.30–32; *ANF* 1.415).

Thus, before the term was ever applied to a discrete collection of apostolic letters, it was in use as a way of describing a particular tradition of Christianity (self-defined as ancient, whole, unified, and true) over against other traditions (which were defined in turn as novel, divisive, and false). The problematic nature of the notions of "orthodoxy" and "heresy" in ancient Christian writings has been well documented in modern research and requires little comment here;[37] my point is simply to emphasize that by the end of the second century, certain fathers of the church understood themselves to stand in continuity with what they understood to be the one, true, whole, "catholic" church, against those teachers and movements who espoused alternative traditions of Christianity.

Given the fact that the "seven-ness" of a letter collection apparently connoted wholeness and completion among patristic writers, and the term "catholic" came to be used as a title for a tradition of Christianity that understood itself to be "whole" against other divisive traditions, it seems quite possible that the ultimate decision to title this seven-letter collection "Catholic" was intended to underscore some related point, either in reference to that collection's nature or its function. It clearly related in some way to the general address of some of its constituent letters; might it also have been intended as a title of demarcation, separating these letters as those belonging to the church called "Catholic," in opposition to other supposedly apostolic texts used by non-Catholics in the early centuries? Is this why the Latin tradition of Christianity tended to call this collection "*Canonical* Epistles" rather than "Catholic Epistles"?[38] Or perhaps the title was meant to say something about the function of the collection? That its inclusion makes complete and brings to consummation an apostolic epistolary witness that would be incomplete and unfinished if limited to those of Paul alone?

Obviously much more will have to be said about this as our study progresses. For now, let it be said that despite the undoubtedly disparate origins of these letters, the literary evidence of the final form suggests that the community that gathered them into a canonical collection did so with a particular sense of their coherence and function in mind. But in an academic environment where the so-called "original historical context" continues for the most part to have hermeneutical priority over the "secondary literary context" of the canon, intertextual readings motivated by the final literary shape of the Bible will only gain limited purchase, primarily among those who are in some way either theologically or methodologically inclined to maintain the integrity of that final shape. But what if a literary reading of the CE

---

[37] The problem was classically defined by W. Bauer in his *Rechtgläubigkeit und Ketzerei im ältesten Christentum*, 1934 (Eng. trans., *Orthodoxy and Heresy in Earliest Christianity* by R. Kraft and G. Krodel [London: SCM, 1971]). For a representative recent discussion of the problem, see B. Ehrman, *The Orthodox Corruption of Scripture* (New York: Oxford University Press, 1993), 3–15.

[38] See B. F. Westcott, *A General Survey of the History of the Canon of the New Testament*, 6th ed. (Grand Rapids: Baker Books, 1980), 539–79, and Augustine's explanation of the term in *Homilies on 1 John*, 7.5 (SC 75.322; Leinenweber, 70).

collection were justified on more substantive historical grounds? It is one thing to reconstruct the process by which *editors* shaped the collection into its current form, but what if it could be demonstrated that the final shape is the result of intentional shaping on the part of a particular *author*? What if it could be shown that there was something about the actual *composition* of one or more of these writings that provided a warrant for the seven being read intertextually as a *collection*? In that case a literary reading would find a more compelling historical justification, and conversely, a hypothetical historical reconstruction might be "proved" by literary means. In turn, the somewhat simplistic modern distinction between composition and collection could be blurred, since the drive to understand the origin of one or more of the texts involved would point back to the collection itself.

As I have already made clear, this book explores the possibility that just such a reality offers a compelling account of the origin of the NT letter of James. Following on several similar scholarly analyses of 2 Peter, this study will explore the hypothesis that the letter of James was composed in the second century in the hope that it might forge together a more literarily coherent and theologically robust collection of non-Pauline letters.

The Shaping of the Catholic Epistle Collection: Canon-consciousness in the Composition of New Testament Texts

Despite the fact that the composition and collection of NT writings are often understood to involve two historically discrete moments, studies have shown that certain biblical texts may have been composed with the shaping of canonical collections in view. Recently David Trobisch has explored the function of several such compositions in his book, *The First Edition of the New Testament*.[39] His study asserts that the earliest complete NT—what he calls the "Canonical Edition"—was "not the result of a lengthy and complicated collecting process that lasted for several centuries," but was in fact circulating in some parts of the church as early as the mid-second century.[40] Rather than follow the typical canon history approach of analyzing external evidence provided by patristic testimony, Trobisch's work focuses almost entirely on literary and bibliographic data derived from the ancient canonical manuscripts themselves. Consistency in the scope, sequence, and titles of these manuscripts, as well as the relatively uniform use of *Nomina Sacra* and the pervasiveness of the codex format, suggest for Trobisch a dependence on an earlier standardized redaction. Further, and more significantly for our purposes, he argues that the editors of this "Canonical Edition" included "editorial notes to the readers" in the text—passages and indeed entire documents that furnish the recipient of the edition with redactional signals designed to buttress the coherence of the final form, and underscore the authority of the individual writings, while

[39] D. Trobisch, *The First Edition of the New Testament* (Oxford: Oxford University Press, 2000).
[40] Trobisch, 6.

emphasizing the harmonious agreement of their apostolic authors. In particular, one of Trobisch's central claims is that the redactional strategy of the editors was primarily concerned with two issues: the harmonization of Paul and the Jerusalem leaders as represented by Peter, and the endorsement of the authority of the Jewish Scriptures for Christian faith.

Trobisch presents 2 Peter as just such a text.[41] Readers of the canonical edition will unavoidably identify the writer as the Apostle Peter, the chief disciple familiar to them from the gospel narratives and the well-known 1 Peter.[42] The letter itself says as much in the way it parallels the opening salutation and closing doxology of 1 Peter,[43] as well as its claim, "This is now, beloved, the second letter I am writing to you" (3:1). The address, "to those who have received a faith of the same kind as ours" (1:1), makes it possible for any reader of the edition to identify themselves as the intended addressee. The comment, "I know that my death will come soon, as indeed our Lord Jesus Christ has made clear to me" (1:14) leads readers to recall Jesus' prophesy of Peter's death in the Gospel of John (21:18-19). The synoptic tradition is twice recalled soon thereafter: when "Peter" says, "I will make every effort so that after my departure you may be able at any time to recall these things" (1:15), readers remember that 1 Peter associated Peter with Mark (1 Pet 5:13) and assume that the "effort" made for recollection of the Petrine message is the Markan gospel. Immediately after that, the author grounds his authority in his being an eyewitness at the Transfiguration (2 Pet 1:16-18), a story only known through the Synoptic witnesses.

Surrounding these allusions to NT texts are claims regarding the authority of the OT: there are references to God's "precious and very great promises" (1:4); readers are told to be attentive to the prophetic message (1:19) that derives from the Holy Spirit (1:21); and a list of OT examples underscores the claim that the OT offers reliable accounts of how God acted in the past and will act in the future (2:1-22). When the author goes on to assert, "[Y]ou should remember the words spoken in the past by the holy prophets, and the commandment of the Lord and Savior spoken through your apostles" (3:2), an important parallel is established for understanding the proper relation between the two testaments of the canonical edition.

While these passages forge intertextual links with the gospels and the OT, other features of the letter illustrate the author's concern to influence the shape of the apostolic letter collection of his day. First, our author chose to incorporate a good deal of the letter of Jude into his text; indeed, nearly all of Jude is reproduced, in

[41] Trobisch, 86–96. The pseudepigraphic origin of 2 Peter is almost universally accepted; see R. Bauckham, "2 Peter: An Account of Research," *ANRW* 2.25.5, 3713–52.

[42] For the influence of 1 Peter on 2 Peter, see, e.g., G. H. Boobyer, "The Indebtedness of 2 Peter to 1 Peter," in *New Testament Essays: Studies in Memory of T. W. Manson,* ed. A. Higgins (Manchester: Manchester University Press, 1959), 34-53; and R. Wall, "The Canonical Function of 2 Peter," *BibInt* 9.1 (2001): 64–81.

[43] Compare 1 Pet 1:2b with 2 Pet 1:2, and 1 Pet 5:11 with 2 Pet 3:18.

modified form, in 2 Peter 2:1-18.[44] Trobisch is uninterested in the source-critical questions that have occupied so many modern interpreters; for his thesis, the simple fact that the two letters echo one another is significant. For readers of the canonical edition, the parallel underscores the sense of apostolic agreement on fundamental aspects of the faith. Just as 1 Corinthians 9:5 mentions Peter together with the brothers of Jesus, and the first eight chapters of the Acts of the Apostles associates Peter with the Jerusalem apostles, so also here we find that Peter and Jude, the brother of Jesus and James, speak with the unified voice of intimate colleagues in ministry. In this way, the links between 2 Peter and Jude underscore Peter's association with the Jerusalem apostolate.

But this is not the only significant apostolic link in the letter, for in closing, the author shows his concern to harmonize Peter and Paul.

> So also our beloved brother Paul wrote to you according to the wisdom given him, speaking of this as he does in all his letters. There are some things in them hard to understand, which the ignorant and unstable twist to their own destruction, as they do the other scriptures. You therefore, beloved, knowing this beforehand, beware lest you be carried away with the error of lawless men and lose your own stability. (3:15b-17)

A good deal is communicated in this short passage. Noting that Paul "also wrote to you," the author indicates not only that Peter and Paul share the same audience, but also that his letter is directed especially toward readers of Pauline letters. His designation of Paul as "our beloved brother" suggests the intimacy of their agreement and echoes the similar designation of Paul in the letter from the Jerusalem leaders in Acts 15, a letter that also underscores the unity of the apostolic kerygma. The reference to "all his letters" indicates that both author and recipient are in the possession of a collection of Pauline writings. The difficulties of Pauline theology are acknowledged: Some of his comments are "hard to understand," and these complexities have enabled some to misinterpret and "twist" his words. Significantly, these people do the same "with the other scriptures." Trobisch is especially interested in two aspects of the communicative intent of this phrase for readers of the canonical edition. First, its presupposition of a collection of writings inclusive of Pauline texts called "scripture" would lead readers to automatically think of the writings of the Old and New Testaments. Second, it specifically identifies the "ignorant and unstable" and "lawless men" of whom readers are to be wary: they are those who misread both Paul and the "scriptures" of the OT.

Again, all of these complex intertextual connections provide redactional signals that evince the coherence of the final form, harmonize Paul and the Jerusalem leaders as represented by Peter, and endorse the authority of the Jewish Scriptures for Christian faith. Trobisch finds the same redactional strategy at work in texts like

---

[44] The dependence of 2 Peter on Jude enjoys widespread scholarly assent, but some continue to challenge the consensus; see, e.g., F. Lapham, *Peter: The Myth, the Man and the Writings* (JSNTSup 239; Sheffield: Sheffield Academic, 2003), 152–58.

the Acts of the Apostles, 2 Timothy, and the Gospel of John.[45] Importantly, this reader-response approach to the NT is not offered without historical justification. According to Trobisch, "This editorial concept expresses the self-understanding of a very specific group within the diverse early Christian community,"[46] namely, that of Irenaeus and Tertullian in their late second-century struggle against Marcion.[47] As is widely known, Marcion was one who championed Paul alone, teaching that Jesus was the revealer of an alien God of love, wholly different than the creator God of the Jews. This doctrine, which effectively drove a wedge of separation between the old and new covenants, led Marcion to omit the "Jewish" elements of Paul's letters, reject the Jewish Scriptures, and with them, the writings of the "Jewish" apostles associated with the Jerusalem mission to the Jews. Catholic theologians like Irenaeus and Tertullian responded to Marcion by placing Paul firmly within the embrace of the Jerusalem apostles and underscoring the continuity of the old and new covenants by insisting on the authority of the OT. The canonical edition of the Christian Bible, according to Trobisch, reflects these same second-century anti-Marcionite tendencies.

Trobisch's position on the canonical function of 2 Peter follows on a number of similar studies, several of which deserve brief mention here. In an article on "The Ecclesial Setting of Pseudepigraphy in Second Peter and its Role in the Formation of the Canon," Dennis Farkasfalvy argued, "the pseudepigraphy of Second Peter stands under the control of a canonical concern."[48] In linking his text with the known "scriptural" texts of his day, the author was "creating scripture" by "matching the status of already canonical epistles."[49] This creation of scripture was motivated by a particular concern that, according to Farkasfalvy, was interested "first of all" in strengthening the link between the Pauline and Petrine traditions in a unified struggle against heresy.[50] The author's community had received a collection of Pauline letters, 1 Peter, and Jude as authoritative. Those of Paul were being misread to support an unorthodox eschatology (cf. 2 Pet 3:1-18), and the eschatological orientation of 1 Peter and Jude were unable to address the new situation. Being "convinced that his understanding of Peter and Paul was correct," and also that "Peter and Paul, as apostles of the Lord who were divinely instructed, must be in agreement with each other," he created a letter in Peter's voice, incorporating elements of the Pauline collection, 1 Peter and Jude, in order to bridge the gap that had formerly existed between them.[51] Like Trobisch, Farkasfalvy also tentatively associates this compositional event with the church's struggle against Marcion.[52]

[45] Trobisch, 78–101.

[46] Trobisch, 77.

[47] Trobisch, 76–77; 105–6.

[48] D. Farkasfalvy, "The Ecclesial Setting of Pseudepigraphy in Second Peter and its Role in the Formation of the Canon," *SecCent* 5 (1985): 3–29, 23.

[49] Farkasfalvy, 9.

[50] Farkasfalvy, 26.

[51] Farkasfalvy, 23.

[52] Farkasfalvy, 13–14; but cf. W. Farmer's response to Farkasfalvy, which supports a more

Marion Soards offers support for this thesis in his "1 Peter, 2 Peter, and Jude as Evidence for a Petrine School."[53] Following on studies that have determined the essential characteristics of an ancient school, Soards analyzes the three very different letters and finds therein the kind of underlying commonalities that point to a shared origin in a particular community. In a rather different manner, Wall's recent study on "The Canonical Function of 2 Peter" demonstrates something quite similar.[54] Regardless of who wrote 2 Peter to whom, it reads as a complementary witness to 1 Peter insofar as it extends the theological reach of that letter. The result is a robust Petrine witness that is more difficult to marginalize in a canon dominated by the Pauline letter collection. Though Wall's literary approach is, again, generally uninterested in producing historical reconstructions of an epistolary *Sitz im Leben*, he concludes by suggesting that the letter is "one tradent's creative attempt to adapt the apostolic message to a later time and different place."[55]

Implicit in all of these studies is the assumption that 2 Peter is pseudonymous; David Meade's study of the practice of pseudepigraphy by ancient Jewish and Christian authors provides a helpful means for us to consider the factors at work in such creations.[56] Meade focuses on apostolic *Vergegenwärtigung* ("actualization," "reimagining," or "realization") as the impetus for the production of canonical pseudepigrapha. The growth of pseudepigraphic apostolic literature in the post-apostolic age was the result of a keenly felt sense of the continuity of authoritative, revelatory tradition. Therein, "tradition" (literary or otherwise) was not received as a static *traditum* that should be rigidly accumulated, but as an ongoing and living *traditio* of revelation that held within it the power to continually readdress new situations.[57] Writers engaged in this task of "apostolic actualization" reinterpreted the tradition according to their own contemporary needs; but the power of their literary creation was dependent on its corresponding veracity to the authoritative source it sought to actualize. That is, the ability of ancient authors to speak to contemporary situations was dependent not simply on the power of the message they had to convey, but also on the maintenance of certain stabilizing elements within that message, namely the preservation of the particular literary, theological, biographical, and historical characteristics associated with that ancient author. The pseudepigrapher was indeed creating a fiction, but not a fantasy; the product needed to be a *historicized* fiction in order to generate an apostolic actualization for a new generation.

---

directly anti-Marcionite compositional concern ("Some Critical Reflections on Second Peter: A Response to a Paper on Second Peter by Dennis Farkasfalvy," *SecCent* 5 [1985]: 30–46).

[53] M. Soards, "1 Peter, 2 Peter, and Jude as Evidence for a Petrine School," *ANRW* 2.25.5. For more thoughts on the "school/circle" behind 2 Peter, see, e.g., R. Bauckham, *Jude, 2 Peter* (WBC 50; Waco, Tex.: Word Books, 1983), 158–62; and J. H. Elliott, *1 Peter* (ABC 37B; New York: Doubleday, 2000), 127–30.

[54] R. Wall, "2 Peter."

[55] R. Wall, "2 Peter," 81.

[56] D. Meade, *Pseudonymity and Canon* (WUNT 39; Tübingen: J. C. B. Mohr, 1986).

[57] Meade, 22.

The presence of such "stabilizing elements" is revealed in what Meade calls the "canon-consciousness" discernable in pseudepigraphic writings—"canon" in this case referring not to a closed collection of fixed texts (Sheppard's "canon 2"), but to an authoritative standard or set of assumptions held by a particular community of believers (canon 1).[58] The components of such a "canon-consciousness" would therefore include texts as well as non-literary traditions. Thus, the "canon-consciousness" of 2 Peter is explicitly evident in its appeal to the "canonical" literature of the author's day (that is, the Jewish Scriptures, the proto-canonical gospels, 1 Peter, Jude, and the letters of Paul) as well as its utilization of certain stabilizing elements found in the Petrine authoritative biography (for example, those deriving from the gospel narratives and 1 Peter, as well as the ecclesial traditions associated with his martyrdom in Rome).[59] Further, the task of apostolic actualization is by its very nature focused primarily on the correct *interpretation* of revelatory, "canonical" sources, a concern that is evident throughout 2 Peter: The "false teachers" who "bring in destructive heresies" (2:1) are guilty of engaging in individualist readings of the Jewish Scriptures (1:19-21), and "twisted" interpretations of the "scriptures" of Paul (3:16). The result is a hermeneutics that renders the apostolic message irrelevant (3:1-4) and false (1:16-21). In writing 2 Peter, the Petrine "tradent" took up the apostolic *traditio* for a new actualization of the apostle Peter, and in doing so, he extended the apostolic letter canon, enabling it to more effectively confront the challenges of his contemporary situation.

Understood as such, a pseudepigraphic, historicized fiction cannot be viewed simply as a crass "forgery," the "false writing" of someone who illegitimately commandeers an ancient authority to transparently correct a contemporary heresy, for the *traditio* continued to hold revelatory power; the old voice continued to speak in the textual actualization of the pseudepigrapher. By extension, the new word would not be read as the obvious address of a pseudepigrapher to a contemporary situation, but as an authentic word from an apostolic authority, the relevance of which was found in its ability to address the historical antecedents of the current heresy.

These studies will undoubtedly give scholars much to debate, but what they bring to the fore is the notion that 2 Peter is not simply a pseudepigraph, but a *canonically motivated* pseudepigraph. It is a document that was created by a particular tradent of authoritative tradition to enable the process of canon formation according to the particular theological needs of his ecclesial readership. Thus, the *historical origin* of 2 Peter points inescapably to its role in the shaping of a *literary collection*. Pseudepigraphic *Vergegenwärtigung* or "actualization" exists, therefore, in a reciprocal relationship with the shaping process of canonization; it is informed by past canon formation and, in turn, contributes to the present and future formation

---

[58] For a useful history of the meaning and use of the word "canon" in the church, see Metzger, *Canon*, 289–93. Generally speaking, my use of the term "canon" in this book will refer to a gathering of authoritative writings, while the term "canonical" will refer to the relative authority of a particular text.

[59] Meade, 181–86.

of that same canon. In the case of 2 Peter, there is no gap between historical origin and canonical collection, for canon and composition go hand in hand.

2 Peter, James, and the State of the Catholic Epistles in Second-century Christianity

Trobisch's book has rightly received a good deal of praise, but there are some short-comings that should be mentioned.[60] In particular, while he may be correct in his assertion that histories of the canon have gone astray through their more narrow concentration on indirect evidence provided by patristic writers, Trobisch commits the equal and opposite sin in his general *exclusion* of such evidence—for it is only by ignoring the patristic use of the proto-CE that one could arrive at the conclusion of when the final form of the canon was achieved.

Trobisch's argument assumes that all seven letters of the CE were included in the Canonical Edition known and used by Irenaeus of Lyon, Tertullian of Carthage, and Clement of Alexandria,[61] but a consideration of their testimony to the CE makes this difficult to accept.[62] As my first chapter will demonstrate, though 1 Peter, 1–2 John (almost certainly along with 3 John), and Jude were clearly known and used by the end of the second century, James and 2 Peter were not. In fact, the first overt witness we have of James, 2 Peter, and 2–3 John is Origen of Alexandria, writing in the early to mid-third century, and the first witness we have to a known seven letter collection called the CE is Eusebius, writing at the beginning of the fourth century. Indeed, as the evidence will show, though the Gospel and Pauline collections were fixed for the most part by the end of the second century, the CE collection remained unstable until the end of the fourth. How then can Trobisch assert the presence of a complete, "Canonical Edition" of the NT before this period? As Gamble notes, "it is very difficult to speak of a New Testament canon having taken any clear shape, whether in conception or in substance, prior to the appearance of this particular collection."[63] A NT canon that does not include a complete CE collection might be rightly called a *first* edition, but it most certainly could not be called the *ultimate* edition. As my first chapter will reveal, Trobisch is not the only modern scholar of canon history to overlook the distinctive development of the CE collection.

Though the relative non-reference to 2–3 John in the second century may be accounted for on the basis of their diminutive size and minimal content, the silence regarding James and 2 Peter is far less easily explained. If those prior to Origen

---

[60] See, e.g., J. K. Elliott's review (*ExpT* 112.12 [2001]: 422–23).

[61] Trobisch, 106.

[62] Also noted by E. Ferguson, "Factors Leading to the Selection and Closure of the New Testament Canon," in *Canon Debate*, 312; and E. Kalin, "The New Testament Canon of Eusebius," in *Canon Debate*, 404.

[63] H. Gamble, "The New Testament Canon: Recent Research and the *Status Quaestionis*," in *Canon Debate*, 288.

were using the complete canonical edition, why do they not seem to know these two letters? It may be countered that the absence of 2 Peter is easily accounted for according to Trobisch's hypothesis, for as an "editorial note" it was perhaps the latest addition to the canon, being the product of the same sort of impulses that animated the theology of Irenaeus and Tertullian. Though they themselves do not seem to quote the letter, they were clearly working with the same assumptions that inspired its creation, as Trobisch's analysis of the letter persuasively reveals.

One such assumption that deserves a closer look is the priority of Peter and Paul among the apostles. Trobisch locates the origin of his Canonical Edition in the second-century interchange between the churches of Rome and Asia Minor. He is right to do so, for it is here, in the Western church associated with Rome, that the elevation of Peter and Paul was most forcefully pressed.[64] Already in *1 Clement*, when Christians are exhorted to consider as examples "the greatest and most upright pillars (στύλοι)" of the church, the Pillars the author has in mind are not the "James, Cephas and John" of Galatians 2:9, but Peter and Paul alone (*1 Clem.* 5.2 [Ehrman, LCL 24.43]). Ignatius subordinates himself specifically under the authority of these two (Ign. *Rom.* 4.3 [Ehrman, LCL 24.275]), and both the *Acts of Peter* and *Acts of Paul* consistently emphasize their shared authority and equal honor.[65] Irenaeus based the priority of the Roman church on the fact that it alone maintained "that tradition derived from the apostles, of the very great, the very ancient, and universally known church founded and organized at Rome by the two most glorious apostles, Peter and Paul" (*Adv. Haer.* 3.3.2 [SC 211.30–32; *ANF* 1.415]), and further, his struggle against the Marcionites was waged primarily by means of harmonizing these two (cf., e.g., *Adv. Haer.* 3.13.1 [SC 211.251]). Furthermore, both he and Tertullian emphasize that the gospels of Mark and Luke are only included among the canonical four because these two were disciples of Peter and Paul (*Adv. Haer.* 3.1.1 [SC 211.31]; *Adv. Marc.* 4.5.3 [CCSL 1.551]). Finally, as will be demonstrated by the end of my first chapter, the Western canon lists from the fourth and fifth centuries (and beyond) all demonstrate the priority of Peter and Paul through their ordering of the canonical books.

In all this we encounter a persistent Western, and perhaps particularly Roman, concern to establish apostolic authority on a harmonious balance of Peter and Paul. Thus, while Trobisch is quite right to claim that the "editorial notes" he identifies seek to harmonize Paul and the Jerusalem apostolate, it is important for us to emphasize that this harmonization occurs specifically *through Peter*. It is a particularly *Western* "First Edition of the New Testament" that Trobisch's work elucidates.

Again, all this helps explain both the particular function and the late "arrival" of 2 Peter. But what can be said about the letter of James? Can a similar set of factors help explain its late canonicity as well? According to Trobisch, one of the reasons the

---

[64] Cf. R. P. C. Hanson, *Tradition in the Early Church* (London: SCM Press, 1962), 144–51; H. Koester, *History and Literature of Early Christianity*, vol. 2 of *Introduction to the New Testament*, 2nd ed. (New York: Walter de Gruyter, 2000), 291–300.

[65] See the analysis in Koester, 327–31.

Western editors of the canonical edition focused on Peter in their harmonization efforts was the fact that readers of the gospels and the Pauline letters found him in a rather "blemished" state. In the gospels, he is rebuked because of his failure to understand the nature of Jesus' messiahship (Mark 8:33; Matt 16:23) and for taking up the sword in the garden of Gethsemane (John 18:10). He alone among the disciples comes closest to Judas' betrayal in his own three-fold denial, a story dramatically emphasized in all four gospels. At least two passages in 1 Corinthians can be read to suggest that Peter and Paul were rival leaders in the early Christian movement (1:12; 9:5). Most damagingly, in Galatians Paul publicly condemns Peter's apparent hypocrisy in withdrawing from table fellowship with Gentiles (Gal 2:1-14), suggesting that Peter did not fully grasp the notion that Christians are "justified by faith in Christ, and not by works of the law" (2:16). In Trobisch's reckoning, the "editorial" texts bear evidence of a concern to correct this tarnished image of the beloved Peter.[66]

But in all this, Trobisch does not address the similarly blemished status of James, the Lord's brother. Despite widespread evidence of his veneration in the second century (evidence which will be explored in detail in my second chapter), he is underrepresented in the gospel and Pauline texts, and what one finds there is easily construed in unflattering ways. Indeed, Peter may have misunderstood Jesus and even denied him, but he was still the first and most prominent among the twelve disciples, the "rock" on whom Christ established the church (see Matt 10:2, 16:18). By contrast, the gospels seem to suggest that James was not a true disciple of the earthly Jesus at all (Mark 3:21, 31-35; John 7:5).[67] Though Peter is condemned for vacillating in Galatians 2, the "Judaizers" who demand Gentile circumcision are explicitly said to have come "from James" (2:12). Even the "harmonizing" tendency of the Acts of the Apostles does little to lift James' status: He is mentioned almost as an afterthought in 12:17, and his main appearances in chapters fifteen and twenty-one show him to be primarily concerned about the right performance of the Jewish law by Paul and the targets of his Gentile mission. If it is concluded that Peter's image in the gospel and Pauline texts required balance and correction, those same texts leave us with the impression that James' image required thorough rehabilitation.

---

[66] Trobisch, 83–84.

[67] While some overstep the evidence to conclude that James was somehow opposed to the work of the earthly Jesus, the opposite attempts by R. Ward ("James of Jerusalem in the First Two Centuries," *ANRW* 2.26.1, 786–90); R. Bauckham (*Jude and the Relatives of Jesus in the Early Church* [Edinburgh: T&T Clark, 1990], 45–57); and J. Painter (*Just James: The Brother of Jesus in History and Tradition* [Edinburgh: T&T Clark, 1999], 11–41) to conclude that Jesus' brothers were in fact *active followers* during this period seem guilty of the same over-extension of the evidence. Regardless of how one reconstructs the historical data, in the end we are left with gospel texts that give the distinct impression that James was not a faithful follower of the earthly Jesus.

We have been able to isolate a particular quarter of second-century Christianity that championed Peter and Paul. Second Peter appears to have come out of this
same environment, and its production may have been part of a concerted effort
to extend the Petrine witness, perhaps in order to create an apostolic letter collection balanced along a Peter-Paul axis. As we will see, however, other Christians of
the period configured apostolic authority along different lines. Indeed, a significant
number of early Christians venerated James and placed him in a position superior
to both Peter and Paul. Might someone among them, noting the blemished, under-
represented state of James in the proto-NT, have written the letter of James through
motivations similar to those that inspired the composition of 2 Peter and the com-
pilation of Trobisch's very Western "Canonical Edition"?

James in the Formation of the New Testament Catholic Epistle
Collection and the Christian Canon: Thesis and Outline

This study presents a composition hypothesis that dovetails the work of Trobisch,
Wall, and others by focusing more closely on the particular role of the letter of James
in the historical formation and literary coherence of the CE collection. As described
above, somewhere in the West, an individual or group of individuals wrote 2 Peter
and included in it a series of intertextual links with 1 Peter, Jude, the Pauline letters, the gospels, and the OT, in order to extend the Petrine NT witness, perhaps to
construct a more theologically coherent apostolic letter collection along a Peter-Paul
axis. We will consider the possibility that somewhere in the East, an individual (or
perhaps even a group of individuals) composed the letter of James, including in it
a series of intertextual links with the contemporary "canonical" Scriptures, in order
to create an apostolic letter collection based not on the dual authority of Peter and
Paul, but on the ancient two-sided apostolic missions of Paul and the Jerusalem Pillars. This hypothesis of the canonical function of the CE, much like that of Augustine's long ago, was originally borne out of literary conclusions inspired by Wall's
work on the intertextual relations of the canonical texts themselves. Subsequent
historical investigation into the formation of the canon and the attendant ecclesial
controversies of the second and third centuries, however, led to the conviction that
these literary hunches might be justified on a more rigorously historical basis.

Obviously, this hypothesis is made up of a number of suppositions that require
defense. Perhaps most importantly, one may begin by wondering whether there is
sufficient justification for entertaining such an unusual hypothesis about the letter
of James in the first place. The answer can only be an unequivocal "yes." No other
letter in the NT contains as many troubling and ambiguous features, and to this
day no scholarly consensus exists regarding its point of origin. Modern scholarship
has long been divided on the authorship of the letter: The majority of twentieth-
century interpreters consider it pseudonymous,[68] though a substantial minority has

---

[68] E.g. J. H. Ropes, *The Epistle of St. James* (ICC; Edinburgh: T&T Clark, 1916); M.
Dibelius, *James*, ed. H. Greeven, trans. M. Williams, rev. ed. (Hermeneia; Philadelphia:

argued for authenticity,[69] and some posit theories of partial authorship.[70] The letter has been dated as early as the decade of the 40s C.E.,[71] as late as the mid- to late second century,[72] and all points in-between.[73] Hypothsized places of composition include Jerusalem,[74] Rome,[75] Antioch,[76] and elsewhere. The letter includes a number of striking literary parallels with other early Christian texts: Some have argued these other texts used James as their source,[77] while some believe James is dependent on the others,[78] though most now opt out of the debate and settle for shared dependence on the so-called "common stock of early Christian tradition."[79]

Fortress, 1976); J. Moffatt, *The General Epistles of James, Peter and Jude* (MNTC; London: Hodder & Stoughton, 1928); A. Meyer, *Das Raetsel des Jakobusbriefes* (Giessen: Töpelmann, 1930); E. Goodspeed, *A History of Early Christian Literature*, rev. and enl. ed. by Robert M. Grant (Chicago: University of Chicago Press, 1966); L. E. Elliott-Binns, *Galilean Christianity* (London: SCM Press, 1956); B. Reicke, *The Epistles of James, Peter, and Jude* (ABC 37; New York: Doubleday, 1964); Balz and Schrage; J. C. M. Cantinat, *Les Épîtres de Saint Jacques et de Saint Jude* (SB; Paris: J. Gabalda, 1973); S. Laws, *The Epistle of James* (BNTC; Peabody, Mass.: Hendrickson, 1980); and C. Burchard, *Der Jakobusbrief* (HNT 15/1; Tübingen: Mohr Siebeck, 2000).

[69] E.g., J. B. Mayor, *The Epistle of St. James*, 2nd ed. (London: Macmillan, 1897); R. Tasker, *The General Epistle of James* (London: Tyndale Press, 1956); F. Mussner, *Der Jakobusbrief* (Freiburg: Verlag Herder, 1964); C. L. Mitton, *The Epistle of James* (London: Marshall, Morgan & Scott, 1966); D. Guthrie, *New Testament Introduction*, 4th ed. (Downers Grove, Ill.: InterVarsity, 1990); E. M. Sidebottom, *James, Jude and 2 Peter* (CBC; London: Thomas Nelson & Sons, 1967); J. B. Adamson, *The Epistle of James* (NICNT; Grand Rapids: Eerdmans, 1976); idem, *James: The Man and his Message* (Grand Rapids: Eerdmans, 1989); P. Hartin, *James and the 'Q' Sayings of Jesus* (JSNTSup 47; Sheffield: Sheffield Academic, 1991); L. T. Johnson, *The Letter of James* (ABC 37A; New York: Doubleday, 1995); and R. Bauckham, *James: Wisdom of James, Disciple of Jesus the Sage* (London: Routledge, 1999).

[70] E.g. W. L. Knox, "The Epistle of James," *JTS* 46 (1945): 10–17; E. C. Blackman. *The Epistle of James* (London: SCM Press, 1957); P. Davids, *The Epistle of James* (NIGTC; Grand Rapids: Eerdmans, 1982); and R. Martin, *James* (WBC 48; Waco, Tex.: Word Books, 1988).

[71] E.g., Mayor.

[72] E.g., A. Harnack, *Geschichte der altchristlichen Literatur bis Eusebius, II: Die Chronologie*, vol. 1 (Leipzig: Hinrichs'sche Buchhandlung, 1897), 486–91; and B. Mack, *The Lost Gospel: The Book of Q and Christian Origins* (San Francisco: Harper, 1993), 259.

[73] See the lists in W. Pratscher, *Der Herrenbruder Jakobus und die Jakobustradition* (FRLANT 139; Göttingen: Vandenhoeck & Ruprecht, 1987), 209 n. 3, and the now rather dated but still useful table in Davids, 4.

[74] E.g., Bauckham, *James*, 11–28.

[75] E.g., Reicke, 6; and Laws, 26.

[76] E.g., Martin, lxxvi; and Hartin, *James and the 'Q' Sayings*, 240.

[77] E.g., Mayor; Meyer; and Sidebottom.

[78] E.g., C. Bigg, *The Epistles of St. Peter and St. Jude* (ICC; Edinburgh: T&T Clark, 1901); and Moffatt, *General Epistles*.

[79] E.g., Ropes; Dibelius, *James*; Mussner, *Der Jakobusbrief*; Davids, *Epistle of James*; and Burchard.

Against the post-Reformation tendency to read James through the "spectacles" of the Pauline letters (a tendency largely enabled throughout the twentieth century by the dominance of Dibelius's commentary), some recent scholars have emphasized the need to read James "as it wants to be read,"[80] and many now endeavor to work with the letter *as though* it were written in the mid-first century by James himself (acknowledging all the while that its authenticity cannot be proven).[81] Sometimes this is pursued as part of a quest for the historical James.[82]

In the midst of all this scholarly diversity lies the widespread agreement that the letter resists confident historical assessment, and in my view, the huge diversity of scholarly opinion allows for a variety of hypothetical reconstructions. I present this in the full knowledge that it will not convince everyone, though it is my hope that some will find here solutions to some of the nagging questions about the canonical letter of James that have persisted over the years.

Each chapter that follows presents material against which my proposed hypothesis will be tested. To begin with, I have to show that my assumption regarding the historical formation of the CE collection is well founded. My first chapter, therefore, offers a thorough analysis of the CE collection's canonical formation. It starts with an in-depth study of the use of the proto-CE by Irenaeus, Tertullian, Clement, Origen, Eusebius, and others from the late second to the early fourth centuries. Since we are interested in the advent of the collection and not that of the individual letters per se, I will not begin with pre-Irenaean "echoes" in order to establish the *terminus ad quem* for any of the individual letters. The scope at this point will simply trace the development of the CE collection beginning with the first overt citation of a proto-CE text (Irenaeus) and ending with the first evidence of the existence of a complete collection called the CE (Eusebius).

Even then, we will still have to investigate "echoes." Though scholars have long noted that James, 2 Peter, and 3 John were not clearly cited until Origen, disagreements exist as to the earlier use of these letters. While many accept the probability that 2 Peter is echoed in texts like the *Acts of Peter* and the *Apocalypse of Peter*, some scholars "hear" evidence of James in the second century, and others do not. Though it cannot be proved definitively, my contention is that there is, in fact, no compelling evidence for James at all until Origen uses it in the first half of the third century. But tracing the early patristic use of NT texts is a difficult (some would say dubious) process, since it so often relies on the discernment of linguistic evidence that may or may not actually exist. I will not be able to avoid such a charge entirely; the evidence only allows for probability, and not certainty. Nevertheless, the avail-

---

[80] A variety of recent approaches are surveyed by K. W. Niebuhr in "A New Perspective on James? Neuere Forschungen zum Jakobusbrief," *TLZ* 129 (2004): 1019–44.

[81] This is the position of Johnson's commentary, continued in *Brother of Jesus, Friend of God: Studies in the Letter of James* (Grand Rapids: Eerdmans, 2004).

[82] See esp. B. Chilton and C. A. Evans, eds., *James the Just and Christian Origins* (Leiden: Brill, 1999); and B. Chilton and J. Neusner, eds., *The Brother of Jesus: James the Just and His Mission* (Louisville: Westminster John Knox, 2001).

able evidence must be attended to. My study hopes to increase the probability of a late date for James by avoiding reliance on the typical echo and allusion counting method often found in histories of the canon. It is not enough to simply refer to a particular patristic comment, note its thematic or even terminological similarity to a verse from James, and conclude that the writer in question was familiar with the letter. We must take a more conservative approach. My study will begin, therefore, with a brief articulation of my more conservative methodology for determining the early patristic use of the proto-CE (including an excursus on the acceptable use of arguments from silence in the task of historical reconstruction).

This account of the development of the CE collection will conclude (a) that the letter group came into existence sometime in the mid- to late-third century in the Eastern church, and (b) that the development of the collection reflects the slow increase of interest in broadening the apostolic witness beyond Paul, first by appeal to Peter (Irenaeus) and then by a more focused appeal to the Pillars of Jerusalem (Tertullian and Clement). Evidence from Tertullian's struggle against Marcion, in particular, will suggest that the ultimate shape of the Pauline and CE collections may have been designed, in an anti-Marcionite move, to reflect the harmony of Paul and the Pillars of the Jerusalem apostolate. Further, Clement's witness to an eleva- tion of James, Peter, and John as leading apostles who received "knowledge" from the resurrected Lord will show that Tertullian's specific elevation of the Jerusalem Pillars was not an isolated phenomenon. From there, after a brief look at the manu- script evidence from the period to ensure that my account of the development of the collection agrees with evidence derived from the extant texts themselves, we will move on to an examination of the canon lists from the fourth and fifth centuries. This will confirm that the CE appears to have been a product of the third-century Eastern church. It will also demonstrate that the seven letters do not appear to have been received in the West until the late fourth century; and further, it will show that several of the Eastern fathers who received the CE collection did so according to a particular understanding of its canonical function in relation to the Acts of the Apostles and the Pauline letter collection, one that appears to mirror Tertullian's anti-Marcionite claims regarding the two ancient Christian missions. The chapter will close with a series of preliminary implications for our understanding of the origin and function of the CE collection.

Among the more mysterious features of the history presented in the first chap- ter is the apparently late "arrival" of the letter of James. Though we cannot find any evidence for it before Origen, within fifty years of his death Eusebius lists it as the lead letter in a collection of seven letters called the CE. The similarly late arrival and acceptance of 2 Peter can be explained, according to Trobisch's hypothesis, because the letter was a perfect fit in a larger Western redactional strategy aimed at an anti- Marcionite reconciliation of Paul and the Jerusalem apostolate through the figure of Peter. Given that both James and the seven-letter CE collection make their first appearance in the East, and that the ultimate collection bears the marks of a similar anti-Marcionite tendency, the first chapter will suggest that James may have been written to perform a function in the East similar to the one that 2 Peter performed in the West.

This hunch will lead us, in chapter two, to a more in-depth consideration of the possible origin of the letter of James. For my hypothesis to be valid, the letter could not have been written by its ostensible author, James, the Lord's brother, for he was martyred in 62 C.E. My hypothesis requires a much later date for the letter, since it assumes that the author was writing with a "canonical" collection of letters in mind that included at least 1 Peter, 1 John, and a Pauline collection. As I have already noted, the majority of scholars consider the pseudonymity of James to be uncontroversial. Others, however, continue to argue that the letter is an authentic epistle from the Lord's brother himself. Those who seek to defend the letter's authenticity, however, have a very difficult time explaining the letter's extremely late reception in the church. Most offer a variety of rationalizations, and so, following on chapter one's analysis of canon history, chapter two will begin with a refutation of these attempts to explain the absence of James before Origen. From there, I will consider the various arguments proffered in support of James' authenticity, those in support of its pseudonymity, and those in support of a first-century date for the letter. This section will conclude by asserting the viability of a second-century provenance for the letter.

The second section of chapter two takes this assessment of pseudepigraphy further in the direction of my larger argument. This segment traces the development of traditions about James through the first and second centuries in order to build up a sense of the differences between his "early" and "later" traditional images. This follows on Meade's identification of the literary, theological, historical, and biographical "stabilizing elements" required for the successful production of an apostolic actualization for a new generation. By considering developments in traditional title, authority, piety, relative independence, and murder, I will isolate various features of the historicized "actualizations" of James held by Catholics, "gnostics," and others, some of which seem specific to the first century, and others of which seem to be later developments deriving from the second century. This will accomplish three things: first, it will increase the plausibility of a second-century date for the letter, for as the final section of chapter two will show, the letter of James contains a number of indications that the author may have been working under the "canon-consciousness" of the later, second-century traditional image of James. Second, it will demonstrate that viewing the letter through this second-century image of its author helps explain many of its notorious ambiguities, most particularly its much maligned lack of christological content. Third, it will help us paint a picture of the difficult situation in which second-century proto-Catholic Christians must have found themselves. For the Pauline witness continued to fuel opinions that led some readers to be out of step with the developing Catholic orthodoxy, having primarily to do with Christianity's relation to Israel and the nature of the freedom provided through justification in Christ.[83] I will argue that the later "historicized" Catho-

---

[83] For a helpful treatment of the problem Paul posed for second-century Catholics, see

lic understanding of James held both problem and promise for second-century proto-Catholicism. On the positive side, they found in him a figure whose apostolicity predated that of Paul, whose "Jewishness" was unquestioned, whose Torah-observant piety was unrivalled, who had himself received a resurrection appearance from the Lord, and who was martyred for his faithful witness to Christ. But conversely, James was more highly venerated by those labeled "Jewish-Christian"[84] and "gnostic"[85] (Christians who placed him above and sometimes in opposition to Peter

---

H. von Campenhausen, *The Formation of the Christian Bible*, trans J. A. Baker (Philadelphia: Fortress, 1972), 144–45, 176–81.

[84] I am fully aware of the imprecise and problematic nature of this term. My limited use here and elsewhere in this study is merely intended to correspond to those various ancient groups that maintained Jewish identity in ways considered unacceptable by contemporary and later Catholic theologians. See the discussions by G. Strecker, "On the Problem of Jewish Christianity," in W. Bauer, *Orthodoxy and Heresy in Earliest Christianity* (London: SCM Press, 1971), 241–85; A. F. J. Klijn, "The Study of Jewish Christianity," *NTS* 20 (1973–1974): 419–31; R. Brown, "Not Jewish Christianity and Gentile Christianity but Types of Jewish/Gentile Christianity," *CBQ* 45.1 (1983): 74–79; and esp. J. Lieu, *Neither Jew Nor Greek? Constructing Early Christianity* (New York: T&T Clark, 2002), whose work on the subject offers one of the most strident challenges to the widely accepted notion that "Christians" and "Jews" had parted ways and were easily distinguishable as separate groups in the second century. As Lieu makes abundantly clear, the historical evidence from the period will allow neither for a simplistic demarcation between "Christians" and "Jews," nor for the existence of a single monolithic group that might be labeled "Jewish-Christian." Such distinctions are rooted in theology more than history; and this, in fact, is what supports my continued use of the term in this book. For we are seeking to enter the minds of the theologians from the second to the fourth centuries who were responsible for the creation of the NT canon, and they were not inclined to join us moderns in drawing sharp distinctions between "history" and "theology." Despite (and surely because of) the actual fluidity between Christianity and Judaism in the second century, many proto-Catholic apologists of the time were deeply concerned to offer a simpler account of the relation between Israel and the church, one that was often unapologetically supercessionist (e.g., *Barnabas* 4.6–14; 14.1–5; Melito of Sardis, *Peri Pascha* 42–43; Justin Martyr, *Dial.* 11.5). Such positions were fuelled by concerns over Christians who maintained their Jewish identity in ways that obscured this theological affirmation. Most often this involved some form of ongoing commitment to ritual observance of Torah, but it could also include an adoptionist christology and the rejection of Pauline teaching (see, e.g., Ignatius's concern to draw a distinction between "old" Judaism and "new" Christianity in *Magn.* 8.1–10.3, and especially Irenaeus's discussion of the "Ebionites" in *Adv. Haer.* 1.26.2). Thus, though the title "Jewish-Christian" is historically problematic, its continued use in scholarly discourse is evidence that it remains theologically useful as a generalized description of those early Christian groups who expressed Jewish identity in ways that threatened developing Catholic orthodoxy. As our analysis of several James traditions from the second century will demonstrate (chap. 2), many of those labeled "Jewish-Christian" looked to James the Just as their apostolic patron. Our hypothesis is that one of the motivating factors behind the production of the NT letter of James was the rehabilitation of James from an exclusive association with these particular Christian groups.

[85] Like the term "Jewish-Christian," so also the viability of the term "gnostic" has been

and Paul), and further, he was terribly under-represented in the existing Catholic
apostolic canon of texts. What was needed, I will suggest, was a new and distinctively Catholic actualization of the Jacobian tradition that would offer an apostolic
defense against the distortions to which the Pauline message proved susceptible. I
propose that the letter of James, and the final form of the CE collection itself, is
the result of this concern that Christian faith be established by appeal to the entire
apostolic witness and not by Paul alone.

Having argued for a late date for the letter, and having constructed a viable
motive for its composition, chapter three will attempt to demonstrate the viability
of the historical hypothesis by means of a literary, intertextual reading of James as
a canon-conscious text. Through a reading of the multiple intertextual linkages
between James, 1 Peter, 1 John, and the Pauline letters, I will demonstrate how our
hypothetical second-century author might have composed a text that would bind
itself to the letters of Peter and John in order to create a theologically robust and
literarily coherent collection of texts from the Jerusalem Pillars of the earliest Christian mission to Jews. Along the way I will show how these many linkages can be read
as an attempt to balance and correct the potential distortions of the Pauline witness. That is to say, my hypothesis is that this letter collection called "Catholic" was
designed to provide a final "consummate" shape to the entire NT letter collection in
order that it might truly be called whole and complete, and thus, fully catholic.

Lastly, in a brief conclusion I will present some final reflections on the letter's
origin and sketch out some of the implications of this study for our understanding of the historical development of the NT canon. Again, it should be recalled
throughout that this book is proposing a hypothesis against which the material discussed in each chapter is being measured. The state of scholarly research on both the
letter of James and the CE collection justifies such a provisional posture, for there
are many different positions put forward and the ground remains unstable. The
position presented here will not provide conclusive answers to all of the debated
questions surrounding these texts, but it is offered in the hope that it might provide
a more compelling alternate answer than some of those frequently provided.

---

questioned lately. See esp. M. A. Williams, *Rethinking "Gnosticism": An Argument for Dismantling a Dubious Category* (Princeton: Princeton University Press, 1996). Though Williams
proposes to replace the painfully inaccurate term "gnosticism" with the more accurate and
less sweeping term "biblical demiurgical," he nevertheless recognizes the usefulness of generic
terms for scholarly discourse and acknowledges the difficulty (if not impossibility) of aban-
doning the term (265). Until Williams's proposed replacement gains purchase, this author
will stick with "gnosticism."

CHAPTER ONE

A Canonical History of the New Testament Catholic Epistle Collection

The central goal of this chapter is to produce a thorough account of the canonical formation of the CE collection. Though assumptions about its development abound in introductory works, and a number of shorter summaries can be found here and there in more scholarly texts, a detailed analysis of all the issues involved is required.[1] The following chapter will begin by considering the early development of the CE collection among patristic sources, then examine manuscript evidence for the collection, continue with a close analysis of the canon lists at the end of the canonizing process, and end with preliminary conclusions about the historical formation and canonical function of the collection.

As was intimated in the introduction, this chapter will focus on the development of the collection itself and not on the establishment of the *terminus ad quem* for its constituent letters. Even so, tracing the patristic use of NT texts is an uncertain endeavor, for church fathers do not always quote their sources in such a way that knowledge and use of a particular text can be firmly established. To borrow Richard Hays's description of intertextual reference, the "volume" of such references can vary widely.

> Quotation, allusion and echo may be seen as points along a spectrum of intertextual reference, moving from the explicit to the subliminal. As we move farther away

---

[1] As I was writing this chapter, J. Schlosser was writing one of his own. See his "Le Corpus Épîtres des Catholiques," in *The Catholic Epistles and the Tradition*, ed. J. Schlosser (BETL 176; Leuven: Leuven Universtiy Press, 2004), 3–41.

from overt citation, the source recedes into the discursive distance, the intertextual relations become less determinate, and the demand placed on the reader's listening powers grows greater. As we near the vanishing point of the echo, it inevitably becomes difficult to decide whether we are really hearing an echo at all, or whether we are only conjuring things out of the murmurings of our own imaginings.[2]

There is an unavoidably subjective aspect to any judgment of patristic use that does not involve direct quotation, and any attempt to itemize such use in the service of a developmental account of canon formation is fraught with difficulty.

This is especially the case with determining the use of the letter of James before Origen, since we possess no direct quotations and are limited to evaluating supposed allusions and echoes. As of yet, there is no scholarly agreement as to exactly how one determines the use of an earlier text by a later writer, or for that matter what differentiates a *quotation* from an allusion or an echo.[3] For our purposes, a quotation will refer to instances in which a writer directly quotes a text (evidenced by nearly exact terminological correspondence), along with either a clear citation formula or some form of direct reference to the author. *Allusion* is a "covert, implied, or indirect reference"[4] to an earlier text, which is intended to remind an audience (consciously or unconsciously) of a tradition or text with which they are presumed to have some measure of acquaintance. Finally, an *echo* refers to those instances where the possibility of an intentional reference exists, but the parallel is so inexact that it remains beyond our ability to determine with anything approaching confidence.

With these definitions in mind, my study will resist the temptation to compile long lists of supposed allusions to and echoes of James from patristic writers as evidence that the letter was known and used before Origen.[5] There are numerous ways of accounting for such parallel material in ancient texts apart from automatically assuming the writer is in some way directly dependent on our letter.[6] Even if a parallel were to be firmly established, it is often difficult if not impossible to

---

[2] R. Hays, *Echoes of Scripture in the Letters of Paul* (New Haven: Yale University Press, 1989), 23.

[3] See the helpful survey in A. Gregory, *The Reception of Luke and Acts in the Period before Irenaeus* (Tübingen: Mohr Siebeck, 2003), 1–20. For the purposes of this study, I will follow an adapted version of the criteria set forward by M. Thompson in his 1991 monograph, *Clothed with Christ: The Example and Teaching of Jesus in Romans 12.1–15.13* (JSNTSup 59; Sheffield: JSOT Press, 1991), 28–36.

[4] *OED* 1.242.3, cited by Thompson (28).

[5] Cf. the far too expansive list of "echoes" in J. B. Mayor's commentary (*The Epistle of St. James*, 2nd ed. [London: Macmillan, 1897], xlviii–lxviii).

[6] For instance, both authors might be appealing independently to an earlier written source or oral tradition that may no longer be extant, as O. J. F. Seitz offers as the best explanation for the parallels between James and the *Shepherd of Hermas* ("The Relationship of the Shepherd of Hermas to the Epistle of James," *JBL* 63 [1944]: 131–40). For a thorough survey of potential pitfalls, along with an analysis of the methodological approaches used to determine the second-century reception of Synoptic material, see Gregory, 1–21.

determine which text is in the dependent position.[7] Instead, we must assume a more conservative approach. First, in the case of uncertain allusions and echoes, I will exegete the broader contexts of the passages in question for assistance in adjudication of dependence. Are there any other indications in the text under review that would support knowledge of the letter? Second, I will refuse to stand on any parallel that can be accounted for on the basis of earlier source material. As I will show, for instance, it is unremarkable that both James and Irenaeus refer to Abraham as the "friend of God," because the tradition was widespread in earlier Jewish literature. It is therefore hardly firm enough ground upon which to make a case for Irenaeus's knowledge of the letter of James.

Third, we note that church fathers often cite apostolic texts intertextually (for example, passages from Paul are often supported by appeal to parallel passages from 1 Peter). I will occasionally point out the use of passages that are closely associated with passages in James (for example, 1 John 3:17-18 and James 2:14-17) to show that the letter is never cited when we might expect it to be if the theologian under investigation was aware of it. Though a solid claim for knowledge or ignorance of a text cannot be grounded entirely in an argument from silence, such silences can be marshaled to support a claim for lack of acquaintance (see the excursus below). Fourth, I will take into consideration other comments the writer makes about the apostolic figure associated with the writing we are exploring. I will do this not only to see if they betray any awareness of an associated letter, but also to see if their comments can tell us anything about their particular understanding of apostolic authority, as well as the state of the apostolic letter collection in their day. Finally, my analysis will investigate how the patristic writer in question used the proto-CE texts themselves. That is, I will not simply note that they appear to have used 1 Peter or 1 John, but I will try to ascertain the hermeneutical assumptions behind their use of those letters to see what, if anything, they might tell us about the perceived "function" of non-Pauline texts.[8]

[7] As an example, consider Luke Johnson's treatment in his most recent book on James (*Brother of Jesus, Friend of God* [Grand Rapids: Eerdmans, 2004], 50). He offers three points of positive criteria that must be met for a literary parallel to be considered positive evidence in the case for dependence: Parallels should bear an overall similarity in outlook, including a certain amount of exact linguistic agreement; the parallels should derive from more than one section of each writing; and the parallels should be sufficiently dense to suggest dependence and not simply coincidence. While such criteria may indeed help us make a claim for some form of literary dependence between texts, they do not help us establish which text is in the dependent position. Johnson does an excellent job of analyzing the parallels between James and texts like *1 Clement* and the *Shepherd of Hermas*, but he makes the mistake of simply assuming throughout that James is the earlier text.

[8] In his call for a "fresh agenda" for canon studies, J. Barton (*Holy Writings, Sacred Text: The Canon in Early Christianity* [Louisville: Westminster John Knox, 1997], 33) has asked, "*How* are such books cited, and what is supposed to follow from the citation?" Similarly, H. Gamble has insisted, "It is more and more widely recognized that what we need is a more thorough understanding of how documents were used. . . . What is at issue here is the

It may be countered, after the analysis of patristic use is complete, that firm conclusions remain beyond our reach. Certainly the church fathers produced far more work than we now possess, and even if we did have a large library of works (as we do, for example, for Tertullian), how can anyone presume to make judgments about what an ancient figure "knew" or "did not know"? Are we not dealing here with an argument from silence? And should we not consider all arguments from silence to be fallacious?

On Arguments from Silence

Arguments from silence attempt to defend a position by capitalizing on the absence of evidence against them. Such arguments are traditionally considered to be fallacious, since a case built on missing evidence relies on something that is not actually "evidence" at all! According to this critique, silences in the historical record make no positive argument and therefore cannot be promoted as actual evidence. One cannot claim that an ancient subject was ignorant of a particular person, text, or event simply because we possess no evidence to the contrary. The fact that Irenaeus shows no awareness of James in his extant texts does not prove that he was unaware of the letter.

But are arguments from silence automatically fallacious? An increasing number of historians and philosophers are willing to admit the opposite—that such arguments can indeed be viewed as appropriate and valuable given the right circumstances.[9] Such a shift in position finds its basis in the simple realization that it is impossible to avoid silences when engaging in the task of historical research.[10] The past is always reconstructed by piecing one "sound" of historical evidence together with another in order to bridge the uncomfortable silence that lies in between. The historian who proposes a reconstructed symphony on the basis of only two or three extant notes may very well be guilty of promoting an illegitimate argument from silence, but such a charge must be made in the acknowledgment that no historical reconstruction ever avoids trading in silences.

Our real task, then, involves distinguishing between fallacious and non-fallacious arguments from silence. Put as a question, we must ask ourselves, "Under what circumstances should these types of arguments be allowed to proceed?" The answer depends, of course, on the "volume" of the silence. The "louder" silences

---

relationship of the history of the canon to the history of interpretation" ("The New Testament Canon: Recent Research and the *Status Quaestionis*," in *The Canon Debate*, ed. L. M. McDonald and J. A. Sanders [Peabody, Mass.: Hendrickson, 2002], 273).

[9] See, e.g., D. Henige, *Historical Evidence and Argument* (Madison: University of Wisconsin Press, 2005), 173–85; D. Walton, "Nonfallacious Arguments from Ignorance," *APQ* 29.4 (1992): 381–87; and idem., "The Appeal to Ignorance, or *Argumentum ad Ignorantiam*," *Argumentation* 13 (1999): 367–77.

[10] As Henige has said, "much of the record of the past is suffused with impenetrable silence, and the bulk of historians' interest is inevitably directed toward the sounds" (175).

demand explanatory hypotheses. Such arguments must always be provisional, but when they are promoted under the right circumstances, arguments from silence may be quite valuable in their ability to open a door of unforeseen lines of inquiry. At the very least, such arguments may expose the tenuousness of other positions, requiring their adherents to make their stand on firmer ground.

With this in mind, let us propose three criteria that must be met for an argument from silence to proceed.[11] First, is the silence *comprehensive*?[12] My James hypothesis is dependent on the claim of its non-use through the period before Origen. Arguments from silence depend upon (and are indeed limited to) careful analysis of extant texts. Even if it is noted that the vast majority of patristic literature has been lost, nevertheless we must offer an account for the evidence we have before us. For example, even though we only have two complete texts from the pen of Irenaeus, if those two texts show no sign that the author knew James, we have no choice but to conclude (pending the arrival of new evidence) that Irenaeus did not use James. When we go beyond the absence of James by Irenaeus to demonstrate the corresponding absence in every other ancient writer before Origen (as this chapter will), the comprehensiveness of the silence will become undeniable and the need for an explanation will become more pressing.

Second, is the silence *counterintuitive*? Given what we already know about the historical situation under analysis, is the silence easily explained, or does create such a disturbance that a rationalization is required? It is commonplace to find a section in commentaries on James devoted to addressing this confusing feature of the letter's historical reception. Those who consider the letter to be pseudonymous present the second-century silence of James as evidence in support of their position. Those who seek to defend authenticity must work hard to downplay the significance of the silence, and often end up focusing the weight of their arguments on internal features of the letter that can be read to support a mid-first-century provenance. Of course, any reconstruction of a text's origin must consider evidence derived from its content—as I will do in my second chapter. But even then, most of those who argue for authenticity on internal grounds feel obligated to provide an account for how an authentic letter from James could have remained largely, if not entirely, unused for two centuries. We will evaluate these rationalizations for the comprehensive and counterintuitive non-use of James before Origen when we turn directly to the letter in the next chapter.

---

[11] My criteria are inspired by Henige's reflections: "The classic argument from silence sees it as reflecting reality and bases specific arguments on that. This works best when the silence is so comprehensive, yet so counterintuitive, that any general argument needs to account for it" (175–76).

[12] According to the *Cambridge Dictionary of Philosophy*, "The strength of any argument from ignorance depends on the thoroughness of the search made" since such arguments "can be used to shift the burden of proof merely on the basis of rumour, innuendo, or false accusations, instead of real evidence" (D. Walton, "Informal Fallacy," in *The Cambridge Dictionary of Philosophy*, ed. R. Audi, 2nd ed. [Cambridge: Cambridge University Press, 1999], 431–35).

Third, is the silence *contextually suggestive*? If the silence is acknowledged to be both comprehensive and counterintuitive, does it allow for a more compelling account that agrees with what we already know about the larger historical context? That is, if one were to abandon the attempt to offer a rationalization *in spite of* the silence, can a more compelling account be made *on the basis of* the silence itself? Many James scholars appear to work with an unspoken commitment to the presumption that all NT texts must be dated within the first century C.E., but the comprehensive and counterintuitive silence of James until Origen requires us to consider the possibility that the letter was composed in the second century. From what we know of the canonical process in the first three centuries of the Christian church, can we establish a *motive* for a second-century actualization of James' apostolic authority? Can we make a case for why it would be that someone would compose *this* letter at *that* time? We will turn to this task in the second half of the second chapter.

Ultimately, the conclusion that the letter of James is entirely absent in the second century is indeed the result of an argument from silence that cannot be proved beyond doubt. Happily it is not my goal here to offer incontrovertible proofs. My goal in this chapter is simply to firm up the already widely accepted notion that use of the letter of James is not found anywhere in the second century, for such a demonstration will allow us to move ahead with our exploration of the hypothesis that the letter of James might have been created in the second century for the purpose of forging together a CE collection.

The Early Patristic Witness to the Formation of the Catholic Epistles Collection

The Earliest Citations: Irenaeus of Lyon (ca. 130–200)

It is widely known that the work of Irenaeus represents a major shift in the formation of the biblical canon, since he was the first Catholic theologian to make authoritative use of (and place limitations on) proto-NT texts. In the process, he offers a fairly clear indication of the state of the Western Catholic canon at the end of the second century.

The Accepted Texts

Irenaeus's *Against Heresies* (hereafter *Adv. Haer.*) is particularly important for our purposes because it is the first writing by an orthodox Christian theologian to cite any of the proto-CE by name as recognized, authoritative texts for the church. Along with his famous argument for a closed four-fold gospel canon (*Adv. Haer.* 3.11.8 [SC 211.161–70]), Irenaeus quoted thirteen letters of Paul and became the first Christian writer to quote 1 Peter and 1 John by name. It must be made clear from the outset that his references to these later epistles are far outweighed by his use of Pauline material.[13] Such is the case for all the church fathers I will consider.

---

[13] H. von Campenhausen (*The Formation of the Christian Bible*, trans. J. A. Baker

There are no clear references to 2 Peter; given Irenaeus's anti-Marcionite focus on securing the continuity of prophets and apostles in the old and new covenants, but it is hard to believe that he *would not* have used the letter had he had access to it (cf. 2 Pet 3.1-2). The same, of course, can be said for Jude (vv. 17-18), of which there are also no quotations or convincing allusions or echoes.

In general Irenaeus is content to initiate quotations by simply saying, "Peter says" or "John, the disciple of the Lord, says," though he occasionally refers directly to the epistles themselves (for example, "Peter says in his epistle" (*Petrus ait in epistula sua*) (*Adv. Haer.* 4.9.2 [SC 100.484]). It is clear that Irenaeus considered the Johannine letters to be prophetic texts that directly addressed the heresies that beset the church of the second century. Not only did John clearly foresee the advent of heretics (3.16.5, citing 1 John 2.18-22), he also detailed the content of their teachings (3.16.8 cites 1 John 4.1-3, 5.1, and 2 John 7-8) and offered directives for Christian interaction with them (1.16.3, citing 2 John 10-11). It is interesting to note that in *Adv. Haer.* 3.16.5–8 Irenaeus fails to differentiate between his citations to the Johannine letters, including a reference to 2 John 7-8 in the midst of a series of quotations from 1 John, and cites all of them as coming from the same "epistle of John" (*Adv. Haer.* 3.16.5–8 [SC 211.308–20]). His confluence of the letters suggests that they may have been received as a single text. Indeed, it is hard to explain the survival of 2–3 John without the assumption that they were always attached to 1 John.[14]

Frequently the references to 1 Peter are offered in such a way that they appear to be secondary support for an apparently more authoritative writing. For example, in 5.7.2 Irenaeus cites 1 Peter 1:8 in support of an already-cited portion of 1 Corinthians 13, introducing the text as something "which has been said also by Peter" (*hoc est quod et a Petro dictum est*) (SC 153.90–92). In 5.36.3 he quotes Romans 8:21 and 1 Corinthians 2:9 and attributes them to "the Apostle" (his preferred designation for Paul), then alludes to the later portion of 1 Peter 1:12 ("things into which angels long to look") in a supporting role without attributing the text to Peter.[15] This later text is a favorite of sorts for Irenaeus: it is also referenced in 2.17.9 and 4.34.1 (SC 294.170 and 100.848, respectively), and in all three uses one gets the sense that the text had become a saying of sorts that functioned as a shorthand

---

[Philadelphia: Fortress, 1972], 195 n. 239) counts 248 from Paul and 8 from CE; B. Metzger (*The Canon of the New Testament* [Oxford: Clarendon, 1987], 154) counts 280 from Paul and 15 from CE.

[14] See J. Lieu's helpful discussion of the history of the Johannine letters in her *The 2nd and 3rd Epistles of John: History and Background* (Edinburgh: T&T Clark, 1986), 1–36. Of particular interest is the evidence that suggests the letters circulated in different combinations, sometimes 1 John by itself, sometimes 1–2 John, and sometimes 1–3 John. More recently, C. E. Hill has written an extensive and valuable analysis of the use of Johannine writings in the second century (*The Johannine Corpus in the Early Church* [Oxford: Oxford University Press, 2004]). Hill discerns an allusion to 3 John in *Adv. Haer.* 4.26.3 (99), but I am not convinced.

[15] SC 153.464; he does the same in 3.16.9 (SC 211.326) and 4.37.4 (SC 100.930).

reference to 1:10-12 and its support for the unity of the prophet's foretelling and the evangelists' forth-telling of Christ.

The Letter of James

Against the opinion of some, it cannot be said that Irenaeus knew the letter of James. The brother of the Lord is never referred to as an author of any text, and the one or two supposed echoes of the letter are better accounted for by other means. As I have already noted, in 4.16.2 Irenaeus writes that Abraham "believed God, and it was imputed unto him for righteousness, and he was called the friend of God" (*credidit Deo et reputatum est illi ad justitiam et amicus Dei vocatus est*) (SC 100.562). Though the language is quite similar to James 2:23, the description of Abraham as the "friend of God" is widespread in earlier Jewish literature.[16] Thus there is nothing to safeguard against the possibility that both Irenaeus and the author of James are each appealing to an earlier source in this instance. Further, here and elsewhere his appeal to the figure of Abraham has a consistently Pauline tone: Abraham is almost always linked with "promise" and not with "works" or even "obedience" (cf., for example, *Adv. Haer.* 4.5.3–5 and 4.7.2). Indeed his entire concern in 4.16 is to explain the Pauline doctrine of justification by faith apart from works of the law in the midst of his ongoing concern to protect the continuity of God's covenants with Israel and the church. The same "friend of God" tradition is noted in 4.13.4, but there it is used in connection with John 15:15, where Jesus calls the disciples "friends." Suggesting that it is entirely appropriate for the Word of God to call human beings friends, Irenaeus appeals to John 8: Abraham witnessed Christ's work ("before Abraham was, I am") and he too was called a friend of God.

Two further points might be raised rather briefly in support of the notion that Irenaeus did not know the letter of James. First, Irenaeus's only references to the person James is in the long discussion of the Acts of the Apostles in 3.12, and his comments there are lifted rather directly from what he has read in Acts 15 and Galatians 2. Second, when he refers to the apostles in relation to Christian scriptural texts in 3.21.3, he only names Peter, John, Matthew, and Paul (SC 211.408). These figures correspond exactly to the apostolic gospels and letters he clearly accepts; if he were aware of a letter from James, would he not have listed him among these four? The complete absence (here and elsewhere) of any kind of reference to the letter of James is sufficient evidence against the possibility that Irenaeus knew of its existence.

Other Ancient Letters Cited

In 3.3.3 Irenaeus mentions *1 Clement*, a "powerful letter" written from Clement of Rome who was "in the third place from the apostles" (*tertio loco ab apostolis episcopatum sortitur Clemens*), that is, bishop of Rome after Linus and Anacletus

[16] Based perhaps on corresponding designations for Abraham in the OT (Isa 41:8; 51:2; 2 Chr 20:7; Dan 3:35), the traditional label is found throughout Jewish literature (e.g. *Sobr.* 56; *Abr.* 89; 273; *Jub.* 19.9; *T. Abr.* [Rec. A] 1.7; 2.3, 6; *Apoc. Abr.* 10).

(SC 211.34). Clement is an important figure for Irenaeus because he forms a link in the chain of succession back to the apostles, and his letter is valuable in this regard because Irenaeus regards it as being older than the teaching of his opponents. Irenaeus is also aware of Ignatius's letter to the Romans (5.28.4), but he does not actually name Ignatius in his quotation of that letter (SC 211.360–62). Polycarp also figures prominently in the work (3.3.4), both because of his status as a disciple of the apostles, and also because of the witness of his *Letter to the Philippians*. While these people are presented as authoritative figures from the past, their authority seems clearly derivative from that of the original apostles. They witness not to Jesus but to the apostolic tradition and are therefore sub-apostolic links in the chain of succession from the first hearers to the present.

The Figures of James, Peter, and John

Given the paucity of CE citations in comparison to the use of Pauline texts, it may be concluded that the *figures* of James, Peter, and John are more important to Irenaeus's argument than the content of their writings. As was the case for most Western writers, Irenaeus considered Peter the chief figure among the three; considered himself to be defending, against the heretics, "the tradition derived from the apostles, of the very great, the very ancient and universally known church founded and organized at Rome by the two most glorious apostles (*gloriosissimi duo apostoli*) Peter and Paul" (3.3.1–2 [SC 211.30–32; *ANF* 1.415]). Though references to Pauline *writings* far outweigh the Petrine, both *persons* are invoked as the "most glorious" dual authorities upon whom the earliest, most authoritative Christian tradition was constituted. In this regard, Peter stands far above his co-Pillars James and John.

The three do play a key role as a unit, however, in the middle chapters of *Adv. Haer.*, book 3, chapters devoted to an extended demonstration of the harmony of apostolic doctrine. While Irenaeus addresses all the major heresies by name at various points along the way, it is clear from this section that the Marcionites are the focus of his concern (*Adv. Haer.* 3.11.7, 9; 12.12; 13.1; 14.4). Against them he called the witness of the Acts of the Apostles (the long chapter 3.12 is devoted to the book), as it enabled a proper, Catholic understanding of Paul as an apostle who worked in harmony along with all the original members of the apostolic mission.[17] Irenaeus's reading of this text focuses particularly on the role of Peter and John as leaders of the twelve; his comments on James, as I said earlier, came directly from Acts 15 and Galatians 12. Add this to the fact that he never shows any awareness of the letter, and we are left with the conclusion that he must not have known it.

For Irenaeus, Peter, John, and James offered an important witness in support of the continuity of salvation history against those who would assert a division between the old and new covenants. His reading of Acts focuses on those passages that demonstrate how the God of Israel was at work in the earliest apostolic mission. After highlighting James' role at the Apostolic Council in Acts 15, he concludes: "From

---

[17] See von Campenhausen (*Formation*, 201–2) for a helpful description of this "catholicizing" function for the Acts of the Apostles.

all these passages, then, it is evident that they [that is, Peter and the apostles associated with James in Jerusalem] did not teach the existence of another Father, but gave the new covenant of liberty to those who had lately believed in God by the Holy Spirit" (*Adv. Haer.* 3.12.14 [SC 211.244; *ANF* 1.436]). Similarly, his discussion of Galatians 2 concludes, "And the apostles who were with James allowed the Gentiles to act freely, yielding us up to the Spirit of God. But they themselves, while knowing the same God, continued in the ancient observances" (3.12.15 [SC 211.248; *ANF* 1.436]). It is on this basis that he defends Peter's infamous withdrawal from Gentile fellowship as a demonstration that the Holy Spirit came from the same God that gave the Jews the Mosaic law. Peter ends up playing the role of the conscientious apostle, concerned about any action that might threaten a proclamation of the continuity of old and new covenants.

It is worth noting that this would have been an excellent opportunity for Irenaeus to speak about the positive presentation of the law in the letter of James, had he known the letter. The language he uses makes it evident that he is fully cognizant of James' high authority in the ancient Jerusalem church. He refers, for instance, to "the apostles who were with James" (*ca. Iacobum*). The *Sources chrétiennes* text includes a Greek fragment of the same passage which reads οἱ δὲ περὶ ᾿Ιακώβου ἀπόστολοι, and the editor rightly notes that the phrase often designates a leading man with his entourage, as it does in reference to Paul in Acts 13:13.32 (SC 211.303). Thus, though James is spoken of as a leader parallel to Peter and Paul, Irenaeus does not refer to the letter attributed to him, even here in what is probably its most applicable context.

He concludes chapter 12 by insisting that the apostles were witnesses of "every action and of every doctrine" (*uniuersi actus et uniuersae doctrinae*) of the Lord (*Adv. Haer.* 3.12.15 [SC 211.248]). The members of the Jerusalem apostolate were always present with the Lord, eyewitnesses to his every action and teaching; therefore their witnesses cannot be excluded as Marcion had insisted.[18] Irenaeus then concluded the discussion in 3.13.1 by reference to two important passages in Paul's own witness to the unity of apostolic preaching.

> With regard to those who allege that Paul alone knew the truth, and that to him the mystery was manifested by revelation [Eph 3:3], let Paul himself convict them, when he says that one and the same God wrought in Peter for the apostolate of the circumcision, and in himself for the Gentiles [*unum et ipsum Deum operatum Petro in apostolatum circumcisionis, et sibi in gentes*; Gal 2:8]. Peter, therefore, was an apostle of that very God whose was also Paul; and Him whom Peter preached as God among those of the circumcision, and likewise the Son of God, did Paul also among the Gentiles. (SC 211.250; *ANF* 1.436)

---

[18] Note that the authors of 1 John and 1–2 Peter predicate their authority on the fact that they were themselves eyewitnesses of Christ's work (1 Pet 5.1; 2 Pet 1.16-18; 1 John 1.1-4).

Paul himself acknowledged a *division of labor* in God's saving work among the apostles, not a *division of doctrine*. Irenaeus then immediately cites 1 Corinthians 15:11, where Paul said in reference to all the apostles who had seen Jesus after the resurrection, "whether it were I or they, so we preach, and so you believed," acknowledging the harmonious unity of their preaching. Even on Paul's own terms, then, one cannot choose a preferred apostle from among the original group. For Irenaeus, the extrication of any one apostle from the unity of the original mission led directly into heretical doctrine.

Conclusion

While he does not set out an explicit agenda for the development of a second apostolic letter collection, Irenaeus does bear witness to its early development: he argues for a broadened apostolic witness beyond Paul, and he accomplishes this by highlighting the role of Peter, John, and James in the Acts of the Apostles as a witness to apostolic unity (though it must be recognized that he has in mind a division of labor primarily according to Paul and Peter, not Paul and the Pillars). Along the way he offers the first unambiguous quotations of 1 Peter and 1–2 John. He does not show any knowledge of James, 2 Peter, 3 John, or Jude.

THE ONGOING STRUGGLE AGAINST MARCION:
TERTULLIAN OF CARTHAGE (CA. 160–223)

We find Irenaeus's line of thought developed in the work of Tertullian of Carthage. Among his most important contributions to the developing NT canon is his work against Marcion's dangerously truncated canon. As we will see, the content of his canon of Christian writings is similar to that of his predecessor. As concerns the CE, Tertullian makes use of 1 Peter, 1 John, and Jude, but there are no clear references to 2 Peter or 2–3 John.

The Accepted Texts

While it is quite evident that Tertullian knew and used 1 Peter, it is surprising that he seems to have only directly quoted the letter on one occasion (*Scorp.* 12.2; CCSL 2.1092). Elsewhere the epistle is alluded to but not directly cited. For instance, the teaching about honoring the emperor (1 Pet 2:13-17) is taken up on several occasions, but only in *Scorp.* 14.3 is the teaching noted to have come from Peter himself. This indirect citation holds for the majority of Tertullian's apparent references to 1 Peter; the letter exists as a felt presence, but attention is rarely drawn to the text itself.[19]

---

[19] CCSL 2.1096; see also *De oratione* 20.2 (CCSL 1.268) in reference to 1 Peter 3:3, *De anima* 7.3 and 55.2 (CCSL 2.790 and 862) in reference to the Petrine tradition of Christ's descent to the dead (1 Pet 3:19 and 4:6), and *Ad nationes* 1.3.2 (CCSL 1.13) in reference to 1 Peter 4:14-16.

The situation is somewhat different when it comes to Tertullian's mention of 1 John, as he refers to him far more frequently than Peter. He is also more likely to refer to the existence of the epistle itself than he was with 1 Peter, though still the vast majority of his references are simply introduced as "John says" or "John teaches." As for 1 John, it must be noted that Tertullian joins Irenaeus in being impressed by the fact that John prophesied the advent of heretics. He shows great interest in the "antichrist" passages; up to half of his citations come from the relevant verses on the subject.[20] Tertullian says that John called heretics "antichrists"(*Ieiun.* 11.5 [CCSL 2.1270]), and goes on to specifically designate Marcion and his followers as antichrists because they denied that Christ came in the flesh (*Adv. Marc.* 3.8.1 [CCSL 1.518], 5.16.4 [CCSL 1.711]). Though John preceded Marcion in time, 1 John is nevertheless read as though it were written to address the Marcionite crisis. As with Irenaeus, Tertullian's references to the "letter" of John are always in the singular. It is striking, however, that 2 John 7 is never cited in this midst of these other "antichrist" quotations.

Finally, Tertullian is the earliest Western witness to the letter of Jude. In *De cultu feminarum* 1.3.1–3 (CCSL 1.346–47), after tracing the roots of feminine ornamentation to the fallen angels described in "the book of Enoch," Tertullian offers a justification for his use of the text. He notes the two known objections to its use: it was not included in the Jewish canon, and it was clearly pseudepigraphic, since an authentic writing of Enoch could not have survived the flood. To these objections he offers the following answers: (1) Jewish rejection is unsurprising, since they always reject that which tells of Christ, and (2) Noah, who was the trustee of Enoch's "preachings" (*praedicata*), may have saved a copy of the document from the flood, or may have renewed it under the Spirit's inspiration after it was destroyed. Should these answers be found unconvincing, to them is added (3) "the fact that Enoch possesses a testimony in the Apostle Jude" (*quod Enoch apud Iudam apostolum testimonium possidet*) (1.3.1 [CCSL 1.347]). Though evidence of use is rather meager, such a statement says much about the status of Jude in Tertullian's day, as the appeal to "the apostle Jude" is presented as the decisive argument to end all arguments. If an apostolic writing approved *1 Enoch*, what Christian can deny its validity?

The Letter of James

Although Tertullian mentions James of Jerusalem at various key points in his text (see below under the *Figures* discussion), he nowhere offers any evidence that he was aware of a letter attributed to that apostle. In *Adv. Marc.* 4.3 and 5.3 (CCSL 1.548–50 and 668–71, respectively), for instance, he speaks at length about the apostolic controversy of Galatians 2, but he says nothing of James' letter. Likewise, in *Scorpiace* 6.10 he quotes Psalm 32:1, "Blessed are they . . . whose sins are

---

[20] Cf. *Adv. Prax.* 31.3 (CCSL 2.1204); *Praescr.* 3.13 (CCSL 1.189), 4.4 (CCSL 1.190), 33.11 (CCSL 1.214); *Ieiun.* 11.5 (CCSL 2.1270); *Carn.* 24.3 (CCSL 2.916).

covered," and immediately refers in 6.11 to 1 Peter 4:8, "love covers a multitude of sins" (CCSL 2.1080). Had he known the letter of James, one would think he might have appealed to the parallel text in James 5:20. As in Irenaeus, so also we find Tertullian calling Abraham a "friend of God" (*Adv. Jud.* 2.7 [CCSL 2.1342]), but as before, given the ubiquity of the tradition, there is no reason to assume this derived from the letter of James. Given Tertullian's rigorous sense of Christian piety, one would think he would have found much of value in the letter had he had access to it.

Other Ancient Letters Cited

Among the available letters beyond the proto-CE, Tertullian also knew of writings attributed to Barnabas. In *De pudicitia*, he amasses support for his denunciation of Pope Calixtus's declaration that the church could forgive adultery and fornication committed after baptism. After listing apostolic support for his position, he turns to the testimony of

> . . . one of the apostles' companions which aptly confirms, as a secondary author-
> ity, the teaching of the masters [*magistri*]. For there is also extant a book entitled
> *To the Hebrews*, written by Barnabas, a man well accredited [*auctorare*] by God
> since Paul associates him with himself in the observance of continence: *Or is it
> only Barnabas and I who have not the right to do this?* [1 Cor 9:6]. And surely the
> epistle of Barnabas has found wider acceptance among the churches than has
> that apocryphal Shepherd of adulterers. (*Pud.* 20.1 [CCSL 1.1321; Le Saint,
> *ACW* 28.115])

He goes on to quote the teaching in Hebrews 6:1-8 against second repentance, con-cluding that Barnabas, as one taught by the disciples, is a witness to their teaching on the subject. Clearly Tertullian needed Hebrews 6 to support his argument, and therefore he appealed to the tradition of its authorship by Barnabas on two grounds. First, he insists that Barnabas was a companion of the apostles who is "well accred-ited by God." Le Saint notes that the word used here, *auctorare*, "is a legal word signifying that one becomes security for another or gives a pledge for another as his bondsman."[21] Thus, in Tertullian's view, though Barnabas is "secondary" in author-ity, he is nevertheless a kind of *legal witness* to the apostolic teaching and is therefore entirely trustworthy. Second, Barnabas can be trusted because he has another epistle (the *Epistle of Barnabas*) that is "generally received among the churches." By con-trast, the *Shepherd of Hermas* allowed for post-baptismal repentance for adultery and had to be rejected.[22] Though he clearly subordinated Barnabas to the apostles, he nevertheless sought to include Barnabas' letters in his broader collection of "legally" authoritative apostolic texts. This author, however, is the only one beyond the apos-tles to be considered; though Tertullian mentions Polycarp and Clement of Rome

---

[21] Le Saint, *ACW* 28.277, n. 605.
[22] *Herm. Vis.* 2.2; Tertullian also says (in *Pud.* 10.12, CCSL 2.1301) that "every council of the Churches" had rejected it.

in *Praescriptione* 32.2 (CCSL 1.213), he seems to have had nothing whatsoever to say about their letters.

The Figures of James, Peter, and John

Like Irenaeus, Tertullian also appealed to the Acts of the Apostles in support of a proper understanding of Paul and castigated Marcion at length for his inability to provide any background information for *his* Paul (*Adv. Marc.* 5.1 [CCSL 1.663–65]). Of crucial importance is the way in which Tertullian moves beyond Irenaeus in his tendency to focus quite narrowly on Paul's relationship with James, Peter, and John in particular, the Pillars of the Jerusalem church as identified in Galatians 2:9. Tertullian's rhetoric against the Marcionites sets forth a mocking demotion of Paul's authority beneath these three whom he calls the *auctores*, the "original" or "primitive authors" (*Adv. Marc.* 4.2.5 [CCSL 1.548]).[23] He insists that Marcion was deficient in his exclusive devotion to Paul and Luke, for Luke was

> not an apostle but an apostolic man [*non apostolus, sed apostolicus*], not a master but a disciple, in any case less than his master, and assuredly even more of a lesser account as being the follower of a later apostle [*posterior apostolus*], Paul, to be sure: so that even if Marcion had introduced his Gospel under the name of Paul in person, that single document would not be adequate for our faith, if destitute of the support of his predecessors. (*Adv. Marc.* 4.2.4 [CCSL 1.548; Evans, 263])

Paul lacks authority on his own. Tertullian sees further demonstration of this in Galatians 2, where it is revealed that Paul, "you understand, who, yet inexperienced in grace (*qui adhuc in gratia rudis*), and anxious lest he had run or was running in vain, was then for the first time conferring with those who were apostles before him [*antecessores*]" (*Adv. Marc.* 1.20.2 [CCSL 1.461; Evans, 51]). This conference was necessary, that is, "perchance he had not believed as they did, or was not preaching the gospel in their manner" (*Adv. Marc.* 4.2.5 [CCSL 1.548; Evans, 263]; cf. *Praescr.* 23 [CCSL 1.204–5]). Tertullian wanted Marcionites to know that Paul *needed* the Jerusalem Pillars: "So great as this was his desire to be approved of and confirmed by those very people who, if you please, you suggest should be understood to be of too close kindred with Judaism" (*Adv. Marc.* 5.3.1 [CCSL 1.668; Evans, 519]). Paul's immaturity in the faith was also to blame for his apparent condemnation of "Peter and those others, pillars of the apostolate," as he was caught up in "his zeal against Judaism" as a "neophyte." But soon he too saw their wisdom, as "he himself was afterwards to become in his practice all things to all men" (*Adv. Marc.* 1.20.2–3 [CCSL 1.461; Evans, 51]; cf. *Praescr.* 24 [CCSL 1.205–6]). Note especially Tertullian's continued insistence that all three apostles (Peter, John, and James) be linked together as a kind of unit; in Tertullian's mind, all three received censure from Paul in Galatians 2, not simply Peter alone (*Adv. Marc.* 1.20.2 [CCSL 1.461]; 4.3.3 [CCSL 1.548]; 5.3.1–6 [CCSL 1.668–69]). In his testimony against

---

[23] Evans (263) offers "original apostles," but the *ANF* (3.348) has "the primitive authors."

Marcion, Tertullian consistently places Paul among and even beneath this triad of apostolic Pillars.

Surely this apparent demotion is more a part of Tertullian's polemical hyperbole than a reflection of his actual opinion.[24] Like Irenaeus, Tertullian's textual appeal is consistently Pauline, with 1 Peter, 1 John, and Jude receiving no more than a handful of citations at best. Beneath the rhetoric, Tertullian is seeking to establish one key point: the separation of Paul and Pillars is based on a division of *labor*, not a division of *doctrine*. When seen in this light, the content of the gospel preached by both missions is revealed to be entirely harmonious. Note how he describes their relationship in the following passages:

> So they gave him their right hands, the sign of fellowship and agreement, and they arranged among themselves a distribution of their spheres of work [*et inter se distributionem officii ordinauerunt*]—not a division of the Gospel. It was not that each should preach something different, but that each should preach to different people, Peter to the Circumcision, Paul to the Gentiles. (*Praescr.* 23.9 [CCSL 1.205; Greenslade, LCC 5.46])

> [I]n respect of the unity of their preaching, as we have read earlier in this epistle, they had joined their right hands, and by the very act of having divided their spheres of work [*officii distributio*] had signified their agreement in the fellowship of the Gospel: as he says in another place, *Whether it were I or they, so we preach* [1 Cor 15:11]. (*Adv. Marc.* 1.20.4 [CCSL 1.461; Evans, 51])

> At length, when he had conferred with the original <apostles>, and there was agreement concerning the rule of the faith [*regula fidei*], they joined the right hands <of fellowship>, and from thenceforth divided their spheres of preaching [*officia praedicandi distinxerunt*], so that the others should go to the Jews, but Paul to Jews and Gentiles. (*Adv. Marc.* 4.2.5 [CCSL 1.548; Evans, 263])

> Well it is therefore that Peter and James and John gave Paul their right hands, and made a compact about distribution of office [*officii distributio*], that Paul should go to the Gentiles, and they to the circumcision. (*Adv. Marc.* 5.3.6 [CCSL 1.669; Evans, 521])

Far from actually demoting Paul, what Tertullian wanted to emphasize was the fact that Paul spoke as a representative of a larger unified group that had nevertheless been amicably divided into different spheres of work. One cannot isolate Paul from this larger apostolic mission, for in doing so, one inevitably falls into heresy. God's truth simply cannot be derived from Paul alone. This concern is underscored by Tertullian's repeated reference to 1 Corinthians 15:11 (*Adv. Marc.* 1.20.4 [CCSL 1.461]; 4.4.5 [CCSL 1.550]; *Pud.* 19.3 [CCSL 1.1320]), a text already cited by Irenaeus. After listing Peter, James, and the others who had seen the resurrected Jesus (15:3-8), and after calling himself "the least of the apostles" (v. 9) but asserting

[24] T. Barnes, *Tertullian: A Historical and Literary Study* (Oxford: Oxford University Press, 1971), 129.

that he "worked harder than any of them" (v. 10), Paul concludes by affirming the harmony of apostolic proclamation: "Whether then it was I or they, so we preach and so you believed" (v. 11).

A passage from *De pudicitia* offers further insight into Tertullian's interest in this Pauline saying. After reconciling an apparent discrepancy between the teachings of Paul and John, he says:

> I am content with the fact that, between apostles, there is a common agreement in rules of faith and of discipline. For, "Whether I," he says, "or they, thus we preach." . . . This harmony of the Holy Spirit whoever observes, shall by Him be conducted into His meanings. (*Pud.* 19:3–4 [CCSL 1.1320; *ANF* 4.94])

The Holy Spirit secures the harmony of apostolic preaching. Likewise, the one who is guided by the Holy Spirit will not, when encountering apparent diversity in the apostolic writings, conclude with Marcion that the apostles preached a different gospel. On the contrary, they arranged "a distribution of their spheres of work—not a division of the gospel. It was not that each should preach something different, but that each should preach to different people" (*Praescr.* 23.9 [CCSL 1.205]).

Conclusion

By way of summary, the witness of Irenaeus and Tertullian demonstrates that 1 Peter and 1 John were widely accepted as authoritative in the early third-century Western churches allied with Rome. Interestingly, Tertullian attributes complete apostolic authority to Jude but shows no awareness of 2 John, while Irenaeus knew 2 John yet shows absolutely no awareness of Jude. It also seems that Hebrews was at this time a letter in search of an author: Irenaeus indirectly cited it as Pauline, but Tertullian attributed it to Barnabas, thereby linking it with a (potential) collection of non-Pauline letters including the "other" *Letter of Barnabas*, 1 Peter, 1 John, and Jude. There are still no clear references to James, 2 Peter, or 3 John. 1 John is appealed to directly in support of his work against the Marcionites, as it was the letter of this apostle that warned the church *in advance* about the coming of Marcion, the Antichrist. 1 Peter emerges as a valuable source for Christian morality in a pagan world. The letter of the "Apostle Jude" is also used in support of Christian morality and is authoritative enough to adjudicate the utilization of questionable texts.

Thus, in Tertullian we do not yet have a CE collection, but we do see an increase in the role of other apostolic letters beyond those of Paul. More importantly, where Irenaeus opened the door for a broader, more diverse apostolic witness through Peter, Tertullian fixed this broadened apostolic witness in the ancient, harmonious division of labor between Paul and the Pillars of the Jerusalem church. One can readily see how this vision of these two missions, which "joined hands in perfect concord" and "preached the same gospel to different people," might eventually become the model for a dual collection of letters, one that similarly preaches the same gospel in different ways. It must be said, however, that Tertullian never makes this connection for us; that is, he nowhere offers any indication that he is applying this "division of labor" to a formal division of apostolic letters for his *novum testamentum*. How could he without possession of a letter from James?

Other Western Witnesses: Hippolytus and Cyprian

A brief look at two other prominent Western writers of the late second to mid-third century will show little difference in letter collections. Like Irenaeus, Hippolytus, the Bishop of Rome (d. 235) cited 1 Peter and 1–2 John, albeit quite sparingly. Some have argued that certain passages may also suggest knowledge of 2 Peter, but this is difficult to establish. His use of "Tartarus" as a description of the place of eternal punishment (*Ref.* 10.33.11 [PTS 25.415]) need not automatically imply knowledge of 2 Peter 2:4, as the term was well known in Hellenistic Pagan and Jewish literature (cf. *1 En.* 20.2; Job 40:20; 41:24; LXX Prov 30:16). The fact that his first two uses of the word are found in quotations from Pagan poets may indicate his source (*Ref.* 1.26.18 [PTS 25.89] and 4.32.20 [PTS 25.120]). More significant is the possible allusion to 2 Peter 2:22, where certain Christians who fell into the Noetian heresy repented, then returned to the false teaching are said to "wallow once again in the same mire [ἐπὶ τὸν αὐτὸν βόρβορον ἀνεκυλίοντο]" (*Ref.* 9.7.16–17 [PTS 25.343]). The proverbial nature of this phrase, however, keeps us from claiming it with any kind of certainty. We are only on certain ground with 1 Peter and 1–2 John.

Similarly, Cyprian, Bishop of Carthage (d. 258) appears to have used only 1 Peter and 1 John.[25] Apart from a number of general allusions and one-off quotations of passages from 1 Peter, Cyprian appeals to the call to maintain good conduct among the Gentiles (2:11-12; *Quir.* 3.11.63 [CCSL 3.102–3]; *Ep.* 13.3.45–49 [CCSL 3B.74]), the example of Christ's sufferings (2:21-23; *Ep.* 8.2.3 [CCSL 3B.41]; *Pat.* 9.169–73 [CCSL 3A.123]; *Quir.* 3.37.3–5 [CCSL 3.131]; *Unit. eccl.* 2.2 [CCSL 3A.249]; *Zel. liv.* [CCSL 3A.81]), the baptismal symbolism of Noah's ark (3:20-21; *Ep.* 69.2.2 [CCSL 3C.472] and 69.12.2 [CCSL 3C.488]; 74.11.3 [CCSL 3C.579]; 75.15.2 [CCSL 3C.595]; *Unit. eccl.* 6.150–51 [CCSL 3.253]), and the call to rejoice in sufferings (4:12-14; *Ep.* 58.2.2 [CCSL 3C.322]; *Fort.* 9.13-20 [CCSL 3.198]). First John is cited even more frequently: Passages on the renunciation of sinful ways in the imitation of Christ (1:8-9; 2:1-2, 6, 15-17) are regularly quoted,[26] as is the teaching on the antichrist (2:18-19; *Ep.* 59.7.3; 69.1.3; 70.3.2 [CCSL 3C.349, 471, 513]). Though he nowhere cites it, he must at least have been aware of 2 John, for it was quoted in his presence at the Council of Carthage in 256. There Bishop Aurelius of Chullabi cited 2 John 10-11 ("Do not receive into the house or welcome anyone who does not bring this teaching . . .") as a teaching

---

[25] See M. Fahey, *Cyprian and the Bible: A Study in Third-Century Exegesis* (Tübingen: J. C. B. Mohr, 1971) for a detailed listing and analysis of Cyprian's NT citations and allusions.

[26] E.g., 1 John 1:8—*Quir.* 3.9.5–6 (CCSL 3.141) and *Op.* 3.54 (CCSL 3A.56); 1 John 2:1-2, 6—*Ep.* 55.18.1 (CCSL 3B.277) and 58.1.3 (CCSL 3B.320); 1 John 2:15-17—*Quir.* 3.11.69–75 (CCSL 3.103) and 3.19.12 (CCSL 3.114).

of the Apostle John regarding the need for lapsed Christians to be rebaptized (*Sent.* 81 [CCSL 3E.103]).[27] There is no evidence as to whether or not he was aware of James, 2 Peter, or 3 John.

The Muratorian Fragment

Finally, I must include a few words about the Muratorian fragment, which has long been considered the earliest discussion of canonical texts in the church.[28] It is generally believed to have originated in the Western church of the late second century, originally written in Greek and carelessly copied into Latin at a later date. It names as "received" the four gospels, Acts, thirteen letters of Paul (excluding Hebrews), Jude, 2 (or possibly 3) epistles of John, the Wisdom of Solomon, and the Apocalypses of John and Peter. The absence of James and Hebrews and the presence of the Apocalypses of John and Peter are generally taken to indicate an early Western origin, as is the fact that *Hermas* is listed as rejected because it was written "but very recently, in our times [*vero nuperrime temporibus nostris*], in the city of Rome, while bishop Pius, his brother, was occupying the chair of the church of the city of Rome."[29] Taken literally, a text written after Pius was bishop of Rome indicates a date sometime after the mid-second century. While the absence of the letters of James, Hebrews, and 2 Peter is understandable in an early Western list, it seems difficult to believe that 1 Peter was intentionally omitted; thus, the generally accepted explanation is that the letter fell out at some point in the process of transmission. When it is included in the list, we see that the non-Pauline letter collection coheres quite nicely with what we have discovered regarding the late second-century Western use of the proto-CE.

It is well known that the traditional date and provenance of the Muratorian fragment has been challenged in recent years, initially through the work of Albert Sundberg and recently extended in a monograph by Geoffrey Hahneman, both of whom propose a fourth-century Eastern provenance for the document. The research presented in this chapter will show that such a theory is highly improbable. However, my reasons for rejecting their thesis will have to wait until after we have considered the state of the canon in the fourth-century Eastern church.

Thus the Western evidence up to the mid-third century demonstrates the primary authority of 1 Peter and 1 John, though 2 John and Jude appear to have been known and used. This will continue to be the case in the West until the African synods of the late fourth and early fifth centuries assert authoritative acceptance of all seven Catholic Epistles, probably based on the authority of Jerome and Augustine.

---

[27] Cf. Lieu, *2nd and 3rd John*, 9.

[28] For text, discussion, and analysis, see G. Hahneman, *The Muratorian Fragment and the Development of the Canon* (Oxford: Clarendon, 1992); Metzger, *Canon*, 305–7; and A. Sundberg, "Canon Muratori: A Fourth-Century List," *HTR* 66.1 (1973): 1–41.

[29] Translation from Metzger, *Canon*, 307.

THE *GNOSIS* OF CHRIST: CLEMENT OF ALEXANDRIA (FL. CA. 190–215)

Clement was a contemporary of Tertullian. Like his Western counterparts, he too was interested in opposing heresy and defending the ecclesiastical tradition. However, while Irenaeus and Tertullian sought the security of a publicly held tradition of apostolic succession and apostolic texts against the secretive speculations of the gnostics, Clement was himself an heir of the Alexandrian gnostic tradition.[30] Though his allegiance to the Catholic Church was clear,[31] Clement nevertheless held that the Christian tradition included that which had been passed down orally by secret "transmission to a few, having been unwritten by the apostles" (*Strom.* 6.7.61.3 [SC 446.186]). His commitment to the scriptural traditions of the church seems to have applied primarily to the inner core of accepted Christian texts. In the third book of the *Stromata*, for instance, he acknowledges the traditional priority of the four-fold gospel: "[W]e do not find this saying in our four traditional gospels [ἐν τοῖς παραδεδομένοις ἡμῖν τετταρασιν εὐαγγελίοις], but in that according to the Egyptians" (*Strom.* 3.13.93.1 [GCS 2.238]). The outer edge of his "canon," however, was intentionally undefined, and this enabled him to appeal to a wide range of texts beyond those later canonized.[32]

The Accepted Texts

When it comes to the later canonical CE, the extant evidence shows that Clement made unambiguous use of 1 Peter, 1–2 John, and Jude. As was the case with the Western writers, so it is for Clement that the proto-CE are cited with far less frequency than other texts. Still, 1 Peter is quoted a number of times with attribution to Peter. Twice he refers to Peter's "epistle" (*Strom.* 3.18.110.1 [GCS 2.247] and 4.20.129.3 [GCS 2.305]), but in general he is content to introduce his citations with a simple "Peter says." The majority of these citations are found in the *Paedagogus*; here it is made evident that Clement valued Peter's letter primarily for its moral instruction. Chapters 11 and 12 of the third book, which are devoted to an extended discourse on moral propriety, are introduced with a reference to 1 Peter 2:12: "We keep in mind these holy words particularly: 'Keep your conduct excellent among the heathens, so that, whereas they slander you as evil-doers, they may, by observing the nobility of your actions, glorify God'" (*Paed.* 3.11.53.3 [SC 158.114]; Wood, FC 23.242). During the course of this discussion Clement supports his moral and ethical exhortations with repeated quotations from the letter.

First John is also quoted numerous times with attribution. He is usually content to introduce the quotation by simply saying, "John says," though sometimes

---

[30] See von Campenhausen's studies in *Formation*, 291–307; and idem., *Ecclesiastical Authority and Spiritual Power* (London: A&C Black, 1969), 196–212; as well as R. P. C. Hanson, *Allegory and Event* (London: SCM Press, 1959), 117–29.

[31] *Strom.* 7.17.107 (SC 428.316–24) is an Irenaeus-like argument for the historic primacy of the Catholic church.

[32] See Otto Stählin's *Citatenregister* for Clement (GCS 39.1–66).

the epistle itself is noted (*Strom.* 3.4.32.2 [GCS 2.210]). He refers in *Stromata* to 1 John as John's "larger epistle" (*Strom.* 2.15.66.4 [GCS 2.148]), and there are short commentaries on both 1 and 2 John extant (these will be discussed below). As usual it is unknown whether or not he was aware of 3 John, though it is odd that he would comment on the second without even mentioning the existence of a third. More often than not, the appeals to Johannine literature are, like 1 Peter, for the purpose of moral exhortation. With John, however, the focus is often more specifically on the nature of Christian love (cf. *Strom.* 4.16.100.4–6 [GCS 2.292]; and *Quis.* 37.6–38.2 [GCS 3.184]).

Finally, the letter of Jude is also the subject of a short commentary (see below). Apart from this, the letter is referred to only a couple of times. Jude 5-6 and 11 is quoted in order to demonstrate how it is that God sets forward the punishment of licentious persons as an example for Christians, so "that we may be kept from sin out of fear of the penalty" (*Paed.* 3.8.44.3-45.1 [GCS 1.262; FC 23.236]). On another occasion we find Clement condemning various heretical views and concluding, "I fancy Jude was speaking prophetically of these and similar sects in his letter when he wrote, 'So too with these people caught up in their dreams' [Jude 8] who do not set upon the truth with their eyes fully open, down to 'pompous phrases pour from their mouth' [Jude 16]" (*Strom.* 3.2.11.2 [GCS 2.200; Ferguson, FC 85.263]).

The Letter of James

Did Clement know the letter of James? There are no overt quotations of the letter, and though a number of potential echoes are often noted in his extant works, none of them allow for certainty. Some have highlighted his characterization of the love command as "kingly" (βασιλικός) in *Strom.* 6.18.164.2 and assumed he was referring to the identification of that command in James 2:8 as the "royal law" (νόμος βασιλικός) (GCS 2.516).[33] The term can be justified on other grounds, however, since in context he is commenting on Jesus' call in Matthew 5:20 that the righteousness of the kingdom must exceed that of the Pharisees. Since Jesus focuses on the love command of Leviticus 19:18 in the course of that sermon (5:43f.), an appeal to James is unnecessary. Likewise the citation of the "scripture" in *Strom.* 3.6.49.2–3, "God opposes the proud, but gives grace to the humble" (GCS 2.218), is hardly a clear reference to James 4:6, since the text itself is Proverbs 3:34, and it is also cited in 1 Peter 5:5. Clement shows no reluctance to refer overtly to other persons and texts (whether or not they were deemed theologically acceptable by his contemporaries); if he had been aware of the letter of James, what would have kept him from citing it? On the face of it, one is led to conclude that Clement must not have known of the epistle.

Nevertheless, three other witnesses are commonly appealed to in support of Clement's use of James. First, Eusebius's *Historia Ecclesiastica* is one of the more

---

[33] See, e.g., L. T. Johnson, *The Letter of James* (ABC 37A; New York: Doubleday, 1995), 129.

important witnesses to the no longer extant *Hypotyposeis of Clement*. Eusebius informs us that the *Hypotyposeis* consisted of eight books in which Clement "has given concise explanations of all the canonical Scriptures [ἐνδιαθῆκοι γραφαί], not passing over even the disputed writings [γραφαὶ ἀντιλεγόμεναι], I mean the Epistle of Jude and the remaining Catholic Epistles, and the Epistle of Barnabas, and the Apocalypse known as Peter's" (*Hist. Eccl.* 6.14.1 [GCSNF 6–2.548; Oulton, LCL 265.47]). Taken at face value, we would conclude that Clement commented on James, which Eusebius had previously identified as "the first of those named Catholic Epistles" [ἡ πρώτη τῶν ὀνομαζομένων καθολικῶν ἐπιστολῶν] (2.23.25 [GCSNF 6–1.174]). But the statement as a whole is casually worded, since we know that Eusebius did not consider all seven of the CE to be disputed. His most carefully constructed passage on the extent of the NT canon (3.25.1–7) lists 1 Peter and 1 John among the acknowledged texts. Can we be certain that he had James in mind when he referred to "Jude and the other Catholic Epistles"? The contribution of our second witness is equally imprecise. The ninth-century Byzantine Patriarch Photius commented on Clement's *Hypotyposeis* in his *Bibliotheca*.[34] In a short paragraph he offers a cursory criticism of Clement's work, calling it impious and unorthodox. After listing several key offenses, he concludes, "the whole purpose of his work is supposedly an interpretation of Genesis, Exodus, the Psalms, St. Paul's epistles, the Catholic Epistles, and Ecclesiastes." The statement as a whole seems too cursory to trust as a reliable source for the precise contents of the work.

The previous witnesses would probably not bear much weight were it not for our third source, the sixth-century Latin writer Cassiodorus. He preserved fragments of Clement's *Hypotyposeis* in a Latin translation entitled *Adumbrationes in Epistolas Catholicas* (GCS 3.203–15; *ANF* 2.567–77), the extant copies of which consist of selected comments on 1 Peter, 1–2 John, and Jude. There is a discrepancy, however, between the *Adumbrationes* and Cassiodorus's comments about it elsewhere. In his *Institutiones divinarum et saecularium litterarum* (ca. 576) he says, "The presbyter Clement of Alexandria . . . has made some comments on the Canonical Epistles, that is to say the first epistle of St. Peter, the first and second epistles of St. John, and the epistle of James."[35] Scholars have long concluded that Cassiodorus mistakenly wrote "James" when he intended to write "Jude," thereby supporting the thesis that Clement did not know James.[36]

Such a conclusion finds further support by a consideration of Clement's use of other apostolic letters. For example, in his *Adumbrationes* on Jude, he notes that

---

[34] *Bibliotheca Photii Patriarchae* cod. 109 (PG 103.384; Wilson, 124).

[35] *De institutione divinarum litterarum* 1.8.4 (R. A. B. Mynors, *Cassiodori Senatoris Institutiones* [Oxford: Clarendon, 1937], 29).

[36] See B. F. Westcott, *A General Survey of the History of the Canon of the New Testament,* 6th ed. (Grand Rapids: Baker Book, 1980), 357–58; Theodore Zahn, *Geschichte des neutestamentlichen Kanons* (2 vols.; Leipzig: Erlangen, 1888–1892), 3.136–38; and Fell's introduction to the *Adumbrations* in PG 9.729–730.

Jude did not claim to be the brother of the Lord, but said that he was the brother of James, and therefore "the brother of the sons of Joseph" (GCS 3.206; *ANF* 2.573). If Clement was aware of the letter of James and had in fact commented on it, it is strange that he does not refer to it as an elaboration of James' identity. As another example, consider Clement's use of 1 John 3:18 in *Strom.* 4.16.100.4–5: "'Little children, let us not love in word, or in tongue,' says John, teaching them to be perfect [τέλειοι], 'but in deed [ἔργῳ] and in truth; hereby shall we know that we are of the truth'" (GCS 2.292; *ANF* 2.427). Clement might well have appealed to the parallel of James 2:14-26 in this instance had he had access to it, especially since the "echo" in James 2:22 uses τελειόω to describe a faith that is perfected by ἔργα. As I have already stated, Clement feels no conflict in citing texts of any doctrinal character, and given his overarching ethical concern, it is extremely difficult to understand why he would not have referred to the letter of James had he known of it. Indeed, as we will see below, the *person* James was quite an important apostolic authority for Clement. The possession of a *letter* from James would no doubt have been a valuable source for him, and the fact that he shows no knowledge of it is support enough for the dominant position that he in fact did not know the letter of James.

The *Adumbrationes* are interesting in their own right. "Selections" is truly the best name for the writings, as they offer a kind of selective running commentary on the letters. The 2 John section is quite short, and the fact that he makes no mention whatsoever of a third letter may support the notion that Clement did not know it. In the Jude commentary Clement draws attention to the fact that Jude's letter justifies the use of the *Assumption of Moses* and *1 Enoch* (GCS 3.207, 208). He also mentions that Jude is the brother of James, but says nothing about a letter by that name. Interestingly, Jude is introduced here for the first time as a "catholic epistle" (GCS 3.206: *Judas, qui catholicam scripsit epistolam . . .*). It is of course difficult to know whether this designation comes from Clement himself or from the translating pen of Cassiodorus. Elsewhere, however, Clement does describe the apostolic encyclical letter in Acts 15 as "the catholic epistle of all the apostles" (ἡ ἐπιστολὴ ἡ καθολικὴ τῶν ἀποστόλων ἁπάντων), which would suggest he understands the term "catholic" to refer to the general address of the two letters (*Strom.* 4.15.97.3 [GCS 2.291]). The only other known second-century writer reported to have used the term in relation to a letter is Apollonius (ca. 197), who apparently condemned someone named Themiso for having "dared, in imitation of the apostle, to compose an epistle general" (*Hist. Eccl.* 5.18.5; GCSNF 6–1.474; Lake, LCL 153.489).[37]

[37] While the *NPNF²* translation says that Themiso composed a "catholic epistle" (1.235), other English translations often strive to differentiate references to epistles addressed generally from comments about the seven Catholic Epistles. Compare, for instance, the translation by Lake offered above with his translation of 2.23.25 and 4.23.1 (LCL 153.179, 379); compare also Rufinus's Latin translation of this text (GCSNF 6–1.475), which has *epistola ad omnes ecclesias*, with 2.23.25 (GCS 6–1.175) which calls the letter of James the first of those named *catholicae*.

Other Ancient Letters Cited

Beyond the use of proto-NT texts, Clement also referred to the *Letter of Barnabas* and *1 Clement*. Clement's use of *Barnabas* indicates a high respect for both the person as well as his work: He regularly calls Barnabas an apostle (*Strom.* 2.6.31.2 [GCS 2.129]; 2.7.35.5–6 [GCS 2.131]; 2.20.116.3 [GCS 2.176]), a bearer of gnostic tradition (*Strom.* 5.10.63.2 [GCS 2.368]), and identifies him as one of the 70 and a fellow worker of Paul (*Strom.* 2.20.116.3 [GCS 2.176]; 5.10.63.1 [GCS 2.368]). The use of allegorical interpretation and the influence of Philo in *Barnabas* has led many scholars to assume an Alexandrian provenance for the letter, which would account for its high standing with Alexandrian fathers like Clement and Origen.[38] Clement's own repeated use of the letter shows that he considered Barnabas to have been a master in the allegorical interpretation of Scripture (cf., for example, *Strom.* 2.15.67 [GCS 2.148] and 5.8.51–52 [GCS 2.361–62]). Barnabas taught "gnostically" that those who think the law is meant to agitate fear failed to properly comprehend the mystical meaning embedded in the text (*Strom.* 2.18.84.3 [GCS 2.157]). Similar use is made of *1 Clement;* most of the references are found in *Strom.* 4.17–18, where he offers an extended string of quotations from the letter (GCS 2.294ff.). Like Barnabas, the author is introduced as "the apostle Clement," and his letter is specified as valuable because in it the author is "drawing a picture of the gnostic" for us. Between the two letters, *Barnabas* is appealed to far more frequently than *1 Clement*.

The Figures of James, Peter, and John

Though Clement's extant writings suggest that he had no knowledge of a letter by James, fragments from his *Hypotyposeis* indicate he was aware of significant traditions about him in relation to Peter and John.

> Peter, James and John after the ascension of the Savior did not struggle for glory, because they had previously been given honor by the Savior, but chose James the Just as Bishop of Jerusalem. (*Hyp.* 6/*Hist. Eccl.* 2.1.3 [GCSNF 6–1.104; Lake, LCL 153.105])

> After the resurrection the Lord gave the tradition of knowledge to James the Just and John and Peter, these gave it to the other apostles and the other apostles to the seventy, of whom Barnabas also was one. (*Hyp.* 8/*Hist. Eccl.* 2.1.4 [GCSNF 6–1.104; LCL 153.105])

These comments will be the subject of closer examination in our analysis of second-century James traditions in chapter 2. For now, let it be noted that Clement, like his North African neighbor Tertullian, was aware of traditions that elevated James, Peter, and John above the rest of the original apostles. For Clement, this elevation

[38] See J. Quasten, *The Beginnings of Patristic Literature* (vol. 1 of *Patrology*; Antwerp: Spectrum Publishers, 1966), 89; and R. P. C. Hanson, *Tradition in the Early Church* (London: SCM Press, 1962), 97–100.

came about on the basis of their having received post-resurrection *gnosis* from Jesus himself. This provides additional evidence for the existence of a widespread elevation of the Jerusalem Pillars in the late second century. Further, Clement's awareness of a tradition that James was one of the primary apostolic recipients of divine *gnosis* makes it even more difficult to understand how he could avoid referring to the letter if he were aware of its existence. Indeed, the evidence requires us to conclude that he must not have known the letter of James.

Conclusion

To sum up, though Clement cites many more texts as inspired than his contemporary Western counterparts, it is significant that his non-Pauline letter collection is not that much different than that of Tertullian. Both accept 1 Peter, 1 John, Jude, and *Barnabas*, though Clement would add 2 John and *1 Clement* to his list, while Tertullian would add Hebrews to his. Clement, however, accepted the dominant Eastern position on Hebrews, that it was Pauline in origin, written first in Hebrew, and then later translated into Greek (*Hist. Eccl.* 6.14.4 [GCSNF 6–2.550]). Similarities between these two are also to be noted in their championing of the letter of Jude as an authentic apostolic authority. Here it is interesting to note the uniformity of their approach to the letter: each appeal to Jude as apostolic support for their rigorous moral exhortation, as well as justification for their use of apocryphal Jewish texts.

Most significant for our purpose is the way in which both Clement and Tertullian view James, Peter, and John as a unity of apostolic authority. Tertullian asserted their combined role as the essential "other half" of the ancient apostolic mission, with whom Paul must be related in order to ensure a complete understanding of apostolic doctrine. Similarly, Clement highlighted these three because of their unique contact with Jesus, for they were the primary recipients of his post-resurrection teachings, which they in turn imparted to the rest of the apostles. Thus, these two fathers offer witness to a late second-century tendency to consolidate non-Pauline apostolic authority in the specific persons of the Jerusalem Pillars. However, neither theologian was in a position to establish these three in a corresponding letter collection, and it makes best sense to assume that this was due to the fact that neither possessed a letter of James.

THE GROWTH OF THE "CATHOLIC LETTER" GENRE:
ORIGEN OF ALEXANDRIA (CA. 185–253)

With Origen we come to what may be considered an entirely new phase in the development of the NT canon. Origen's extant work reflects knowledge of church practices throughout the Greco-Roman world.[39] He also applied all the available critical insights of his day to Scripture study, including careful versional analyses,

[39] Hanson, *Allegory*, 308; W. G. Kummel, *Introduction to the New Testament* (London: SCM Press, 1975), 495.

linguistic studies, and historical investigations that influence interpretation. Most importantly, Origen was the first ancient churchman to have offered some comment on all twenty-seven writings that are now a part of the NT canon. With Origen we hear for the first time explicit reference to James, 2 Peter, and 2–3 John, though as we will see, his acknowledgement of their existence cannot be equated with an acknowledgment of their apostolic authority.

The Accepted Texts

It should not surprise us that Origen makes extensive use of 1 Peter and 1 John. We have no room for a thorough collation of his many references to these texts, so instead we will focus on the passages that may shed light on Origen's contribution to the development of this canonical sub-unit. Of greatest importance is the fact that Origen is the first witness to use the word "catholic" in association with some of the proto-CE. 1 Peter is called a "catholic epistle" several times (*Sel. Ps.* 3 [PG 12.1128]; *Comm. Jn.* 6.175.9 (SC 157.260),[40] as is *Barnabas* on one occasion (*Cels.* 1.63.9 [SC 132.250]); however, the designation is most frequently used for 1 John, which is referred to in this way frequently (for example, *Comm. Jn.* 1.138 [SC 120.132] and 2.149 [SC 120.304]; *Sel. Dt.* [PG 12.817]) in the Greek texts (which do not as easily fall under scholarly suspicion for possible interpolation by Latin translators).[41] Origen himself never explains what it is he means by the title, but the fact that it is used primarily for 1 John suggests that he understood the term as a description of a letter that is addressed "generally." This usage is significant, of course, because it offers witness to the development of a *category* of letters falling under a genre called "catholic."

Quotes from 1 Peter are rarely introduced by reference to a text; most often Origen introduces the passages with a simple "Peter says." Citations of 1 John, by contrast, are frequently introduced as coming from "the epistle of John," apparently in order to differentiate these quotes from his more frequent appeals to "the gospel" of John. While Origen quotes a variety of passages from 1 Peter and 1 John, a survey of those which receive repeated citation may tell us something about Origen's attitude toward the letters. Origen's favorite verses from 1 Peter, 2:5 and 2:9, are quoted

---

[40] Further, Eusebius preserves a fragment from the first book of the Matthew commentary (*Hist. Eccl.* 6.25.5; GCSNF 6–2.576) in which Origen cites 1 Peter 5:13 as coming from Peter's Catholic Epistle.

[41] Most of Origen's writings have not survived in Greek, the majority being known only through the fourth century Latin translations of Rufinus and Jerome. What was passed down, when compared to the extant Greek texts, can be shown to be more akin to edited paraphrases than careful translations (see, e.g., Rufinus's own comments in the preface to *De principiis*). Some of the departures from the Greek have merely to do with the addition of rhetorical flourishes, but G. W. Butterworth notes, "Sometimes, when [Scripture] texts are quoted, he will add an extra one that occurs to him or insert a fresh illustration" (*Origen On First Principles* [London: SPCK, 1936], xxx). We must consider all of Origen's extant works, but in doing so we must proceed with caution.

or alluded to at least thirteen times each. These verses themselves offer the kind of Christian typological reading of the OT that Origen seeks to perform elsewhere, thereby functioning not only as crucial intertextual linkages between the OT and NT, but also as scriptural affirmations of Origen's distinct brand of spiritual exegesis. The former verse is referred to whenever Origen seeks an allegorical interpretation of the Jerusalem temple (for example, *Comm. Jn.* 10.229 [SC 157.520]; *Cels.* 8.19.23ff. [SC 150.216]). Frequently this linkage is used by Origen to find instructions for the Christian "priesthood" hidden in the OT descriptions of priestly duties in the temple cult (cf. *Hom. Lev.* 9.9 [PG 12.521]; *Hom. Num.* 4.3 [PG 12.601]; *Hom. Josh.* 1.5 [PG 12.830]).

Unsurprisingly, the largest gathering of references to 1 John is found in the *Commentary on John*, where they are generally used to offer corroboration with the gospel text being explored. In that commentary, passages from the letter echo and blur with texts from the gospel to offer an expanded, more robust witness to Johannine Christology. In particular, what is declared about Jesus' divinity in these Johannine texts is that he is "the lamb of God who takes away the sin of the world" (John 1:29). As this text is repeated over twenty times in the commentary, it is understandable that among the 1 John passages cited most frequently are the two passages on Jesus' atonement for sin: 1 John 2:1-2 is cited eight times, and 3:8 is cited six times. 1 John's association with the gospel probably explains why it is that Origen cites this letter more frequently than any of the other CE. It also suggests that Origen is not yet thinking of the Johannine letters as belonging to a discrete collection of non-Pauline letters, categorizing them instead as part of the larger Johannine witness.

Among the remaining CE, Origen demonstrates nothing but approval for the letter of Jude: "And Jude, who wrote a letter of few lines, it is true, but filled with the healthful words of heavenly grace, said in the preface, 'Jude, the servant of Jesus Christ and the brother of James'" (*Comm. Mt.* 10.17.40ff. [SC 162.218; *ANF* 10.424]). A survey of Origen's works reveals around fourteen references to the letter, many offered with attribution to Jude (cf., for example, 10.24.30 [SC 162.260]; *Princ.* 3.2.1.7 [SC 268.152]). On only one occasion does he suggest that the letter is doubted by some, introducing a quote by saying, "and if indeed one were to accept the epistle of Jude" (εἰ δὲ καὶ τὴν Ἰούδα προσοῖτό τις ἐπιστολήν) (*Comm. Mt.* 17.30.9–10 [GCS 10.672]). If he held doubts of his own they are nowhere apparent.

The situation was different for 2 Peter and 2–3 John. Origen is our first overt witness to the existence of these letters, though it is doubtful that he accepted them as authentic. Eusebius preserves a fragment of Origen's *Commentary on John* that says Peter "has left one acknowledged [ὁμολογουμένη] epistle, and, it may be, a second also; for it is doubted [ἀμφιβάλλεται]" (*Hist. Eccl.* 6.25.8 [GCSNF 6–2.578; Oulton, LCL 265.77]). Though this passage does not offer any clear indication of his own opinion regarding the dispute, it has been pointed out before that Origen nowhere quotes or even mentions 2 Peter in any of his own writings that have come down to us in Greek.[42] Unsurprisingly, the Latin texts offer more for us to consider. *De principiis* 2.5.135 has Origen saying "Peter himself says this in his first epistle" (SC 252.298); the Greek texts always refer to Peter's epistle in the singular, so the distinction here is noteworthy. More clearly, *Homilies on Leviticus* 4.4.18 quotes 2 Peter 1:4, attributing the text to Peter (SC 286.170). Origen speaks of 2–3 John in the Eusebian fragment just mentioned: John "left also an epistle of a very few lines, and, it may be, a second and third; for not all say that these are genuine [γνήσιοι]" (*Hist. Eccl.* 6.25.9 [GCS NF 6–2.578; LCL 265.77]). While there are no references to 2 Peter in the Greek texts, the lack of clear references to 2–3 John in either the Greek *or* the Latin texts may lead us to conclude that he did not accept either as authentic.

The Letter of James

Origen is the first early theologian to make clear use of the letter of James. There are, however, some interesting variants that require explanation. In the Greek manuscripts he directly quotes the letter on numerous occasions with attribution to James.[43] Though the designation of James as an "apostle" occurs most frequently in the Latin texts, its presence in at least two of the Greek texts suggests that this title was not simply an insertion by a Latin translator.[44] Commentators have been troubled, however, by certain passages that seem to qualify Origen's acceptance of the letter. A common example has been in the *Commentary on John* where Origen quotes James 2:17 and offers what has appeared to some to be a rather hesitant attribution, saying the quote is found ἐν τῇ φερομένῃ Ἰακώβου ἐπιστολῇ (*Comm. Jn.* 19.23.152 [SC 290.140]). While this text may suggest that Origen had doubts about the letter when the text is translated "the so-called epistle of James," it should be noted that φερομένος does not necessarily carry the implication of doubt. In fact, Lampe prefers "in circulation," "extant," "the work of" or "attributed to."[45] Further, elsewhere in the commentary Origen applies the same word in relation to all of the available apostolic letters (*Comm. Jn.* 1.15 [SC 120.64]). Dibelius, who offers the translation "the letter of James which is current," suggests that Origen's cautious language here is simply due to his awareness that the letter was not universally accepted.[46] Such an assessment is supported later in the commentary, where

---

[42] Metzger, *Canon*, 139; Westcott, 363.

[43] Among the numerous examples, see *Sel. Ps.* 30:6 (PG 12:1300), citing James 2:26; *Sel. Ps.* 118.153 (PG 12:1621), citing James 4:10.

[44] *Comm. Jn. Frag.* 126; *Sel. Ps.* 65.4 (PG 12.1500), citing James 5:13; Latin examples are *Hom. Ex.* 3.3 (PG 12.316); *Hom. Lev.* 2.4 (PG 12.418); 13.2 (PG 12.546); and *Hom. Josh.* 10.2 (PG 12.881).

[45] G. W. H. Lampe, *A Patristic Greek Lexicon* (Oxford: Clarendon, 1961), 1473.

[46] M. Dibelius, *James*, ed. H. Greeven, trans. M. Williams (Hermeneia; Philadelphia: Fortress, 1976), 52.

Origen says that a particular position "would not be conceded by those who accept the saying as authoritative [ὑπὸ τῶν παραδεχομένων], 'Faith without works is dead'" (*Comm. Jn.* 20.10.66 [SC 290.188; Heine, FC 89.219–20]). Thus, while there is no need to conclude that Origen himself doubted the letter of James, these comments do offer witness to the incomplete acceptance of the letter in the first half of the third-century Eastern church. He implies hesitancy because he knows that acceptance of the letter is not universal. This is an important point, because it recognizes that in Origen's day the letter was still in its early use and was not fully authoritative even to those in Origen's audience. *Pace* Johnson, Origen's use of the letter cannot be used to support the assumption that it had been used long before him in the Alexandrian church.[47] Indeed, his appeal to the letter is that of a document recently arrived.

More difficult to explain is *Commentary on Matthew* 10.17.27ff., where Origen addresses the topic of the brothers of Jesus (SC 162.214–20). He identifies James as the one whom Paul referred to in Galatians 1:9, and goes on to describe him using information from Josephus's *Antiquities*, but never mentions any letter by James. Immediately thereafter, Jude is identified as the one who wrote a letter referring to himself as the "servant of Jesus Christ and the brother of James." The same occurs in *Celsus* 1.47.17ff.; Origen refers to Josephus's account of James and then to Paul's note in Galatians 1:9 without mentioning any associated letter (SC 132.198–200). What would have kept Origen from referring to the letter of James in these writings? Dibelius wonders if this is an indication that Origen thought the letter was written by another James,[48] and Painter cites the *Commentary on Matthew* passage as proof that Origen believed the letter was indeed written by someone else,[49] but this is difficult to accept since the *Commentary on Romans* 4.8.30 identifies a quotation from the letter as being from "James, the brother of the Lord" (*VL* 33.328). After considering which texts include references to James, Laws attempts to solve the mystery by asserting that Origen's references to the epistle come only in works that were written *after* his move to Caesarea; Origen must therefore have come to know the letter later in life through his contact with the Palestinian church.[50] However, Origen may have cited James 4:17 in *De principiis*, a work written at the beginning of his career while still residing in Alexandria (*Princ.* 1.3.6.185 [SC 252.156]),[51] and Eusebius tells us that *Celsus* and the *Commentary on Matthew* were written at the end of his life whilst residing in Caesarea (*Hist. Eccl.* 6.36.1 [GCSNF 6–2.590]). According to Laws' theory, he should have known and accepted the letter of James by that time, but as I have just shown, the letter is glaringly absent in both works.

---

[47] Johnson, *James,* 130; *Brother of Jesus,* 45.

[48] Dibelius, *James,* 52 n. 201.

[49] J. Painter, *Just James: The Brother of Jesus in History and Tradition* (Edinburgh: T&T Clark, 1999), 235.

[50] S. Laws, *The Epistle of James* (BNTC; Peabody, Mass.: Hendrickson, 1980), 24.

[51] Again, we must be concerned about Rufinian interpolation.

In the end, any conclusion must remain tentative. Since (a) Clement did not seem to know of James, and (b) Origen's own comments show that acceptance of the letter was not universal in his day, we cannot assume that Origen inherited it from prior use in the Alexandrian church, so his on and off use of the letter must reflect his sensitivity to its uncertain status among his readers and hearers. Clearly Eusebius noted the discrepancy; Origen is perhaps his chief resource when it comes to canon history, and he had access to a far greater selection of Origen's works than we do. The fact that Eusebius ultimately placed James in his "disputed but known" category may give us a good indication of Origen's ultimate perspective on the letter. Regardless, it seems to have been Origen's use of the letter that cemented its place in the NT canon. From his time onward James is everywhere present in the writings of the Eastern church.

I do not have the space to offer a full summary of Origen's use of James, so instead I will focus on two texts in particular. The first has just been mentioned; in the *Commentary on John* (20.10.66) Origen offers the following comments on Jesus' command that children of Abraham should "do the works of Abraham" (John 8:39).[52]

> Let those who fasten on to one of Abraham's works, such as the statement, "Abraham believed God, and it was reckoned to him for justice," and think that this is what is referred to in the command, "Do the works of Abraham" (even if it be conceded to them that faith is a work, which would not be conceded by those who accept the saying as authoritative, "Faith without works is dead," nor by those who understand that to be justified by faith differs from being justified by works of the law) explain why it was not said in the singular, "If you are children of Abraham, do the work of Abraham," but in the plural, "Do the works of Abraham." This is equivalent, I think, to saying, "Do all the works of Abraham." (*Comm. Jn.* 20.10.66 [SC 290.188])[53]

Here Origen seems to appeal to James as part of a larger concern to reconcile Jesus' call to good works with the Pauline teaching on justification by faith. Jesus commanded Christians to do *all the works* of Abraham, Origen insists, and not simply the single "work" of believing intellectually in God, which, he notes, is not really a work at all according to James. He suggests that those who might argue such a thing do not really understand the difference between justification by faith and justification by works of the law. The implication, of course, is that being justified by faith does not exempt one from the obligation to perform good works.

The *Commentary on Romans* offers yet more evidence that Origen found James useful because of its ability to shape a particular reading of the Pauline teaching on

---

[52] Though the accepted text of John 8:39 has the imperfect ἐποιεῖτε, R. E. Heine (*Origen's Commentary on the Gospel According to John, Books 12–32* [FC 39; Washington D.C.: Catholic University of America Press, 1993], 219 n. 66) notes that Origen (along with a number of other ancient witnesses) has the imperative ποιεῖτε.

[53] Eng. trans. R. Heine, FC 89.219–20.

justification.[54] He notes that Romans is difficult to interpret "because he makes use of expressions which sometimes are confused and insufficiently explicit [*confusi et minus expliciti*]" (1.1.3–4 [*VL* 16.37.3–4; Scheck, FC 103.53]), but also because it is "about Israel according to the flesh and about the Israel not according to the flesh, about the circumcision of the flesh and of the heart, about the spiritual law and the law of the letter" (1.1.92–96 [*VL* 16.41.92-96; FC 103.57]). This complex shifting between spiritual and literal comes particularly to the fore in his discussion of circumcision. Origen says it symbolizes the Christian's refraining from evil deeds; but it is not enough to refrain from evil, for one must do "the works of faith" to avoid having one's circumcision become uncircumcision (Rom 2:25). "If anyone in the church . . . should afterwards become a transgressor of Christ's law, his baptismal circumcision shall be reckoned to him as the uncircumcision of unbelief; for it says, 'Faith without works is dead'" (Jas 2:17, 26; *Comm. Rom.* 2.9.59ff. [*VL* 16.149.59–150.63; FC 103.143]).

But then he raises a possible objection to this allegorical reading of circumcision: Some have noted that Ezekiel 44:9 says, "No son of a foreigner, uncircumcised in heart and uncircumcised in flesh, of all the sons of foreigners who are among the house of Israel, shall enter my sanctuary." Since the prophetic text itself speaks of two kinds of circumcision, "we are compelled to assign form and kind to both circumcisions, in accordance with the laws of allegorical interpretation" (*Comm. Rom.* 2.9.390 [*VL* 16.165.390; FC 103.156]). He answers that circumcision of the heart has to do with justification by faith, and circumcision of the flesh has to do with justification by works.

> This would mean that the one who does not have faith would be uncircumcised in the heart and the one who does not have works would be uncircumcised in the flesh. For one without the other is condemned, seeing that also faith without works is called "dead" [*quia et fides sine operibus mortua dicitur*; cf. Jas 2:17, 26], and that no one is justified before God by works without faith [*et ex operibus sine fide apud Deum nemo iustificatur*; cf. Rom 3:20; Gal 2:16]. Thus I am convinced that the prophetic word shall be properly applied to that people which is made up of believers, to whom it is being said, "No foreigner who is among you in the midst of the house of Israel, who is uncircumcised in heart and uncircumcised in flesh, shall enter my sanctuary." Doubtless this is what the Lord also says in the Gospel, "He who believes in me keeps my commands" [John 14:15, 21, 23]; and again, "he who hears these words of mine and does them" [Matt 7:24]; and likewise, "why do you say to me, 'Lord, Lord,' and do not do what I say?" [Luke 6:46]. You see, then, that everywhere faith is joined with works and works are united with faith. (*Comm. Rom.* 2.9.396-408 [*VL* 16.165.396–166.408; FC 103.156])

In a brilliant intertextual reading, Origen reconciles James and Paul by appeal to Ezekiel 44 and the gospels. Since no one "uncircumcised in heart and uncircumcised in flesh" can enter the sanctuary of the Lord, both James and Paul must be cor-

---

[54] It too comes down from the pen of Rufinus, so caution is required.

rect in their teachings on justification: Since "everywhere faith is joined with works and works are united with faith," the one who is uncircumcised in the heart lacks justification by faith (Romans/Galatians), and the one who is uncircumcised in the flesh lacks justification by works (James). Origen seems to glory in his allegorical reconciliation of the scriptural word when he goes on to point out that "Marcion, who is a man who takes no pleasure at all in allegorical interpretation, is completely at a loss when explaining the Apostle's words, 'Circumcision is of value' [Rom 2:25]. Not even concerning the details which are mentioned was he able to give an account in any respect whatsoever" (*Comm. Rom.* 2.9.460–63 [*VL* 16.168.460–169.463; FC 103.159]). Origen *was* able to give such an account, thanks particularly to the emphasis on justification by works as found in the letter of James.

Origen wanted his readers to know, however, that Paul also insists on works. Pointing out that Paul makes it clear that Abraham was justified by faith, he goes on to insist:

> Now you should not imagine that if someone has such faith . . . that he would be able at the same time to have unrighteousness with it as well. For there is no common ground between faith and infidelity; there is no communion of righteousness with wickedness, just as light can have no fellowship with darkness. . . . Therefore the proof of true faith is that sin is not being committed, just as, on the contrary, where sin is being committed, there you have proof of unbelief. For this reason then it is also said of Abraham in another passage of Scripture that he was justified by the works of faith [*Propterea ergo et in alio scripturae loco dicitur de Abraham quia ex operibus fidei iustificatus*; cf. Jas 2:21-22]. (*Comm. Rom.* 4.1.63–73 [*VL* 33.272.63–273.73; FC 103.239])

Origen goes on to read that justification by faith means that Christians "have peace with God through our Lord Jesus Christ" (Rom 5:1) and insists that no one who has peace with God will go on to partake in the things that are hateful to God.

> Paul himself teaches you when he says, 'The wisdom of the flesh is hateful to God, for it is not subjected to the law of God' [Rom 8:7]. And so, if you are wise in a fleshly manner, or if you expose your life to the lusts of the flesh and release the floods of luxury . . . then you have become God's enemy through the wisdom of the flesh. Not only Paul writes such things in his letters. Listen also to James, the brother of the Lord, testifying in similar fashion when he says, 'Whoever wants to be a friend of this world makes himself an enemy of God' [Jas 4:4]. . . . Therefore the person in whom these things exist cannot have peace with God. On the contrary, he awakens those hostilities which Christ came to destroy. (*Comm. Rom.* 4.8.22–37 [*VL* 33.328.22–329.37; FC 103.280])

Justification by faith does indeed bring peace with God, but that peace does not entail the end of struggle against the seductive powers of the devil. Origen goes on to insist:

> We enter more into peace with God at that time when we are persevering in warlike hostility against the devil and when we struggle furiously against vices of the

flesh. After all, in this manner the apostle James says, 'Resist the devil and he will
flee from you; come near to God and he will come near to you' [Jas 4:7-8]. Thus
you can see that he thought that one would be near to God at that very moment
when he is resisting the devil. (*Comm. Rom.* 4.8.64–69 [*VL* 33.330.64–69; FC
103.281])

From these passages we can see that the letter of James was useful to Origen on
numerous counts. It provided him with a corrective foil to antinomian readings of
Paul and, in doing so, enabled a more thoroughly intertextual reading of the apostolic writings, most particularly by reconciling the "justification by faith" passages
of Paul with the ethical injunctions of the gospels. It is also not insignificant that
Marcion is brought up in this context: Origen was able to circumvent an anti-Jewish
reading of "circumcision of the flesh" by appeal to Paul's claim that "circumcision
is of value"; but Origen was only able to "value" fleshly circumcision allegorically
by equating it with the teaching on justification by works as it is proclaimed in the
letter of James. It is extremely significant that the earliest known overt tradent of
James employed the letter in this particular fashion, for it suggests that James found
its canonical "home" when it was read as a corrective to those who misread Paul in
an antinomian or anti-Jewish manner.

Other Ancient Letters Cited

Origen does not refer to *Barnabas* nearly as frequently as did his predecessor Clement, though that is the only factor that might lead us to qualify his acceptance.
Other considerations lead us to assume that he had an extremely high view of the
letter. *De principiis* 3.2.4.238–40 cites the letter as part of an extended proof from
"the testimony of holy scripture" (SC 268.169). It is clear from Clement's use that
Origen inherited his high view of *Barnabas* from the Alexandrian tradition. Though
within fifty years Eusebius will choose to place the letter in the "rejected" category
of writings, its (roughly contemporaneous) presence among the CE in the stichometric list found in Codex Claromontanus shows that Eusebius was not speaking
on behalf of the entire Eastern church.

I sense a diminution of authority, however, in Origen's references to *1 Clement*.
De principiis 2.3.6.226 has Origen citing the letter and referring to Clement as a
later "disciple of the apostles" (*apostolorum discipulus*) (SC 252.264). In *Commentary on John* 6.54.279, he authorizes his use of *1 Clement* by appeal to Paul's reference to a "Clement" in Philippians 4:3.161 (SC 157.340–42). Interestingly, he does
not predicate Clement's authority in his role as Bishop of Rome; his appeal to the
Philippians text suggests Origen needed to defend his use of the letter on the basis
of Pauline authority. Another reference to Clement, this time in a fragment from
his *Homily on Hebrews* preserved by Eusebius, has Origen suggesting that "Clement, bishop of the Romans" may have written the anonymous letter (*Hist. Eccl.*
6.25.14 [GCSNF 6–2.580]). Here, however, there is no mention whatsoever of
another well-known letter written by the Bishop. Can we infer that Origen's theory

of Clementine authorship is predicated on his awareness that Clement had written *1 Clement*? If that was Origen's intention, Eusebius did not preserve it for us.

Two Latin Canon Lists

At this point, I will briefly consider the NT lists that come down to us embedded in Latin homilies from late in Origen's career. The first is from the seventh *Homily on Joshua*. After describing the seven priests carrying seven trumpets at the conquest of Jericho, he says:

> So too our Lord Jesus Christ . . . sent his apostles as priests carrying well-wrought trumpets. First Matthew sounded the priestly trumpet in his Gospel. Mark also, and Luke, and John, each gave forth a strain on their priestly trumpets. Peter moreover sounds with the two trumpets of his Epistles; James also and Jude. Still the number is incomplete, and John gives forth the trumpet sound through his Epistles and Apocalypse; and Luke while describing the deeds of the apostles. Latest of all, moreover, that one comes who said, 'I think that God has set us forth as the apostles last of all', and thundering on the fourteen trumpets of his Epistles he threw down, even to their very foundations, the walls of Jericho, that is to say, all the instruments of idolatry and the dogmas of the philosophers. (GCS 7.327–28)[55]

Similarly, the thirteenth *Homily on Genesis* refers to Genesis 26, where Isaac unstops wells closed by the Philistines and digs new ones. Moses, David, and the prophets also opened fountains that gave life to God's people, but like the Philistines, Origen insists, the Jews stopped these up with earthly concerns.

> So then he dug new wells; and so did his servants. Isaac's servants were Matthew, Mark, Luke and John; his servants are Peter, James and Jude; his servant is also the Apostle Paul; who all dug wells of the New Testament. But those who mind earthly things strive ever for these also, and suffer not the new to be formed, nor the old to be cleansed. They gainsay the sources opened in the Gospel: they oppose those opened by the Apostles. (GCS 6.115–16)[56]

Both of these homilies come down to us from the pen of Rufinus, and though the style is clearly that of Origen, most scholars do not trust the details afforded.[57] In the former "trumpets" list, we have no safeguard against the possibility that Rufinus filled in the gaps to make Origen set forth exactly the twenty-seven books that were accepted as NT Scripture in his own day. It should be noted that the unusual

---

[55] Metzger, *Canon*, 139.

[56] Westcott, 361–62.

[57] See the discussions in E. Kalin, "Re-Examining New Testament Canon History: 1) The Canon of Origen," *CurTM* 17 (1990): 274–82; Metzger, *Canon*, 139–40; L. M. McDonald, *The Formation of the Christian Biblical Canon*, rev. ed. (Peabody, Mass.: Hendrickson, 1995), 203–5.

ordering of the CE in this first list (Peter, James, Jude, John) has only one other parallel in canon history: that of Rufinus's own canon list in his *Commentarius in symbolum apostolorum* (ca. 400) (*Symb*. 35 [CCSL 20.171]). Though it could be argued that Rufinus was following an Origenist tradition in his listing, it is more likely that Rufinus has presented his own NT list in the voice of Origen. There is little, however, to keep us from accepting the list set forth in the second "wells" passage. While the precise enumeration of the former list calls it into question, the more general nature of the latter lends it credibility. He simply refers to names of authors, not numbers of letters; and as I have shown, the authors listed correspond almost exactly with the writings cited elsewhere in his works. The only exception would be *Barnabas*; as the author of a "catholic epistle," we might expect to see his name listed here amongst the other "wells." But again, it is probable that "catholic" is used here as a descriptor and not a formal title, so we should not assume its use was meant to function as an indicator of *Barnabas*'s authority.

Conclusion

With Origen we have, for the first time, evidence of the existence and use of all seven proto-CE. We see that Origen's non-Pauline collection certainly included 1 Peter, 1 John, James, Jude, and *Barnabas*. He was also quite clearly aware of 2 Peter and 2–3 John, though he expressed doubts about them and seems to have avoided using them in his work. This non-Pauline letter usage represents a clear development beyond Clement: where James was not evident in Clement's work, by Origen's day it was in process of being accepted; where Clement showed little distinction between *Barnabas* and *1 Clement*, Origen's critical discernment seems to have relegated Clement of Rome to a sub-apostolic position; where Clement knows only 1 Peter and 1–2 John, Origen is able to add 2 Peter and 3 John.

We also see in Origen the emergence of a category of letters, called "catholic," which included 1 Peter, 1 John, and *Barnabas*. Though the meaning of the title is never directly explained, the fact that 1 John is the most frequent recipient of the designation leads us to assume that the traditional interpretation of "general (address)" is probably accurate. If this were the only meaning of the term, however, one wonders why James and Jude were not also called "catholic," for they are no less universally addressed than 1 Peter, 1 John, and *Barnabas*. Might this reality be attributed to Origen's awareness that the letters were not universally accepted? If so, it suggests that he may have understood the "catholicity" of a letter to refer not merely to its universal address but also to its widespread acceptance. Regardless, Origen's extant work makes it clear that in his day the CE was a collection on its way to completion.

Finally, we note again that Origen is the first church Father to make use of the letter of James. In his use we find support for my hypothesis: the first person to appeal to the letter found it useful because (1) it enabled a balance of Paul's teaching on justification by faith with the ethical injunctions found elsewhere in apostolic teaching, and (2) it enabled an anti-Marcionite reading of Paul that vindicated the authority of the Jewish Scriptures. We must note, however, that despite having all the ingredients in his possession, Origen shows no awareness of a discrete canonical collection called the CE. Indeed, his occasionally hesitant references to the letter of James may indicate that the epistle was not yet authoritative enough to anchor the collection. As we will see, however, within fifty years of Origen's death the situation had changed.

THE FIRST WITNESS TO THE CATHOLIC EPISTLE COLLECTION:
EUSEBIUS OF CAESAREA (CA. 270–340)

Among the many contributions of Eusebius's *Historia Ecclesiastica*, one of the most important is its attempted large-scale categorization of ancient Christian writings. Geoffrey Hahneman offers a helpful description of the changed historical situation represented in his work on the canon: "Rather than considering a few books one by one as Origen had done, he considered the *categories* one by one, fitting the individual books into each."[58] This is what makes Eusebius so important for our concerns: he represents the beginning of the final stage in canon development, the effort to close the canon by officially declaring some books as accepted and canonical, and others as rejected. Those who create such lists may appeal to a variety of criteria in their discernment, but Eusebius the historian seems to have had one criterion that took precedence over all others: the testimony of οἱ πάλαι πρεσβύτεροι, "the ancient elders."[59] As we read Eusebius's account of the extent of the canon, we are reminded again and again that he is a scholar of history first and foremost. What he offers in the *Historia Ecclesiastica* is his critical assessment of the ancient attestation for or against the acceptance of ancient Christian writings. Though he is capable of functioning as a literary critic or a judge of doctrine, he seeks to offer a balanced consideration of his scholarly findings in the hope that his information will help settle the question as to the extent of the new Christian Scriptures. This must be remembered when one attempts to offer an account of "Eusebius's NT canon."

Eusebius's Classification of Available Texts

With this in mind, let us consider his most careful and systematic treatment of the canon as it is found in *Hist. Eccl.* 3.25.1–7.[60] Here again he classifies the writings into three categories. The first group contains those writings that are "recognized."

---

[58] Hahneman, 140 (italics mine).

[59] On Eusebius's use of ancient authorities see Kalin, "Eusebius," 386–404; R. M. Grant, *Eusebius as Church Historian* (Oxford: Clarendon, 1980); idem., "Early Alexandrian Christianity," *CH* 40 (1970): 133–44; B. Gustafsson's "Eusebius' Principles in Handling His Sources as Found in His Church History, Books I–VII," *TU* 79 (1961): 429–41; and D. S. Wallace-Hadrill's *Eusebius of Caesarea* (London: Mowbray, 1960).

[60] GCSNF 6–1.250–52; Lake, LCL 153.257–59 (unless otherwise noted).

In the first place should be put the holy tetrad of the Gospels. To them follows the writing of the Acts of the Apostles. After this should be reckoned the Epistles of Paul. Following them the Epistle of John called the first [ἡ φερομένη Ἰωάννου προτέρα⁶¹], and in the same way should be recognized the Epistle of Peter. In addition to these should be put, if it seem desirable, the Revelation of John, the arguments concerning which we will expound at the proper time. These belong to the recognized books [καὶ ταῦτα μὲν ἐν ὁμολογουμένοις] (3.25.1–2).

The passive participle of the verb ὁμολογέω refers to something that is *being accepted* or *recognized* in a confessional sense; the "recognized" writings are those that belong to the group described previously as having universal support among the ancient elders. Though he notes a difference of opinion regarding the Apocalypse of John, for now he is simply presenting the historical evidence (Eusebius's own opinion that it does not belong in this first group will become clear later on in the *Hist. Eccl.*).⁶²

The next category contains writings described as "disputed" yet "known to most":

Of the disputed books which are nevertheless known to most [ἀντιλεγομένων γνωρίμων δ᾽ οὖν ὅμως τοῖς πολλοῖς] are the Epistle called of James [ἡ λεγομένη Ἰακώβου φέρεται⁶³], that of Jude, the second Epistle of Peter, and the so-called [ἡ ὀνομαζομένη] second and third Epistles of John which may be the work of the evangelist or of some other with the same name (3.25.3).

We note immediately that the writings of the first two groups make up exactly the twenty-seven writings eventually canonized. But why are these five separated from the previous twenty-two? As we saw earlier, the "disputed" are writings that do not enjoy the same exalted status of the "accepted." The word ἀντιλεγόμενα conveys the sense of contradiction and doubt in patristic use.⁶⁴ Eusebius probably intended the term to suggest that he discovered a debate of sorts among the historical witnesses, which may make sense of his qualification that they are "nevertheless known to most" (that is, not all of the ancients knew of them, but most did). This is the sense in almost every instance where a text is called "disputed": though some find the writing valuable and account it among the Scriptures, it lacks unqualified ancient attestation.⁶⁵ Such a categorization makes complete sense when one recalls the fact that Origen used James but Tertullian did not, or that Tertullian used Jude but Irenaeus did not.

It is possible, however, to place more weight on the "known to most" as a distinguishing mark of this group of writings. For while γνώριμος can simply mean

---

⁶¹ Or "circulating as the earlier."

⁶² For a thorough analysis of Eusebius's opinion of the Apocalypse, see Grant, *Eusebius*, 130–36.

⁶³ Or "in circulation as James."

⁶⁴ Lampe, 154–55.

⁶⁵ Cf. 3.24.17–18 (GCSNF 6–1.250) in regard to the writings of John.

"known" or "familiar," it can also be used to classify something as "well-known,"[66] "notable," or "distinguished."[67] In that case, we should understand Eusebius to be saying that though these writings have a "disputed" historical record, they are nevertheless "well-known" and "distinguished" in comparison to the writings that follow. He immediately goes on to say:

> Among the νόθα must be reckoned the Acts of Paul, the work entitled the Shepherd, the Apocalypse of Peter, and in addition to them the letter called of Barnabas and the so-called Teachings of the Apostles. And in addition, as I said, the Revelation of John, if this view prevail. For, as I said, some reject it, but others count it among the recognized books [ἐν ὁμολογουμένοις]. Some have also counted the Gospel according to the Hebrews in which those of the Hebrews who have accepted Christ take a special pleasure. (3.25.4–5)

How is the designation νόθα to be understood? Eusebius probably intended the word as a subset of the ἀντιλεγόμενα, since elsewhere he gathers texts from both groups together under this broader heading;[68] yet in this more careful, systematic presentation he can be seen to draw a distinction between the two. The word νόθος translates literally as "bastard." In this case the notion of illegitimate descent is implied metaphorically: These writings, valued as they are in many churches, are not to be counted as legitimate offspring of the historic, apostolic church and ought to be rejected from consideration for the canon. This is crucial: Eusebius uses the term here as a designation of canonical status and not necessarily as a value judgment or a description of literary integrity. Though the word sometimes carried such meanings in patristic usage and even elsewhere in the *Historia Ecclesiastica*,[69] the translations "ingenuine"[70] and the even more common "spurious"[71] seem insufficiently precise, or at least unnecessarily negative. Since the topic of discussion is canonicity, the best translation in this context is "illegitimate." Again, in this discussion of the limits of the canon, Eusebius is acting as a historian; when it comes to works that circulated among orthodox Christians, ancient attestation is his primary concern and not literary or theological criticism per se. In fact, there is no indication

[66] See Lampe, 318.

[67] See LSJ, 167.

[68] Cf. 6.13.6 and 14.1 (GCSNF 6–2.548), though the point is itself "disputed"; see Kalin, "Eusebius" (394–97), who argues that the ἀντιλεγόμενα andt he νόθα are in fact one single group.

[69] In some other contexts he uses the term to mean "false" or "unorthodox." In 5.16.8 the prophecies of Montanus are described as νόθα ἐκφωνήματα, "false utterances." In 3.31.6 he uses the term to describe unorthodox texts, though even in that context, "rejected" is still the best interpretation. See the discussion in Lampe, 918.

[70] See Lake (257) and Grant (*Eusebius*, 128); it could be argued that they are "ingenuine" precisely because they lack early citation, but the point would be the same. Eusebius is more interested in canonicity than literary criticism, and "ingenuine" is suggestive of literary quality, not canonical status.

[71] See the Lawlor (87) and Williams (89) editions, as well as Kalin ("Eusebius," 390).

here that Eusebius is using either ἀντιλεγόμενα or νόθα in a pejorative sense at all; they are simply gradations along the scale of canonization: the ὁμολογούμενα are universally recognized, the ἀντιλεγόμενα are the subject of some dispute but are nevertheless "known" or "distinguished by most," and the νόθα have such a marginal history that they are to be considered "illegitimate."

The fact that the first three categories are related along canonical lines becomes all the more clear when he goes on to present his opinion regarding an altogether different group of writings:

> These would all belong to the disputed books, but we have nevertheless been obliged to make a list of them, distinguishing between those writings which, according to the tradition of the Church, are true, genuine, and recognized, and those which differ from them in that they are not canonical but disputed [οὐκ ἐνδιαθῆκοι μὲν ἀλλὰ καὶ ἀντιλεγομέναι], yet nevertheless are known to most of the writers of the Church [ὅμος δὲ παρὰ πλείστοις τῶν ἐκκλησιαστικῶν γιν-ωσκόμεναι],[72] in order that we might know them and the writings which are put forward by heretics under the name of the apostles [*a series of "heretical" texts are listed*]. To none of these has any who belonged to the succession of the orthodox ever thought it right to refer in his writings. Moreover, the type of phraseology differs from apostolic style, and the opinion and tendency of their contents is widely dissonant from true orthodoxy and clearly shows that they are the forgeries of heretics. They ought, therefore, to be reckoned not even among the νόθα but shunned as altogether wicked and impious (3.25.6–7).

Here the value judgments begin. As usual he gives priority to the historical witness, but this time he moves on to literary and theological criticism. This group of writings represents an entirely different situation than that of the first three; they are to be cast aside because they are heretical and impious. The former categories, however, contain writings that are orthodox and have a history of acceptance in some or most quarters of the Christian world.

To sum up: groups one through three are orthodox books categorized according to canonical status, all of which are set against group four which contains heretical writings that are deemed heretical and unorthodox. While the distinction between groups one and four is quite clear (universally accepted against universally rejected), the differentiation between the second and third categories requires further clarification. They are all writings that have been accepted by some and rejected by others, but what seems to set the five ἀντιλεγόμενα texts apart from the others is the fact that they are "known by most": James, 2 Peter, 2–3 John and Jude cannot really be placed with the νόθα because they belong to an already "distinguished" and "known" collection called the seven Catholic Epistles. Eusebius has already told us as much: he is the first witness to the existence of a seven letter collection known as the Catholic Epistles, headed by James and including letters of Peter, John, and Jude.

---

[72] Eusebius seems to be speaking here of both the νόθα and the ἀντιλεγόμενα as a single group.

Such is the story of James, whose is said to be the first of the Epistles called Catholic [πρώτη τῶν ὀνομαζομένων καθολικῶν ἐπιστολῶν] . . . as is also the case with the Epistle called Jude's, which is itself one of the seven called Catholic [μία τῶν ἑπτὰ λεγομένων καθολικῶν]. (2.23.25; GCSNF 6–1.174)

There is little room to doubt that Eusebius had the canonical seven in mind when he referred to "the seven called Catholic." Though all seven of them were "recognized by most" in his day, his historical analysis showed that only 1 Peter and 1 John were worthy of the complete confidence afforded by universal ancient attestation. Notice his language in 3.3.1:

> [B]ut the so-called second Epistle [of Peter] we have not received as canonical [τὴν δὲ φερομένην δευτέραν οὐκ ἐνδιάθηκον μὲν εἶναι παρειλήφαμεν], but nevertheless it has appeared useful to many, and has been studied with the other Scriptures. (GCSNF 6–1.188)

The tradition he is following may be Origen's, as he cites him saying as much in 6.25.8: "And Peter, on whom the church of Christ is built . . . has left one acknowledged [ὁμολογουμένη] epistle and, it may be, a second also; for it is doubted [ἀμφιβάλλεται]." Yet, despite Origen, he nevertheless acknowledges the fact that these disputed texts are known and used—that is, they *function* canonically—by most. This is also the case with James and Jude. Thus, in the canon discussion of 3.25, he cannot place them with the νόθα texts because the five disputed CE were in his day generally accepted, indeed were part of an increasingly recognized subunit of the NT canon called the "Catholic Epistles," while the others were subject to increasing marginalization.

The double placement of the Apocalypse of John offers further illumination of the logic behind his categories. At first glance it seems nonsensical: how can a text be "universally accepted" and "rejected" at the same time? If it were disputed, would it not make more sense to place it in the second group with those that are "disputed yet recognized by most"?[73] A consideration of the canonical history of the Apocalypse, however, shows that it cannot be placed in the second group. According to the logic behind the categories, the ἀντιλεγόμενα group represents writings that had a history of dispute but were being used in the churches. The apocalypse of John, however, had the opposite history: it was once universally recognized as canonical but had become disputed in Eusebius's day. Eusebius is not "confused" as to the status of this text;[74] on the contrary, he is trying to be precise: some consider it ὁμολογούμενα, universally recognized, while others consider it νόθα, illegitimate.

---

[73] Kalin argues, of course, that the Apocalypse is counted among the disputed texts, since he believes the νόθα and the ἀντιλεγόμενα should not be separated in any substantive way ("Eusebius," 395).

[74] *Pace* Hahneman, who sees Eusebius's double placement of the Apocalypse in this light (139–40).

Our knowledge of the historical development of the CE to this point makes it difficult to accept Kalin's recent claim that the ἀντιλεγόμενα and the νόϑα are not divided "in any substantial way."[75] He is of course correct to note that the two are essentially related and that Eusebius conflates the two elsewhere in the *Historia Ecclesiastica*; but he has overlooked the crucial difference that the existence of the CE collection has made on Eusebius's thinking. Indeed, it makes sense to assume that it was the status of the CE in Eusebius's day that required the existence of a "disputed" category at all. Eusebius *himself* may have believed that the "disputed" and the "illegitimate" were in fact one group, but he could not classify them as one because the five ἀντιλεγόμενα texts included in the CE had achieved a higher level of authority by their use in the churches. Similarly, Gamble, who also does not draw any distinction between the ἀντιλεγόμενα and the νόϑα, says:

> It seems that little development had taken place during the third century: The writings placed in the "acknowledged" group are precisely those which had come to be generally recognized by the end of the second century. Apart from 1 Peter and 1 John, the other "catholic epistles" had not gained general recognition even by Eusebius' time.[76]

Indeed, Eusebius's classification of the CE suggests that they *had* gained general recognition, and it was precisely that recognition that demanded the complexity of his categorization.

The difficulty in interpreting Eusebius's canonical comments is fuelled by the fact that elsewhere his terminology is blurred. In his conclusion to the canon discussion (3.31.6) he refers to "sacred writings" (ἱερὰ γράμματα), those that are "disputed" (ἀντιλεγόμενα), and those that are παντελῶς νόϑα, in this case apparently using the term not to mean "illegitimate" but "altogether fictitious" (GCSNF 6–1.266). Here we find no third "orthodox but illegitimate" category, the term νόϑα instead being used to describe the fourth "unorthodox" group. Further, in 6.13–14 he lists together a variety of books from the second and third groups but calls them all ἀντιλεγόμενα. The fact that Eusebius uses the terms quite specifically in 3.25 and quite loosely elsewhere underscores the fact that he himself believed the ἀντιλεγόμενα and the νόϑα to be of the same larger group. In 3.25, however, they are used to describe subtle variations in contemporary canonical status, variations that required him to draw a distinction between them.

Conclusion: The "Arrival" of the Catholic Epistle Collection

It was in the East then, sometime in the period between Origen and Eusebius, that the CE collection was shaped into the canonical seven and titled "the Catholic Epis-

---

[75] Kalin, "Eusebius," 392–97.

[76] See H. Gamble, *The New Testament Canon: Its Making and Meaning* (Philadelphia: Fortress, 1985), 53. His opinion had not changed by the printing of McDonald and Sanders, *Canon Debate* (287).

tles." If in fact the first edition of the *Historia Ecclesiastica* was completed sometime in the years before 300,[77] and the CE collection was "known to most" by that time, then we can consider this sub-section of the canon to have been a relatively fixed entity in certain quarters of the East sometime in the latter third of the third century. Yet we must not overstate the situation: though Eusebius witnesses to a CE collection that had developed beyond Origen, it was not so well established that he was willing to place all its letters among the ὁμολογούμενα. As will be demonstrated in the next section, however, from Eusebius onward the Eastern churches show an amazing amount of uniformity of opinion regarding the canonical status of the CE, while the Western churches will take another century to formalize the group.

What happened in the intervening years to the other Eastern candidates for inclusion in the CE, the letters of *Barnabas* and *1 Clement*? I have shown that Origen's CE collection included *Barnabas* at least, but Eusebius suggests that the tradition of the church in his time did not consider either of these writings to be canonical. He has rather little to say about *Barnabas*; of the man himself, Eusebius notes that he was one of the seventy disciples of the Lord (1.12.1), and quotes Clement of Alexandria's comment that he was one of those who received from the apostles the "knowledge" (γνῶσις) imparted from the Lord post-resurrection (2.1.4). Of the letter, Eusebius reflects no debate on the matter: it is among the third νόθα group of disputed texts that are orthodox and known by many, but not canonical (3.25.4).

The picture is far clearer when it comes to Eusebius's view of *1 Clement*. He has nothing but praise for the letter: in 3.16 he calls it "accepted" (ὁμολογουμένη)[78] and "wonderful" (θαυμασία), saying it is "used publicly in a great many churches both in former times and in our own." Still, it is not under consideration for canonicity; *1 Clement* is not even mentioned in the canon discussion of 3.25, and in 6.13.6 he groups it with the other ἀντιλεγόμενα texts. Eusebius understands the letter to be post-apostolic because of its reliance on the letter to the Hebrews, and therefore ranks it with the letters of Ignatius (cf. 3.38.1). Clearly these books enjoyed widespread popularity in the East before and after Eusebius's time. Origen used both and included *Barnabas* in particular in his nascent CE collection; and as we will see, this tradition persisted in some quarters well into the fourth century. It may have been Eusebius's treatment of these writings, however, that sealed their fate as νόθα texts. Further, Constantine's request (ca. 332) that Eusebius orchestrate the production of fifty uniform copies of the "Sacred Scriptures" for use in the growing churches of Constantinople must have had a unifying effect on the state of the canon in the East.[79] From the evidence set forth in the *Historia Ecclesiastica*, it

---

[77] On this point there is general agreement among the principal Eusebius scholars.

[78] "Accepted," that is, in relation to *2 Clement*; see 3.38.4–5.

[79] Eusebius's version of events is in his *Life of Constantine*, 4.34–37. The emperor is said to have requested "fifty copies of the sacred scriptures" which Eusebius says were "magnificent and elaborately bound." Similarly, Athanasius had volumes prepared for the Emperor Constantius during the exiled Bishop's stay at Rome (339–46) amidst the Arian crisis (*Defense before Constantius*, 4). See also the discussions in F. F. Bruce, *The Canon of Scripture* (Downers

makes sense to assume that *Barnabas* and *1 Clement* were not included in Eusebius's edition of the NT.

Textual Evidence for the Catholic Epistles

Before we turn to post-Eusebian canon lists, it is a good idea to compare our findings with the textual evidence from the period.

THE GREEK PAPYRUS MANUSCRIPTS

Given the paucity of its patristic usage, one might be surprised to discover that portions of the letter of James are found among the earliest papyrus fragments of the CE.[80] P[20] (containing Jas 2:19–3:2, 4-9), P[23] (containing Jas 1:10-12, 15-16), and P[100] (containing Jas 3:13–4:4 and 4:9–5:1) are all dated to the third century and show that the letter of James was available in Egypt at that time. If their dating is accurate, they support the evidence for the letter's availability by Origen's day.

P[72] (Bodmer Papyrus VII–VIII) offers the earliest textual evidence *in Greek* for 1–2 Peter and Jude.[81] These writings were bound together in a single codex along with a number of other texts in the following order: the Nativity of Mary, the third letter of Paul to the Corinthians, the eleventh Ode of Solomon, Jude, the Homily of Melito on the Passover, a Hymn, the Apology of Phileas, Psalms 33 and 34, and 1 and 2 Peter. Though it was bound together sometime in the fourth century, the paginations indicate that it is composed of at least three previous collections, the orthographical peculiarities of which suggest that the writings themselves were copied sometime in the third century in Egypt.[82] The size and contents of the book, as well as the rather careless scribal hand, has led scholars to conclude that P[72] is a collection of texts bound for private use. Though it is textually important as an early witness to Jude and the Petrine letters, it is canonically significant for other reasons. First, it shows that the CE sub-canon was not entirely fixed in every quar-

---

Grove, Ill.: InterVarsity, 1988), 203–5; McDonald, 182–89; Metzger, *Canon*, 206–7; and K. L. Carroll, "Toward a Commonly Received New Testament," *BJRL* 44 (1962): 327–49, esp. 341f.

[80] General information about the early papyri and codices is available from a number of sources; see B. Metzger, *Text of the New Testament* (Oxford: Clarendon, 1992); K. Aland, *Kurzgefasste Liste der griechischen Handschriften des Neuen Testaments* (Berlin: Walter de Gruyter, 1963); K. and B. Aland, *Text of the New Testament* (Grand Rapids: Eerdmans, 1987) and the textual apparatus from NA 27th ed.

[81] As we will show in our discussion of the early versions, the Coptic MS 193 should probably be considered the earliest witness to 1 Peter.

[82] Cf. E. J. Epp, "Issues in the Interrelation of New Testament Textual Criticism and Canon," in McDonald and Sanders, *Canon Debate*, 485–515; F. W. Beare, "Some Remarks on the Text of 1 Peter in the Bodmer Papyrus (P[72])," *SE* 3 [= *TU* 88] (1964): 263–65; Jerome D. Quinn, "Notes on the Text of the P[72]," *CBQ* 27 (1965): 241–49, dates it to 250, but NA 27th edition lists it as third or fourth century.

ter of Christian Egypt by the end of the third century, as these letters at least were still capable of semi-independent movement. Second, these proto-canonical texts were obviously not so highly regarded at this point as to make it inappropriate for someone to bind them together with a miscellaneous assortment of canonical, apocryphal, and contemporary writings. Finally, Epp notes the unlikelihood that the same scribe produced the three letters, suggesting that each of them derived from other manuscripts.[83] Were we to form judgments on the basis of this codex alone, we might be tempted to conclude that 1–2 Peter and Jude fell into a category of texts labeled "miscellaneous."

P[78] (OP 2684) is a fragment of Jude found at Oxyrhynchus.[84] It is a single double-leaf page (containing Jude 4-5 and 7-8) from what was originally a small codex written sometime from the mid-third to the early fourth century. The construction of the fragment suggests that it did not originally contain the whole of Jude but was probably made up of either a collection of verses or simply a partial copy of the letter. The poor spelling, odd format (5.3 cm. wide and 2.9 cm. high), and amateurish script has led to the conclusion that the codex was probably created for use as an amulet. While we cannot know what else the little book contained, it is tempting to conclude on the basis of the Jude text involved that the amulet was intended to protect the wearer from the condemned false teachers who had secretly gained admission to the church (Jude 4).

A perusal of the list of papyrus witnesses in the twenty-seventh edition of the Nestle-Aland Greek NT (1993) shows that the CE are little represented in this period compared to the manuscripts preserving the gospels and Pauline letters. Forty-six papyri are dated from the third to fourth century or earlier; of these, twenty-four are witnesses to the gospels and Acts, fourteen are Pauline, five are CE, and three are of the Apocalypse. Four of the five CE papyri are tiny fragments that preserve only a few verses each.[85] The only one of substance is the aforementioned P[72] that preserves the whole of 1–2 Peter and Jude. There are no Greek papyrus witnesses to 2 or 3 John from this period, the earliest being P[74], a seventh-century codex of Acts and all seven CE.

THE GREEK UNCIAL MANUSCRIPTS

The earliest extant collections of NT texts derive from the East and date from the fourth and early fifth centuries. While they are quite uniform, their variations illustrate the status of certain texts in the stage just prior to the period when the canon

---

[83] Epp, 491–93; he notes that this manuscript diversity is consistent with many other manuscripts of the CE, which also often do not share a uniform textual character; see also Aland, *Text*, 48ff.

[84] The following information on P[78] came from L. Ingrams, et al., *The Oxyrhynchus Papyri* (Egypt Exploration Society, 1968) 34.4–6.

[85] P[9] contains 1 John 4:11-12, 14-17; P[20] has James 2:19–3:9; P[23] preserves James 1:10-12, 15-18; P[78] has Jude 4-5, 7-8; and P[72] has all of 1–2 Peter and Jude.

had reached its final form. Codices Sinaiticus (ℵ) and Vaticanus (B) both date from no later than the mid-fourth century, though the latter is generally considered to be slightly older due to its lack of ornamentation.[86] The two are quite similar in style and may have originated from the same scriptorium, though the differences keep them from being too closely linked. Both were most likely written in Alexandria, and they display evidence of having been corrected at a later date in Caesarea.

Sinaiticus's contents appear in the following order: four gospels, fourteen Pauline letters (with Hebrews between 2 Thessalonians and 1 Timothy), Acts, seven CE (in the canonical order James–Peter–John–Jude), Revelation, followed by the letter of *Barnabas*, and part of *Hermas*. It is unknown whether or not any writings were included thereafter. There is a space of over one and a half columns separating *Barnabas* from *Hermas*, and though some have suggested this indicates a lower view of the latter text, it must be noted that a similar gap exists after Acts and before James.[87] Vaticanus follows what has come to be known as the traditional Eastern ordering: gospels, Acts, CE (James–Peter–John–Jude), and some of the Pauline letters. As in Sinaiticus, Hebrews is included after 2 Thessalonians; however the manuscript ends abruptly at 9:13, so we are left wondering what the codex ultimately contained. It should also be noted that the text of Vaticanus contains an ancient system of division that arranges the writings into portions akin to chapters. Second Peter is not divided according to this system, which may indicate some uncertainty regarding the canonical status of this epistle.

Codex Alexandrinus (A) is later than ℵ and B, probably dating from the first half of the fifth century. The codex as a whole is made up of a variety of text types, though the volume itself is traditionally assumed to have originated in Egypt. Alexandrinus orders its books in the following manner: four gospels, Acts, seven CE (James–Peter–John–Jude), fourteen Pauline letters (like the others, with Hebrews between 2 Thessalonians and the pastorals), Revelation, *1–2 Clement*, and the *Psalms of Solomon* (the latter text is no longer a part of the codex, but a table of contents verifies its former presence).

The evidence suggests that third century Christians would not have had the entire Bible in one volume, having instead several codices containing different collections, gospels in one, Pauline letters in another.[88] In the fourth century, however, we witness a shift to large, professionally made and undoubtedly very expensive Bibles, a shift possibly related to the official state sanctioning of the church at that time. What role did the production of these complete Bibles have on the final formalization of the NT canon? Bruce Metzger, arguing on the assumption that the canon was essentially complete by this time in the East, says they had little effect on selection but may have had a unifying effect on the sequence of books.[89] Other

---

[86] Metzger, *Text*, 47.

[87] Hahneman, 67.

[88] A. Souter, *The Text and Canon of the New Testament* (London: Duckworth, 1913), 11.

[89] Metzger, *Canon*, 109, n. 79.

scholars, who are committed to a later canon, argue that this move must have played a more determinative role regarding the final contents of the NT.[90] Yet surely both conclusions were the case: the fact that the canon was essentially complete in one part of Christendom need not imply that these impressive codices did not help to secure that canon elsewhere. It is hard to believe otherwise; such "official" codices had to have a unifying effect, at least where they were used in the "official" churches of the East.

The Early Versions

Among the many manuscripts of ancient versions of the NT available to us today, three in particular are of interest to my study and therefore require brief comment.[91] The first is the Crosby-Schøyen codex (MS 193), a papyrus document written in Coptic uncial and containing the entire book of Jonah, 2 Maccabees 5:27–7:41, 1 Peter, Melito's *Homily on the Passover*, and an otherwise unknown Easter sermon.[92] Noting the comparable subject matter of the various texts included (sorrows, passion, Easter), Hans-Gebhard Bethge supposes that the codex was designed to function as a liturgical text for the Easter season.[93] Its significance for NT studies lies principally in the fact that it may represent the oldest manuscript attestation for 1 Peter. While Metzger dates it "no later than the turn of the third and fourth centuries,"[94] and the Alands place it "probably ca. 400,"[95] Bethge notes other opinions placing it as early as the late second century.[96] If the text is indeed that early, its underlying Greek exemplar would probably have been only a generation or two away from the original text.

We must also consider the well-known and much debated Codex Bezae Cantabrigiensis (D).[97] The manuscript, dated to the late fourth or early fifth century, is a bilingual two-columned text in Greek and Latin containing most of the four

---

[90] Gamble, *Canon: Making and Meaning*, 67 attributes these larger manuscripts to improvements in codex technology, while McDonald, 182–89, highlights the political interests of the emperor.

[91] I am grateful to Dr. Peter J. Williams of the University of Aberdeen for having alerted me to the importance of this particular evidence.

[92] For information on the codex, see J. E. Goehring, *The Crosby-Schøyen Codex, MS 193* (CSCO 521; Louvain: Peeters, 1990), and Hans-Gebhard Bethge, "Der Text des ersten Petrusbriefes im Crosby-Schøyen-Codex (Ms. 193 Schøyen Collection)," *ZNW* 84 (1993): 255–67.

[93] Bethge, 257.

[94] B. Metzger, *The Early Versions of the New Testament* (Oxford: Clarendon, 1977), 111.

[95] Aland and Aland, *Text*, 197.

[96] Bethge, 258.

[97] See the recent thorough analysis of the codex by D. C. Parker, *Codex Bezae: An Early Christian Manuscript and its Text* (Cambridge: Cambridge University Press, 1992) and the collection of essays edited by Parker and C.-B. Amphoux, *Codex Bezae: Studies from the Lunel Colloquium, June 1994* (Leiden: Brill, 1996).

gospels (in the order Matthew, John, Luke, Mark) and, after a significant lacuna, the last verses of 3 John (in the Latin column only) followed by most of the Acts of the Apostles. The question of what was included in the original manuscript cannot be concluded with certainty. In his annotated edition of the text, Scrivener noted his supposition that the original must have included the seven CE,[98] but the recent study by Parker notes that Scrivener's hypothesis was supplanted long ago by that of John Chapman.[99] Noting (a) that the seven CE are not long enough to fill in the missing leaves, and (b) that the available patristic evidence makes it historically unlikely that a Latin biblical text of the time would have included James and 2 Peter, Chapman went on to argue, by calculation of relative line length, that it is far more likely that the lacuna included the Apocalypse and 1–3 John. Acknowledging the unavoidable uncertainty of the matter, Parker nevertheless concludes that "Chapman's case remains the most scientifically argued and acceptable that we have."[100] My own demonstration of minimal CE attestation among Latin church fathers (especially in light of the next section) leads us to the same estimation of Chapman's hypothesis. It is highly unlikely that Codex Bezae ever contained the entire CE collection.[101]

Though the canon list found in the sixth-century Codex Claromontanus is more appropriately considered in the next section, it is presented here as an interesting contrast to the preceding manuscripts, written slightly earlier than these at a time roughly contemporaneous with the first edition of Eusebius's *Historia Ecclesiastica*. The codex (D^P or D^2) is a sixth-century Greek and Latin manuscript of the Pauline epistles that was found to contain a stichometric list of the books of the Bible written in Latin, the original of which is believed to have been written

---

[98] F. H. Scrivener, *Bezae Codex Cantabrigiensis: being an exact Copy, in ordinary Type, of the celebrated Uncial Graeco-Latin Manuscript of the Four Gospels and Acts of the Apostles, written early in the Sixth Century, and presented to the University of Cambridge by Theodore Beza A.D. 1581. Edited, with a critical Introduction, Annotations, and Facsimiles* (Cambridge: Cambridge University Press, 1864).

[99] J. Chapman, "The Original Contents of Codex Bezae," *Exp* 6 (1905): 46–53.

[100] Parker, 9.

[101] It has also been brought to my attention that the fifth-century old Latin manuscript Codex Floriacensis (*h*; also known as the Fleury Palimpsest) bears textual similarities with Cyprian of Carthage. Though the codex only contains portions of Revelation, Acts, 1–2 Peter and 1 John, if the same text type were found in old Latin manuscripts of James, 2–3 John, and Jude, it might be argued that a Latin text of the CE collection as a whole was extant in the third century. Cf. the comments of W. Thiele, "Probleme der Versio Latina in den Katholischen Briefen," in *Die Alten Übersetzungen des Neuen Testaments, Die Kirchenväterzitate und lektionare*, ed. K. Aland (*ANTF* 5; Berlin: Walter de Gruyter, 1972), 93–94; and B. Fischer, *Beiträge zur Geschichte der Lateinischen Bibeltexte* (*VL* 12; Freiburg: Verlag Herder, 1986), 191–92. Obviously such an investigation lies beyond the scope of this study; but given the overwhelming evidence we have provided (and will continue to provide in the next section against the knowledge of James by Latin churchmen before the fourth century, it seems (at this point at least) that Floriacensis poses little threat to our hypothesis.

in Greek around the year 300 in the vicinity of Alexandria.[102] The list recognizes the "four gospels" (presenting them in the so-called Western ordering of Matthew, John, Mark, and Luke), along with the epistles of Paul (with several Pauline letters missing, perhaps due to the carelessness of the scribe). The list continues as follows: 1–2 Peter, James, 1–3 John, Jude, *Barnabas*, the Revelation of John, the Acts of the Apostles, *Hermas*, the *Acts of Paul*, and the *Apocalypse of Peter*. There are short horizontal lines marking off 1 Peter, *Barnabas*, *Hermas*, the *Acts of Paul*, and the *Apocalypse of Peter*. Metzger notes that while the mark next to 1 Peter is probably a Greek paragraph mark drawing attention to the fact that the following do not belong to the Epistles of Paul, the other may isolate texts of disputed authority.[103] While the ordering of the gospels, the Petrine priority in the CE, and the scribal marks can most likely be attributed to a later Latin editor, the fact that *Barnabas* is listed in the midst of the CE may be indicative of a period in the later stages of the third century when the collection was in its last stages of formal development.

While it would be unwise to draw substantive conclusions from fragmentary textual data, we can nevertheless say with some confidence that the evidence supports the conclusions from the previous section. The third-century papyrus material suggests a period in which the CE sub-canon had not been fixed and the letters were capable of somewhat independent movement. As we move from the list in Claromontanus through the "great manuscripts" of the fourth and early fifth centuries, we witness movements toward stabilization. *Barnabas* is listed among the CE in Claromontanus, but in Sinaiticus it has been moved to the end, and it is missing altogether from the later Alexandrinus. Several points should be noted regarding the canonical order and sequence of the CE: (1) The sequence James–Peter–John–Jude is prevalent in the great manuscripts; (2) we note that Acts is not listed with the CE in Claromontanus but introduces them in the great manuscripts; and (3) Vaticanus and Alexandrinus place the Acts and the CE immediately after the gospel collection and before the Pauline letters. As we will see in the next section, this particular canonical ordering appears to have been the tradition in the East.

The Catholic Epistles in the Closing of the Canon: The Fourth and Fifth Centuries

The years after Eusebius witness an increase in attempts to close the NT canon through the production and dissemination of authoritative canon lists. More thorough treatments of the canon lists are available in the standard editions;[104] for our purposes a summary of the evidence will suffice.

---

[102] See the discussion in Zahn, 3.157–72; Metzger, *Canon*, 230; and Hahneman, 140–43.

[103] Metzger, *Canon*, 230 and 310 n. 9.

[104] Where references to critical editions are not given, the canon list information was culled from Westcott (548–90), Metzger (*Canon*, 305–15) and Hahneman (132–63).

The Eastern Church

In agreement with the earliest major manuscripts (Vaticanus, Sinaiticus, and Alexandrinus), most of the Eastern lists from this period witness the existence of a relatively fixed CE collection, titled "the Catholic Epistles" and include seven letters in the canonical order of James, Peter, John, and Jude (see the chart on pp. 92–93). This is the case with Cyril of Jerusalem (*catech.* 4.33, ca. 350), the Synod of Laodicea (Canon 60, ca. 365), Athanasius of Alexandria (*Ep.* 39 of 367), and Gregory of Nazianzus (*Carm.* 12.31, ca. 390). We can also add Amphilochius of Iconium (*Iambi ad Seleucum* ca. 289–319), who says,

> Of the Catholic Epistles some say we must receive seven, but others say only three should be received—that of James, one, and one of Peter, and those of John, one. And some receive three [of John], and besides these, two of Peter, and that of Jude a seventh.[105]

It is probably the case that the "others" are representatives of the Syrian churches, whose canon lists will be discussed in the next section. Epiphanius of Salamis (*Panarion* 76.5, ca. 375) offers an interesting catalog: after listing four gospels and fourteen epistles of Paul without actually naming any of them, he then lists the CE *by name* (in canonical order) but refrains from numbering them.[106] As I noted in my introduction, *numbering* the letters in a collection is important, especially if that number happens to be "seven." One gets the sense in patristic writings that a canonical collection has achieved a level of completion when a number becomes part of the title: There are *seven* CE, not two or three; there are *four* gospels, not three or five; and depending on the tradition of the writer in question, there may be *thirteen* or *fourteen* Pauline letters, but *seven* churches are addressed. A number in the title seems to indicate a limit. Thus, Epiphanius's reluctance to number the CE may reflect his awareness of differing opinions regarding the proper number of Petrine and Johannine epistles.

The widely observable development of the CE in the East is precisely why I cannot accept Sundberg and Hahneman's proposed fourth-century Eastern provenance for the Muratorian fragment. While there is no room here to enter more fully into the debate, we can at least conclude from the evidence that their hypothesis is severely damaged by the fact that one would expect to see a more fully developed CE collection in a fourth-century Eastern list. Apart from the conspicuous absence of a title or a number, Hahneman's conclusion that "the absence of James and Hebrews and 1 Peter is inconclusive because of defects in the fragment" is a convenient way of avoiding a serious problem in his thesis, for the evidence shows that the absence

---

[105] καθολικῶν ἐπιστολῶν τινὲς μὲν ἑπτά φασιν, οἱ δὲ τρεῖς μόνας χρῆναι δέχεσθαι· τὴν Ἰακώβου μίαν, μίαν δὲ Πέτρου τῶν τ᾽ Ἰωάννου μίαν. Τινὲς δὲ τὰς τρεῖς καὶ πρὸς αὐταῖς τὰς δύο Πέτρου δέχονται, τὴν Ἰουδα δ᾽ ἑβδόμην (PTS 9.39.310–13; Metzger, *Canon*, 314).

[106] See the text in Westcott, 551.

of these letters makes no sense whatsoever in a fourth-century Eastern list.[107] Quite simply, the "Eastern" hypothesis that requires the accidental removal of Hebrews, James, *and* 1 Peter is far harder to accept than the "Western" hypothesis that only 1 Peter was lost in transmission.

Two other lists that differ from the dominant pattern deserve mention. The NT list in the apostolic canons (Canon 85, ca. 380) lists the CE as follows: "two of Peter, three of John, one of James, one of Jude."[108] Metzger has noted that this peculiar listing seems to order the letters according to the total stichometric length of the writings *by author*.[109] The list in Codex Claromontanus has already been addressed; its order lists 1–2 Peter, James, 1–3 John, Jude, and *Barnabas*. As will be made clear in the next section, this particular ordering reflects the Western tendency to give Peter priority of place over the other CE.

From the above lists we can note two further Eastern tendencies beyond that of title, number, and sequence. First, we see that the Acts of the Apostles is almost always linked with the CE (Cyril, Athanasius, Synod of Laodicea, Epiphanius, Vaticanus, Sinaiticus, and Alexandrinus). Second, we see that the Acts + CE collection follows the gospels and precedes the Pauline epistles in all of the above except Sinaiticus. Metzger has pointed out that "virtually all Greek manuscripts" of the NT follow this pattern, which has come to be recognized as the traditional Eastern canonical ordering.[110]

While the sequence of NT books is often considered to be ad hoc,[111] some of the commentary from the above lists suggest otherwise. Cyril of Jerusalem has this to say:

> Receive also the Acts of the Twelve Apostles; and in addition to these, the seven Catholic Epistles of James, Peter, John, and Jude [δέχεσθε . . . πρὸς τούτοις δὲ καὶ τὰς ἑπτά, Ἰακώβου, καὶ Πέτρου, καὶ Ἰωάννου, καὶ Ἰούδα καθολικὰς ἐπιστολάς]; then, as a seal upon them all, and the last work of disciples [ἐπισφράγισμα δὲ τῶν πάντων, καὶ μαθητῶν τὸ τελευταῖον], the fourteen Epistles of Paul. (4.36)[112]

The gospels, Acts, and CE seem to belong to an earlier period (in fact, his limitation of Acts to that of "the twelve Apostles" explicitly excludes the work of Paul), while the Pauline epistles represent "the last work of disciples" and function as "a seal" upon the other writings. How is it that Paul's work can be considered *last* among

[107] Hahneman on James, 25–26; on Hebrews, 110–25.
[108] Text in Westcott, 542; Eng. trans. by Metzger, *Canon*, 313.
[109] Metzger, *Canon*, 299, lists 403 Petrine stichoi, 332 of John, 247 of James, and 71 of Jude.
[110] Metzger, *Canon*, 295–96.
[111] See introduction; Bruce, *Canon*, 211 comments: "The temptation to find theological significance in what was originally a fortuitous or mechanical arrangement of biblical books is one to which some readers yield even today."
[112] Reischl and Rupp, 130; McCauley and Stephenson, FC 61.137.

the apostles? Such a way of putting things makes perfect *narratological* sense according to the Eastern ordering. The narrative flow of Acts begins with the apostles in
Jerusalem and moves outward from there, culminating in the work of Paul. This
narrative logic is thus imprinted in the Eastern ordering of the NT writings: following the Acts narrative, the CE represent the literary deposit of the Christian
mission to Jews inaugurated in Jerusalem, and the Pauline writings represent the
"later" Gentile mission. The fact that Peter and John are traditionally associated
with Rome and Ephesus, respectively, does not change the fact that they both continued to be associated with the Jewish mission in Jerusalem, as some other patristic
comments make clear.[113] One also notes Galatians 1:17, where Paul calls the Pillars
of Jerusalem "those who were apostles *before* me," as well as Paul's self-designation
in 1 Corinthians 15:8 as "*last* of all," that is, after Peter, the twelve, James, and
the remaining apostles. Regardless, Cyril's presentation seems to insist that Acts
be linked with the CE, with the latter functioning as representative writings of the
twelve. These writings then appear to find their fulfillment in Paul's letters, which
function as "a seal upon them all."

In a similar fashion, Athanasius's list links Acts with the CE and separates them
from the Pauline epistles:

> Then after these [εἶτα μετὰ ταῦτα], Acts of the Apostles and seven letters,
> called Catholic, by the apostles [καὶ ἐπιστολαὶ καθολικαὶ καλούμεναι τῶν
> ἀποστόλων ἑπτά], namely one by James, two by Peter, then three by John, and
> after these, one by Jude. After these [πρὸς τούτοις] there are fourteen letters by
> Paul. (PG 26.1137)[114]

Here there are no chronological claims as in Cyril ("after these" may be translated
"in addition to," and in the end either reading refers simply to the canonical ordering), but we find the same notion that Acts + CE have to do with "the apostles" in
a way that seems designed to distinguish them from Paul. This also can be seen to

---

[113] Peter and John continued to be associated with the Jewish mission in Jerusalem,
at least historically (via the witness of Acts and Galatians) but sometimes also whilst they
resided elsewhere. Note, for instance, the words of Origen in *Against Celsus* 2.2.1: "Now,
since we are on the subject of Peter, and the teachers of Christianity to the circumcision,
I do not deem it out of place to quote a certain declaration of Jesus taken from the gospel
according to John . . ." (*ANF* 4.430). Consider also Didymus the Blind's opening comments
in his commentary on the CE: "It is right that James the apostle to the circumcised writes to
those of the circumcision, just as Peter, who was well known as an apostle to the same, also
writes to Jews located in the dispersion; for these things, which are written to them, can be
adapted also for those who are secretly spiritual Jews. For John was an apostle with James, and
he also discoursed about spiritual Israelites and their tribes in the Apocalypse" (PG 39:1749).
Though it was traditionally believed that John wrote the Apocalypse from Patmos (i.e., *Hist.
Eccl.* 3.20.2) and the gospel from Ephesus (i.e., *Adv. Haer.* 3.1.1), nevertheless Origen and
Didymus could continue to associate them with the Jewish mission to the circumcised.

[114] Translation by D. Brakke, *Athanasius and the Politics of Asceticism* (Oxford: Clarendon,
1995), 329.

have been inspired by Acts, where the name "apostles" is typically reserved for the original disciples of Jesus living in Jerusalem and working in the mission to Jews (see especially Acts 9:27, ch. 15, and 16:4). Finally, Epiphanius's list begins with the four gospels and fourteen letters of Paul but follows with "those that come before these [ἐν ταῖς πρὸ τούτων], including the Acts of the Apostles in their times [σὺν ταῖς ἐν τοῖς αὐτῶν χρόνοις Πράξεσι τῶν ἀποστόλων] and the Catholic Epistles of James, Peter, John, and Jude" (*Panarion* 76.5).[115] Here again the CE are separated from the Pauline letters and are specifically linked with the text that tells of the (earlier) Acts of the Apostles "in their times."

The comments of Cyril, Athanasius, and Epiphanius imply that the Acts + CE collection was placed before the Pauline collection in the East as a structural instantiation of the narrative logic of Acts, which midway through turns away from the apostolic mission to Jews in order to focus exclusively on Paul's Gentile mission. As Richard Bauckham has suggested, such an ordering should not be taken to imply a subordination of the Jewish mission, but instead emphasizes the priority of the center (Jerusalem) in relation to the movement out from the center (Gentile mission) according to Paul's own formulation of priority in the Christian mission: "to the Jew first and also to the Greek" (Rom 1:16).[116] The logic of this ordering finds further expression in those Eastern writers who underscore the connection by using the title "Catholic" in relation to the Acts of the Apostles itself. Amphilochius refers to "the catholic Acts of the apostles" in his list (*Iambi ad Seleucum* 297 [PTS 9.38.297]). Cyril of Jerusalem, in a discourse advising against the eating of meat that had been sacrificed to idols, refers to the apostolic letter of Acts 15 as the "catholic epistle to all the Gentiles."[117] Over a century before Cyril, Clement of Alexandria referred to the Acts 15 apostolic letter in the same way (*Strom.* 4.15.97.3 [GCS 2.291]). The evidence clearly suggests that Acts + CE were considered in the East to be a discreet canonical unit, separate from the gospels that came before and the letters of Paul that followed them in canonical order. The fact that the sequence James–Peter–John echoes Paul's own description of the leaders of the Jewish mission in Galatians 2:9 underscores the point that the two epistolary collections were meant to be associated with the two-sided mission of the ancient apostolate as it is described in the Acts of the Apostles.

THE SYRIAN CHURCHES

The unique situation of the Syrian church represents a significant departure from the canonical traditions of the rest of contemporary Eastern Christianity (see the chart on p. 91).[118] We must begin by distinguishing between the Greek-speaking

[115] Text by Westcott, 551.

[116] Bauckham, *James*, 116.

[117] *Catechetical Lectures* 4.28 (Reischl-Rupp, 120).

[118] See Metzger's excellent survey in *Early Versions*, 3–98; Jeffrey Siker, "The Canonical Status of the Catholic Epistles in the Syriac New Testament," *JTS* 38 (1987): 311–40; Julius

Christianity of Western Syria (centered at Antioch) from the Syriac-speaking Christianity of Eastern Syria (centered around the cities of Edessa and Arbela). Though Antioch lay within the boundaries of the Roman Empire and was very much a part of the broader Greek church, Eastern Syria was an independent kingdom until the early third century. Hence, differences in language, government, and culture allowed the churches of Eastern Syria to develop independently of the major Christian traditions of their day.

This independence is perhaps most notable in their canon history. Apart from the well-known issues surrounding the long acceptance of Tatian's *Diatessaron*, the Syrians prior to the fifth century appear to have either rejected or remained ignorant of most or all of the CE collection.[119] The evidence is admittedly sparse: we have no real canon lists before the turn of the fifth century, and we have little by way of versional evidence beyond the fact that no extant manuscripts of the Old Syriac include any of the CE. The picture becomes clearer when we consider the Syrian version of the Bible known as the Peshitta, which was in circulation by the early fifth century in both Greek-speaking western and Syriac-speaking eastern Syria. Among the CE, the Peshitta included the three "major" epistles in the Eastern order James–Peter–John, after the gospels and before the Pauline letters; however, the "minor" CE (2 Peter, 2–3 John, Jude) and Revelation were excluded. Later, in 508, Philoxenus the Bishop of Mabbug undertook a revision of the Peshitta in the interest of bringing the Syrian NT in line with the Greek text. This version included the minor CE and Revelation. Both versions circulated in the Syrian church throughout the sixth century; but since Philoxenus was a Monophysite, the version he commissioned only circulated in the Western, Monophysite church. The Eastern Nestorian church holds to the Peshitta version with its twenty-two-book NT to this day.

A canon list from the Syriac-speaking East may be representative of the period before the dominance of the Peshitta version. The *Doctrine of Addai*, traditionally dated around the year 400, includes a proscription against reading anything other than

> the Law and the Prophets and the Gospel, which you read every day before the people, and the epistles of Paul which Simon Peter sent us from the city of Rome, and the Acts of the twelve apostles which John the Son of Zebedee sent us from Ephesus: From these writings you shall read in the Churches of the Messiah, and besides them nothing else shall you read, as there is not any other in which the truth that you hold is written, except these books, which keep you in the faith to which you have been called.[120]

A. Brewer, "The History of the New Testament Canon in the Syrian Church II: The Acts of the Apostles and the Epistles," *AJT* 4 (1900): 345–63; and Barbara Aland, *Das Neue Testament in Syrischer Überlieferung 1. Die Grossen Katholischen Briefe* (*ANTF* 7; Berlin: Walter de Gruyter, 1986).

[119] B. Aland complains, "Wir haben uns bemüht, die Zitate vollständig zu sammeln. Jedoch gibt es eindeutige Zitate aus syrischen Autoren vor dem 5. Jarhundert ebenfalls nicht" (96).

[120] Translation adapted from Brewer, 345.

Apart from the interesting fact of the singularity of the "gospel" in this canon list (undoubtedly the *Diatessaron* is in mind) it is intriguing that the prohibition against reading anything beyond the Pauline epistles and Acts is anchored in the fact that these writings were directly received from Peter and John, who apparently championed the letters of Paul without ever mentioning their own!

The Western, Greek-speaking students of the Antiochene School in the early to mid-fifth century offer witness in agreement with the Peshitta version to a minimal three-letter CE collection, though none have left us an official canon list. The NT citations in the large collection of writings attributed to John Chrysostom (d. ca. 407) show no appeal to any of the minor CE.[121] Though this does not offer proof of rejection, the fact that his usage agrees with the contents of the Peshitta version suggests he agreed with its limits. The same can be said for the later Antiochine Theodoret (d. ca. 466), who also seems to know only James, 1 Peter, and 1 John. Even then his citations of these letters are minimal, especially in James, where we find only one unattributed quotation (*Interpretatio in Psalmos* 26.6 [PG 80:1053A]). The little we have of the writings of Theodore of Mopsuestia (d. 428), however, shows no use of any of the CE at all.[122] Though such a small amount of available data will not allow for confidence, comments from his opponents support the notion that he actually rejected all of them.[123] As already mentioned, it was probably his awareness of the status of the CE in Syria that led Amphilochius (writing ca. 396 from nearby Iconium) to comment in his list, "some say we must receive seven, but others say only three should be received."

THE WESTERN CHURCH

By contrast to the Greek East, the Latin West produced far fewer canon lists in this period (see the chart on pp. 94–95). The first Western canon post-Eusebius is a North African stichometric list known as the Mommsen catalogue (or, "Cheltenham list"), which probably dates from sometime in the latter third of the fourth century.[124] Following the gospels, thirteen unnamed epistles of Paul, Acts, and Revelation, the list concludes with the three epistles of John and the two epistles of Peter. There is no mention of James or Jude, and it is assumed that Hebrews is the missing letter in the Pauline collection. On the lines below each of the Johannine and Petrine letters, there are separate lines that repeat the phrase *una sola*, "one only." It is generally assumed that the *una sola* indicates a scribal protest against accepting any CE beyond 1 John and 1 Peter. Such a protest shows that the CE collection in the West had not developed much in the century and a half since Irenaeus.

---

[121] See Westcott, 442; and Metzger, *Canon*, 214–15.

[122] The citation register in CCSL 88A shows no sign of any CE usage.

[123] Leontius of Byzantium (d. ca. 620) accused Theodore of having rejected "the epistle of James and the other CE that followed it" (*Against the Nestorians* 3.14). Likewise, Isho'dad of Merv (ca. 850) mentioned in his *Commentary on the Epistle of James* that Theodore never made use of them (see Metzger, *Canon*, 215).

[124] T. Mommsen, "Zur Lateinischen Stichometrie," *Hermes* 21 (1886): 142–56.

The situation was quite likely changed as the result of the contact between Athanasius and Western church leaders instigated by the Arian crisis.[125] The similarity between Vaticanus and Athanasius's list has already been mentioned; regardless of whether or not the manuscript can be convincingly connected with the scriptures prepared by Athanasius during his exile in Rome, the event nevertheless represents a significant point of contact between East and West wherein the Alexandrian bishop could certainly have transmitted Eastern traditions concerning the extent of the canon. Similarly, when certain Western anti-Arian leaders supported Athanasius against Emperor Constantius (who supported the Arians), they were exiled eastward and thereby came into contact with Eastern traditions. One of the earliest of these was Hilary, Bishop of Poitiers (d. ca. 368), an anti-Arian theologian who had been influenced by the work of Athanasius.[126] He was exiled to the East from 356 to 360 and became one of the most important bridges between East and West upon his return. Hilary's Eastern influences are apparent in his post-exilic work: against the dominant Western opinion he championed the letter to the Hebrews as Pauline, he cited 2 Peter as an authentic writing of the apostle Peter (*De Trinitate* 1.18.3 [CSEL 62.18] cites 2 Peter 1:4), and he was the first theologian in the West to cite the letter of the "apostle James" as Scripture (*De Trinitate* 4.8.28 [CSEL 62.108)] cites James 1:17). Since the form of the James passage Hilary quotes does not correspond with any extant ancient Latin translation, it suggests that Hilary was translating the text himself from the Greek[127]—providing still further evidence that the letter was not available in the west prior to his day.

Soon after this period many other Western writers begin to demonstrate an acceptance of some of the formerly disputed CE. The otherwise unknown Pseudo-Ambrose, in his commentaries on the Pauline epistles (written in Rome during the Papacy of Damasus, sometime between 366 and 384), cite all the CE except Jude, explicitly ascribing 2 John to "John the apostle" and 2 Peter to "Peter the apostle."[128] Filaster, Bishop of Brescia (writing ca. 385), includes all seven CE in his canon list (*Liber de haeresibus* 88 [CCSL 9.255]), as does Rufinus (ca. 400) (*Symb.* 35 [CCSL 20.171]). However, none of them applies the title "Catholic Epistles" to the letters, and the sequences within their lists vary.

---

[125] Though we came to this conclusion independently, see J. P. Yates's extended defense of this position in his essay, "The Reception of the Epistle of James in the Latin West: Did Athanasius Play a Role?" in Schlosser, *Catholic Epistles and the Tradition*, 273–88.

[126] Information on Hilary comes from A. Di Berardino, *The Golden Age of Latin Patristic Literature From the Council of Nicea to the Council of Chalcedon* (vol. 4 of *Patrology*; Westminster, Md.: Christian Classics, 1986), 36–61; and W. G. Rusch, *The Later Latin Fathers* (London: Duckworth, 1977), 11–17.

[127] Ropes, 101; J. B. Adamson, *James: The Man and His Message* (Grand Rapids: Eerdmans, 1989), 149–50.

[128] Second John is attributed to "the Apostle John" in the *Commentary on Romans* 12.18.2 (CSEL 81.1.413), and 2 Peter is attributed to "the Apostle Peter" in the *Commentary on Philippians* 1.3–5 (CSEL 81.1.3.131) and the *Commentary on 1 Timothy* 2.4.2 (CSEL 81.1.3.260).

Among all the Western figures that played a role in the development of the NT canon, the most important of them was Jerome. Though he was trained as a scholar in the Latin tradition, significant periods of residence in the East informed him of the major canon traditions of the church of his day and must have enabled his role as a mediator between the East and the West. His letter to Paulinus (written from Bethlehem in 394) includes a list of biblical texts, the NT of which begins with the gospels and Paul's letters (including Hebrews) followed by Acts, the CE (in the Eastern order), and Revelation. Though he does not call them "Catholic Epistles" in this context, it is noteworthy that he links them with Acts, orders them in the Eastern sequence, and praises them as a whole without noting any dispute: "The apostles James, Peter, John, and Jude, have published seven epistles at once spiritual and to the point, short and long, short that is in words but lengthy in substance so that there are few indeed who do not find themselves in the dark when they read them" (*Ep.* 53.9 [LaBourt, 3.23.5–8; *NPNF²* 6.102]).

Elsewhere he is more forthright concerning the disputes that existed over some of the letters. His *De viris illustribus* (393) includes short chapters on all the major figures of church history. Peter "wrote two epistles which are called Catholic, the second of which, on account of its difference from the first in style, is considered by many not to be his" (1.3 [PL 23.607; Halton, FC 100.5]). In another writing he defended the Petrine authorship of 2 Peter by arguing that the apostle used different amanuenses for each letter (*Ep.* 120 [LaBourt 6.156.13–17]). As for James, he "wrote a single epistle, which is reckoned among the seven Catholic Epistles, and even this is claimed by some to have been published [*edita*] by someone else under his name, and gradually as time went on to have gained authority" (*Vir. ill.* 2.2 [PL 23.609; FC 100.7]). Jude, "the brother of James, left a short epistle which is reckoned among the seven Catholic Epistles, and because in it he quotes from the apocryphal book of Enoch, it is rejected by many. Nevertheless by age and use it has gained authority and is reckoned among the Holy Scriptures" (4.1–2 [PL 23.614–15; FC 100.11]). John "wrote also one epistle . . . which is esteemed by all who are men of the church or of learning. The other two . . . are said to be the work of John the presbyter in whose memory another sepulcher is shown at Ephesus to the present day, though some think that the two memorials belong to this same John the evangelist" (9.4–5 [PL 23.623–25; FC 100.19-20]).

One immediately notes that Jerome's notion of canonicity differs from many of his forebears in that he appears to have been untroubled by doubts over authorship. He is content with the fact that texts once considered dubious had "by age and use" gained authority as canonical Scripture. His comments in another letter regarding the dispute over Hebrews can be safely extended to the CE:

> It makes no difference whose it is, since it is from a churchman, and is celebrated in the daily readings of the churches. And if the usage of the Latins does not receive it among the canonical scriptures, neither indeed by the same liberty do the churches of the Greeks receive the Revelation of John. And yet we receive both, in

that we follow by no means the habit of today, but the authority of ancient writers, who for the most part quote each of them. (*Ep.* 129.3)[129]

His argument for accepting both Hebrews and Revelation involves a compromise between Eastern and Western traditions. For the good of the whole church, the criterion of ancient attestation should be applied universally; the West should accept the texts that were traditionally supported by the East and vice-versa. This reasoning may be extended to the disputed CE: the Latin church may have been in the habit of restricting its complete confidence to 1 Peter and 1 John, but from Jerome's perspective the CE tradition of the Greek church was over a century old and demanded acceptance.

Though Jerome maintains Pauline epistolary priority in his letter to Paulinus, the influence of the Eastern tradition on his list is made evident when one compares his placement of Acts and the CE with other Westerners of his generation. Filaster (ca. 385) orders them Peter, John, Jude, and James. Augustine's NT canon list (ca. 396) begins with the gospels and Paul's letters, following them with 1–2 Peter, 1–3 John, Jude, James, Acts, and Revelation (*De doctrina Christiana* 2.13 [CCSL 32.40]). Rufinus (ca. 400) lists them in the order Peter, James, Jude, and John (*Symb.* 35 [CCSL 20.171]). The canon of Pope Innocent I (ca. 405) closely mirrors Augustine's by listing the gospels and Pauline letters first, and Acts and Revelation last, but differs by ordering the CE as 1–3 John, 1–2 Peter, Jude, and James.[130] The canon lists of the three North African Councils (393 in Hippo; 397 and 419 in Carthage) resemble the ultimate order by placing Acts after the gospels and before the Pauline letters, but they order the CE as Peter, John, James, and Jude.

Given the widespread Western evidence of Pauline priority in the letters and Petrine priority within the CE, Jerome's sequence appears to be unique among the Latin churchmen of his day. This apparent commitment to the traditional Eastern ordering may be due to the method he employed in his work of revising the Latin Bible, to which he was commissioned by Pope Damasus in 383. Jerome's preface to his edition of the four gospels (produced in 384) tells us something about the nature of his task: he was not to produce a Latin translation of the Greek, but a revision of the existing Latin texts by appeal to the more authoritative Greek manuscripts.[131] It is probably here that Jerome's Eastern tendencies with the CE come into play: agreement with the Greek original must have included, at least in part, agreement with the sequence tradition of the Greek manuscripts.

Further, Jerome is the only Westerner of this period to use the Eastern "CE" title in his writings. The preferred Latin title, where one was used, was *epistulae canonicae*, "Canonical Epistles." This title was used less frequently, though it was preferred by Augustine (ca. 415), Junilius (ca. 545), Cassiodorus (d. ca. 565), the later writers John of Salisbury (1165), and Hugo of St. Victor (1140).[132] Augustine

---

[129] LaBourt, 8.161.7–15; Metzger, *Canon*, 236.

[130] *Letter to Exsuperius* (Hahneman, 136).

[131] Metzger, *Early Versions*, 333.

[132] See Westcott, 539–79.

gives us a sense of his understanding of this title in his *Seventh Homily on 1 John*: "This is God's scripture, dear friends. This letter is canonical [*canonica est ista Epistola*]; all peoples read it [*per omnes gentes recitatur*[133]]. It is held by universal authority, it has edified the whole earth" (*Homilies on 1 John*, 7.5).[134] Here "canonical" clearly designates not "universal address" but "universal acceptance." The fact that Augustine used this title on occasion for all the NT letters suggests that the term should be taken rather literally, that is, as a way of describing the letters that are universally included in the NT canon.[135]

Though it is unclear how much of the ultimate Vulgate can be attributed to Jerome himself,[136] it is certainly the case that its dominance in the Western church was the ultimate factor in the fixing of the NT book sequence. That this final sequence came about in the Western church by habit of use and not by convictions regarding the internal logic of the ordering is demonstrated by the fact that subsequent Western lists continued to vary in order. Among later Westerners, Cassiodorus (sixth century) maintained Petrine priority in the CE sequence; Isidore of Seville (d. 636) followed the Eastern order of the CE but placed Acts at the end with Revelation;[137] and Alfric, Abbot of Cerne (d. 1006) listed the CE after the gospels with Petrine priority, followed by Pauline letters, Acts and Revelation. Even as late as the Council of Trent (1546) Petrine priority was retained in the CE sequence.[138] If the Easterners had indeed ordered their NT books according to a particular sequential logic, the Westerners as a whole did not pick up on it.

Conclusion

My conclusion will present a short summary of the historical evidence for the development of the CE by focusing on what can be determined concerning the following components: the process of emergence; the sequence within the collection and within the canon; and the witness to a canonical function for the collection.

THE EMERGENCE OF THE CATHOLIC EPISTLE COLLECTION

While the gospel and the Pauline collections achieved a relatively fixed form through the second century it seems that the CE collection was not formed until the later third century, and did not find widespread acceptance until the late fourth. Prior to Origen, we witnessed minimal usage, in both the East and the West, focused

---

[133] Or perhaps "throughout all nations it is recited."

[134] SC 75.322; Leinenweber, 70.

[135] Brevard Childs, *The New Testament as Canon: An Introduction* (Valley Forge, Pa.: Trinity Press International, 1985), 495; Robert Webb, "Catholic Epistles" (*ABD* 2.570; ed. D. N. Freedman; New York: Doubleday, 1992).

[136] See the discussion in Metzger, *Early Versions*, 356–62.

[137] Westcott, 574–75.

[138] Westcott, 579.

primarily on 1 Peter, 1 John, and Jude. With Origen we have, for the first time, an unambiguous witness to the existence and use of all seven letters, though Origen himself seemed truly confident of only James, 1 Peter, 1 John, and Jude. To this we must also add the *Letter of Barnabas*, which was apparently valued for its allegorical interpretations of the OT Scriptures. The testimony of Eusebius leads us to believe that the CE collection as it now stands came into existence in the East sometime in the period between 250 and 300. However, while it is clearly the case that the CE was a known quantity in the Eastern churches of his day, Eusebius himself considered the new collection to be rather unstable. Five of the seven letters had a disputed history, and Eusebius, at least, was not ready to accept them all as canonical. Nevertheless, this "disputed" status was overcome rather quickly; the next Eastern canon lists (Cyril and Athanasius, et al.) show no sign of instability whatsoever. By then the CE was a fully canonical collection, fixed in content and sequence.

Elsewhere the collection took longer to arrive at its final form. On the evidence of the Mommsen Catalogue, it seems that 1 Peter and 1 John were still the only accepted CE in the West up until the mid-fourth century. While there is evidence that the Eastern CE tradition began to spread westward through this period, it not until the end of that century that we find acceptance of the seven letters in Jerome, Filaster, Rufinus, Augustine, Pope Innocent, and the North African Councils. The Syrian churches, meanwhile, lagged behind the rest of Christendom as regards the CE collection. The Peshitta version seems to have established the place of the three "major" CE in both the western Greek-speaking and the eastern Syriac-speaking church by the beginning of the fifth century. The "minor" CE, however, only found a place in western Syria with the dominance of the Philoxenian version in the sixth century.

It should be noted once again that a number of recent studies on the canon have lacked a thorough consideration of the particular issues surrounding canonical emergence of the CE collection. Trobisch was led to assume that his "Canonical Edition" was available by the end of the second century, which we have shown to be an impossibility given the state of the CE at that time. The Sundberg-Hahnemann thesis regarding the date and provenance of the Muratorian fragment only works if one ignores the status of the CE in the fourth-century Eastern church. Kalin and Gamble overlooked the particularities of its development, and it led them to deny any "substantive" distinction between Eusebius' ἀντιλεγόμενα and νόθα categories. Greater attention must therefore be paid to the role of the CE collection when scholars account for the rise of the NT canon. Indeed, as I have already mentioned, the CE collection should be considered that which is ultimately constitutive of the NT as a whole, since it was the last section of the canon to achieve its final shape.

The Sequence within the Collection and within the Canon

The order *James–Peter–John–Jude* has been shown to be of Eastern origin, and the canon lists post-Eusebius demonstrate that this order was standardized in the East from a very early period. Other sequences prevailed in the West, though they varied widely, having only Petrine priority in the CE as their common denominator. As for the sequence of canonical collections, nearly every Eastern list and manuscript of the NT orders the collections *Gospels–Acts–CE–Paul–Apocalypse*. Comments from some of the Eastern list-makers (i.e., Cyril, Athanasius, and Epiphanius) linked Acts with the CE in such a way as to suggest that they conceived of the relationship between the CE and Pauline letter collections according to the early Jewish and Gentile missions as depicted in the Acts of the Apostles. The fact that the sequence within the CE collection mirrors Paul's listing of the Pillars of the Jerusalem church in Galatians 2:9 supports this reasoning.

The Eastern sequence of canonical collections did not ultimately prevail. Other orderings placed Paul after the gospels, and before the CE, and placed Acts at the end of the canon with the Apocalypse (Codex Claromontanus, Apostolic Canon 85, Jerome, Augustine, and Pope Innocent I). The ultimate ordering *Gospels–Acts–Paul–CE–Apocalypse* found several earlier witnesses (Gregory of Nazianzus, Amphilochius, Rufinus, and the North African Councils) and was the sequence ultimately chosen for the Vulgate version that came to dominate the Western church. Though we can make assumptions about the Eastern ordering based on the comments of certain Eastern theologians, no one from this period offers any "explanation" for the decision to break up the Acts + CE collection in order to give Paul priority. Indeed, the wide variety of sequences in the West (even after the dominance of the Vulgate) suggests that canonical ordering was not of great significance for the majority of Western patristic witnesses.

Nevertheless, the final sequence makes sense historically. As the patristic citation patterns indicate, the Pauline writings were *always* "first" in authority, even among those who championed the sequence that placed the CE before his letters. The decision to give Paul priority in the NT letter collection undermines the logic that ordered the letters according to the Acts narrative in favor, perhaps, of an overriding theological concern. Augustine's comments in *De fide et operibus* may therefore provide an accurate depiction of the logic behind the ultimate ordering (that the CE were *added to* Paul as a means of correction) but it seems that the historical evidence will not allow us to substantiate this claim any further.

THOUGHTS ON THE CANONICAL FUNCTION OF THE COLLECTION

Augustine believed the CE were "deliberately aimed" at the correction of a "treacherous" Paulinism that allowed Christians to exist under "the illusion that faith alone is sufficient for salvation." My close survey of the evidence prior to Eusebius gives us little reason to doubt that many church fathers shared his opinion about some of these letters. Though James, 2 Peter, and 2–3 John were little used, 1 Peter, 1 John, and Jude were regularly cited in support of ethical exhortation, as was James once it found a champion in Origen. His *Commentary on Romans* in particular offers us clear evidence that the letter was used as a counterweight against unorthodox readings of Paul that denigrated the role of "works" in the Christian life. Nevertheless,

Augustine's understanding of this collection must not be allowed to overshadow the other themes that presented themselves in association with the use of these letters in the patristic church. Five other points must also be considered as we develop our understanding of the canonical function of this collection.

Some of our writers were concerned to establish the essential harmony of the apostolic proclamation. While Irenaeus argued this more generally (primarily with the use of the Acts of the Apostles), Tertullian focused this concern explicitly in the relationship between Paul, the apostle to the uncircumcised, and James, Peter, and John, the apostles to the circumcised. Far from being at odds with one another, Tertullian argued, these in fact preached the same gospel to different persons, as Paul himself acknowledged when he said "whether then it was I or they, so we preach" (1 Cor 15:11). Origen continued this trend in his commentary on Romans, where the Pauline "justification by faith" and the Jacobian "justification by works" were understood allegorically to represent the two circumcisions required of any-one entering the sanctuary of God, that is, the "circumcision of the heart" and the "circumcision of the flesh." Thus the two apostolic letter collections function as a literary testimony to the Catholic vision of apostolic unity in diversity.

In this regard, "the evidence" offers support for the notion that these letters were gathered together as a literary witness to the Jerusalem mission to Jews. The sequence that came to dominate (James–Peter–John–Jude) suggests that most East-ern Christians picked up on the Galatians 2:9 echo. Further, the Eastern tendency to link Acts with the CE as a prelude to the Pauline corpus, combined with the comments of certain Eastern fathers, suggests that they structured the NT letter col-lection to mirror the narrative logic of Acts, which begins with the activities of the Jewish mission and continues on with the work of Paul and the Gentile mission.

An important component of the recognition of the Jerusalem apostolate was the concern that Christian traditions include the testimony of eyewitnesses to Jesus' earthly ministry. It was on this point that Irenaeus highlighted the unique author-ity of Peter and John, "whom the Lord made witnesses of every action and of every doctrine" (*Adv. Haer.* 3.12.15 [CS 211.248; *ANF* 1.436]). Tertullian went on to insist, against a denigration of the Jerusalem apostolate in the name of Paul, that Paul needed the support of the "original apostles" for his testimony to be valid. Even if we had a gospel by Paul's own hand, that "document would not be ade-quate for our faith, if destitute of the support of his predecessors" (*Adv. Marc.* 4.2.4 [CCSL 1.548]).[139] Turning to the letters themselves, we see that 1–2 Peter and 1 John explicitly predicate their authority on the fact that they were eyewitnesses of Christ's earthly life and ministry (1 Pet 5:1; 2 Pet 1:16-18; 1 John 1:1-3), James and 1 John each appear to carefully recapitulate the teachings of the earthly Jesus (for example, Jas 5:12; 1 John 3:23), and 1 Peter explicitly sets the earthly Jesus forward as the primary example of Christian discipleship (for example, 1 Pet 2:21).

We see in the use of the letters an appreciation for their prophetic role vis-à-vis the advent of heresy. Irenaeus, Tertullian, and Cyprian saw 1 (and 2) John in this

---

[139] E. B. Evans, 263.

light, and Clement noted the same in Jude. Similarly (though without the prophetic emphasis), Origen used James to correct unorthodox readings of Paul, and Augustine claimed the same for the collection as a whole. That most if not all of the seven letters articulate concerns regarding "deceivers," "false prophets," "teachers," and "antichrists" may also help to explain the delayed "arrival" of this collection, as a developing Catholic orthodoxy increasingly found itself in conflict with the doctrinal claims of emerging alternative Christianities.

Finally, all of these themes may be joined together in the ongoing concern to demonstrate the unity of salvation history, which included a defense of its textual articulation in the unity of the Old and New Testaments. Most of these letters incorporate OT texts, themes, and images in a way that enables a greater sense of continuity between the two covenants.[140] That this unity be defended was one of the central points of contention in the writings of Irenaeus and Tertullian. Origen's use of James and 1 Peter showed that he valued the letters for this very reason. It is also the best explanation for the popularity of *Barnabas* in Clement and Origen, as its allegorical reading of the OT enabled their defense of the harmony of the two testaments. Finally, the fact that Jude was often cited in defense of the use of apocryphal Jewish texts demonstrates a concern to keep Jewish traditions alive.

These six themes might be seen to coalesce indirectly around the church's struggle against Marcion. While the four-fold gospel and Pauline collections were already on the road to completion by the time Marcion's work reached fruition, my analysis shows that the CE collection developed at the same time that the church was struggling against his teaching. Though Harnack's famous claim that "the Christian NT is an anti-Marcionite creation on a Marcionite basis" has been long overturned, might it be historically justifiable to suppose that the formation of the CE collection was at least indirectly influenced by anti-Marcionite polemics? This significant question will require further comment, so I will have to return to it in the conclusion.

What is particularly striking in all of this is the way in which James, 2 Peter, 2–3 John, and Jude, texts that were previously "disputed," quickly rose to "canonical" status in the late third and early fourth centuries as components of the CE collection. James and 2 Peter are the real enigmas among these five, for they appear to have arrived latest. Trobisch's work suggests that 2 Peter found acceptance because it was a good fit in a larger Western redactional strategy aimed at an anti-Marcionite reconciliation of Peter and Paul. Given that both James and the seven letter CE collection make their first appearance in the East, we are left with the strong hunch that the rise of the CE collection as a whole is attributable to a similar phenomenon as that which gave rise to the acceptance of 2 Peter in the West. As Origen's use of James in the *Commentary on Romans* suggests, once James was added to the other letters, a "fit" was made that enabled a particularly potent anti-Marcionite reading strategy grounded in the structure of the NT letter collection itself. Indeed, without James

---

[140] 1–3 John are exceptions to this, though we will nevertheless suggest in chapter 3 that the emphasis in 1 John on commandment keeping may have been heard in reference to the commandments of God in the OT.

the NT letters would include a Pauline collection, a Petrine collection linked with Jude, a Johannine collection, and a receding list of semi-authoritative letters headed by *Barnabas* and *1 Clement*. By adding James to that group, the Petrine and Johannine collections are merged under a Pillars of Jerusalem rubric, one that would act as a theological counterweight to the Pauline collection and provide a meaningful category by which these may be differentiated from other available letters, so that the apostolic letter collection might be closed. This hypothesis regarding the canonical function of James requires a good deal of further substantiation, of course, so my next chapter will focus exclusively on the question of that letter's origin.

SYRIAN CHURCH

Century	Church Father	Death/ Date of Writing	Non-Pauline letters known/used	Aware of a discrete collection?	Title for the collection?	Reference to a number?	Sequence within the Canon	Sequence within the CE
3rd	*Peshitta* in circulation		Jas, 1 Pet, 1 Jn	n/a	n/a	n/a	A-CE-P	Jas-Pet Jn
4th–5th	*Doctrine of Addai*	ca. 400	None	No	No	No	n/a	n/a
	John Chrysostom	d. ca. 407	Jas, 1 Pet, 1 Jn	No	No	No	n/a	n/a
5th	Theodore of Mopsuetia	d. 428	None	No	No	No	n/a	n/a
	Theodoret	d. ca. 466	Jas, 1 Pet, 1 Jn	No	No	No	n/a	n/a
6th	Philoxenus revision of *Peshitta*	508	Jas, 1–2 Pet, 1–3 Jn, Jd	n/a	n/a	n/a	A-CE-P	Jas-Pet-Jn-Jd

EASTERN CHURCH

Note: *Italicized* text indicates deviation from the apparent norm

Century	Church Father/ Manuscript	Death/ Date of Writing	Non-Pauline letters known/used	Aware of a discreet collection?	Title for the collection	Reference to a number?	Sequence within the Canon	Sequence within the CE
Late 2nd	Clement of Alexandria	d. ca. 215	1 Pet, 1–2 Jn, Jd, Barn, 1 Clem	No, but calls Jd + letter of Act 15 "CE"	No	No	n/a	n/a
3rd	Origin of Alexandria	d. ca. 253	Jas, 1 Pet, 1 Jn, Barn, 1 Clem; knows 2–3 Jn and 2 Pet, but doesn't accept	No, but calls 1 Jn, 1 Pet & Barn "CE"	No	No	n/a	n/a
	Eusebius of Caesarea	ca. 300	1 Jn & 1 Pet listed as "accepted"; Jas, 2 Pet, 2–3 Jn & Jd are "disputed"	Yes	"Catholic Epistles"	"Seven"	*A-P-CE*	Jas-Pet-Jn-Jd
	Codex Vaticanus	early 4th?	Jas, 1–2 Pet, 1–3 Jn, Jd	n/a	n/a	n/a	A-CE-P	Jas-Pet Jn-Jd
	Codex Sinaiticus	early 4th?	Jas, 1–2 Pet, 1–3 Jn, Jd	n/a	n/a	n/a	*P-A-CE*	Jas-Pet-Jn-Jd

Period	Source	Date	Letters					
4th	Cyril of Jerusalem	ca. 350	Jas, 1–2 Pet, 1–3 Jn, Jd	Yes	"Catholic Epistles"	"Seven"	A-CE-P	Jas-Pet-Jn-Jd
	Synod of Laodicea	ca. 365	Jas, 1–2 Pet, 1–3 Jn, Jd	Yes	"Catholic Epistles"	"Seven"	A-CE-P	Jas-Pet-Jn-Jd
	Athanasius of Alexandria	367	Jas, 1–2 Pet, 1–3 Jn, Jd	Yes	"Catholic Epistles"	"Seven"	A-CE-P	Jas-Pet-Jn-Jd
	Epiphanius of Salamis	ca. 375	Jas, 1–2 Pet, 1–3 Jn, Jd	Yes, but knows of dispute	"Catholic Epistles"	None: lists names but doesn't number	A-CE-P	Jas-Pet Jn-Jd
	Apostolic Canon #85	380	Jas, 1–2 Pet, 1–3 Jn, Jd 1–2 Clem.	No	No	Numbers individual letters only	*P-CE-A*	*Pet-Jn-Jas-Jd*
	Gregory of Nazianzus	390	Jas, 1–2 Pet, 1–3 Jn, Jd	Yes	"Catholic Epistles"	"Seven"	*A-P-CE*	Jas-Pet Jn-Jd
	Amphilochius of Iconium	ca. 396	Jas, 1–2 Pet, 1–3 Jn, Jd	Yes, but knows of dispute	"Catholic Epistles"	"Either seven or three"	*A-P-CE*	Jas-Pet-Jn-Jd
Early 5th	Codex Alexandrinus	early 5th?	Jas, 1–2 Pet, 1–3 Jn, Jd	n/a	n/a	n/a	A-CE-P	Jas-Pet-Jn-Jd

WESTERN CHURCH

Century	Church Father/ Manuscript	Death/ Date of Writing	Non-Pauline letters known/used	Aware of a discrete collection?	Title for the collection?	Reference to a number?	Sequence within the Canon	Sequence within the CE
Late 2nd	Irenaeus of Lyon	d. ca. 200	1 Pet, 1–2 Jn	No	No	No	n/a	n/a
Late 2nd	Muratorian Fragment	ca. 200	Jd, 1–2 (or 3?) Jn	No	n/a	No	A-P-Jd-Jn	Jd-Jn
3rd	Tertullian of Carthage	d. ca. 223	1 Pet, 1 Jn, Jd	No	No	No	n/a	n/a
3rd	Hippolytus Alexandria	d. ca. 235	1 Pet, 1-2 Jn; maybe – Pet?	No	No	No	n/a	n/a
3rd	Cyprian of Carthage	d. ca. 258	1 Pet, 1 Jn	No	No	No	n/a	n/a
4th	Mommsen Catalogue/ Cheltenham Canon	mid-late 4th	1–2 Pet, 1–3 Jn; scribal marks indicate only 1 Pet & 1 Jn accepted	No	n/a	n/a	P-A-Rev-Jn-Pet	Jn-Pet
4th	Hilary of Poitiers	d. ca. 368	1st in West to use Jas & 2 Pet; cites Heb as Pauline; also knows 1 Pet & 1 Jn	No	No	No	n/a	n/a

Century	Author	Date						
5th	Pseudo-Ambrose	mid-late 4th	Jas, 1–2 Pet, 1–3 Jn, Jd	No	No	No	n/a	n/a
	Jerome	394	Jas, 1–2 Pet, 1–3 Jn, Jd	Yes	"Catholic Epistles"	"Seven"	P-A-CE	Jas-Pet-Jn-Jd
	Augustine of Hippo	ca. 396	Jas, 1–2 Pet, 1–3 Jn, Jd	Yes	Canonicae Epistulae	No	P-CE-A	Pet-Jn-Jd-Jas
	Filaster of Brescia	ca. 397	Jas, 1–2 Pet, 1–2 Clem.	Yes?	No	"Seven letters"	A-P-CE	Pet-Jn-Jd-Jas
	N. African Canons	393, 397, 419	Jas, 1–2 Pet, 1–3 Jn, Jd	No	No	No	A-P-CE	Pet-Jn-Jas-Jd
	Rufinus of Aquileia	404	Jas, 1–2 Pet, 1–3 Jn, Jd	No	No	No	A-P-CE	Pet-Jas-Jd-Jn
	Pope Innocent	405	Jas, 1–2 Pet, 1–3 Jn, Jd	No	No	No	P-CE-A	Jn-Pet-Jd-Jas
6th	Junilius Africanus	ca. 545	Jas, 1–2 Pet, 1–3 Jn, Jd; gives priority to 1 Pet & 1 Jn	Yes	Canonicae Epistulae	2; 5 others "added by very many"	P-CE	Pet-Jn; Jas-Pet-Jd-Jn
	Cassidorus	d. ca. 565	Jas, 1–2 Pet, 1–3 Jn, Jd; doubts	Yes	Canonicae Epistulae	No	A-CE-P	Pet-Jd-Jas-Jn

KNOWLEDGE / USAGE CHART UP TO THE TURN OF THE FIFTH CENTURY

d. = died   ca. = circa

■ = Uses/Accepts   ■ = Rejects

??? = Cites something that *sounds a bit like* this text: possibly an echo?

■ = Never mentions the writing; probably does not know it.

Century	Eastern Church Father/Manuscript	Jas	1P	2P	1J	2J	3J	Jude
Late 2nd	Clement of Alexandria (d. ca. 215)							
3rd	Origen (d. ca. 250)							
	Eusebius (writing ca. 300)							
4th	Codex Vaticanus (early 4th?)							
	Codex Sinaiticus (early 4th?)							
	Cyril of Jerusalem (writing ca. 350)							
	Synod of Laodicea (ca. 365)							
	Athanasius (writing 367)							
	Epiphanius of Salamis (writing ca. 375)							
	Apostolic Canon #85 (380)							
	Gregory of Nazianus (writing 390)							
	Amphilochius of Iconium (writing ca. 396)							

Century	Western Church Father/Manuscript	Jas	1P	2P	1J	2J	3J	Jude
2nd	Muratorian Fragment (ca. 200?)							
	Irenaeus (d. ca. 200)							
3rd	Tertullian (d. ca. 223)							
	Hippolytus (d. 235)							
	Cyprian (d. 258)							
4th	Mommsen/Cheltenham (mid-late 4th?)							
	Hilary of Poitiers (d. 368)							
	Pseudo-Ambrose (mid-late 4th?)							
Early	Jerome (writing 394)							
	Augustine (writing ca. 396)							
5th	Filaster of Brescia (writing ca. 397)							
	North African Canons (393, 397, 419)							

CHAPTER TWO

EARLY JAMES TRADITIONS
AND THE CANONICAL LETTER OF JAMES

Though the authenticity of the letter of James was generally taken for granted by many church leaders after Augustine, we have seen that several noteworthy patristic figures recorded for posterity their doubts about the document. Origen was the first on record to accept the letter, but comments acknowledging that other churchmen of his time rejected it cast a shadow over his glowing approval (for example, *Comm. Jo.* 20.10.66 [SC 290.188]). Though Eusebius explicitly acknowledged that by his day James was the canonical head of the CE, he nevertheless had his own scholarly concerns about the letter based on its lack of attestation among his earliest historical witnesses. This concern kept him from supporting its candidacy for the canon (*Hist. Eccl.* 2.23.25 [GCSNF 6–1.174]). Though its status as NT Scripture was subsequently fixed, clearly Eusebius intended his doubts about James to live on in the *Historia Ecclesiastica* he left behind.

An even more important witness in this regard is Jerome, the internationally known biblical scholar and monk of Bethlehem. In 393 Jerome wrote his widely popular literary history, *De viris illustribus.* As the preface tells, it was written to establish the philosophical and literary heritage of the Christian church against the slander of those who "accuse our faith of such rustic simplicity" (*Vir. ill.*, pref. [PL 23.605–6; FC 100.4]). Though his intention was to found the church on solid historical ground, it is significant that he did not establish the letter of James on an equally sure foundation: as we have seen, he wanted his readers to know that the letter "is claimed by some to have been published [*edita*] by someone else under his name" (*Vir. ill.* 2.2 [PL 23.609; FC 100.7]).[1] Only 2 Peter received similar treatment; Jerome anchored every other NT text in the authority of the historic, apostolic tradition.[2] Like Eusebius, Jerome was concerned that the Catholic Church be an institution of historical and intellectual integrity; and yet, like Eusebius, he felt it important to record the persistent doubts of his day about the authorship of James.

Similar authorial apprehensions resurfaced during the Reformation and have long since found a permanent home in biblical scholarship. To this day there exists no scholarly consensus on the authorship and provenance of the letter. As I described in my introduction, a survey of twentieth-century positions on its dating reveals opinions ranging from as early as 40 C.E. all the way to the middle of the second century.[3] Proposed places of origin are equally widespread, placing the letter in Jerusalem, Antioch, Rome, and elsewhere.[4] If anything like a scholarly consensus does exist, it is that the letter appears to resist easy historical assessment.

In this chapter I seek to strengthen the claim that the letter of James is a pseudepigraph of the second century. Twenty-five years ago this thesis would not have posed that great of a problem, as the magisterial work of Martin Dibelius was still holding court over analysis of the text. Dibelius's form-critical study of the letter argued that it is an example of paraenesis, which he understood to involve an eclectic and discontinuous string of general ethical exhortations held together by catch-word associations. From this perspective the letter is not an "actual" letter at all, and it was clearly not written by James, the brother of the Lord, before his death in 62 C.E.; it is simply an assortment of teachings with an epistolary prescript attached, having no overarching "theology" and addressing no actual social context. Over the last twenty-five years, however, Dibelius's position on James has been largely dethroned.[5]

[1] In light of this, it is amazing that J. B. Adamson (*James: The Man and His Message* [Grand Rapids: Eerdmans, 1989], 40) can assert that "no historical facts support" the theory that a later editor published traditional James material.

[2] He lists traditions attributing Hebrews to Barnabas, Luke, or Clement; and on authority of Papias he explains that 2–3 John were written by John the elder and not the disciple of the Lord. The origins of James and 2 Peter, however, are left afloat in mystery.

[3] Again, see the introductory note, as well as the list in W. Pratscher (*Der Herrenbruder Jakobus und die Jakobustradition* [FRLANT 139; Göttingen: Vandenhoeck & Ruprecht, 1987], 209 n. 3) and the table in P. Davids (*The Epistle of James* [NIGTC; Grand Rapids: Eerdmans, 1982], 4).

[4] Locales suggested, respectively, by Richard Bauckham, *James: Wisdom of James, Disciple of Jesus the Sage* (London: Routledge, 1999), 11–28; R. P. Martin, *James* (WBC 48; Waco, Tex.: Word Books, 1988), lxxvi; and S. Laws, *The Epistle of James* (BNTC; Peabody, Mass.: Hendrickson, 1980), 26.

[5] Several studies in ancient Jewish and Greco-Roman epistolary customs have shown that James is much more like an actual letter than Dibelius assumed (e.g., F. O. Francis, "The Form and Function of the Opening and Closing Paragraphs of James and 1 John," *ZNW* 61 [1970]: 110–26; D. Verseput, "Genre and Story: The Community Setting of the Epistle of James," *CBQ* 62.1 [2000]: 96–110; K. W. Niebuhr, "Der Jakobusbrief im Licht fruehju-

Karl-Wilhelm Niebuhr has noted that this shift in opinion has been enabled by the removal the "Pauline spectacles" that have dominated readings of the letter since the Reformation.[6] James did not look like an "actual letter" and appeared to have a deficient theology because it was read under the shadow of Paul's letters. The removal of this presumptive lens has allowed interpreters to read James "on its own terms," according to the way the letter presents itself, and the many fresh perspectives generated since have taught us a great deal more about the text.

Most notably, these new perspectives have enabled more than a few contemporary scholars to turn against the widespread modern opinion that James is a pseudepigraph. Now it is more common to find interpreters who will argue that there is little reason to conclude that James the Lord's brother could not have written this letter himself.[7] While I have great respect and admiration for the contributions of scholars since Dibelius who have enabled a clearer understanding of the text, it is my opinion that none of them offer a convincing explanation for the complete lack of attestation before the *terminus ad quem* provided by Origen in the early third century. The earlier one tries to place the letter, the more problematic this *terminus* becomes; therefore it seems that the burden of proof lies with those who want to secure an early date against this formidable difficulty. As the first section will show, no one has been able to offer a convincing explanation. Further, I will describe how many scholars remain convinced that the letter contains elements that point unavoidably to a pseudepigraphic origin. In order to strengthen this claim, the second half of the chapter will explore first- and second-century traditions about James in order to demonstrate the possibility that the author of the letter was working under the "canon-consciousness" of the second-century historicized James. A second-century frame, we will see, will help to explain many of the most persistent ambiguities of the letter, most particularly its lack of christological content. Further, it will fill out our understanding of the second-century context wherein a new actualization of James was desperately needed by Catholic Christianity.

---

discher Diasporabriefe," *NTS* 44 [1998]: 420–43). Likewise, further study into the nature and function of paraenesis have sensitized us to the fact that such writings can and do address a particular social situation (e.g., L. Perdue, "Paraenesis and the Epistle of James," *ZNW* 72 [1981]: 241–56; W. Popkes, "James and Paraenesis, Reconsidered," in *Texts and Contexts: Biblical Texts in Their Textual and Situational Contexts*, ed. T. Fornberg and D. Hellholm [Oslo: Scandinavian University Press, 1995], 535–61), and closer analyses of the letter itself have shown that James is not simply a loose collection of sayings, but a deliberately composed piece of rhetoric that is in fact held together by an overarching literary and conceptual logic (e.g., E. Baasland, "Literarische Form, Thematik und geschichtliche Einordnung des Jakobusbriefes," *ANRW* II.25.5, 3646–84).

[6] K. W. Niebuhr, "A New Perspective on James? Neuere Forschungen zum Jakobusbrief." *TLZ* 129 (2004): 1019–44.

[7] Most prominent among these are the recent commentaries by L. T. Johnson and R. Bauckham; P. Davids and R. P. Martin have defended theories of partial authenticity that will be explored later in our argument.

Arguments for and against the Authenticity of James

The following section will consider the arguments made in favor of the authenticity of the letter of James. We will begin with a brief consideration of the various ways scholars have attempted to explain the lack of external witnesses for the letter. These explanations are often set forward in an attempt to mute the force of evidence which calls the letter's authenticity into question.

The Lack of External Evidence:
Explaining the Late Canonicity of James

Though the issues involved here were thoroughly examined in chapter one, a brief consideration of the pertinent points will be of value in assessing the various ways defenders of authenticity seek to explain the canonical history of the letter. The first church father to offer any overt evidence for the existence of James was Origen. Most scholars willingly acknowledge this, but some have attempted to brush its significance aside by amassing any and all possible "echoes" of the text from writings before his day. The classic example of this trend is found in Mayor's influential commentary,[8] but others have followed his example. These defenders of authenticity hope that the accumulated evidence will convince the reader of James' early presence among the canonical texts, even though few if any of the examples can be called persuasive.[9] As Brooks has pointed out, however, this sort of mass listing typically has the opposite effect from what is intended. "If in fact James was known to most of the Christian writers between Clement of Rome and Origen, it is impossible to explain why there is not a single unmistakable reference to the book during this period."[10] Rather than impress, such long lists give the impression of grasping after straws. It must be stated unapologetically that we can find no references to this letter before Origen.

[8] J. B. Mayor, *The Epistle of St. James.* 2nd ed. (London: Macmillan, 1897), xlviii–lxviii. M. Dibelius (*James*, ed. H. Greeven, trans.M. Williams [Hermeneia; Philadelphia: Fortress, 1976], 30 n. 99) rightly calls the length of Mayor's list "misleading."

[9] See, e.g., L. T. Johnson's primary treatments of the issue (*The Letter of James* [ABC 37A; New York: Doubleday, 1995], 66–80, 124–40; *Brother of Jesus, Friend of God: Studies in the Letter of James* [Grand Rapids: Eerdmans, 2004], 45–100, esp. 88ff.). His ultimate argument in support of literary dependence among the Apostolic Fathers presumes throughout that James is the earlier text ("Where does this come from if *not* from James?" *James*, 128). See also *James*, 136–37, where he substantiates earlier Western use of James by appeal to texts long known to be later forgeries. This trend continues in *Brother of Jesus* (96): He presents an undifferentiated list of questionable allusions and overt citations from third-century Western writers, but then acknowledges in a footnote, "The problem with this and other 'papal' letters cited is that they are among the 'False Decretals,' undoubtedly medieval forgeries. I include them simply because, even if spurious, they associated James with Rome in an intriguing way."

[10] James Brooks, "The Place of James in the New Testament Canon," *SJT* 12 (1969): 47: "There is no certain or even probable evidence for the use of James prior to the beginning of the third century."

For some, the lack of evidence from the period of canonization is proof enough that we are dealing with a late, pseudonymous work. Those who seek to defend authenticity downplay its significance, focusing the weight of their arguments on factors internal to the letter that can be read to support a mid-first-century provenance. Once the plausibility of James' authorship has been demonstrated on internal grounds, they go on to offer a wide variety of rationalizations for the letter's missing external evidence. Some, however, avoid addressing the problem of the missing external attestation altogether.[11] Indeed, Richard Bauckham attempts to avoid a detailed analysis of canon history by insisting that reasons for late canonicity "can only be inferred."[12] After noting the scholarly tendency to count its late arrival as a factor against authenticity, he attempts to neutralize the issue by saying, "By the late second-century Christians are unlikely to have had any means of assessing authenticity which are not also available to us."[13] Though other scholars offer more substantive explanations, they are for the most part equally unimpressive.

One of the more common explanations supposes that James was not cited because it lacked useful material for use in doctrinal debate and apologetics.[14] This explanation is misleading, for it wrongly over-associates usefulness with doctrinal concerns. As my historical analysis has demonstrated, apostolic letters were cited in support of moral exhortation as much as for theological debate. This is particularly the case for Tertullian and Clement, who are as much moralists as theologians; they consistently cite 1 Peter and 1 John in support of calls to an embodied faith, a distinctive social ethic, and concern for the poor, yet there is no reference whatsoever to the related passages in James. A particularly important example is found in Clement's aforementioned use of 1 John 3:18 in *Stromata* 4.16: "'Little children, let us not love in word, or in tongue,' says John, teaching them to be perfect [τελείους], 'but in deed [ἔργῳ] and in truth; hereby shall we know that we are of the truth.'" Surely Clement would have appealed to James 2:14-26 in this instance had he had access to it, most especially because the "echo" in 2:22 uses τελειόω to describe a faith that is perfected by ἔργων (GCS 2.292; *ANF* 2.427).[15] Further, it has been shown that a central feature of later second-century

---

[11] See, e.g., the commentary of E. M. Sidebottom, *James, Jude and 2 Peter.* (CBC; London: Thomas Nelson & Sons, 1967), as well as M. J. Townsend, *The Epistle of James* (London: Epworth Press, 1994).

[12] Bauckham, *James*, 112–13.

[13] Bauckham, *James*, 216 n. 1.

[14] E.g., Adamson, *Man and His Message*, 38; Brooks, "James," 50; D. Guthrie, *New Testament Introduction: Hebrews to Revelation* (London: Tyndale, 1964), 723ff.; and Douglas Moo, *The Letter of James* (PNTC; Grand Rapids: Eerdmans, 2000), 4. Laws says James "may have been known, but, because of its general ideas and lack of distinctly Christian interpretation, not lent itself to quotation" (20).

[15] Dibelius's explanation (*James*, 53f.) that paraenetic texts are not often quoted because they "contain fewer religious and theological proof-texts" should be questioned, for some of

doctrinal debate was the concern to locate Paul in relationship with the Pillars of the Jerusalem church; yet though letters of Peter and John are utilized, no one mentions anything about a letter from James. One is left with the impression that the content of James as well as the mere existence of such a letter would in fact have been extremely *useful* for their purposes (as it clearly was for Origen) had they had access to it. But as we have seen, there is no indication that they had any knowledge of the letter's existence.

Another familiar rationalization asserts that James was known and used early on (hence the oft-cited supposed echoes in *1 Clement* and the *Shepherd of Hermas*) but fell into disuse in the second century and was temporarily forgotten. Most suggest this state of affairs came about as a result of the decline of the Jewish church and the increasingly Gentile makeup of the early Christianity,[16] but other factors are also presented, including the possibility that it was accidentally neglected and left unnoticed by its initial recipients.[17] There are at least two problems with this "once known but forgotten" theory. First, it is extremely difficult to accept the notion that an authentic letter from James, the brother of the Lord, was somehow forgotten in the second century, for (as I will demonstrate later in this chapter) it was precisely in this period that the figure of James grew in stature and authority among Catholic, "gnostic" and "Jewish-Christian"[18] circles. There was an explosion of hagiographical writings attached to James in the second century; yet in all of this there is no evidence of the letter we now attribute to him. The fact that the letter came into common use *after* the period when most of these non-canonical James writings were penned certainly suggests that its production was instigated by the same sort of concerns, namely, that he be claimed as an apostolic spokesperson for a later Christian tradition. Moreover, *1 Clement* and *Hermas* went on to become widely popular texts in the patristic era. Are we to believe that their authoritative source—an authentic letter of James, the brother of Jesus and the central figure of Christianity in Jerusalem—was forgotten, while a letter from the fourth bishop of Rome and a visionary text from a little known Roman prophet went on to have a place of great honor in patristic use? Such a reconstruction may be possible but against the evidence it seems rather improbable.

Some have suggested that the letter may have suffered from *confusion over the identity of the author*. Moo says, "Early Christians tended to accord special prominence to books written by apostles; and James was such a common name that many probably wondered whether the letter had an apostolic origin or not."[19] There is

---

Clement's favorite material comes from the paraenetic sections of 1 Peter (e.g., *Paed.* 3.11–12; *Strom.* 3.11).

[16] Cf. Mayor, li; Adamson, *Man and His Message*, 166; Brooks, "James," 50–51; Laws, 25; and Davids, *James*, 22.

[17] Brooks, "James," 50; Davids insists, "a theory of limited interest in and circulation of the epistle would also explain the evidence" (*James*, 8).

[18] See my caveat at the end of the introduction regarding the use of these terms.

[19] Moo, 4; Mayor (li) notes that the letter "did not profess to be written by an Apostle."

little to suggest, however, that anyone would have associated this James with anyone other than the brother of the Lord, as no other James held such authority in
primitive Christianity. The other early Jameses are easily disqualified as candidates:
James of Zebedee was martyred (Acts 12:2) at a point too early to be considered
a plausible author, and James of Alphaeus and the father of Judas are simply too
obscure to be a likely candidates (Luke 6:16; Acts 1:13). One must also consider
the way the authors of Acts and Jude can speak of "James" without offering further
identification; clearly the person was so well known that they knew the unadorned
name would be sufficient. At the very least it can be said that there existed no confusion on this point once the letter was finally in use. Though many have wondered
whether James of Jerusalem actually wrote the letter, no one anywhere appears to
have been confused over the identity of its ostensible author.

At the other end of author-related rationalizations, some have suggested the
letter's acceptance may have been hindered because of its association with James
of Jerusalem. Some suppose that the letter was questioned because of James' connection with heterodox Christianity, but interest in James was also strong among
certain early Catholic churchmen, and an authentic, orthodox writing in his name
would have been a valuable bit of evidence for their position. Others have wondered
if the letter suffered from James' traditional conflict with Paul (Gal 2:12) and his
perceived stance against the Pauline justification formula (Jas 2:14-26).[20] As we saw
in the late second century writings of Irenaeus and Tertullian, there was a concern
among Catholic writers to assert the unity and harmonious proclamation of the first
apostles, and this assertion often involved a "clarification" of Galatians 1–2.24 (*Adv.
Haer.* 3.12–13; *Prescr.* 23–24; *Adv. Marc.* 1.20; 4.2–3; 5.3). Still, there is little evidence that the earliest champions of James felt the need to apologize for it; Origen's
use of the letter relies heavily on the "faith and works" passages; and the Western
church, once introduced to the letter, appears to have accepted it warmly.[21] Even if
the letter was maligned along these lines, one would still expect to hear something
of it before Origen.

Some have posited that the letter may have suffered because James was not a
missionary-founder of a church; hence it would have been viewed as less important, and by extension, there would be no clear "recipient" to preserve and champion the letter. Tasker says, "Its author might indeed speak with authority and be
addressing a wide audience on important matters, but that authority could never
be quite the same as that of apostles who had first spoken to them the gospel of
God."[22] Such an explanation is hardly possible when the author in question is

[20] Mayor, li.
[21] Dibelius, *James*, 53 n. 204; Brooks, "James," 50: "There is no evidence . . . that the
early church saw in James a conflict with the theology of Paul and that for this or any other
theological reason was slow to accept the book."
[22] R. Tasker (*The General Epistle of James* [London: Tyndale, 1956]. 19) followed by C.
L. Mitton, *The Epistle of James* (London: Marshall, Morgan & Scott, 1966), 227–28, and
Guthrie (725).

James of Jerusalem. Richard Bauckham has persuasively shown that James was a figure of central importance in early Christianity; such a letter would have been received as a correspondence from the leader of the mother church in Jerusalem.[23] Surely such an important letter would have been extremely valuable.

In the end it may be argued that any one of the above rationalizations for the late arrival of James is possible, but as I have shown, all of them are little more than conjectures offered up on the basis of preconceptions about the authenticity of the letter. None of them are compelling enough to convincingly explain the lack of external attestation.

THE INTERNAL EVIDENCE

Given the dearth of external evidence for the letter, scholars seeking to defend its authenticity are forced to limit their investigations to internal evidence; and though an analysis of such evidence cannot prove that James of Jerusalem was the author of the letter, much attention has been focused on an attempt to establish the plausibility of a mid-first-century Palestinian provenance. If I am to build my historical hypothesis on a late date for James, a reconsideration of the internal arguments for and against its authenticity is required. We begin, therefore, with a review of the arguments that favor authenticity. From there we will consider those that favor pseudonymity, and finally, we will reflect on the arguments that favor a first-century dating. This will then lead directly into the next section, which will try to make the case that James is more at home in the second century than the first.

Assessment of Arguments That Favor Authenticity

Several arguments are promoted as evidence in favor of the letter's authenticity. Some have suggested that the author does not appear to be trying to be pseudonymous. Adamson says, "If the document had been forged, we would expect a more sophisticated effort to stress his authority."[24] In fact, the authority of the author *is* stressed throughout the letter, not only through the accumulation of at least fifty-five imperative verbs over 108 short verses, but also by its rather exalted prescript (which will be analyzed more closely as my study progresses). Johnson adds, "James lacks any of the classic signs of late, pseudonymous authorship," naming the fictional elaboration of the author's identity and authority, a rationalization for the delay of the parousia, clear evidence of doctrinal development, an understanding of tradition as having a fixed content, attacks on doctrinal deviance, and evidence of

---

[23] Richard Bauckham, "James and the Jerusalem Church," in *The Book of Acts in its First Century Setting*, ed. R. Bauckham (Grand Rapids: Eerdmans, 1995), 415–80, see 417ff. His own argument in this article damages the authenticity of the letter that he claims elsewhere, for how could a document from such an important figure in early Christianity be lost, set aside, or forgotten?

[24] Adamson, *Man and His Message*, 39.

an elaborate institutional structure.[25] Against these we should begin by pointing out that studies have moved far beyond such limited understandings of pseudonymity, as our introductory comments have suggested. These classic signs fit some forms of pseudepigraphy, but not all.[26] But even if one were inclined to search for Johnson's classic signs, might they not be present in the concern about "teachers" (3:1f.), the warning against seduction by the wisdom of the world (3:13-17), the encouragement to seek out the return of apostates (5:19), and the exhortation to be patient in waiting for the Parousia (5:7-11)?[27] Of course, neither the absence nor the presence of eschatological expectation is an indicator of an early date, as it is present in first and second century texts alike.[28] Finally, Mitton has argued that if the letter were in fact pseudonymous, the author "would have been at much greater pains to ensure that every reader would know which James was intended."[29] Again, the supposed "problem" of the author's identity did not appear to have existed in the early centuries. Indeed, a comparison of the canonical letter with various James traditions from the second century will demonstrate that the letter can be seen to include a number of veiled identity references that may derive from second-century traditions about James.

Another point of focus for defenders of authenticity has to do with the letter's use of sayings of Jesus that appear to pre-date the canonical gospels. L. E. Elliott-Binns has said, "Although the epistle is full of reminiscences of the sayings of Jesus as contained in the Synoptists, there is seldom verbal agreement, a circumstance which strongly suggests that they come from a period before the sayings had become stereotyped in a literary form."[30] Regardless of their position on the authenticity of the letter, all scholars recognize that James appeals to the teaching of Jesus.[31] The

[25] Johnson, *James*, 118.

[26] See D. Meade, *Pseudonymity and Canon* (WUNT 39; Tübingen: J. C. B. Mohr, 1986); and also, e.g., Richard Bauckham, "Pseudo-Apostolic Letters," *JBL* 107 (1988): 469–94, who identifies five different categories of inauthentic letters, not all of which include the "classic signs" of pseudepigraphy to which Johnson refers.

[27] B. Reicke, *The Epistles of James, Peter, and Jude* (ABC 37; New York: Doubleday, 1964), 5.

[28] So W. Pratscher, *Der Herrenbruder Jakobus und die Jakobustradition* (FRLANT 139; Göttingen: Vandenhoeck & Ruprecht, 1987), 210; cf., e.g., *Did.* 10.6; 16.1ff.; *Barn.* 4.1ff.; *Herm. Vis.* 2.2ff.

[29] C. L. Mitton, *The Epistle of James* (London: Marshall, Morgan & Scott, 1966), 229.

[30] L. E. Elliott-Binns, *Galilean Christianity* (London: SCM Press, 1956), 47.

[31] For a list of potential parallels, see J. Painter, *Just James: The Brother of Jesus in History and Tradition* (Edinburgh: T&T Clark, 1999), 260–62. See also J. S. Kloppenborg's helpful list of alternative positions on the relationship between Jesus and James in his "The Reception of the Jesus Tradition in James," in *The Catholic Epistles and the Tradition*, ed. J. Schlosser. (BETL 176; Leuven: Leuven University Press, 2004), 93–141.

close, yet inexact parallels with the synoptics (particularly Matthew's Sermon on the Mount,[32] though others lean toward Luke[33] or Q[34]) has led many to conclude that James was probably written before the existence of authoritative written gospels.[35] While such evidence may seem persuasive at first glance, it cannot be used to support an early date for our letter. To begin with, the author of James does not *quote* Jesus, he *echoes* his teaching. When a church father says, "The Lord says," and then cites the words of Jesus, we might be justified in trying to determine his gospel source on the basis of literary parallels. The author of James does not quote Jesus in this way; indeed, Jesus is never cited in the letter at all! There are simply unsecured echoes and allusions, and divergence between an echo and its supposed source can tell us little about the relative date of the texts involved.

We must recall that during most of the second century the proto-canonical gospels were considered transcripts of Jesus tradition, not the supremely authoritative written texts they eventually came to be. Jesus' *words* were more authoritative that the various receptacles that transmitted them.[36] Indeed, even well after the dominance of the four-fold gospel tradition, unwritten sayings of Jesus persisted for centuries,[37] and the fathers continued to "quote" Jesus without exactly reproducing his words as they are found in the extant gospels.[38] Further, recent studies on orality and textuality in the ancient world have shown that oral and written traditions interacted and supported one another to a far greater degree than was once assumed.[39] We must therefore avoid the form-critical trap of reducing the possibilities to a stark contrast between "literary sources" and "pre-literary oral traditions." Even if it could be shown that particular echoes of Jesus in James derive from a very early period, all that would demonstrate is the fact that our author had access to early sources; it does not prove that the letter itself was produced at an early date (especially given the numerous elements in the letter that point to a later

---

[32] E.g., M. H. Shepherd, "The Epistle of James and the Gospel of Matthew," *JBL* 75 (1956): 40–51.

[33] Davids, *James*, 49; Adamson, *Man and His Message*, 188–90; Painter, *Just James*, 244–46.

[34] P. J. Hartin, *James and the 'Q' Sayings of Jesus* (JSNTSup 47; Sheffield: Sheffield Academic, 1991); Kloppenborg.

[35] Martin, lxxiv–lxxvii; Davids, *James*, 16; Johnson, *James*, 119–20; Hartin, *James and the 'Q' Sayings*, and the critique of Hartin in Todd Penner, *The Epistle of James and Eschatology* (JSNTSup 121; Sheffield: Sheffield Academic, 1996), 116–20.

[36] Shepherd, "Epistle of James," 48; J. Barton, *Holy Writings, Sacred Text: The Canon in Early Christianity* (Louisville: Westminster John Knox, 1997), 79–91.

[37] See the list of "agrapha" in L. M. McDonald, *The Formation of the Christian Biblical Canon*, rev. ed. (Peabody, Mass.: Hendrickson, 1995), 293–98.

[38] E.g., in *Strom.* 2.18.91, Clement of Alexandria writes "the Lord says" and then strings together a whole series of phrases that do not exactly correspond with any one gospel.

[39] See esp. Harry Gamble, *Books and Readers in the Early Church: A History of Early Christian Texts* (New Haven: Yale University Press, 1995), 1–41, 203–18; and Risto Uro, *Thomas at the Crossroads* (Edinburgh: T&T Clark, 1998), 8–32.

composition). At best, it seems safest to conclude that the author simply intended to allude to Jesus' teachings, knowing that his readers were familiar with them and would recognize the "voice" being echoed. For our purposes, a far more interesting question is exactly why it was that our author appears to have taken up the voice of Jesus without drawing explicit attention to him in any way (as he does also, I would argue, with the voices of Paul, Peter, and John). I will address this issue directly later in this chapter. For now, however, let it be concluded that though our letter is clearly dependent in some way on the teaching of Jesus, the notion that one can confidently date the letter based on his use of this material is questionable.

Some try to support authenticity on the basis of words and images that are seen to reflect a first-century Palestinian context.[40] Johnson lists the following examples: proximity to the sea (1:6; 4:13); the effect of the burning wind on vegetation (1:11); the existence of salt and bitter springs (3:11); the cultivation of figs, olives, and grapes (3:12); the presence of day laborers in fields (5:4); the reference to the early and late rains (5:7).[41] But how is it that such illustrations *necessarily* point to first-century Palestine? Is it not the case that these images could be said to reflect almost any area of Mediterranean life from almost any period? As Burchard has rightly insisted, "local color" is missing in the letter of James.[42] Similarly, the appearance of "synagogue" (2:2), "Gehenna" (3:6), and "elder" (5:14) do not necessarily imply an early date for the letter. They may derive from the letter's sources, or they may simply be part of the rhetorical world of the Jacobian actualization constructed by the pseudepigrapher. Regardless, they cannot be used as proof of an early date.

Finally, we can mention a series of other considerations that are seen to support the letter's authenticity. Mayor saw the lack of reference to the fall of Jerusalem as an indication of an early date,[43] yet it could be suggested that the effectiveness of the pseudonymity required the author to avoid referring to events that took place after James' death. More pointedly, the lack of reference to Jerusalem or the temple cult at all might likely indicate a period well after the fall of that city marginalized its centrality in the life of early believers. It has also been asserted that James' focus on Jesus' teaching instead of christological reflection points to a more "primitive" doctrine than the later Pauline and Johannine soteriological formulations,[44] but against this it has been noted that the ethical tone of the letter is quite in line with the tendencies of known second-century texts.[45] In the end it must be concluded

---

[40] Recently Peter Davids, "Palestinian Traditions in the Epistle of James," in *James the Just and Christian Origins*, ed. B. Chilton and C. A. Evans (Leiden: Brill, 1999), 33–57; see also Martin, lxxiii.

[41] Johnson, *James*, 120–21.

[42] Christof Burchard, *Der Jakobusbrief* (HNT 15/1; Tübingen: Mohr Siebeck, 2000), 7.

[43] Mayor, cxxii.

[44] Martin, lxxiii; Sidebottom, 13–14.

[45] J. Moffatt, *An Introduction to the Literature of the New Testament* (Edinburgh: T&T Clark, 1918), 471.

that though some of the foregoing evidences may be used to *support* an argument for an early date for James, none of them *require* an early date; and it is most certain that none of them require us to accept James of Jerusalem as the actual author of the letter. Most of them are simply attempts to militate against the significant list of features that point toward the letter's pseudonymity.

Assessment of Arguments That Favor Pseudonymity

We have already made much of the late canonicity. This must be taken more seriously than it often is. But lack of attestation is not the only good reason to consider James to be a pseudepigraph. The language of the letter has long been considered a stumbling block to accepting authenticity.[46] The Greek of the text is among the most sophisticated of the NT,[47] and though it includes various Aramaisms, Hebraisms, and Semitisms,[48] its complex catchword organization requires a Greek original document.[49] For many years it was assumed that James, an Aramaic speaker, would have lacked the proper training to write such a stylized Greek work, but a number of scholars have undercut this assumption by demonstrating the extent to which Greek language and culture dominated Palestine in the first century C.E.[50] This fact, combined with the aforementioned Semitic features, has been used by some to support the possibility of authorship by James of Jerusalem. But even if we can account for the widespread use of Greek in James' day, the letter was written by a writer for whom Greek was clearly *Muttersprache*. Further, the letter was produced by a true literary stylist, someone who had quite likely received secondary rhetorical education.[51] Especially when one notes the comparatively simple Greek of Paul's letters,[52] it seems unlikely that James of Jerusalem could have produced such a docu-

---

[46] Among many other older studies, Reicke, 4; E. C. Blackman, *The Epistle of James* (London: SCM Press, 1957), 26; W. G. Kummel, *Introduction to the New Testament* (London: SCM Press, 1975), 406; and J. Ropes, *The Epistle of St. James* (ICC; Edinburgh: T&T Clark, 1916), 50.

[47] Mitton (234) calls it "elegant Greek," and Mayor (ccxvi) places it along with Heb. as the nearest to classical Greek in the NT, though N. Turner (*Style*, vol. 4 of *A Grammar of New Testament Greek* [Edinburgh: T&T Clark, 1976], 115) calls this an exaggeration. Dibelius (*James*, 34–35) calls it "polished Greek," with a vocabulary of "linguistic cultivation" and a style that approaches "literary Koine."

[48] See Turner, 117–19.

[49] Dibelius, *James*, 6–11, 17.

[50] M. Hengel, *Judaism and Hellenism*, vol. 1; trans. J. Bowdon (London: SCM Press, 1974); J. N. Sevenster, *Do You Know Greek? How Much Greek Could the First Jewish Christians Have Known?* (NovTSup 19; Leiden: E. J. Brill, 1968).

[51] So argues D. Watson; see "James 2 in Light of Greco-Roman Schemes of Argumentation," *NTS* 39 (1993): 94–121; and idem., "A Reassessment of the Rhetoric of the Epistle of James and its Implications for Christian Origins" (unpublished essay, read at the 2005 Annual Meeting of the Society of Biblical Literature).

[52] Pratscher, 210–11.

ment. On this point, even the staunchest defenders of authenticity often admit that James had to have received some help.[53] Despite recent arguments to the contrary, it is still the case that the language of the epistle is supporting evidence in favor of pseudonymity.

A more persuasive consideration has to do with the letter's attitude toward the law and the Gentiles. The contrast between the content of the letter and the portrait of James we receive from canonical and non-canonical sources are too great for many to accept that the person described wrote the letter attributed to him. Of primary concern is the letter's lack of interest in the ritual aspects of the law:[54] As we will explore more closely below, (a) the James of Acts is concerned that both Jewish and Gentile Christians observe the appropriate purity laws; (b) Paul tells of "certain men from James" (Gal 2:12), whom he associates with "the circumcision party"; (c) Josephus says Torah-observant Jews (possibly Pharisees) defended James at his execution (*Ant.* 20:199f.); and (d) Hegesippus's portrayal of James presents him as a figure especially revered for his legal purity and temple observance (*Hist. Eccl.* 2.23).

In contrast to this well-attested traditional characterization, our author focuses entirely on the moral aspects of the law (1:25; 2:8-13; 4:11-12), ignores any ritual aspect, and characterizes the law as "the law of liberty" (1:25). The fact that he can exhort his readers to fulfill "the entire law" (2:10) without referring in any way to ritual and purity regulations makes it clear that he has a very different concept of "law" in mind.[55] It is widely noted that the purity language of the temple cult is used figuratively to support ethical injunctions (καθαρός and ἀμίαντος in 1:27; καθαρίζω and ἁγνίζω in 4:8).[56] Related to this is the complete absence of anything in the letter suggesting that the author is devoted to the temple cult in Jerusalem, as numerous sources suggest was the case for James of Jerusalem.[57] Additionally, Konradt draws tentative attention to the "worldly" believers in the letter who are rich (1:9-11; 5:1-5), travel about as business people seeking profit (4:13-17), and are condemned as "adulterers" and "friends of the world" (4:4). If the author actually had "the entire law" in mind, would we not expect him to be concerned that these

[53] Mayor, ccxxxvii; F. Mussner, *Der Jakobusbrief* (Freiburg: Herder, 1964), 8; Bauckham, *James*, 24; Johnson (*James*, 117), however, insists there is no need to invoke a secretary or deny authenticity on the basis of language.

[54] Cf. Ropes, 51; Blackman, 25; Reicke 4; Kummel 290; W. Marxsen, *Introduction to the New Testament: An Approach to its Problems* (Oxford: Basil Blackwell, 1968), 229; Laws, 40–41.

[55] Martin, lxx.

[56] See also D. C. Allison, Jr., "Exegetical Amnesia in James," *ETL* 86 (2000): 162–66, who argues that the phrase διὸ ἀποθέμενοι πᾶσαν ῥυπαρίαν καὶ περισσείαν κακίας in James 1:21 is a metaphorical application of circumcision language. In this he follows W. J. Dalton's argument about the parallel phrase in 1 Peter 3:21 (*Christ's Proclamation to the Spirits: A Study of 1 Peter 3:18–4:6* [AnBib. 23; Rome: Pontifical Biblical Institute, 1989], 205).

[57] Burchard, 1, 6–7.

"worldly" believers might transgress the laws associated with cleanliness, diet, and Sabbath keeping?[58] Though none of these points are entirely conclusive on their own, the general picture they paint suggests a period after the law had ceased to function ritually for Christians.

A corollary to this is the fact that there is no mention at all of a mission to the Gentiles in the letter. Mayor saw this as proof that the epistle was written before the advent of the Gentile mission,[59] but it is enough to counter that the omission is just as easily (if not more easily) explained as indicating a period well after the establishment of the Gentile mission. This is especially the case when one considers the treatment of parallel material between James and Paul (explored below). Like the lack of concern for ritual purity, the absence of any comment as to the admission of Gentiles in a letter that exhorts readers to fulfill "the entire law" is suggestive of a very late date indeed.

The *form* of the letter also requires comment. Since the prescript is the only immediately identifiable epistolary element in the text, many have considered the "letter" of James to be little more than a loose collection of moral maxims "dressed up" to fit the existing model of an apostolic letter.[60] Some even argue that the prescript itself was added later.[61] Others have produced studies of ancient Greco-Roman epistolary customs showing that James can be seen to exhibit features of actual ancient letterforms.[62] Among these, many have placed James in the "diaspora letter" strand of ancient Jewish literature: Such letters took the form of encyclicals, written from authorized persons in Jerusalem to Jews in the diaspora, giving directions on cultic and legal matters.[63] Examples include Jeremiah 29:1-23 (the prototype of the tradition), the apocryphal Epistle of Jeremiah, 2 Maccabees 1:1–9 and 1:10–2:18, and *2 Baruch* 78–86. Though distinctions might be made between various types of diaspora letters, all of them typically offer consolation in tribulation and admonitions that are motivated by the hope of future restoration.[64] Similarly, James clearly presents itself as a diaspora letter from an authority, presumably in

---

[58] M. Konradt, *Christliche Existenz nach dem Jakobusbrief* (SUNT 22; Göttingen: Vandenhoeck & Ruprecht, 1998), 204.

[59] Mayor, cxxii–cxxiii.

[60] H. Balz and W. Schrage, *Die Katholischen Briefe* (NTD 10; Göttingen: Vandenhoeck & Ruprecht, 1973), 6.

[61] Recent advocates include Elliott-Binns, *Galilean Christianity,* 47–48; and S. R. Llewelyn, "The Prescript of James," *NovT* 39 (1997): 385–93.

[62] Most prominent is that of F. O. Francis, which argued that James fits an ancient "literary letter" genre that followed a well defined structure and content. Francis's argument will be considered in detalin in the next chapter.

[63] Recent analyses include Verseput, "Genre and Story," 96–110; Niebuhr, "Der Jakobusbrief"; Bauckham, *James,* 11–25, and "James and the Jerusalem Church," 423–25; and W. Popkes, "The Mission of James in His Time," in *The Brother of Jesus: James the Just and His Mission,* ed. B. Chilton and J. Neusner (Louisville: Westminster John Knox, 2001), 89.

[64] Verseput, "Genre and Story," 101.

Jerusalem, to believers scattered abroad. Yet we immediately note that the prescript of James is rather more idealized than the other available examples of the genre, which for the most part bear more concrete addresses to specific persons and locales. The exception is *2 Baruch*, which is clearly not historical and bears a more idealized address similar to James.[65] Especially when other idealized elements of the prescript are noted (as they will be in the last section of this chapter), it seems plain that we are dealing here with a fictionalized, "literary" diaspora letter created in imitation of the traditional genre.

One of the most crucial issues in determining the authenticity of the letter has to do with James' relationship to Paul and Pauline theology. The passage in focus, of course, is 2:14-26 (though as we will see in chapter three, many other sections of the letter can be explained against a Pauline backdrop). A number of questions have arisen: is James responding to Paul, to Paulinists, or has he come to discuss this issue quite apart from any Pauline influence? If the comments do have a Pauline referent, does the author's understanding of Pauline theology rely on oral testimony or on an acquaintance with the letters themselves? Since our current interest involves determining the authenticity of the letter, only one question need be addressed at this time: does this section envisage a post-Jacobian context? If it can be shown that the letter of James does indeed interact with Pauline letters, it would support a date of composition later than the traditional death date of James in 62 C.E. The following arguments can be made in favor of the view that the author of James is indeed interacting directly with Pauline letters.

We begin with an examination of the terminological and grammatical parallels between James 2:21-24, Romans 3:28 and 4:1-3, and Galatians 2:16.

> **Jas 2:21**: Was not Abraham our father justified by works . . . ?
> Ἀβραὰμ ὁ πατὴρ ἡμῶν οὐκ ἐξ ἔργων ἐδικαιώθη . . . ;
>
> **Rom 4:1-2**: What then shall we say of Abraham, our forefather . . . ? For if Abraham was justified by works . . .
> Τί οὖν ἐροῦμεν εὑρηκέναι Ἀβραὰμ τὸν προπάτορα ἡμῶν. . ., Εἰ γὰρ Ἀβραὰμ ἐξ ἔργων ἐδικαιώθη . . .
>
> **Jas 2:23**: the Scripture was fulfilled which says *Abraham believed God, and it was reckoned to him as righteousness.*
> ἡ γραφὴ ἡ λέγουσα ἐπίστευσεν δὲ Ἀβραὰμ τῷ θεῷ καὶ ἐλογίσθη αὐτῷ εἰς δικαιοσύνην.

[65] Indeed, as A. Deissmann wryly noted, "a 'letter' . . . inscribed 'to the twelve tribes which are scattered abroad' would be simply undeliverable" (*Light from the Ancient East* [Grand Rapids: Baker, 1980], 242).

> **Rom 4:3**: For what does the Scripture say? *Abraham believed God and it was reckoned to him as righteousness.*
> τί γὰρ ἡ γραφὴ λέγει ἐπίστευσεν δὲ ᾽Αβραὰμ τῷ θεῷ καὶ ἐλογίσθη αὐτῷ εἰς δικαιοσύνην.
>
> **LXX Gen 15:6**: ἐπίστευσεν ᾽Αβραμ τῷ θεῷ καὶ αὐτῷ εἰς δικαιοσύνην.
>
> ---
>
> **Jas 2:24**: You see that a man is justified by works and not by faith alone.
> ὁρᾶτε ὅτι ἐξ ἔργων δικαιοῦται ἄνθρωπος καὶ οὐκ ἐκ πίστεως μόνον.
>
> **Gal 2:16**: Yet we know that a man is not justified by works of the law but through faith in Jesus Christ . . .
> εἰδότες δὲ ὅτι οὐ δικαιοῦται ἄνθρωπος ἐξ ἔργων νόμου ἐὰν μὴ διὰ πίστεως ᾽Ιησοῦ Χριστοῦ . . .
>
> **Rom 3:28**: For we hold that a man is justified by faith apart from works of the law.
> λογιζόμεθα γὰρ δικαιοῦσθαι πίστει ἄνθρωπον χωρὶς ἔργων νόμου.

The second set of parallels in the series is the least strong since it deals with a quotation of Genesis 15:6; nevertheless we find that Paul and the author of James agree in the citation form against the LXX: Both use the name ᾽Αβραάμ instead of ᾽Αβραμ, and both add a postpositive δέ after ἐπίστευσεν. The force of this agreement is muted somewhat by the fact that all NT references to Abraham use his full (post-Genesis 17) name, and further, Philo also cites Genesis 15:6 including the postpositive dev (*Mut.* 177).[66] It is the first and third parallels that are more promising. In the first, the discussion of Abraham is introduced using very similar language in the form of an opening rhetorical question. Apart from the rather common description of Abraham as "our (fore)father," it should be noted that ἔργον and δικαιόω are found together in the NT only in Romans (3:20, 28; 4:2), Galatians (2:16), James (2:21, 24, 25), and Matthew 11:19, where Jesus insists, "wisdom is justified by her works." In the third set of parallels, attention has been drawn to the phrase ἐκ πίστεω, which occurs only once in the LXX (at Habakkuk 2:4), and twenty-three times in the NT: twelve times in Romans (once in 1:17, in a quotation of Hab 2:4),[67] nine times in Galatians (once in 3:11, in a quotation of Hab 2:4),[68] once in Hebrews (10:38, a quotation of Hab 2:4), and

---

[66] See Penner, 66.
[67] Rom 1:17 (x2); 3:26, 30; 4:16 (x2); 5:1; 9:30, 32; 10:6; 14:23 (x2).
[68] Gal 2:16; 3:7, 8, 9, 11, 12, 22, 24; 5:5.

once in James 2:24. Elsewhere in early Christianity the phrase is found only in the *Shepherd of Hermas Vision* 3.8.7, ἐκ τῆς πίστεως γεννᾶται ἐκγράτεια ("self-control is born out of faith"; even here the addition of the article marks out a difference from the canonical occurrences).[69] Further, Romans 3:28, Galatians 2:16, and James 2:24 are the only verses in all of Christian Scripture where the substantives πίστις and ἔργον are paired with the verb δικαιόω.

For many, this overwhelming concentration of parallel words and phrases provides sufficient ground for an assumption of literary dependence between the writings involved. But on top of this impressive verbal equivalence, one also notices a remarkable degree of structural agreement between James 2 and Romans 2–4.[70]

1. Preparatory echoes and parallels
   a) Partiality forbidden: Rom 2:11   Jas 2:1
   b) On being doers of the law/word
      and not hearers: Rom 2:13   Jas 1:22-25
   c) Condemnation of partial law-keeping: Rom 2:21-23   Jas 2:8-11

2. Acknowledgment that some have
   misunderstood the Pauline message "Why
   not do evil that good may come of it?":   Rom 3:8

3. Precise sequential agreement between
   James 2:14-24 and Romans 3:27–4:22
   a) Issue posed in terms of faith and works: Rom 3:27-28   Jas 2:14-18
   b) Significance of claiming "God is one":   Rom 3:29-30   Jas 2:19
   c) Appeal to "father" Abraham as
      authoritative test case: Rom 4:1-2   Jas 2:20-22
   d) Citation of proof text—Gen 15:6:   Rom 4:3   Jas 2:20-22
   e) Conflicting interpretations of the
      proof text: Rom 4:4-21   Jas 2:23
   f) Conclusion of the argument: Rom 4:22   Jas 2:24

One of Penner's arguments for denying Jacobian dependence on Romans states, "the writer of the epistle does not seem to indicate a familiarity with large sections of either Galatians or Romans, but only with isolated expressions."[71] Clearly he did not notice the way in which the key "isolated expressions" in James and Romans fit within a

[69] J. T. Sanders, *Ethics in the New Testament: Change and Development* (London: SCM Press, 1975), 119–20.
[70] Section 3a–f has been pointed out by J. D. G. Dunn, *Romans 1–8* (WBC 38A; Waco, Tex.: Word Books, 1988), 197. I have adjusted his citations and added the parallels in sections 1 and 2.
[71] Penner, 71.

broader framework characterized by precise sequential agreement. Not only do the two authors use the same language, they do so according to a shared rhetorical outline.

Finally, while the above arguments point strongly in the direction of literary dependence, evidence from *religion history* appears to secure a post-Pauline date for James. As will be made abundantly clear in the exegetical analysis presented in the next chapter, James 2:14-26 teaches that faith and works cannot exist as two separate entities: "faith by itself, if it has no works, is dead" (2:17). It has long been demonstrated that nowhere in Jewish thought before Paul do we find a separation of these two key ingredients in the life of the believer.[72] In ancient Jewish thought, faith was never something that could be separated from works. Regarding Abraham, numerous examples have been culled to demonstrate how the exegetical tradition interpreted Genesis 15:6 (Abraham "believed God, and it was reckoned to him as righteousness") in light of Abraham's obedience, focusing particularly on the story of the offering of Isaac in Genesis 22 as the culminating demonstration of Abraham's faith.[73] So, for example, 1 Maccabees 2:51–52 states, "Remember the works of the fathers, which they did in their generations. . . . Was not Abraham found faithful *when tested*, and it was reckoned to him as righteousness?"[74]

Likewise the author of James appeals to Abraham in agreement with this exegetical tradition. However, the particular appeal to Abraham in James 2:21-24 offers a new twist on the traditional theme: "You see that faith was active along with his works, and faith was completed by works. . . . You see that a man is justified by works [ἐξ ἔργων δικαιοῦται] and not by faith alone [οὐκ ἐκ πίστεως μόνον]." The passage reveals that our author assumes a disruption in the tradition, for apparently it was possible for someone to conceive of πίστις and ἔργα as two different entities. Such a distinction would only make sense if someone had previously separated the two by suggesting that it was possible for someone to have "faith" apart from "works," and it is widely agreed that Paul is the first person in the Jewish tradition to suggest such a thing. Thus, the rejection of justification ἐκ πίστεως μόνον only makes sense in a post-Pauline context.[75] The letter of James

---

[72] Cf. Dibelius's important excursus on the subject, *James*, 168–80; cf. Ropes, 35f.; J. Jeremias, "Paul and James," *ExpT* 66 (1954–1955): 368f.; Laws, 15–18.

[73] See M. Soards, "The Early Christian Interpretation of Abraham and the Place of James within That Context," *IBS* 9 (1987): 18–26; R. Ward, "The Works of Abraham: James 2:14-26," *HTR* 61 (1968): 283–90; D. Verseput, "Reworking the Puzzle of Faith and Deeds in James 2:14-26," *NTS* 43 (1997): 97–115; and I. Jacobs, "The Midrashic Background for James 2:21-23," *NTS* 22 (1976): 457–64.

[74] Italics added. See also *Jub.* 17:15–18; 18:15–16; Sir 44:19–22; 1 Macc. 2:52; *m. Kidd.* 4:14; *Abr.* 167; *Deus.* 1.4; *Ant.* 1.223, 233–34.

[75] Davids (*James*, 21) and Penner (63–65) point to the aforementioned 1 Maccabees passage to demonstrate how the author of James could have developed his discussion of faith and works apart from any Pauline influence. All the parallel shows, however, is the extent to which the authors of both texts were reliant on the same traditional understanding of Abraham's faith. The fact that the ideas presented in 2:14-26 were commonplace in ancient Jewish literature cannot be used to obscure the fact that the particular language used to present these

was therefore written sometime after Paul's publication of his distinctive justification formula, and James' "not by faith alone" is actually meant to connote "not by
Paul alone"—at least, not by the "Paul" of those who championed him in ways that
distorted authentic apostolic faith. As I will argue below, the author of James does
not have the historical Paul in view here; his letter is not an anti-Pauline polemic,
but a polemic against particular Paulinists.

There is widespread scholarly agreement that the letter to the Romans was written sometime between 55 and 58 C.E.,[76] and it is, of course, not entirely impossible
that the letter, once received, had quickly circled around to Jerusalem within the
four to seven years before James' death in 62. But a consideration of the parallel
passages in Romans shows that Paul's "faith and works" concerns are tied directly to
the inclusion of the Gentiles among the covenant people of God: Paul opposes the
notion that anyone can be justified by fulfilling the works *of the law* (Rom 3:28; Gal
2:16). I have already shown that the faith and works discussion in James post-dates
that of Paul; had James himself written the letter, we would expect to find its discussion of faith and works cast in some way against a similar background. In fact, however, the Jew/Gentile issue is nowhere present in James, and I have already suggested
that his treatment of the law seems to indicate a later period wherein the Torah had
ceased to function ritually for Christians. While Paul separated faith from *works of
the law*, the caricatured person of faith in James can be seen to have extended this
formula to separate faith from all works, not simply ἐξ ἔργων νόμου. Further, the
Pauline understanding of a faith that transforms the believer χωρὶς ἔργων νόμου
has been weakened in James into a faith that involves mere cognitive assent to doc-
trines (2:19). Such a divergence makes sense when understood according to a temporal matrix wherein the letter of James follows those of Paul at a rather significant
distance. Thus, the parallels between James and Romans offer strong support for the
pseudonymity of the letter. Indeed, as I will demonstrate in chapter three, numerous other points of contact with Romans, 1 Corinthians, Galatians, 1 Peter, and 1
John (the latter two most likely written well after 62 C.E.) will substantiate even
further the supposition that the author of James was literarily dependent not only
on Romans but on a whole collection of first-century apostolic letters.

Finally, a note must be made of what has become a popular intermediate position between authenticity and pseudonymity, that is, that the letter is an edited,
two-stage production composed of what may have been authentic sayings of
James.[77] Beyond benefiting from the historical attestation offered by Jerome (that

---

ideas is found elsewhere only in Romans and Galatians. Further, the passages in James and
Paul are oriented around soteriological concerns, while the 1 Maccabees passage is not.

[76] See the list in Dunn, *Romans 1–8*, xliii.

[77] This is the position presented by Davids, *Epistle of James*, and Martin; Mitton (236–
41), via Tasker, suggested the letter might have been a transcript of James' sermons that was
then transmitted as a tract-like "letter" within his own lifetime. The notion of a two-stage *late*
composition involving the reworking of potentially authentic James material received earlier
exposition by Marxsen, 231; W. L. Knox, "The Epistle of James," *JTS* 46 (1945): 10–17.

the letter was "*edita*" by someone else), this theory is valued as a means of accounting for the features of the letter that point to a pseudepigraphic basis. The problem, of course, is that the theory cannot be substantiated in any methodologically acceptable fashion. As Penner rightly insists, "no attempt has been made in these studies to reconstruct the hypothetical original Semitic document which was later redacted, and for good reason since there is no consistent pattern to the so-called Semitisms in James; they appear throughout the document in a variety of places and ways and bear little overall relation to one another."[78] It is difficult to avoid the sense that behind this theory there lurks a scholarly discomfort with the many features of the letter that point to pseudonymity; the theory functions as a partial concession, a means of acknowledging the inescapable evidence of late production whilst retaining a limited claim of authenticity for the text. Regardless, while it may be the case that the writer appealed to existing source material, and while some of that material may have derived somehow from the historical James of Jerusalem, in the end someone else composed the canonical letter. As Rob Wall has pointed out, the letter of James

> hardly results from an arbitrary compilation of sayings, as some have suggested in the past . . . nor, on the other hand, is it the exact copy of some former speech faithfully recalled. Indeed, if a two-stage composition is followed, one should probably assume that the editor had specific theological, sociological, and literary intentions, which are then reflected by the letter's final shape and subject matter.[79]

Ultimately, theories regarding the supposed "prehistory" of the letter of James are of little consequence, and those who support a two-stage hypothesis must acknowledge that their hypothetical editor is the actual author of the letter.

Assessment of Arguments That Favor a First-century Dating

If I am correct in my conclusion that the historical James could not have written the letter of James, what evidence is there to favor a first-century provenance for the letter? Since (a) the letter shows possible dependence on other apostolic letters, and (b) we hear nothing of its existence until Origen, what is to keep us from assigning a second-century provenance? The strongest argument put forward in favor of a first-century dating is the conviction that James was known and used by the apostolic fathers, most particularly the authors of *1 Clement* and the *Shepherd of Hermas*. Much has been made of these connections in attempts to secure a *terminus ad quem* for our letter, for if James can be shown to have been a source for any of these texts it would demand an earlier date, given the need to allow for a period of dissemina-

---

Blackman (26–28), and has since become a working option for some James scholars (see, e.g., R. Wall, *Community of the Wise: The Letter of James* [Valley Forge, Pa.: Trinity Press International, 1997], 9–11; and P. Hartin, *James of Jerusalem: Heir to Jesus of Nazareth* [Collegeville, Minn.: Liturgical Press, 2004], 93).

[78] Penner, 43 n. 3.
[79] Wall, *James*, 10.

tion. Unsurprisingly, there is little agreement on these matters; those arguing for authenticity also tend to argue in favor of literary dependence on James, while those who consider James to be pseudonymous are content to admit the inconclusiveness of the evidence. Most commentators consider dependence by *1 Clement* (ca. 96) to be unlikely,[80] but some consider dependence by the author of the *Shepherd of Hermas* (ca. 130–140) to be a strong possibility. As we might expect, however, here too there is a good deal of disagreement on the matter. James Moffatt[81] and Sophie Laws[82] present *Hermas* as a possible anchor for dating James, and Johnson goes even further, saying it is "virtually certain" that Hermas used the letter.[83] Against this, Dibelius,[84] Peter Davids,[85] and Todd Penner,[86] while agreeing that *Hermas* presents the best case available, nevertheless rightly conclude that the evidence is inconclusive, and a number of other scholars have argued against the existence of any literary dependence whatsoever.[87]

With these latter scholars, I agree that there are far too many uncertainties to appeal to *Hermas* as a confident *terminus ad quem*. There are indeed many conceptual and terminological similarities between the two texts, but these "parallels" seem more suggestive of a shared milieu than direct literary dependence.[88] This becomes especially apparent when one compares Hermas's supposed use of James with, for instance, Polycarp's use of 1 Peter in his *Letter to the Philippians*, where the repeated correspondence of entire phrases makes his dependence on 1 Peter largely indisputable.[89] The supposed parallels in *Hermas* allow for no such confidence. Laws admits as much when she says,

> Hermas has no exact quotation of James. . . . Nor does he derive distinctive ideas
> from the epistle; the *Mandates* like James draw on the common stock of ethical

[80] J. Drummond, *The New Testament in the Apostolic Fathers* (Oxford: Oxford University Press, 1905), 103–33; Dibelius (*James*, 32–33), Brooks ("James," 47), and Laws (21) offer negative conclusions; Johnson, *James*, following D. Hagner (*The Use of the Old and New Testaments in Clement of Rome* [NovTSup 34; Leiden: Brill, 1973], 248–56), admits, "the case is not conclusive" (75), but asserts nevertheless that "probability" allows for 1 Clement's knowledge of James. The "probability," of course, is based on Johnson's presupposition that James is early.

[81] J. Moffatt, *The General Epistles of James, Peter and Jude* (MNTC; London: Hodder & Stoughton, 1928), 1.

[82] Laws, 42 n. 3.

[83] Johnson, *James*, 79, and *Brother of Jesus*, 56–60.

[84] Dibelius, *James*, 32.

[85] Davids, *James*, 8–9.

[86] Penner, 103.

[87] Drummond, 103–33; Ropes, 88–89; Brooks, "James," 45–47.

[88] There are too many supposed "parallels" listed in Mayor (lviii–lxii). Laws's (22–23) and Johnson's (*James*, 75–79) presentations are more accessible.

[89] Compare, for instance, *Poly. Phil.* 1.3 (LCL 24.334) with 1 Peter 1:8, 8.1-2 (LCL 24.344) with 1 Peter 2:21-24, and the allusions in 10.1-3 (LCL 24.346) to 1 Peter 2:12, 17 and 5:5.

teaching, and though both make much use of the Jewish theme of doubleness as a cause of sin, Hermas' exploration of this in terms of two spirits or two desires, though it has Jewish parallels . . . is foreign to James.

Despite these and other points of difference, she goes on to conclude:

> The strong impression is, however, that Hermas is familiar with James, that the language of the epistle colors his exposition of his ideas, and that where he once takes up an expression, other reminiscences tend to follow.[90]

The data suggests that the two texts are *related* in some way; Laws's "strong impression" that "Hermas is familiar with James" can only derive from the presupposition that James is the earlier document. That is to say, even if such "parallels" are somehow established, one cannot say for sure which text is in the dependent position. And even if the similarities between the texts are judged to involve some kind of dependence, a number of theoretical possibilities are available to explain the relationship. O. J. F. Seitz, for one, has made the case that both James and *Hermas* were dependent on yet another source,[91] and J. H. Ropes and Dibelius argued that both texts were simply passing on some of the same traditional paraenetic material.[92]

Indeed the case could even be made that the author of James used *Hermas* as a source. Consider, for instance, the oft-cited strongest parallel in their shared use of the rare term δίψυχος: James uses the word twice (1:8; 4:8), but Hermas uses δίψυχος nineteen times, διψυχεῖν twenty times, and διψυχία sixteen times; the word and its cognates are repeated so frequently that the concept develops into a major sub-theme of the book. When we compare the extensive popularity of *The Shepherd of Hermas* in the early centuries with the comparable obscurity of the letter of James, is it more likely that Hermas developed this theme from its occurrence in James, or that the author of James appealed to what, by his time, had become a well-known idea thanks to its use in texts like the widely admired *Shepherd of Hermas*? Indeed, if we accept the notion that the Roman writers Hermas and Clement appealed to James as an authoritative source, we are then forced into the unlikely conclusion that the letter was a quotable authority in the Western church by the end of the first century but was somehow subsequently neglected for over 200 years until it was reintroduced by Hilary of Poitiers in the fourth century.

The fact is, the evidence does not allow for certainty one way or the other, and arguments about the date of James made on the basis of literary affinities with the apostolic fathers have entirely to do with presuppositions about the relative date of the texts involved. For my purposes, I simply conclude that the letter shares similarities of word and thought with known second-century texts. When this is combined with our knowledge of an increase in James-related material in the second century

[90] Laws, 23.

[91] O. J. F. Seitz, "The Relationship of the Shepherd of Hermas to the Epistle of James," *JBL* 63 (1944): 131–40.

[92] Ropes, 88–89; Dibelius, *James*, 32.

(explored below), evidence of its literary dependence on known first-century apostolic writings (demonstrated in chapter three), and the letter's canonical "arrival" in the third century, it simply makes sense to conclude that James' *Sitz im Leben* is more likely the second century than the first. At the very least, it must be acknowledged that the available evidence supports my hypothesis at a number of points and ought not keep us from pursuing it to the end.

This first section has demonstrated the following points: (1) Scholarship has offered no compelling explanation for the lack of external attestation for James before the early third century; (2) common means of supporting the authenticity of the letter are not persuasive enough to overturn the credible evidence in favor of pseudonymity; and (3) arguments in support of a first-century provenance for the letter have primarily to do with scholarly presuppositions concerning the acceptable range for the dating of NT writings. Indeed, the research presented thus far allows for the strong possibility that the letter of James is a second-century text. Such a claim, however, would be much stronger if I could present actual features of the canonical letter that demonstrate the author's knowledge of second-century realities. Just such a demonstration is the objective of the next section.

James of Jerusalem in History and Tradition

The following material is covered in detail in a number of other sources, and the reader is directed to them for more thorough analyses.[93] My intention is not to supply an in-depth study of the various texts under review, but to trace the development of particular aspects of the James tradition (the pseudepigraphic "stabilizing elements" identified by Meade) with a view toward locating the letter of James in the context of the second century rather than the first. The evidence I present will make it quite clear that James of Jerusalem was an important figure for Catholic, "Jewish-Christian," and "gnostic" Christians of the time. While we are on safe enough ground locating the NT sources and Josephus in the first century, the other materials are generally agreed to be later, most of them falling into the second century. I will present these "later" sources by means of a spectrum ranging from "Broadly Catholic" through "Mixed" (that is, containing a mixture of elements deemed "orthodox" and "unorthodox" by Catholic theologians) and on to "broadly gnostic," in order to see if we can isolate different tendencies among the *Jakobusbild* appealed to by adherents of these traditions.[94] We will analyze the image presented in each text according to the following five categories:

[93] Cf. Painter, *Just James*; Pratscher, *Der Herrenbruder*; R. Ward, "James of Jerusalem in the First Two Centuries." *ANRW* II.26.1, 779–812; Martin, xli–lxxvii; and G. Luedemann, *Opposition to Paul in Jewish Christianity*, trans. M. E. Boring (Minneapolis, Minn.: Fortress, 1989). Hartin (*James of Jerusalem*, 115–40) provides a similar tradition-historical overview of the development of James traditions but assumes throughout that the canonical letter predates the later traditions.

[94] This useful German term is borrowed from Pratscher.

1) How is James *named* in the text under review?
2) What kind of *authority* is attributed to James in each text?
3) How is his *piety* depicted?
4) Some of the sources present James as a rather *independent* figure in relation to Jesus and the broader Christian movement. What standing does
   he have in these portraits?
5) How is James' *murder* depicted?

The five points of analysis will not always be applicable to every text, and on occasion we will struggle to meaningfully relate these writings to one another under a
single scheme, since they derive from such radically different communities who were
interested in radically different aspects of the available *Jakobusbild*. Still, it is hoped
that the accumulated portrait will provide an accurate picture of the James traditions in the first two centuries. Once complete, we will see how the canonical letter
of James fits into the broader depiction of his identity and character as it developed
over the first two centuries. We begin with those traditions deemed "early."

EARLY JAMES TRADITIONS

The James traditions that can be fairly firmly located in the first century are limited
to two certain sources: his appearances in the relevant NT texts, and the reference
to him in Josephus's *Antiquities of the Jews*.

The New Testament

James is explicitly *named* in only eight NT passages (Matt 13:55; Mark 6:3; Acts
12:17; 15:13-29; 21:17-26; 1 Cor 15:7; Gal 1–2; Jude 1:1). In Matthew and Mark,
Jesus' countrymen recognize Jesus as being the son of Mary and the brother of
James, Joseph/Joses, Simon, and Judas (Matt 13:55; Mark 6:3). While the other
two gospels make reference to brothers of Jesus, they do not offer any associated
names. The Acts narrative offers no title beyond "James," though he is sometimes
mentioned in tandem with the Jerusalem leadership, that is, "James and the brethren" (12:17), or "James and all the elders" (21:18). Readers are probably meant to
see an implicit inclusion of James in Acts 1:14, since it says that Jesus' mother Mary
and his brothers were present with the apostles praying in the upper room on the
day of Pentecost, though it must be acknowledged that Luke does little to enable
the connection. Paul identifies James as the Lord's brother (Gal 1:19), resident in
Jerusalem (Gal 1:18-19; 2:1) as a Pillar (στῦλος) of the church there along with
Peter and John (Gal 2:9). He was also known by Paul to have received a resurrection
appearance (1 Cor 15:7). The final reference to James in the NT is from the letter of
Jude, where the author identifies himself as "servant of Jesus Christ and brother of
James" (v. 1). Tradition has always associated this James and Jude with the brothers
of Jesus identified in Matthew and Mark.[95]

---

[95] Cf. Richard Bauckham, *Jude, 2 Peter* (WBC 50; Waco, Tex.: Word Books, 1983),

Though James is something of a marginal figure in these texts, the *authority* accorded him appears rather high. On several occasions he is simply named "James" (Acts 12, 15, 21; 1 Cor 15:7; Jude 1:1), and the lack of corresponding identification suggests a level of prominence in the eyes of the readers. His initial appearance in Acts is typical of this tendency. Luke begins chapter 12 by reporting the execution of the only prominent "James" in the gospels, James the brother of John (12:2), and in so doing clears the way for the only other prominent "James" in the early church, the brother of the Lord. After his escape from prison (12:6-11), Peter instructs his comrades to tell the news "to James and the brethren" (12:17). Peter then immediately departs Jerusalem for "another place" (12:17), suggesting that James functions as the leader of the Jerusalem church. This hunch is confirmed three chapters later in the Apostolic Council of Acts 15, where James' leadership position is abundantly clear: he is the last among the leaders to give his opinion on the matter at hand, and his speech concludes the debate with an authoritative judgment which is immediately obeyed (15:13-29). Though Peter, Barnabas, and Paul all relate experiential testimony regarding God's work among the Gentiles, it is James who offers key scriptural support for their inclusion among the eschatological people of God (15:13-21).[96] He appears again in his leadership role in 21:17-26, when Paul offers a report on his Gentile mission to James in the presence of the elders of Jerusalem.

Paul's letters corroborate James' authority. He is listed as a recipient of a resurrection appearance in 1 Corinthians 15:7, and the presence of his unadorned name alongside the similarly unembellished "Cephas" suggests that Paul felt no need to offer further identification for these well-known figures. In Galatians Paul calls James "the brother of the Lord" and regards him as one of a trio "reputed to be pillars" (οἱ δοκοῦντες στῦλοι εἶναι) of the Jerusalem church.[97] Among them, the fact that James is mentioned before Peter and John might be seen as a recognition of his relative authority over even these two leading apostles. Further, the fact that the "certain men" who "arrived from James" (ἐλθεῖν τινας ἀπὸ Ἰακώβου) were able to sway Peter, Barnabas, and "the rest of the Jews" into altering their

---

24–25; J. N. D. Kelly, *A Commentary on the Epistles of Peter and Jude* (BNTC; London: A&C Black, 1969), 242.

[96] See the careful studies of James' speech in Acts 15:13-21 in R. Bauckham, "James and the Gentiles," in *History, Literature, and Society in the Book of Acts*, ed. B. Witherington (Cambridge: Cambridge University Press, 1995), 154–84; and J. Adna, "James' Position at the Summit Meeting of the Apostles and the Elders in Jerusalem (Acts 15)," in *The Mission of the Early Church to Jews and Gentiles*, ed. J. Adna and H. Kvalbein (Tübingen: Mohr Siebeck, 2000), 125–61.

[97] It has been argued that the title "Pillar" (στῦλος) should be understood against the backdrop of the early church's self-understanding as the eschatological temple of God, as found elsewhere in early Christian literature (e.g., 1 Cor 3:16-17; Eph 2:19-22; 1 Pet 2:4-5). See C. K. Barrett, "Paul and the 'Pillar' Apostles," in *Studia Paulina*, ed. J. N. Sevenster and W. C. van Unnik (Haarlem: De Erven F. Bohn N.V., 1953), 12; and Bauckham, "James and the Jerusalem Church," 442–50.

table fellowship with Gentile Christians suggests that James was an authority to be obeyed (Gal 2:11-14).

We are given some indication of James' *piety* in these passages, as the texts depict James as one who was concerned that the Christian mission be grounded in conformity to the Torah. We have already mentioned James' appeal to Israel's scriptures at the Apostolic Council of Acts 15; though this act alone demonstrates his concern to ground the earliest Christian mission in the continuity of God's salvation history, his listing of four "necessary things" for Gentile observance offers further insight. The four requirements listed in Acts 15:20 and 29 (abstinence from food sacrificed to idols, blood, things strangled, and unchastity) are not "necessary" because they enable table fellowship between Jews and Gentiles[98] (in fact they do not enable such fellowship[99]); nor are they to be understood merely as a "concession" by Jewish Christians, enabling Gentile Christians to be released from the "burden of the law."[100] They are "necessary" for James because they are the only four requirements the law placed upon Gentiles dwelling in the midst of the Jews.[101] Further, in Acts 21:17-26 James informs Paul of rumors among Jewish brethren "zealous for the law" that he teaches Jews to forsake the law and subsequently orders him to demonstrate his commitment by a public performance of purification rituals (21:23-24). In both passages, James is revealed to be an advocate for ongoing Christian conformity to the Torah as appropriate for Jews and Gentiles alike. Likewise, in Galatians 2:12, the "certain men who arrived from James" are identified as "those from the circumcision" (τοὺς ἐκ περιτομῆς). The passage is unclear as to the extent of James' direct association with those agitating for Gentile circumcision, but it cannot be ignored that Jewish believers agitating for Gentile circumcision are identified as having been sent "from James."

Certain aspects of these texts present James as an *independent* figure in earliest Christianity. First, the gospels leave readers with the clear impression that James was not a faithful disciple during Jesus' lifetime.[102] Mark seems especially intent on casting Jesus' family in a negative light (3:21, 31-35; 6:1-6), while Matthew softens the critique (compare the Matthean redaction in 12:46 and 13:57). Though James

---

[98] Argued by J. Munck, *The Acts of the Apostles* (ABC 31; New York: Doubleday, 1967) 140, and H. Conzelmann, *The Acts of the Apostles* (Hermeneia; Philadelphia: Fortress, 1987), 118.

[99] As demonstrated by Bauckham, "James and the Jerusalem Church," 464.

[100] M. Dibelius, *Studies in the Acts of the Apostles* (London: SCM Press, 1956), 97.

[101] E. Haenchen, *The Acts of the Apostles: A Commentary* (Philadelphia: Westminster, 1971), 469; Bauckham, "James and the Jerusalem Church," 458–60.

[102] But see Richard Bauckham, *Jude and the Relatives of Jesus in the Early Church* (Edinburgh: T&T Clark, 1990), 45–57; Ward, "James of Jerusalem," 786–90; and Painter, *Just James*, 11–41, who offer historical reconstructions that attempt to reduce the plain sense of the text in favor of the notion that James may well have been a follower during Jesus' lifetime. Whether one finds their arguments plausible or not, here we are concerned not with what "really happened" but with the *traditions* about James that develop through the first and second centuries.

is not named in John, the rejection of Jesus is generally maintained, for though John 2:12 tells us that his mother and brothers traveled with Jesus and the disciples from Cana to Capernaum, by 7:5 we are told, "even his brothers did not believe in him." Secondly, we should consider Luke's enigmatic presentation of James. He is not named as a brother of the Lord in the gospel, and it is an intriguing fact that we are not told how it is that James attained the high position reflected in Acts; he simply appears in that position when he arrives in chapter 12. Similarly, while Luke presents James as the leader of the Jerusalem church, he nowhere gives James a formal title beyond his association with the brethren and the elders. While Luke's avoidance of the "family critique" may have been due to his high view of Jesus' mother as the first faithful disciple, it may also have been the case that Luke himself did not quite know where to place James. He knew James was the first leader of the Jerusalem church and exerted some measure of authority over the earliest apostles, yet it seems he also believed that this James did not qualify as a true "apostle." Consider Acts 1:20-22: in seeking a replacement for the betrayer Judas, Peter says,

> So one of the men who have accompanied us during all the time that the Lord Jesus went in and out among us beginning from the baptism of John until the day when he was taken up from us—one of these men must become with us a witness to his resurrection. (Acts 1:21-22)

James does not meet these qualifications and therefore cannot be joined with this particular group, which 1:26 identifies as the "apostles." This title appears twenty-eight times in the first sixteen chapters of Acts in reference to the disciples encircled around Peter (for example, 2:37, 5:29). It is true that on one occasion Paul and Barnabas are called apostles (14:14), but this is an anomaly, for they are generally differentiated from this group (9:27; 15:2, 4, 22; 16:4). The passage describing the Apostolic Council consistently lists "the apostles and the elders" as two different groups (15:2, 4, 6, 22, 23; 16:4), and as I have already noted, James is associated with the latter set (21:18). For Luke, James was the leader of the Jerusalem church and an ecclesial authority, but not an apostle.

Paul, however, seems to have considered James an apostle. In 1 Corinthians 15:5, Paul says that Jesus "appeared [ὤφθη] to Cephas, then [εἶτα] to the twelve"; then in 15:7, he says, "he appeared [ὤφθη] to James, then [εἶτα] to all the apostles." The parallel syntax suggests that Paul considered James an apostle in the same way that he himself was one, that is, as one directly commissioned by the resurrected Lord.[103] In Galatians 1:18-19, Paul describes the period immediately after his calling, saying that when he went to Jerusalem to stay with Cephas, he also saw "James the Lord's brother." There is some scholarly debate about the proper translation of this passage: Paul says, "ἕτερον δὲ τῶν ἀποστόλων οὐκ εἶδον εἰ μὴ Ἰακωβον τὸν ἀδελφὸν τοῦ κυρίου." Some have argued that Paul is being intentionally ambiguous here, saying something like, "I saw none of the other apostles—unless

---

[103] Johnson, *James*, 94.

you count James as an apostle."[104] Still others believe Paul is not calling James an apostle at all, translating the verse, "Other than the apostles I saw none except James, the Lord's brother."[105] Most English translations, however, render the phrase as something akin to, "I saw none of the other apostles except James the Lord's brother," the straightforward sense of which agrees with 1 Corinthians 15:7 that Paul considered James an apostle.

Nonetheless, a tension between Paul and James is present behind Galatians 1–2 that indicates some measure of separation between them. First, whether the association is direct or indirect, Paul names James in the same breath with those "of the circumcision" who led Jewish believers into hypocrisy with Gentile Christians. Further, after Paul introduces himself as one who was "an apostle not from men nor through man, but through Jesus Christ and God the Father" (1:1), he refers on four occasions to those who were "of repute" among the Jerusalem Christians (2:2, 6a, 6c, 9), then calls the authority of these leaders (identified as James, Cephas, and John in 2:9) into question when he contrasts human reputation with God's impartiality (Gal 2:6). Still, Paul's claim that the Pillars extended to him and Barnabas the right hand of fellowship (Gal 2:9) suggests that any ultimate division between James and Paul is untenable.

To summarize the NT witness, then, we may note the following: the gospels and Paul agree on *naming* James "the brother of Jesus." His *authority* as leader of the Jerusalem church is clearly implied, but the process by which he attained this leadership role is not described. Both Luke and Paul treat his leadership as a fact that is so well known it requires no substantive comment. His *piety* is linked with concern for appropriate Torah-observance among Jews and Gentiles alike. James is depicted as a somewhat *independent* figure in early Christianity. The gospels inform us that he was not a believer during Jesus' lifetime. Further, he is differentiated from the twelve, and though Paul considered him an apostle, Luke did not. There is also an indication that tensions of some kind existed between James and Paul, and that James was behind a delegation sent to Antioch to curtail Peter; though it also seems clear that James generally supported Paul's mission, and Paul respectfully recognized James' authority.

Josephus

Another source for James traditions from the first century is Josephus's *Antiquities of the Jews*, written sometime around 93/94 C.E.[106] From him we receive the earliest report of the martyrdom of James at the hands of the high priest Ananus, who grasped the opportunity during a temporary break in Roman leadership after the

---

[104] W. Schmithals, *The Office of an Apostle* (Nashville: Abingdon, 1965), 65, followed by Martin, xxxviii.

[105] L. P. Trudinger, "ΕΤΕΡΟΝ ΔΕ ΤΩΝ ΑΠΟΣΤΟΛΩΝ ΟΥΚ ΕΙΔΟΝ, ΕΙ ΜΗ ΙΑΚ-ΩΒΟΝ: A Note on Galatians i:19," *NovT* 17.3 (1975): 200–202.

[106] S. Mason, *Josephus and the New Testament*, 2nd ed. (Peabody, Mass.: Hendrickson, 2003), 99.

death of Festus in 62 C.E. The authenticity of the report is strengthened by information from his *Life*, where we learn that he was a young Pharisee in Jerusalem at
the time (*Life*, 12–13). In the *Antiquities*, Josephus reports,

> [Ananus] convened the judges of the Sanhedrin and brought before them the
> brother of Jesus who was called Christ, whose name was James [τὸν ἀδελφὸν
> Ἰησοῦ τοῦ λεγομένου Χριστοῦ, Ἰάκωβος ὄνομα αὐτῷ], and certain others. He
> accused them of having transgressed the law and delivered them up to be stoned.
> Those of the inhabitants of the city who were considered the most fair-minded
> and who were strict in observance of the law were offended at this. They therefore
> secretly sent to King Agrippa urging him, for Ananus had not even been correct in
> his first step, to order him to desist from any further such actions. (*Ant.* 20:200–1
> [Niese 20.200–1; Feldman, LCL 433.496–97])

It should be noted that while Jesus is qualified as the one who is "called" Christ,
James is *named* "the brother of Jesus" without qualification; this is not only indicative of the authenticity of the passage (for what Christian scribe would allow such a
qualification of Jesus' identity to stand?), but also of the solidity of the "brother" tradition in the first century.[107] In this regard, it should be noted that Josephus's application of the name "James" is almost secondary; he is first and foremost "the brother
of Jesus." Even among non-Christian first-century sources, James was apparently
known primarily by this title.

The *authority* of James is less clear from this source. The narrative suggests that
James was caught up in internecine conflicts within the Jewish leadership, and though
he is not clearly identified as a leader of Jerusalem Christians, the fact that he was
murdered during a political struggle suggests that he was viewed as a figure whose

---

[107] Painter, *Just James*, 136. It is possible of course that the qualification of Jesus' title is
only apparent, for this is the second time Josephus has spoken of him. The famous *Testimonium Flavianum* (18.63–64) speaks of Jesus amidst the story of Pilate, saying of him "This
man was Christ." Though scholars take up a variety of opinions as to the authenticity of
the *Testimonium*, Mason notes, "The vast majority of commentators hold a middle position
between authenticity and inauthenticity, claiming that Josephus wrote *something* about Jesus
that was subsequently edited by Christian copyists" (235). J. P. Meier ("The Testimonium:
Evidence for Jesus Outside the Bible," *BRev* 7/3 [1991]: 23) has proposed an emendation of
the text that removes the three phrases most widely affirmed to be Christian interpolations,
leaving us the following: "At this time there appeared Jesus, a wise man. For he was a doer of
startling deeds, a teacher of people who receive the truth with pleasure. And he gained a following both among many Jews and among many of Greek origin. And when Pilate, because
of an accusation made by the leading men among us, condemned him to the cross, those who
loved him previously did not cease to do so. And up until this very day the tribe of Christians,
named after him, has not died out." If Meier's reconstruction is correct, it would suggest that
the "Christ" phrase from our passage should likewise be considered an interpolation. Indeed,
removing it gives the phrase a more straightforward feel: "the brother of Jesus, whose name
was James." The other possibility is that the original had "He was *called* Christ" in 18.63,
which would then be echoed in 20.200, "Jesus, who was called Christ."

removal would benefit those in power. Further, Josephus's mention of him by name
suggests his prominence in the Jerusalem of his day. The identity of these rival fac-
tions may tell us something about James' *piety*. Josephus makes it clear that the Sad-
ducees were a brutal sect (*Ant.* 20.199), and notes elsewhere that the Pharisees were
milder in punishments and more accurate in their enforcement of the law (13.294;
17.141; *War* 1.110; 2.162; *Life,* 191). Thus, while the Sadducean leadership considered him a lawbreaker, at least some among the Pharisees did not; and what unavoidably emerges above the clash is the fact that James was known as a keeper of the law
whose death was precipitated by a debate concerning its proper maintenance.

When it comes to James' *independence*, it is striking that Josephus offers no
associated comment regarding a Christian movement or other figures associated
with that movement. Indeed, the only association with Jesus is James' identification
as his brother; otherwise James is a Jew among Jews, caught up in the debate over
the proper adherence to Torah. He is an important enough figure for Josephus to
remember him, but his remembrance does not include his identity as a follower of
Christ; if Josephus were our only source of knowledge about Jesus and James, we
would assume that James was the figure of importance and not his brother. Finally,
it almost goes without saying that this is our earliest source for the *murder* of James.
Josephus's presentation of James' death makes at least three points clear: (1) James
was killed during a temporary break in Roman leadership after the death of Festus
in 62 C.E.; (2) the legality of his execution was questionable; and (3) those who
came to his support were most probably Pharisees (who, significantly, are not identified as fellow Christians).

Summary of Early Sources

Let us briefly summarize the evidence from our earlier sources of James tradition.
Matthew, Mark, Paul, and Josephus agree on *naming* James the "brother" of Jesus.
James' *authority* is shown to be quite high, but he is not given a formal title, and his
ascent to leadership is nowhere explained. His *piety* can best be described as Torah-
observant. This is supported by his demand that both Jews and Gentiles conform
to the demands of the law, and by the fact that law-abiding Pharisees protested
against his execution as a law-breaker by the Sadducean leadership. His depiction
as an unbeliever in the gospels, his unexplained leadership in Acts, his uncertain
apostolicity in Luke and Paul, and his depiction as a Jew among Jews in Josephus
all combine to present him as a somewhat obscure, *independent* figure in the earliest
church. His *murder* is not related in the NT, though Josephus makes brief mention
of it in his *Antiquities*.

LATER JAMES TRADITIONS

As already stated, the exact origins of the following texts are frequently debated, as
is the succession of influence among them. My interest here is simply to read them
as evidence of later James traditions among the various Christian groups that cham-

pioned him as an apostolic hero. We begin with broadly Catholic sources, followed by sources including theologically "mixed" material, and conclude with sources that can be considered broadly "gnostic."

Later Broadly Catholic Sources

The Protevangelium of James[108]

The so-called *Protevangelium of James* has, at first glance, rather little to say about James himself, focused as it is on proclaiming the purity of his mother Mary. James is asserted to be the author of the text, as the final section makes clear:

> Now I, James, am the one who wrote this account at the time when an uproar arose in Jerusalem at the death of Herod. I took myself off to the wilderness until the uproar in Jerusalem died down. There I praised the Lord God, who gave me the wisdom to write this account. (*Prot. Jas.* 25:1–3 [Hock, 76–77])

Though he is not *named* beyond the authorial "James" signature at the end, it seems that readers are expected to associate this James with the sons of Joseph mentioned throughout the text (9:8; 17:2, 5). It is here that we find a significant development in the James tradition, as the *Protevangelium* (focused as it is on proclaiming the perpetual virginity of Mary) is intent on denying any blood relationship between James and Jesus. In this manner Joseph is depicted as an aging widower with grown sons of his own by the time he is chosen to be the guardian-husband of the pregnant Mary. Thus, the infancy gospel demonstrates a growing fascination among Catholic Christians with the virginity of Mary, and an associated disquiet with the notion that Jesus had siblings in the flesh. The document has little to say about James' *authority*, save that he is named without elaboration and described as residing in Jerusalem. His authority is therefore implied more than asserted. Yet it is clear that God's dispensation of the "wisdom to write this history" is as much an authorizing of James as the gospel he has purportedly written. Further, as evidence of James' *piety*, it could be argued that his account of Jesus' miraculous birth supports his early belief in Christ (indeed, while Jesus was still an infant!), against available portraits that might suggest otherwise.

The Gospel According to the Hebrews[109]

This gospel only exists for us in fragments passed down via the writings of others. Clement of Alexandria (*Strom.* 2.9.45), Origen (*Com. Jn.* 2.12), Eusebius (*Hist.*

---

[108] R. Hock, the editor of the critical text (*The Infancy Gospels of James and Thomas*, Scholar's Bible, vol. 2 [Santa Rosa, Calif.: Polebridge Press, 1995], 11–12), dates the work to the latter half of the second century, as does Pratscher (224 n. 69) and O. Cullman (in E. Hennecke and W. Schneemelcher, *New Testament Apocrypha*, ed. R. McL. Wilson, 2 vols. [London: Lutterworth, 1963], 1.372). However, the fact that Clement clearly knows the book (*Strom.* 7.16.93, SC 428.284) should probably push us back toward the middle of the second century.

[109] P. Vielhauer ("Jewish-Christian Gospels," in Hennecke-Schneemelcher, 1.163) seems

Eccl. 3.25.5; 39.17; 4.22.8), Epiphanius (*Pan.* 29–30), and Jerome (*Vir. ill.* 2.3.16) all cited a gospel by this name. This title intermingles in the patristic sources with citations from other so-called "Jewish" gospels, making it extremely difficult to know whether they are all referring to the same text. It is probably the case that they are not.[110] Nevertheless, there are gathered together a number of quotations attributed to a gospel by this name. Of importance for our purposes is the one cited by Jerome in his chapter on James in the *De viris illustribus*.

> Also the gospel which is called the *Gospel According to the Hebrews* . . . after the account of the resurrection says, "The Lord, however, after he had given his grave clothes to the servant of the priest, appeared to James, for James had sworn that he would not eat bread from that hour in which he drank the cup of the Lord until he should see him rising again from among those that sleep"; and again, a little later, it says, "'Bring a table and bread,' said the Lord." And immediately it is added, "He brought bread and blessed and broke it and gave it to James the Just and said to him, 'My brother, eat your bread, for the Son of Man is risen from among those that sleep.'" (*Vir. ill.* 211–13 [PL 23.611–13; Halton, FC 100.8])

Though Jesus refers to James as "my brother," we find for the first time in our study that he is *named* "the Just" (ὁ δίκαιος). As we will see, this name will come to dominate through the second-century materials. Along these lines it is worth mentioning that Jerome certainly did not believe that Jesus' reference to James as "my brother" was to be taken literally. He begins his chapter on James by saying that though some people *called* James "the brother of Jesus," he was in fact *surnamed* "the Just." The depiction of James' *authority* is quite significant: First, against the tradition handed down by Paul that James received a resurrection appearance *after* Peter and the twelve (1 Cor 15:3-7), it is suggested here that James was *first* among the apostles to meet the resurrected Lord; second, it seems that James attended the Last Supper, as the meeting described was the result of his apparently bold assertion after the meal that he would not eat again until Jesus was raised. The parallel between James' dinner oath and Jesus own words at the meal (Luke 22:18) suggests that this assertion functions as a claim for the faithful *piety* of James vis-à-vis the other apostles. Plainly, this source is a witness to the *independent* elevation of James that took place in certain early circles. Consider the implications: contrary to the canonical accounts, James was a disciple and an attendant at the last supper; further, he was the first to see the risen Lord, and likewise, the first celebration of the

---

to speak for the majority when he dates this gospel to the first half of the second century. R. Cameron (*The Other Gospels: Non-Canonical Gospel Texts* [Philadelphia: Westminster, 1982], 84), however, is willing to date it anywhere from the mid-first to the mid-second century. Its earliest certain witness comes at the end of the second century with Clement of Alexandria, though Eusebius reports that Papias and Hegesippus used it (see, e.g., *Hist. Eccl.* 3.39.17 and 4.22.8).

[110] See Vielhauer's discussion ("Jewish-Christian Gospels," in Hennecke-Schneemelcher, 1.117–39), and my earlier caveat on the use of the term "Jewish-Christian" (27 n. 84).

Eucharist was a private event shared between the two brothers.[111] Such a tradition indicates an extremely high view of James, certainly higher than the other apostles, though significantly, none are mentioned.

Hegesippus

Hegesippus, fragments of whose writings are preserved for us in the *Historia Ecclesiastica* (GCSNF 6–1.166–70; Lake, LCL 153.170–74), is said by Eusebius to have been "in the first generation after the apostles" (2.23.3), though several other indicators from his testimony lead most historians to place his writing somewhere in the third quarter of the second century.[112] Indeed, it is not at all clear that Hegesippus is the early convert from Judaism Eusebius apparently believes him to be (*Hist. Eccl.* 4.22.8), for as we will see, Hegesippus's testimony includes a number of statements that suggest he is ignorant of certain basic Jewish realities.[113]

Eusebius appeals to Hegesippus for information about second-century heresies (4.7–8, 11, 22), as well as information about the relatives of Jesus (3.11–12, 19–20, 32; 4.22), and for biographical information regarding the character and martyrdom of James (2.23).

> The charge of the Church passed to James the brother of the Lord, together with the Apostles. He was called the "Just" by all men from the Lord's time to ours, since many are called James, but he was holy from his mother's womb. (2.23.4)

As in the *Gospel According to the Hebrews*, James is referred to as "the brother of the Lord," but is explicitly *named* "the Just." The title is explained, in part, by reference to his *piety*:

> He drank no wine or strong drink, nor did he eat flesh; no razor went upon his head; he did not anoint himself with oil, and he did not go to the baths. He alone was allowed to enter the sanctuary [τὰ ἅγια], for he did not wear wool but linen, and he used to enter alone into the temple, and be found kneeling and praying for forgiveness for the people, so that his knees grew hard like a camel's because of his constant worship of God, kneeling and asking forgiveness for the people. So from his excessive righteousness he was called the Just and Oblias, that is in Greek, "Rampart of the people and righteousness," as the prophets declare concerning him. (2.23.5–7)

Hegesippus's description of James in this passage is a conflation of stereotypical OT images of heroic holiness reminiscent of the Jewish priesthood and the Nazirite vow (abstinence from wine, the wearing of linen, the unshaved head; cf. Lev 10:9; Num 6:1-5; Ezek 44:17, 20-21). Some of the characteristics listed do not fit either of these models (vegetarianism, no oil or baths),[114] and are probably more indicative of

---

[111] These points are drawn out by Painter, *Just James*, 185.

[112] See, e.g., the comments in Martin (xlviii–xlix) and Painter (*Just James*, 119).

[113] Martin, xlix–l; Luedemann, *Opposition to Paul*, 167.

[114] Martin, l; Painter, *Just James*, 125–26.

Hegesippus's idealizations of Jewish piety than anything else.[115] As OT texts associate oil with gladness and an avoidance of oil with mourning (2 Sam 14:2; Ps 92:10; Isa 61:3), we may interpret James' refusal to anoint himself as consonant with his repentant posture as one "beseeching forgiveness for the people."

It should be noted that there is nothing explicitly Christian about James' piety as it is described here. Much is said, however, of Hegesippus's view of James' *authority*: "He alone was permitted to enter the sanctuary, for he did not wear wool but linen, and he used to enter alone into the temple, and be found kneeling and praying for forgiveness for the people." One cannot miss the allusion to the description of the high priest on the Day of Atonement, who would enter alone into the Holy of Holies wearing only linen in order to beseech forgiveness for the people of Israel (cf. Lev 16). This fact, as well as subsequent interpretive tradition, supports the view that the "sanctuary" Hegesippus describes is in fact the "Holy of Holies."[116] Such a statement not only betrays a basic ignorance of temple architecture, it also reads very much like an idealization of Jewish holiness made by a non-Jew: are we really to believe that the non-priestly James was permitted to enter the Holy of Holies whenever he liked? Regardless, James is described here as a high priestly figure, a characterization that is strengthened later in Hegesippus's testimony by the Scribes and Pharisees, who three times affirm James to be one "to whom we all owe obedience" (2.23.10–12). Julius Scott has observed that Hegesippus's description of James in the guise of a high priest corresponds to the expectation of certain pre-Christian Jewish groups that an eschatological priest figure would appear to signal the end of the age, a "priest like Aaron" to accompany the messianic "prophet like Moses."[117] His study demonstrates that these Jewish expectations "provided a fertile seedbed" from which traditions with priestly connotations could have grown up around an early Christian leader, and Hegesippus's account (as well as that of others[118]) suggests that James was the early church figure onto whom these expectations were fastened.

Hegesippus's description of James' death ends by saying, "and immediately Vespasian began to besiege them" (2.23.18). Mainstream Christian tradition typically considered the destruction of Jerusalem to have been punishment for the death of Christ; nevertheless, numerous sources indicate that there also existed a persistent tradition associating the destruction of Jerusalem with the death of James.[119]

---

[115] But cf. Irenaeus (*Adv. Haer.* 1.24.2) and Epiphanius (*Pan.* 30.15), who associate vegetarianism with deviant gnostic and Jewish sects.

[116] The Syriac and Latin translations of the *Hist. Eccl.* seek to clarify the place by saying explicitly that James entered the Holy of Holies, as do Epiphanius (*Pan.* 88) and Jerome (*Vir. ill.* 2.5).

[117] J. Scott, "James the Relative of Jesus and the Expctation of an Eschatological Priest," *JETS* 25.3 (1982): 323–31. Epiphanius makes James' priestly role even more explicit by depicting him wearing the high priestly "petalon" headdress (*Pan.* 88; cf. LXX Exod 28:36).

[118] *Pseudo-Clementine Recognitions* 1.43,67–74; 4.35; *Apocr.*; the *Teachings of the Apostles* (*ANF* 8.668 and 671); traditions associated with James passed down by Clement and Origen.

[119] *1–2 Apoc.*; Origen (*Comm. Matt.* 10.17; *Cels.* 1.47; 2.13).

Eusebius echoes this tradition in a modified form, saying that the intercession of James "and the apostles" provided a strong protection for the city (3.7.8), and the destruction of Jerusalem was not punishment for James' death, but came about because James and the other apostles were no longer there to hold it back with their righteous prayers. Not only does this tradition support the "eschatological high priest" view of James as one who offered effective intercession before God, it also helps us understand why Hegesippus reports that James was called "Oblias" (which he translated as "rampart of the people"): James' intercession was comparable to a wall of protection against the wrath of God.

Though James is presented as a stereotype of OT heroic piety, he is *murdered* as the result of his confession of Christ. Hegesippus's story unfolds as follows: the growth of the Christian community began to alarm the Scribes and the Pharisees, who, interestingly, go to James for help. As I have already noted, James is presented as a pious Jew; and though we are told he was involved in the conversion of the Jewish people (2.23.9), the leadership seems to have been completely untroubled by this activity. They are not unaware of his relation to Jesus, however; indeed, they appeal to James as a kind of authority on Jesus. They say to him,

> We beseech you to restrain the people since they are straying after Jesus as though he were the Messiah. We beseech you to persuade concerning Jesus all who have come for the day of the Passover, for all obey you. For we and the whole people testify that you are a righteous person and do not respect persons. So do persuade the crowd not to err concerning Jesus, for the whole people and we all obey you. (2.23.10)

It seems that James' particular Christian commitments, whatever they were, did not threaten the vision of Judaic orthodoxy promoted by his contemporaries in Jewish leadership. The leaders call on James to offer a right *teaching* about Jesus, not to deny him per se: they want James to "persuade the crowd not to err concerning Jesus." The problem is not following Jesus' teaching, for instance, but "straying after Jesus as though he were the messiah." The issue presented to James is not one of Jesus versus Judaism but a correct understanding of Jesus vis-à-vis Judaism. The implication is not that he had thus far never said anything about Jesus, but that what he had said to that point (publicly at least) was fully orthodox and inoffensive by the standards of Jewish orthodoxy.

James is instructed to take his stand on the "parapet of the temple"[120] so that all the people might hear him. To the chagrin of the Scribes and Pharisees, however, James proclaims a faithful witness to Jesus that is a plain echo of Jesus' own testimony before Caiaphas (Matt 26:64) as well as Stephen's words just before his own martyrdom (Acts 7:56): "Why do you ask me concerning the Son of Man? He is sitting in heaven on the right hand of the great power, and he will come on the

---

[120] πτερύγιον τοῦ ἱεροῦ, the place where Jesus was tempted by the devil; Matt 4:5; Luke 4:9.

clouds of heaven." The Scribes and Pharisees, shocked at this turn of events, say to one another,

> "We did wrong to provide Jesus with such testimony, but let us go up and throw him down that they may be afraid and not believe him." And they cried out saying, "Oh, oh, even the Just One erred!" (2.23.15)

Casting narrative plausibility aside, it is clear that the Jewish leadership in this story expected James to witness about Jesus in accordance with his presentation as a righteous Jew. How did they make such a mistake? Hegesippus's story suggests one of two possibilities: either James had heretofore existed as a kind of "secret Christian" (like Nicodemus and Joseph of Arimathea; John 3:1-2; 12:42; 19:38-39), one who confessed Jesus yet continued to live publicly as a prominent and exemplary Jew, or that his particular devotion to Jesus was entirely non-soteriological and fully in line with orthodox Judaism. When the crucial point presented itself, however, James offered a witness to Jesus that resulted in his martyrdom. Yet (as in Josephus's account) even then the leadership is not completely unified in its murder of James: as they are stoning him, "one of the priests of the sons of Rechab, the son of Rechabim, to whom the prophet Jeremiah bore witness, cried out saying, 'Stop! What are you doing? The Just One is praying for you'" (2.23.17). Again it is worth noting that Hegesippus seems to be confused, for Jeremiah does not suggest that the Rechabites were a priestly family. Further, the reference to "the sons of Rechab, the son of Rechabim" also seems confused, since "Rechabim" is the Hebrew plural and merely creates an unnecessary repetition.[121]

Hegesippus's account also offers insight into James' *independent* status vis-à-vis the early Christian movement. It is noteworthy that Hegesippus does not call James an apostle and makes no mention of his receipt of a resurrection appearance. Though we are told James' leadership was shared with the apostles, the latter set has no real presence in the Hegesippian narrative. James' actual colleagues are the Jewish leaders, who consider him the supremely authoritative "Just One" to whom all owe obedience. Further, his lifestyle is presented in accordance with an almost superhuman holiness that has nothing overtly Christian about it. As the narrative presents it, whatever witness he offered concerning Jesus before his martyrdom did not incite any concern on the part of the Jewish leadership; indeed, they appeal to him in the hopes of stopping the spread of an errant sect! This independence from Jesus himself is most clearly instantiated by the tradition that asserts the destruction of Jerusalem was punishment not for the murder of Jesus but for the murder of James.

Before moving on from Hegesippus, one final important point must be made. We are told that James' martyrdom was a fulfillment of "the scripture written in Isaiah: 'Let us remove the Just One, for he is unprofitable to us; therefore they shall eat the fruit of their works'" (2.23.15). This citation offers a second indication of Hegesippus's understanding of James' title "the Just": apart from his extraordinary

---

[121] Martin, xlix; K. Lake, *Eusebius I: The Ecclesiastical History, Books I–V* (LCL 153; Cambridge, Mass.: Harvard University Press, 1926), 174–75 n. 2.

piety, James is "the Just" because his death was the fulfillment of prophecies about a "Just One." Though Hegesippus attributes the prophetic text to Isaiah, only the latter half ("therefore they shall eat the fruit of their works") clearly derives from that prophet (Isa 3:10). The first phrase, ". . . the Just One, for he is unprofitable to us," is also found in Wisdom 2:12.

Isa 3:10 LXX: δήσωμεν τὸν δίκαιον, ὅτι δύσχρηστος ἡμῖν ἐστιν, τοίνυν τὰ γενήματα τῶν ἔργων αὐτῶν φάγονται.

Wis 2:12 LXX: ἐνεδρεύσωμεν τὸν δίκαιον, ὅτι δύσχρηστος ἡμῖν ἐστιν, καὶ ἐναντιοῦται τοῖς ἔργοις ἡμῶν.

Hist. Eccl. 2.23.25: ἄρωμεν τὸν δίκαιον, ὅτι δύσχρηστος ἡμῖν ἐστιν· τοίνυν τὰ γενήματα τῶν ἔργων αὐτῶν φάγονται.

Yet again, one wonders if Hegesippus is mistaken, for in the context of Isaiah 3, what is described is the collapse of Israel's leadership and their inability to guide the people of God. It makes no mention of killing the Just One but simply says, "Let us bind the Just One [δήσωμεν τὸν δίκαιον], for he is unprofitable to us; therefore they will eat the product of their works." It is the Wisdom passage, however, that offers a far closer reflection of what Hegesippus describes in his narrative and may be what he had in mind when he said that James' death was a fulfillment of Scripture. In that passage we find a Just One (2:10, 12, 18) who is hunted because of his opposition to the unrighteous (2:12); his words are tested (2:17); and he is condemned to a shameful death (2:20). This potential Wisdom connection will prove significant when we turn back to the letter at the end of this chapter.

The testimony of Hegesippus is extensive enough to merit its own brief summary, at least concerning three central aspects of his contribution to the second-century *Jakobusbild*. First, Hegesippus's picture of James' authority, related as it is to the depiction of his heroic piety, presents James as a high priestly figure whose unsurpassable devotion demands the obedience of the entire Jewish leadership. This is related, secondly, to Hegesippus's contribution to the tradition of James' relative independence from the earliest Christian mission: the description of his authority and piety is more reflective of an idealized Judaism than anything overtly Christian; he is not depicted as working within the embrace of the apostles; his colleagues are not Christians but Scribes and Pharisees; his defenders are Jewish priests; and though his ultimate confession of Christ led to his martyrdom, the tradition conveys the sense that his public Christology was entirely inoffensive to Jewish orthodoxy. Third, and finally, I refer once again to the preceding paragraph's discussion concerning the influence of Wisdom 2 on Hegesippus's narrative, since we will be returning to it in our discussion of the canonical letter of James.

Irenaeus of Lyon

We must briefly return to Irenaeus's relevant comments, for while he evidently either lacked or rejected the sort of James traditions encountered thus far, what little he did have to say about him will nevertheless offer something to our study of the "broadly Catholic" picture of James. Irenaeus appears to have rejected Jerusalem-centered traditions as being associated entirely with Jewish Christian heresies. For instance, he notes with disdain that the Ebionites are "so Judaic in their style of life that they even adore Jerusalem as if it were the house of God" (*Adv. Haer.* 1.26.2). By contrast, he makes his perspective clear that Jerusalem has only a past and a future role: once salvation history produced the "fruit" of Christ and the Apostles, Jerusalem was rightly forsaken by God (4.4.1). At the end of time it will be temporarily under the reign of the Antichrist (5.25.4; 30.4), until the Parousia, when Jerusalem will be redeemed and become a city of saints (5.34.4f.). Thus Jerusalem does not exist as an ecclesial city for Irenaeus as do Rome, Ephesus, and Smyrna. These cities are centers of ongoing apostolic witness, but Jerusalem in Irenaeus's day was "no longer useful for bringing forth fruit" (4.4.1–2).

As for James, Irenaeus had nothing to contribute beyond what he found in Acts 15 and Galatians 2. Yet even in this context we learn something about the function of James in Irenaeus's ecclesial circle. James plays no meaningful individual role in his writings (indeed, Irenaeus would have been profoundly skeptical of any claim for elevating one apostle over another), but as part of a collective including Peter and John he offered an important witness in support of Irenaeus's defense of the continuity of salvation history against those who would assert a division between the old and new covenants. His reading of Acts focuses on those passages that demonstrate how the God of Israel was at work in the earliest apostolic mission. After highlighting James' role at the Apostolic Council, he concludes: "From all these passages, then, it is evident that they [the disciples other than Paul] did not teach the existence of another Father, but gave the new covenant of liberty to those who had lately believed in God by the Holy Spirit" (3.12.14). Similarly, his discussion of Galatians 2 concludes, "And the apostles who were with James allowed the Gentiles to act freely, yielding us up to the Spirit of God. But they themselves, while knowing the same God, continued in the ancient observances" (3.12.15). It is on this basis that he defends Peter's withdrawal from Gentile fellowship, since it demonstrated his conviction that the Holy Spirit came from the same God that gave the Jews the Mosaic Law. It seems that Irenaeus rejected the sort of James traditions that saw him as a figure of ongoing apostolic authority, quite likely believing that both James and Jerusalem belonged to an earlier "fruitful" period that by his day had ceased to be productive.

Clement of Alexandria

Our final witness to second-century Catholic James traditions is Clement of Alexandria. As we saw in the first chapter, Clement's extant writings suggest that he had no knowledge of a letter by James; but, as it is made clear in the fragments from his *Outlines*, he was aware of traditions about James. The Eusebian passages are presented again for the benefit of the reader.

> Peter, James and John after the ascension of the Savior did not struggle for glory, because they had previously been given honor by the Savior, but chose James the Just as Bishop of Jerusalem. (*Hyp.* 6/*Hist. Eccl.* 2.1.3 [GCSNF 6–1.104; Lake, LCL 153.105])

> After the resurrection the Lord gave the tradition of knowledge to James the Just and John and Peter, these gave it to the other apostles and the other apostles to the seventy, of whom Barnabas also was one. (*Hyp.* 8/*Hist. Eccl.* 2.1.4 [GCSNF 6–1.104; LCL 153.105])

Unsurprisingly, James is three times *named* "the Just"; and though we are only dealing with fragments, it is nevertheless significant that there is no mention of James being the brother of the Lord. In fact, Clement only mentions James a few times in his available writings, and among these, it is only in the *Adumbrations* "commentary" on Jude that James' relationship with Jesus is discussed. The view of the *Protevangelium* can be detected in that text: Clement points out that Jude did not claim to be Jesus' brother, and he calls both of them "sons of Joseph" (*Adum.* 2 (GCS 3.206).[122]

Like Hegesippus, Clement's testimony appears to be focused on an explanation of James' great *authority*; yet Clement's information is rather different than that of Hegesippus. First, we are told that James was chosen to be Bishop of Jerusalem by the highest-ranking apostles, Peter and the brothers James and John. Second, we hear that James, along with Peter and John, was a recipient of post-resurrection "knowledge" from Jesus, which was in turn passed down to the rest of the church. Though Eusebius tells us that the first quote precedes the latter in the course of the *Hypotyposeis*, each relates a different time period for the events described: while the impartation of divine knowledge took place *after the resurrection*, the election to the bishopric took place *after the ascension*. Though Eusebius's presentation suggests that the election of James took place before his receipt of knowledge (implicitly subordinating our James to Peter, James, and John), Clement suggests that events took place in the reverse order; that is, James the Just, John, and Peter received knowledge from the resurrected Jesus, and sometime after this, James was elected Bishop of Jerusalem. It is also worth noting that though Peter is listed first in the former quotation, James is listed first in the latter. Thus, while Clement significantly diminishes James' *independent* status by drawing him more closely into the embrace of the larger apostolic circle, his autonomy as an authoritative recipient of resurrection knowledge is indirectly upheld.[123]

---

[122] See, further, *Strom.* 7.16.93 (SC 428.284), where it is made evident that Clement knows the *Protevangelium* (Hock, 11).

[123] It is tempting to agree with Painter's suggestion that Clement's placement of James within the larger apostolic embrace is an example of "a gnostic tradition transformed into an anti-gnostic weapon" (*Just James*, 116).

Apart from the minor differences in Clement's account of James' *murder*, the only matter of significance is the way in which his reference assumes that the manner of James' death is as well known as that of the other James whose death is mentioned in Acts 12.

Summary of the Later "Broadly Catholic" Jakobusbild

In summary, the *Gospel According to the Hebrews* and Hegesippus make reference to the fact that James is Jesus' brother, but they both quite clearly *name* James "the Just." Clement seems to know him only as "the Just," and his comments suggest he accepted the position of the influential *Protevangelium* that denied any blood relationship between the two. All four sources then witness to the passing of the "brother" tradition that was so dominant in the first century, in favor of the "Just" tradition that is nowhere present among our first-century texts. James' *authority* is unambiguously high in these texts, particularly in the *Gospel According to the Hebrews*, which plainly infers that he is first in priority among the apostles. Hegesippus takes this even farther; he does little to contrast James with the apostles, yet here more than anywhere else he is a larger than life figure, a kind of super-pious high priest of the Messiah, the Just One to whom all owe obedience. Clement's portrayal of James, while nowhere near as grandiose as that of Hegesippus, is likewise intended to present him as a leader in the company of the other apostles, and by doing so, to plant him firmly within the apostolic succession of the church. Yet even in that frame he is presented as having an authority that appears to have given him precedence even over Peter. Though the *Gospel According to the Hebrews* offers some hint of James' *piety*, again it is Hegesippus who presents us with the image of James as a man of extraordinary holiness, leading the Jerusalem church as a kind of OT hero figure. The first-century sense of James' *independence* is intensified in these later Catholic texts: the *Protevangelium* and the *Gospel According to the Hebrews* make no mention of any other apostles; Hegesippus mentions other apostles but presents James working independently of them among the other leaders of the Jews; and though Clement places James firmly within the embrace of the other apostles, it is still implied that James' leadership was due to his receipt of a resurrection appearance. Finally, only Hegesippus and Clement make mention of his *murder*, and the broad details of their accounts are similar. Yet Clement only refers to James' death as a means of identifying him; Hegesippus, on the other hand, presents a fully developed, hagiographical account of James' death as a martyr.

Later Mixed Material

The Gospel of Thomas

The *Gospel of Thomas*[124] is a collection of Jesus' sayings and contains very little nar-

[124] Text and translation by B. Layton, *Nag Hammadi Codex II.2–7*, vol. 1 (NHS 20; Leiden: Brill, 1989). Dating *Thomas* is difficult due to its highly redacted character; H.-Ch. Puech ("Gnostic Gospels and Related Documents," in *New Testament Apocrypha*, ed. E. Hennecke and W. Schneemelcher, trans. R. McL. Wilson [Philadelphia: Westminster,

rative from his life and ministry. Logion 12 is of particular interest for our investigation of James traditions.

> The disciples said to Jesus, "We know that you will depart from us. Who is to be our leader?" Jesus said to them, "Wherever you are, you are to go to James the Just, for whose sake heaven and earth came into being" (Logion 12; II.34.25–30).

As in most of the other later sources, so once again we find James *named* "the Just," and there is no mention whatsoever of his being Jesus' brother. This, as we have come to expect from our analysis of the broadly Catholic material, is typical of later James traditions. While some earlier sources refrained from explaining the path of James' ascent to *authority* in the Jerusalem church, *Thomas* makes it explicit: before his death, Christ himself ordained James the leader of the apostles. The phrase "for whose sake heaven and earth came into being" has clear roots in second temple and rabbinic Judaism: it is applied to Israel (*4 Ezra* 6:55; 7:11; *Gen. R.* 1.4), to the Righteous (*2 Bar.* 14:19) and the Torah (*As. Mos.* 1.12), as well as Abraham, Moses, David, and the Messiah (*2 Bar.* 15:7; 21:24; *Gen. R.* 1.7; 12:9; *b San.* 98b); thus we find it applied especially to those exceptionally important individuals who functioned as mediators in salvation history.[125] Such a phrase also suggests something quite important about James' *piety*, since its application to individuals is nearly always related to that individual's exemplary Torah observance.[126]

Its application to James reveals a good deal about his stature in the communities that championed him. The tradition may have competed with Matthew's elevation of Peter as the foundation of the church, the one who possessed the keys to the kingdom of heaven and had the power to bind and to loose in heaven and on earth (Matt 16:17-19). Having said that, the difference between Matthew and *Thomas* on this score could not be more striking. In Matthew, Peter is left in charge, but his authority is provisional in that it is grounded in the ongoing presence of the resurrected Jesus, who remains "with you always, to the end of the age" (28:20).

1963], 1.305) warns, "It is hazardous, and probably indeed misguided, to seek to visualize its original form and determine its origin," and cautiously places its earliest redaction to around 140. Layton (*The Gnostic Scriptures* [ABRL; New York: Doubleday, 1987], 377) notes that while many scholars place it in the mid-second century, "one qualified expert" recently dated the text to the first century. J. D. Crossan (*The Historical Jesus: The Life of a Mediterranean Jewish Peasant* [Edinburgh: T&T Clark, 1991], 427ff.) divides *Thomas* into two layers of tradition, the earlier being composed in the 50s under James' authority, from which Logion 12 derives. After James' death, a second layer was added under "the Thomas authority" as early as the 60s. While we cannot enter fully into the debate, our research suggests that a first-century date is too early, for as we have seen, the tradition of naming James "the Just" is found nowhere among our first-century sources and seems to be a later phenomenon, as is the failure to mention anything about James' blood relation to Jesus. Further, the appellation "for whose sake heaven and earth came into being" is reflective of the high regard for James that is less apparent in the earlier James traditions.

[125] See esp. Pratscher, 154–56; cf. Martin, xliv; Painter, *Just James*, 163 n. 10.
[126] Pratscher, 155.

By contrast, the *Thomas* logion underscores Jesus' *absence*: "We know that you will depart from us," say the disciples to Jesus. "Who is to be our leader?" Like John the Baptist, Jesus points the way to one coming after him: "Wherever you are, you are to go to James the Just, for whose sake heaven and earth came into being." James is apparently not one of "the disciples" who ask the question, pointing once again to the tradition of his *independence* from the other members of the Christian mission. His presentation as the one on whose behalf the divine act of creation itself was undertaken seems to place James as an authority just below Jesus himself; he is Jesus' deputy, functioning as Jesus' replacement.

The Pseudo-Clementine Recognitions[127]

Though the extant version of the *Pseudo-Clementine* literature is to be dated no earlier than the fourth century, it is widely held that the section *Recognitions* 1.27–71 derives from an earlier "Jewish-Christian" source, to be dated somewhere in the second century.[128] Though James is *named* "the Lord's brother" elsewhere in the *Recognitions* (4.35.1 [GCS 51.164]), this older section makes use of neither "the brother" nor "the Just" as a title. Instead, James is referred to as "the Bishop" of the Jerusalem church (1.66:2, 5; 70:3), and, in contrast to Caiaphas the "chief of priests," James is called the "chief of bishops" or the "Archbishop" (1.68), a title which corresponds quite nicely with Hegesippus' depiction of James as a high priest.[129] Such a title indicates the extremely high view of his *authority* found throughout the Pseudo-Clementine literature. Like the *Gospel of Thomas* (and against Hegesippus and Clement), the *Recognitions* make it clear that James was "ordained by the Lord" to leadership of the Jerusalem church (1.43). He receives reports from the twelve and calls them to gather for debate against the Jewish leadership (1.44). It is here that James' *independence* is made evident, as he is surrounded by apostles and yet consistently separated from them (cf. 1.40.4; 1.43.3–44.1). In the Pseudo-Clementine material deemed later than the second century, James' superiority over all the apostles is intensified: he commands Peter to do his bidding (1.72), Peter calls him "the Lord and bishop of the holy church," and Clement calls him "the Lord and bishop of bishops, who rules Jerusalem, the holy church of the Hebrews, and the churches everywhere excellently founded by the providence of God."[130] Still other passages proclaim James to be the chief teaching authority of the church, and it is only by his imprimatur that a person is authorized to preach the gospel (for example, *Rec.* 4.35.1 [GCS 51.164]).

---

[127] Critical text by B. Rehm and F. Paschke, *Die Pseudoklementinen II: Rekognitionen* (GCS 51; Berlin: Akademie-Verlag, 1965), 23–49; Eng. trans. and critical analysis by F. S. Jones, *An Ancient Jewish-Christian Source on the History of Christianity: Pseudo-Clementine Recognitions 1.27–71* (Atlanta: Scholars Press, 1995).

[128] See the extensive review of research in Jones, 1–38.

[129] Jones (104) notes that while the Latin has "chief of bishops," the Syriac reads "Archbishop."

[130] See the prescripts to the epistles of Peter to James, and that of Clement to James (GCS 51.375).

He is (unsurprisingly) depicted as being an untiring advocate for the conversion of the Jewish people, and here we find yet another instance of the traditional notion that James had "inside support" among the Jewish leadership: in this case it is Gamaliel, described as a "chief of the people" who was "secretly our brother in the faith, but by our advice remained among them" (1.65). Gamaliel's words introduce those of James, who in his seven-day discourse to the Jewish Leadership (1.66–69) insists that proof of Jesus' messiahship must be based in Scripture:

> The chief of the priests asked of James, the chief of the bishops, that the discourse concerning Christ should only be drawn from the Scriptures; "that we may know," said he, "whether Jesus is the true Christ or not." Then said James: "We must first inquire from what Scriptures we are especially to derive our discussion." Then he, with difficulty, at length overcome by reason, answered, that it must be derived from the law; and afterwards he made mention also of the prophets. . . . And when he had discussed most fully concerning the law, and had, by a most clear exposition, brought into light whatever things are in it concerning Christ, he showed by most abundant proofs that Jesus is the Christ, and that in Him are fulfilled all the prophecies which related to His humble advent. (1.68–69)

His reading of Scripture proved so persuasive that "all the people and the high priest" hastened "straightway to receive baptism" (1.70). As in the Acts of the Apostles, so also here James is depicted as an authoritative interpreter of Israel's scriptures for the defense and governance of the early church.

Of course the people do not make it to the point of baptism in the *Recognitions*, because a "hostile person" (Saul of Tarsus?) enters the temple leading a mob of people intent on disrupting the evangelization. Though James attempts to reason with the hostile leader, he cannot restrain the man, who in turn grabs a brand from the altar and begins a violent riot. In the process James is thrown down from the highest flight of stairs; but amazingly, he is not actually *murdered*. As in Hegesippus's version of events, James survives the fall; but unlike Hegesippus's account, James survives in the *Recognitions*, and goes on to rule over the ongoing expansion of the church from his throne in Jerusalem.

Summary of the Later "Mixed" Material Jakobusbild

Most of what we encounter in this "mixed" material offers confirmation for what we have come to expect in later James material, so my summary will be brief. *Thomas* maintains our expectations for James' *name*: he is titled "the Just" and there is no mention of his being Jesus' brother. The *Recognitions*, by contrast, does not name him according to our expectations, though the title offered, "chief of bishops," corresponds quite nicely with Hegesippus's depiction of James as a high priest. His exceedingly high *authority* comes likewise as no surprise, save one striking difference: in these two texts, *Jesus himself ordains James* to leadership over the apostles. Both texts link his *piety* with careful adherence to the Mosaic Law. In each he is *independent* of the other apostles insofar as he is clearly not numbered among them but differentiated from them as their divinely ordained supreme leader. Finally, his *murder* is not related in the short *Thomas* logion, and while the *Recognitions* is clearly in contact with the same martyrdom traditions as Hegesippus and Clement, it varies greatly: the James of the *Recognitions* is too resilient to kill, for he lives on, ruling the world-wide church from his throne in Jerusalem. In conclusion, it is important to draw our attention to one particular aspect of these materials: in contrast to the Catholic sources, here one encounters the unabashed elevation of a single apostle to a position of supreme authority. As we saw, the Catholic emphasis on a harmonious, plural apostolic authority revealed a tension of sorts with the tradition of James' independent authority. In these "mixed" materials, however, there is little tension at all; and as the gnostic James material will demonstrate, the further one drifts away from the Catholic position, the more one encounters this sort of solitary apostolic elevation.

Broadly Gnostic Material

The Apocryphon of James[131]

This text presents us with a new type of James tradition, that of the revelatory discourse.[132] James himself is the author of the text (1.1–18), which is presented in the form of a letter that narrates an encounter of James and Peter with the resurrected Christ. Jesus does most of the talking, and the discourse is punctuated throughout by questions from these two disciples. Though Jesus calls both James and Peter "my brothers" (9.10), James' own status as Jesus' brother is not directly referred to, and he is nowhere *named* "the Just." He is simply "James." Though the document depicts both James and Peter receiving a direct revelation of higher gnosis from Jesus (which corresponds with Paul's highlighting of these two in 1 Cor 15), James is clearly shown to be the more *authoritative* disciple: he is the author of the text (1.1); he refers to a previous book containing knowledge Jesus revealed to him alone (1.28–35), to which Jesus himself refers on two occasions (8.30-36; 13.36f.); words of Peter from the canonical gospels are put in James' mouth (4.25f.); where he and Peter are mentioned together, James is always named first; and James is the one to direct instruction to the other disciples (16.7). In this manner he is cast in the guise of the truly gnostic leader of the apostles: "Blessed are those," he says, "who will be saved through faith in this discourse" (1.26–28).

---

[131] R. Cameron's historical and tradition-critical analysis of the text (*Sayings Traditions in the Apocryphon of James* [Philadelphia: Fortress, 1984]) leads him to place *Apocryphon of James* somewhere between the end of the first and the middle of the second century (123). His judgment is followed in the critical edition of the text produced by D. Kirchner, *Epistula Jacobi Apocrypha: Die zweite Schrift aus Nag-Hammadi-Codex I* (Berlin: Academie-Verlag, 1989), 6; Engl. trans. J. M. Robinson, *The Nag Hammadi Library in English* (Leiden: Brill, 1977), 29–36.

[132] Some have debated whether or not the *Apocryphon* should be considered a gnostic document at all, especially in light of 1.6.1–7, where Jesus says, "none will be saved unless they believe in my cross." Yet the presence of other evidently gnostic features make it acceptable to place the document in the "broadly gnostic" camp. See Puech's discussion in Hennecke-Schneemelcher (1.333–38).

Once again, the elevation of James presents him as an *independent* figure. For instance, since he has been set apart in his reception of the revelation, he asks the reader to be similarly set apart in his or her transmission of the discourse: "Take care not to recount this book to many—this which the Savior did not desire to recount to all of us" (1.20–25). The narrative begins with James and the twelve sitting down to write books about Jesus, "remembering what the Savior had said to each of them, whether secretly or openly" (2.7–15). Suddenly Jesus appears and asks James and Peter to come with him "in order that I may fill them." The other disciples are told to get back to their writing (2.17–39); thus they are depicted as writing books based on memories of the historical Jesus' teaching. That Jesus selects James and Peter from among them to be "filled" with resurrection teaching plainly implies that the memorial writings of the other apostles are "empty." After a lengthy teaching (2.40–15.5), James and Peter return to the remaining disciples to relate what the Lord had said. The other disciples believe but become jealous (16.3–5), so James sends them all away to another place, while he himself goes to Jerusalem to wait and pray, that he might "obtain a portion with the beloved who are to be revealed" (16.5–11).

Finally, it should be noted that the *Apocryphon of James* offers no substantive mention of James' *murder*. Jesus speaks of James and Peter's coming sufferings, saying that they will be "shut up in prison, and condemned unlawfully, and crucified without reason, and buried shamefully, as was I myself" (5.10–35; 6.1–20). Thus there is in this description no indication that the author was aware of the other known martyr-traditions associated with James.

The First Apocalypse of James[133]

This document, called the *"First" Apocalypse of James*, is one of two Nag Hammadi texts titled simply *Apocalypse of James*. In contrast to the *Apocryphon*, here the revelatory dialogue comes to James alone: "James, after these things I shall reveal to you everything, not for your sake alone but for the sake of the unbelief of men, so that faith may exist in them" (29.19–25). Most of the document is made up of typically arcane gnostic revelatory material, but along the way we learn much about the "gnostic" image of James. As we have come to expect, James is referred to as Jesus' brother but *named* "the Just." The materiality of their "brother" relationship, however, is denied: "For not without reason have I called you my brother, although you are not my brother materially" (24.14–15). We find in this text an explanation for the title, "the Just," though an unfortunate lacuna makes it difficult to completely understand. As James is in prayer, the Lord appears to him; James stops praying to embrace him and kiss him, and Jesus says this in response:

---

[133] Critical text by A. Veilleux, *La Première Apocalypse de Jacques et la Seconde Apocalypse de Jacques* (BCNH 17; Québec: Les Presses de l'Université Laval, 1986); Engl. trans. Robinson, 242–48. Though Veilleux does not assign a fixed date to the two documents, he places them well within the second century in his insistence that they both reflect the teaching of the Valentinian school, and in particular, the branch of that school represented by the *Excerpts from Theodotus*.

The just . . . is his servant. Therefore your name is "James the Just." You see how you will become sober when you see me. And you stopped this prayer. Now since you are a just man of God, you have embraced and kissed me. Truly I say to you that you have stirred up great anger and wrath against yourself. But this has happened so that these others might come to be (31.30–32.10).

Though the passage is far from straightforward, the title "Just" is evidently related to being a "servant," and to having a particular attentiveness to and intimacy with Christ, which results in the opposition and anger of others. Yet this opposition is somehow redemptive and happens "so that these others might come to be."

As for his *authority*, James is presented as residing in Jerusalem (25.15), and it is suggested that he is the leader of the apostles (42.20–24), but the focus of his authority is maintained throughout by the repeated reference to his having been chosen to be a revealer figure (for example, 25.6; 26.8–10; 29.19–26). His authority is related to his presentation as one whose *piety* is related to his suffering, which is certainly the dominant theme of the text. In this way James is presented as a kind of mirror figure for Jesus: he is told that his own suffering and death, like Jesus', will be redemptive for himself (29.12–13; 32.28) as well as for others (32.12). In similar fashion, Jesus, who identifies himself as the "image of Him Who Is" (25.1), tells James that his death will enable him to reach "Him Who Is" and will transform James from his fleshly state into "the One Who Is" (27.10). Even James' actions emphasize this "mirror" role as he teaches his own disciples on a mountain, eventually dismissing them to be in prayer, "as was his custom" (30.13–31.1).[134]

It is worth noting that James is entirely *independent* in this text. Disciples of Jesus are mentioned (36.2; 38.16–17), but they play no significant role in the discourse. James resides in Jerusalem, but Jerusalem and its associated apostles are depicted in a negative light: James must rebuke the disciples to "cast out of them contentment concerning the way of knowledge" (42.20–24). Likewise, powers of evil are associated with Judaism and Jerusalem, the city that "always gives the cup of bitterness to the sons of light" (25.15–29), the very cup from which James himself must drink (30.13f; 32.13–22). Further, as in the testimony of Hegesippus, there is a connection made between James' fate and that of Jerusalem: "When you depart, immediately war will be made with this land. Weep, then, for him who dwells in Jerusalem" (36.16–19).

Finally, in distinction from the *Apocryphon*, this text speaks quite directly of James' *murder*. Early in the document, James' own redemptive suffering is predicted (25.13-21), and later, his opponents are described as a "multitude" led by "three who will seize you, they who sit as toll collectors. Not only do they demand toll, but they also take away souls by theft" (33.1–10). These "toll collectors" are associated with the twelve apostles (36.2). After a rather substantial lacuna at the end of the document, we find ourselves in the middle of what appears to be a description of his trial and death.

[134] M. Franzmann, *Jesus in the Nag Hammadi Writings* (Edinburgh: T&T Clark, 1996), 177.

And the majority of them . . . when they saw, the messenger took in. . . . The others . . . said, ". . . him from this earth. For he is not worthy of life." These, then, were afraid. They arose, saying, "We have no part in this blood, for a just man will perish through injustice." James departed so that . . . look . . . for we . . . him (43.7–44.9).

The content is difficult to decipher, but two points in particular stand out. First, the phrase, ". . . him from this earth; for his is not worthy of life" sounds very similar to Hegesippus's claim that James' murder fulfilled the prophecy of Isaiah, "Let us take the Just One, for he is unprofitable to us" (*Hist. Eccl.* 2.23.15). Second, the subsequent quotation ("we have no part in this [man's] blood . . .") indicates yet another example of the tradition (found already in Josephus, Hegesippus, and the *Recognitions*) that James had supporters in the midst of his murderous opponents.

The Second Apocalypse of James[135]

It is not without reason that this Apocalypse has been identified as the "Second": where the first stresses the period prior to the martyrdom of James and focuses on predictions of his death, the second describes the suffering and death of James in detail. Further, where the first presented Jesus as the primary speaker, James does most of the talking in the second. He is repeatedly *named* "the Just." The text begins, "This is the discourse that James the Just spoke in Jerusalem, which Mareim, one of the priests, wrote. He had told it to Theuda, the father of the Just One, since he was a relative of his" (44.13–19). Apparently James' father is not Joseph but "Theuda," a relative of "Mareim" the priest. Still, James' status as brother of the Lord is in some sense maintained:

Once when I was sitting deliberating, he opened the door. That one whom you hated and persecuted came in to me. He said to me, "Hail, my brother; my brother, hail." As I raised my face to stare at him, [my] mother said to me, "Do not be frightened, my son, because he said 'My brother' to you. For you [pl.] were nourished with this same milk. Because of this he calls me 'My mother'. For he is not a stranger to us. He is your step-brother." (50.5–23)

Obviously the author is aware of the "brother" tradition, though it is not clearly explained how James and Jesus are "step-brothers." The text offers further information about "the Just" title: after speaking of the Lord's role in judgment, James says, "I am the Just One, and I do [not] judge. I am not a master, then, but I am a helper" (59.21–24). Again, as in the *First Apocalypse*, the title "Just" is related to being a servant or a "helper." Later he says, "The Lord has taken you captive from the Lord, having closed your ears, that they may not hear the sound of my word; yet you will be able to pay heed in your hearts, and you will call me 'the Just One'" (60.5–12). It seems then that James' role as revealer of Christ makes him a non-judging "helper," and it is on that basis that he is to be known as "the Just."

[135] Critical text by Veilleux; Eng. trans. Robinson, 249–55. See the above note (133) under the *First Apocalypse* for a discussion of dating.

In comparison with the *First Apocalypse*, the James of the *Second Apocalypse* is accorded an even higher *authoritative* status in his depiction as a gnostic Revealer and Redeemer. The *Second Apocalypse* depicts James teaching in a sitting position "from above the fifth flight of steps, which is highly esteemed" (45.23–25). Later we are informed that the location described is in the temple (61.21–22). In contrast to the *Pseudo-Clementine* and Hegesippian accounts of James' teaching in the temple, here his words are unmistakably gnostic in character:

> I am he who received revelation from the Pleroma of Imperishability. [I am] he who was first summoned by him who is great, and who obeyed the Lord—he who passed through the worlds. (46.6–13)

> Now again am I rich in knowledge and I have a unique understanding, which was produced only from above. . . . That which was revealed to me was hidden from everyone and shall (only) be revealed through him. (47.7–19)

Later Jesus is reported to have told James,

> I wish to reveal through you and the spirit of power, in order that he might reveal to those who are yours. And those who wish to enter, and who seek to walk in the way that is before the door, open the good door through you. And they follow you; they enter and you escort them inside, and give a reward to each one who is ready for it. . . . You are an illuminator and a redeemer of those who are mine, and now of those who are yours. You shall reveal [to them]; you shall bring good among them all. (55.3–25)

James is thus the "escort" who guides the gnostic through the door of the heavenly kingdom. Again it is possible to see in Jesus' designation of James as "the door" a contrast with Peter, whom Jesus called "the rock" and the keeper of the keys of heaven (Matt 16:19). And as we have seen before, so also here the death of James is associated with the destruction of Jerusalem; only here, the semi-divine James himself pronounces the judgment of "doom to destruction and derision" against Jerusalem (60.13–24).

As in the other two gnostic texts, there is little specific information about James' *piety* in the *Second Apocalypse*. We find him associated with the temple in his teaching, as well as by the note in the prescript that his father Theuda was a relative of priests, but these issues are secondary at best behind the central focus on James' role as gnostic Revealer and Redeemer. The focus is so strong on this role that the document includes no mention at all of any other leaders of the Jesus movement. James acts entirely *independently* of any other disciples, standing alone in the revelatory spotlight.

After James' revelation is complete, we are told that the people were left disturbed and unpersuaded (61.1–4). Eventually the priests turn against him and he is *murdered*. Mareim, the priestly scribe of the discourse, narrates the scene to us:

> And I was with the priests and revealed nothing of the relationship, since all of them were saying with one voice, "Come, let us stone the Just One." And they

arose, saying, "Yes, let us kill this man, that he may be taken from our midst; for he will be of no use to us." And they were there and found him standing beside the columns of the temple beside the mighty corner stone. And they decided to throw him down from the height, and they cast him down. . . . They seized him and struck him as they dragged him upon the ground. They stretched him out and placed a stone on his abdomen. They all placed their feet on him, saying "You have erred!" Again they raised him up, since he was alive, and made him dig a hole. They made him stand in it. After having covered him up to his abdomen, they stoned him in this manner. (61.9–62.12)

The many similarities to other martyrdom sources are undeniable. Further, the figure of Mareim is continuous with the tradition of James having a supporter within the Jewish leadership. In contrast, however, to both the protesting Pharisees in Josephus and the priestly supporter "Rechab" in Hegesippus, the insider Mareim of the *Second Apocalypse* remains silent during James' murder. The words of the priests ("let us kill this man, that he be taken from our midst; for he will be of no use to us") are again reminiscent of the similar phrases in the *First Apocalypse* (". . . him from this earth; for he is not worthy of life") and Hegesippus ("let us take the Just one, for he is unprofitable to us). Finally, the *Second Apocalypse* closes with James' lengthy dying prayer, in which he asks God for resurrection and deliverance from judgment, the "humiliating enemy," and the "sinful flesh" (62.12f.). This should be contrasted to the dying prayer in Hegesippus, in which he prays for the forgiveness of his enemies.

Summary of the "Broadly Gnostic" Jakobusbild

Though the *Apocryphon* makes no mention of any brother relationship and offers no traditional *name* beyond the simple "James," the *First* and *Second Apocalypse* assume a brother relationship (of some kind) and explicitly call him "the Just." In these latter texts the title is elaborated by appeal to his status as a revelatory "servant" or "helper" of Jesus. James is colossally *authoritative* in the gnostic material, appearing in all three texts as an almost supernatural Revealer and Redeemer figure. In contrast to other sources, these texts portray his superiority over the other apostles without clearly ranking him with a title such as leader, archbishop, or chief priest. It is noteworthy that the gnostic texts do not focus on James' piety in the way other sources do. Though the *First Apocalypse* presented him as a kind of righteous sufferer, the *Apocryphon* and the *Second Apocalypse* offer little to nothing beyond the fact that the *Second Apocalypse* associates him with the temple. In these texts James functions *independently*, such that no other apostolic leader can share the limelight. The other disciples play little to no role here; when they do appear they are either shown to be empty in comparison to James' fullness (*Apocryphon*), unworthy of divine gnosis, or in need of his rebuke (*First Apocalypse*). In the case of the *Second Apocalypse* especially, one notes the tendency shared with Josephus and Hegesippus associating James more with organized Judaism than Christianity. Similarly, all three of these texts present someone within the Jewish leadership supporting James against his murderous oppressors. This *murder* was not depicted in the *Apocryphon*, though it was briefly described in the *First Apocalypse* and elaborated on in the *Second*. In those texts that relate the event, his death is depicted as being redemptive for himself as well as others.

2FIRST- AND SECOND-CENTURY JAMES TRADITIONS:
SUMMARY AND CONCLUSIONS

Let us conclude this section by summarizing the traditions surrounding James in the first two centuries of the church. In the first century, the tradition of his being *named* "the Brother of the Lord" was dominant (NT, Josephus). In the second century, James' status as "brother" developed into a point of contention due to the popularity of the sort of teachings promoted in the *Protevangelium*. "Gnostic" and "Jewish-Christian" sources continued to make use of it, but Catholics showed their concern for the title by either ignoring it or undermining it. The title that predominated in the second century was "the Just," being found in six of the nine primary sources investigated. This title is nowhere to be found in the first century. It is related to his being a "servant" or "helper" (*1* and *2 Apoc*), to his intimate openness to Christ (*1 Apoc.*), to his role as a righteous sufferer (Hegesippus, *2 Apoc.*), and to his legendary piety (*G. Thom.*, Hegesippus).

As far as his *authority* is concerned, James was known in the first century as the leader of the Jerusalem church (NT). In the second century, however, this developed into more official and elaborate roles. In almost every arena his stature grew to immense proportions, being cast as the chief of bishops (*Ps. Clem.*), a high priest (Hegesippus), first among the apostles (*G. Heb.*), their sole leader (*G. Thom.*, *Ps. Clem.*), and the Revealer and Redeemer (*Apocr.*, *1–2 Apoc.*). In some of these texts, James is ordained to this position by the direction of the Lord himself (*Ps. Clem.*, *G. Thom.*), while others offer explanations that attempt to place him within the fold of the early apostolate (Hegesippus, Clement).

We saw that traditions surrounding James' *piety* were limited in the first century to his being a Torah-observant Jew concerned that Israel's scriptures continue to shape the theology and practice of the nascent church. But like depictions of his authority, depictions of his piety were also intensified in the second-century sources. Foremost among these is Hegesippus, who accentuated this feature more than any other in his presentation of James. For Hegesippus, James is a supremely righteous figure styled after the heroes of the OT. He was known less for the content of his teaching than for the holiness of his life. By contrast, the gnostics tended in the reverse direction, avoiding elaborate depictions of his lifestyle in favor of the revelatory content of his teachings.

The tradition of James' *independent* status was continuous through the first and second centuries. This was manifest in a number of features from the first-century sources: We saw that he was not a true believer during Jesus' lifetime; he was not a member of the twelve; his apostolicity was uncertain; his ascent to leadership was unexplained; and he was indirectly associated with Jewish groups such as "the circumcision" and the Pharisees. By the second century this independence required explanation. The gnostics did so by appeal to his capacity as a revealer of divine truth; on this basis he either stood at odds with the other apostles (*Apocr.*, *1 Apoc.*) or had little to do with them at all (*2 Apoc.*). Other groups explained his leadership by saying that the Lord himself ordained him to the position (*G. Thom.*, *Ps. Clem.*). In contrast to the heterodox tendency to elevate particular apostles, the Catholic sources consistently reflect a concern to locate him more firmly within the apostolic succession to avoid any sense of competition. On this basis Hegesippus simply says that leadership of the Jerusalem church "passed to James the brother of the Lord, together with the apostles"; Clement reflects an even greater catholicizing trend in his contention that it was Peter and the brothers James and John who chose James to be leader. Even then, a number of other "independent" traditions persisted: For instance, that he had supporters within the Jewish leadership (Hegesippus, *Ps. Clem.*, *2 Apoc.*), and that he was seen to work in isolation from the other apostles (*G. Heb.*, Hegesippus, *1–2 Apoc.*).

We have also seen that James' independence extended in some way to Jesus himself. We have noted that Josephus's presentation leaves the reader with the sense that James is as important if not the more important figure. In some second century sources James is presented as the one who takes Jesus' place (*G. Thom.*), and indeed, in certain cases his authority seems to overshadow that of Jesus (*1–2 Apoc.*). In others his particular confession of Jesus did not threaten his placement within the collegium of the Jewish leadership. Indeed it is most significant that James' supporters are generally found therein (*Ps. Clem.*, Hegesippus, *2 Apoc.*). His title points to his exemplary Judaism and does nothing to directly associate him with Christianity. In many of these writings, James comes across as a supremely pious Jew who also just happens to be a Christian.

Finally, it was also known in both centuries that James was *murdered*. Josephus is our only first century witness to this event, though it is a common feature of the second century narratives. He may have been thrown down from a high place (*Ps. Clem.*, *2 Apoc.*, Hegesippus, Clement), stoned (Josephus, *2 Apoc.*, Hegesippus), crushed (*2 Apoc.*), and/or beaten to death (Hegesippus, Clement). Some understood his death in relation to the destruction of Jerusalem (*1–2 Apoc.*, Hegesippus).

Before we move on to our analysis of the canonical letter, one final important point must be made about this second century material. If James were, in fact, an early letter, should we not expect to find some indication of its availability somewhere in the midst of all these sources? Yet we find no indication that the authors of these texts had any knowledge of the canonical letter. If James were in fact available and authoritative by the second century, is there not a good chance that it would have served as a model for subsequent James-oriented writings seeking to gain acceptance? The other known "letter" of James, the *Apocryphon*, could not be more different than the canonical letter.[136] Compare by contrast the use of Pauline letters as source material for the pseudepigraphic *Letter of Paul to the Laodiceans*: it is little more than a cut and paste version of Galatians and

---

[136] Laws, 41–42.

Philippians.[137] Similarly, the third-century apocryphal correspondence between Paul and Seneca is clearly dependent on 1 Corinthians in a number of places.[138] An analysis of the *Acts of Peter* reveals a similar dependence on the Petrine letters.[139] The lack of attestation for James in the second century is thus an even more damaging blow to the defenders of authenticity than most are willing to admit, for amidst an explosion of contemporary interest in him, neither orthodox nor heterodox churchmen show any awareness of it. When one considers the overwhelming fame of the man in this period, it is improbable that an authentic, orthodox letter would have remained hidden, ignored, or lost for nearly two centuries. It would have been far too valuable a resource.

The Canonical Letter and the Later James Tradition

According to my introductory comments, pseudonymous authors appealed to various biographical, historical, literary, and theological "stabilizing elements" associated with their ostensible author in order to ensure an effective apostolic actualization for a new generation. Does the canonical letter of James betray any awareness of the particular "stabilizing elements" of James the Just that rose to the fore in the second century? According to Ward,

> the Letter of James does not fit into any of the trajectories we have traced. Either it came from James of Jerusalem and thus supplements what we know of the "historical James," or it represents a later, independent development which had no interest in James as apostle, recipient of a resurrection appearance, brother of Jesus, leader of the Jerusalem *ekklesia*, or martyr.[140]

Nevertheless, in addition to the numerous features of the letter that point to a later date, I am able to note three potential points of contact with the second century *Jakobusbild* that stand out as significant.

James' Name and Murder:
You Have Condemned, You Have Killed the Just One

As for the name presented in the letter, we note immediately that our author is not identified in the prescript by any of the titles we have come to know, such as "the Just" or "the Brother" or "the Bishop."[141] If this text were written in the first century, why does James not identify himself as "the brother of the Lord" as he is

---

[137] Hennecke-Schneemelcher, 2.128–32.
[138] Hennecke-Schneemelcher, 2.133–41.
[139] The linkages are too numerous to mention here; see the list in Bauckham, *Jude, 2 Peter*, 149.
[140] Ward, "James of Jerusalem," 812.
[141] P. Davids ("Palestinian Traditions," 34 n. 5) insists its simplicity fits a first-century *Sitz im Leben*.

known in almost every other first-century source? It has been suggested that his failure to do so was due to his modesty,[142] his awareness that knowledge of Jesus in the flesh was "no longer important,"[143] or similarly, his recognition that a physical relationship to Jesus was not a valid basis for authority in the earliest church.[144] What is generally not considered is the controversial nature of this claim among second-century Catholics schooled in the *Herrenbruder* teachings promoted in texts like the *Protevangelium*. Such a title simply could not be used in a second-century text that sought acceptance in Catholic circles. Post-*Protevangelium*, James had to be championed under a different name.

As we have seen, the title chosen was "the Just One." For defenders of authenticity, the absence of this title in the prescript is just as much a detriment to a second century provenance as the absence of "the brother of the Lord" damages an early one. But is there no "Just One" in the canonical letter of James? In one of the final passages of the letter (5:1–6), the author condemns the rich for their trust in riches, and the related abuse of laborers and harvesters through the withholding of their pay, and comes to a climax in v. 6, saying, "You have condemned, you have killed the Just one; he does not resist you" (κατεδικάσατε, ἐφονεύσατε τὸν δίκαιον, οὐκ ἀντιτάσσεται ὑμῖν). Two factors in particular make this verse a rather awkward transition. First, it is difficult to see how the withholding of wages described in vv. 1–5 constitutes the condemnation and murder described in v. 6. Some have tried to overcome this by suggesting the phrase is symbolic, yet this is highly unlikely on semantic grounds, for the language is suggestive of a corrupt legal process: καταδικάζω is forensic in nature, suggesting "the condemnation of the innocent poor by an abuse of justice" (*TDNT* 3.621–22);[145] when φονεύω is added, we see that we are dealing not with a lawful execution but an unjust judicial murder.[146] The letter has already spoken of people being dragged into court (2:6), but how does the withholding of a laborer's wages amount to a literal judicial murder? The second factor that makes v. 6 an awkward transition is the singularity of ὁ δίκαιος. In context the accused as well as the abused are plural. Who then is represented by the singular ὁ δίκαιος in this verse?

The widely held answer to the question proposes that ὁ δίκαιος in context is designed to function as a "collective singular" as it is occasionally found in the OT "piety of the poor" tradition.[147] In such texts God's righteous ones are typically described as poor, innocent, and defenseless, with their opponents contrasted as

[142] Mayor, 29; Mitton, 11.

[143] Guthrie, 736.

[144] Bauckham, *James*, 17. Such a claim is hard to accept, given the clear sense in the *Historia Ecclesiastica* that it was precisely this relationship that enabled James' authority in Jerusalem, and Simeon's after him.

[145] Cf. Davids, *James*, 179; Martin, 181.

[146] Davids, *James*, 179; cf. Martin, 181; Reicke, 51.

[147] E.g., Dibelius, *James*, 239; Laws, 206; Balz and Schrage, 51; Mussner, 198–99; Davids, 180; Johnson, *James*, 304; Wall, *James*, 232.

wicked abusers. Some of these texts use the singular ὁ δίκαιος as a collective reference to God's numerous righteous sufferers (LXX Ps 36:12, 17; Isa 3:10; 57:1; Wis
2:20). What is appealed to in James 5:6, then, is the well-known image of the righteous poor standing defenseless before unrighteous oppressors. Stock images from
the tradition have already been recalled in the letter (1:9-11; 2:3-7, 15-16) and it
is therefore completely appropriate to find them raised again here at the end. And
yet, even with the "piety of the poor" precedent in mind, v. 6 still reads as a rather
surprising leap in the context of vv. 1-5. What motivates the language here?

Most commentators recognize that Wisdom 2 is the particular piety of the
poor text behind James 5:6.[148] In that passage we also find a Just One (2:10, 12, 18)
who is characterized as poor (πένητα, 2:10); he is hunted down and tested because
of his opposition to the unrighteous (2:12–19) and is condemned to a shameful
death (θανάτῳ ἀσχήμονι καταδικάσωμεν, 2:20). The verbal correspondence
between this text and James 5:1-6 is immediately recognizable. What is of utmost
significance for our purpose is the fact that it is this very Wisdom passage that Hegesippus seems to be referring to in his claim that James' murder was a fulfillment
of OT prophecy. Thus, James 5:6 and the martyrdom account of Hegesippus are
linked together by shared references to Wisdom 2; and while it might be argued that
Hegesippus picked up on the link between James 5:6 and Wisdom 2 and alluded
to it in his narrative, it seems more likely that the second-century author of James
included in 5:6 a veiled reference to the known link identifying James with the
"Just One" of Wisdom 2. It cannot be accidental that a letter purportedly written
by James, a man known throughout the second century as "the Just One" who was
murdered by a perversion of justice, would culminate in this particular condemnation. Following Greeven, Martin, and Painter,[149] it is submitted that the reference
to ὁ δίκαιος in 5:6 is in fact a thinly veiled allusion to the purported author of the
letter. This supports a second century provenance.

JAMES' AUTHORITY: TO THE TWELVE TRIBES IN THE DISPERSION

It can also be argued that the authority of the implied author of James corresponds
to the second-century view of James the Just. The letter is addressed "to the twelve
tribes in the dispersion." The restoration of the δώδεκα φυλαῖς which had been
scattered ἐν τῇ διασπορᾷ (a widely observable focus of Jewish eschatological hope
[for example, Jer 31:7-10; Ezek 37:15-28; *Pss. Sol.* 17:28; 1QS 8:1, *Sib. Or.* 3.249;

---

[148] NA[27]; Mayor, 154–55; Dibelius, *James*, 239-40; Laws, 204; Johnson, *James*, 304;
Painter, *Just James*, 259. We disagree with Davids (*James*, 179) and Mitton (182) who assert
that Sirach 34:26–27 (where withholding an employees' wages [μισθόν] is equated with
murdering him [φονεύων]) is to be preferred over Wisdom 2, for the Sirach text addresses the
acceptability of ill-gained offerings, and the "murder" described is metaphorical. By contrast,
καταδικάζω in Wisdom 2 and James 5 requires a more literal murder of the righteous one
at the hands of the wicked.

[149] Dibelius, *James*, 240 n. 58; Martin, 182; Painter, *Just James*, 259.

Ant. 1.221]), reflects an early Christian appropriation of Israel's self-understanding (for example, Matt 19:28; Luke 22:30; Rev 7:5-8). An address to "the twelve tribes in the dispersion" invites the readers to consider themselves members of the eschatological Israel who remain dispersed among the nations. I have already mentioned that James fits the format of a diaspora letter written from Jewish authorities in Jerusalem to Jews living abroad, and we have seen how the second-century *Jakobusbild* presented him as an eschatological high priest or chief bishop of Jerusalem. In a similar manner, the letter address casts the author in an idealized, exalted role as one who stands in a uniquely privileged position in relation to all of Israel. As the first and greatest among the apostles (*G. Heb.*, Hegesippus, *G. Thom.*, *Ps. Clem.*, *1–2 Apoc.*) James is certified to write an authoritative diaspora letter to the whole people of God throughout the earth. Who else could address the eschatological Israel in this authoritative manner but the eschatological high priest of the Messiah, James the Just?

This idealization of James may also be evident in his designation as δοῦλος θεοῦ, a common LXX title for Israel's past heroic leaders. There it is used for Moses (3 Kgdms 8:53, 56; Ps 104:26, 42 [LXX]; Dan 9:11; Mal 3:24; 4:4), David (2 Sam 7:5f.; 1 Kgs 8:66; 1 Chr 17:4; Ps 77:70; 88:4; 131:10; 143:10 [LXX]; Jer 33:21; Ezek 34:23; 37:25), and God's prophets (Jer 7:25; 26:4f.; 44:4; Ezek 38:17; Joel 3:2; Amos 3:7; Jonah 1:9; Zech 1:6); the term is attributed to the heroes of Israel's past who functioned as mediators between God and God's people.[150] Indeed, the overall verbal mood of the letter corresponds with the historicized picture of James as the one to whom "all owe obedience": there are fifty-five imperative verbs in this short 108-verse tractate.[151] While our early sources clearly portray James as the leader of the Jerusalem church, they do not present him in these exalted terms. I will return to the prescript for further analysis in chapter three; for now, I simply conclude that the exalted address of the letter of James seems to reflect the second-century elevation of James the Just.

JAMES' PIETY AND INDEPENDENCE: A NON-CHRISTOLOGICAL CHRISTIANITY?

I noted how the second-century *Jakobusbild* presented us with a picture of James as a leader who fervently kept the law, had associates within the Jewish leadership, and lived in their midst in such a way that his particular Christian witness caused no offense. The letter of James conforms to this later depiction of James' piety and relative independence, most particularly in its rather glaring lack of explicitly christological content.

---

[150] Cf., e.g., Dibelius, *James*, 65–66; Laws, 45; Martin, 4, 7; Johnson, 168; Wall, *James*, 41; Niebuhr, 422.

[151] Davids (*James*, 58) finds 49, Mayor (ccii) and Johnson (*James*, 8) find 59; my search found 55.

The Ambiguous Christology of James

This puzzling feature was a contributing factor to Luther's well-known rejection of the letter on the basis that it did not "show Christ." In the more recent past, it has led some scholars to hypothesize that James was a non-Christian Jewish document that had been lightly reworked for a later Christian audience.[152] While such hypotheses have been widely rejected (for James shows far too great a dependence on Christian sources to have originated entirely within non-Christian Judaism), such concerns about James' Christianity are understandable given its many "silences." Dale Allison has presented us with a helpful list:[153] James names "Jesus" only twice in 108 verses; there is no mention of Jesus' crucifixion or resurrection; no mention of his earthly deeds or discussion of his character; his teaching seems to be present, but it is reworded and presented without citation to him; further, there are no references to basic Christian realities such as baptism, the Lord's Supper, or the Holy Spirit. Instead, one finds repeated appeals to the law (1:25; 2:8-13; 4:11-12), but no reference to the gospel; OT prophecy is highlighted (1:9-11, 27; 4:4; 5:1-6, 10), but there is no indication that prophecy has been fulfilled; Jewish wisdom is a major source for the letter (for example, 3:13–4:6; 5:20), but there is no reflection on Jesus as the incarnation of God's wisdom.[154] Many OT heroes are set forth—Abraham and Rahab as examples of faith in action (2:21-25), the Prophets as examples of suffering and patience (5:10), Job as an example of endurance (5:11), Elijah as an example of the powerful prayer of the righteous (5:16-18)—but Jesus is nowhere listed among them.

Some have defended the Christology of James by pointing out that it is "implied" or indirect.[155] Others have gone even further to argue that the letter includes a very "high" Christology indeed, at least for those who have eyes to see.[156] When the passages that reflect this Christology are explored more closely, however, one finds that most of these passages are more accurately characterized as "ambiguous" than "implied."[157] For instance:

---

[152] Principally argued by F. Spitta, *Der Brief des Jakobus untersucht* (Göttingen: Vandenhoek & Ruprecht, 1896); and L. Massebieau, "L'epitre de Jacques: est-elle l'oeuvre d'un chretien?" *RHR* 31–32 (1895). A. Meyer (*Das Raetsel des Jakobusbriefes* [Giessen: Toepelmann, 1930]) argued in similar fashion that the letter was an allegorical address of the patriarch Jacob to his twelve sons.

[153] D. C. Allison, Jr., "The Fiction of James and its *Sitz im Leben*," *RB* 4 (2001): 555.

[154] B. Witherington, *Jesus the Sage: The Pilgrimage of Wisdom* (Edinburgh: T&T Clark, 1994), 246.

[155] E.g. Mussner, 250–54.

[156] See R. Bauckham, "James and Jesus," in Chilton and Neusner, *The Brother of Jesus*, 131–35.

[157] Allison draws attention to A. H. McNeile (*An Introduction to the Study of the New Testament*, 2nd ed. [Oxford: Clarendon, 1953], 201–13), who provided a similar list; mine is an expansion of his.

1) The address "to the twelve tribes in the dispersion" (1:1) could be read as an address to the literal (that is, non-Christian) Israel, but Christian readers could read it as a figurative address to the messianically restored "spiritual Israel" made up of Jews and Gentiles alike.

2) The κύριος is named fourteen times; and though twice it is specifically tied to Jesus (1:1; 2:1), the rest (1:1, 7; 3:9; 4:10, 15; 5:4, 7, 8, 10, 11, 14, 15) could be taken to refer to either God or Jesus.

3) The claim that the "Father of lights . . . gave us birth by the word of truth" (1:17-18) could be heard in reference either to the original creation or to Christian regeneration.

4) In the exhortation to be "doers of the word and not hearers only" (1:22), non-Christian Jewish readers would think of the word of the law (see 1:25) while Christians would think of the word of the gospel.

5) The "royal law according to the scripture, 'you shall love your neighbor as yourself'" (2:8) refers directly to the text of Leviticus, but Christians would hear the "summary of the law" teaching of Jesus.

6) Συναγωγή in 2:2 could suggest a literal "synagogue" but it could also refer simply to an "assembly" or "meeting" of believers; likewise the use of the term ἐκκλησία in 5:14 is in no way uniquely Christian, for it is used throughout the LXX to refer to the congregation of Yahweh (for example, Deut 23:2ff.; 1 Chr 28:8; Neh 13:1; Mic 2:5).

7) The "honorable name which was invoked over you" in 2:7 might lead Christian readers to think of baptism (though the sacrament is not mentioned), but non-Christian Jewish readers would be reminded of the theme as it is found recurrently in the LXX (for example, Gen 12:8; Deut 28:10; 1 Kgs 8:43; 1 Macc. 7:37; Ps 78:6; Isa 43:7; Jer 7:10-14; Joel 3:5; Amos 9:12).

8) The "coming of the Lord" in 5:7 and the "judge standing at the doors" in 5:9 would be heard by Christians as a reference to the parousia of Christ, but since such images find their precedent in Jewish eschatology (for example, Isa 19:1; 30:27; 66:15; Hab 3:3, 13; Amos 5:18-20; Zeph 1:15-18; 2:2; Mal 3:5), such an inference is not required of the reader.

Obviously much hangs on the only two overtly "Christian" verses in the letter, 1:1 and 2:1. Both have been argued at various times to be later additions,[158] the first because it provides the only clear epistolary element of the letter, and the second because its awkward succession of genitives (τὴν πίστιν τοῦ κυρίου ἡμῶν Ἰησοῦ Χριστοῦ τῆς δόξης) makes it look as though something had been added to what had once been a well-formed sentence. But ultimately there is little solid ground for theories of interpolation apart from the oddity of the verses themselves, and most

---

[158] 1:1 was argued to be such principally by Harnack (*Geschichte der altchristlichen Literatur*, 487f.) and more recently by Llewelyn; Spitta and Massebieau claimed both 1:1 and 2:1 were interpolations.

scholars now take them both to be original. Having said that, the fleeting quality
of these appearances of the "Lord Jesus Christ" must be taken more seriously than
they often are, for apart from these two verses, the letter of James is a text without
any explicitly Christian elements.

Explaining the Lack of Explicit Christological Content

Since the letter acknowledges the Lord Jesus Christ in 1:1 and 2:1, appears to rely
heavily on the teaching of Jesus, and has numerous connections to other early
Christian writings, it makes little sense to claim it is a non-Christian Jewish text
later reworked for a Christian readership. Recently, Richard Bauckham has sought
to explain the christological ambiguity by appeal to genre: James is an example of
wisdom paraenesis, and as such it treats the Jesus tradition as though it were part
of accumulated Jewish wisdom that was regularly taken up and developed by each
new generation of sages.[159] Jesus is not cited in James because wisdom writers do
not cite their sources; the parallels to the Jesus tradition in James are not verbatim
because James the Sage was simply reexpressing the teaching of Jesus the Sage for his
own context.[160] John Kloppenborg argues something similar by appeal to ancient
rhetorical practices, suggesting that the author is paraphrasing, emulating, or recit-
ing Jesus' words according to a commonly utilized strategy.[161] Emphasize these rhetorical strategies along with the "implied" high Christology of the letter, and the
puzzling theological ambiguity of James disappears. Impressive as these arguments
often are, they do not provide an adequate account for what appears to be the intentional ambiguity of the passages identified as christological; for while the reader may
infer the presence of high christological commitments in the letter, such inferences
are by no means *required* on the part of the reader. Outside of 1:1 and 2:1, the
reader must pick up on echoes and fill in gaps in order to make James read as an
overtly Christian text. Indeed, it seems obvious that the writer *expects* readers to fill
in these gaps. But why has he chosen to write so obliquely in the first place?

A. H. McNeile explained the mystery of James by suggesting the author of the
letter simply wanted to reach as wide an audience as possible among both Jews and
Christians: "He desires to prove nothing doctrinal, and to 'proselytize' no one, but
to show that the highest standard of ethics for Jew and for Christian could be one
and the same."[162] But what would be the motivation for such a correspondence?
Allison takes McNeile one step further: the orientation of James is similar to that
of Matthew, which reflects the tensions between Jewish Christians and Rabbinic
authorities over their respective influence in the synagogues. Both books are representative of "Jewish Christianity," both speak positively of the Jewish law and
regard it as still in force, both contain material that can be read as anti-Pauline, both
oppose oaths, and both appeal to similar sources for sayings of Jesus. However, in
contrast to Matthew's opposition between the Christianity and Judaism of his day,

[159] Bauckham, "James and Jesus"; see also Witherington, 236–47.
[160] Bauckham, *James*, 91.
[161] Kloppenborg, "The Reception of the Jesus Tradition in James."
[162] McNeile, 207–8.

James . . . likely emerged from a group that, in its place and time, whether that time was before or after Matthew, was still seeking to keep relations irenic. It was yet within the synagogue and so still trying to get along as best as possible with those who did not believe Jesus to be the Messiah. . . . The emphasis upon convictions rooted in the common religiosity of the wisdom literature, the omission of potentially divisive Christian affirmations, and the passages that can be read one way by a Christian and another way by a non-Christian would make for good will on the part of the latter and also provide edification for the former.[163]

Allison concludes his study by suggesting that the community behind James may have been similar to the secret Christians identified by J. Louis Martyn and Raymond Brown in their studies of the Johannine community. These Christians attended the synagogue and did not proselytize but worked "from within to bring . . . offended synagogue leaders back to a tolerance toward Christians that had previously existed."[164] James is written likewise by a "crypto-Christian" and addressed to both Christian and non-Christian Jews of the diaspora synagogues of the mid- to late first century.

Allison's analysis provides an attractive explanation for why the author would submerge his Christology as he does. But it also falls short at a couple of key points. First, it fails to account for the "ethicized" view of the law present in the letter. If the readers were all observant Jews there would be no reason to be ambiguous on this point. Though it could be countered that the ritual laws are implied, once again we are left wondering why the author needed to avoid mentioning them, especially given the evidence that most Christian Jews in the first century continued to keep the whole Torah. More importantly, while communal tensions are an important focus of the letter's exhortation, there is no indication whatsoever that the tensions were between Christian and non-Christian Jews. According to Allison, the author describes the tension as being between rich and poor because he "wants them [non-Christian Jews] to recognize in their opposition to Christians the unjust oppression of the poor so fervently condemned by the Hebrew prophets. . . . In other words, the epistle seeks not to proselytize but to promote tolerance, to gain sympathy for Christians in a context where there is perhaps growing antipathy."[165] But there is no supporting evidence for reading James as a first-century apology to non-Christian Jews from the Christians in their midst, and further, there is little basis for reading the economic critique of the letter figuratively. When one adds to this the strong evidence for a second-century dating, Allison's theory proves less persuasive.

The Ambiguity of James in Second-century Context

An alternative explanation of the ambiguous Christianity of the letter is afforded by the research presented thus far: the second-century author of James desired the

---

[163] Allison, "Fiction of James," 565–69.

[164] Allison, "Fiction of James," 569, quoting R. Brown, *The Community of the Beloved Disciple* (New York: Paulist, 1979), 71–73.

[165] Allison, "Fiction of James," 568.

content of the letter to comport closely with the historicized James of his day, a James who was somewhat ambiguous about his Christianity. According to that image, James the Just was a rather independent Christian; he was more oriented toward the law than the gospel; he was more often associated with the Jewish leadership than the apostles of Jesus; indeed, he was not known as an "apostle" nor even a "disciple," but as a character of heroic piety and power, a "servant of God" akin to the patriarchs and prophets of old; he was a supremely pious Jew of high priestly authority who was also at some level a follower of Christ. A letter supposedly written by him needed to present itself in accordance with this second-century image in order to be an effective actualization of apostolic teaching. In this regard, it is quite possible that both the author of the canonical letter and Hegesippus were working in different modes with the same traditional picture of James. Hegesippus wrote of James in a retrospective, biographical mode, and this led him to present James in idealized OT imagery as the pinnacle of priestly and Nazirite ritual holiness. The author of our letter appealed to this same OT-oriented traditional depiction but needed to create a "teaching of James" that would speak to his contemporary *Gentile* Christian readership.

But if it was not intra-synagogue tensions that motivated the composition of the letter of James, what did? Several points must be made. To begin with, we note that the letter offers both continuity and correction to the traditional *Jakobusbild*. In continuity with that image, we find that James is indeed a supremely authoritative Jewish leader who is deeply committed to the ongoing significance of Israel's scriptures for the Christian church. Through its constant appeal to the law, the prophets, wisdom literature, and OT exemplars, James highlights the centrality of the Jewish Scriptures for Christian life and practice. However, in what must have been a much needed correction to the commonly held portrayal, Gentile Christian readers discover an adherence to Torah that is entirely amenable to Gentile Christianity, for it is not the ritual laws of the Jewish Scriptures that are binding, but the moral law that is compulsory. This view of Israel's Torah was entirely consonant with the broader Christian understanding of the law's enduring relevance (cf. Matt 5:17-48; Rom 13:8-10; Gal 3:19; 5:14; 1 Tim 1:8-11). In this manner James the Just could be shown to maintain his traditional law-oriented independence while speaking in basic harmony with the larger apostolic proclamation.

Nevertheless, in contrast to this broader NT understanding, the canonical James is oriented toward the law in a generally non-christological manner. Like the James of Hegesippus, it could be that the author assumed the Christianity of the historical James was basically non-soteriological, that he understood Jesus to be a *teaching* messiah of an ethicized Judaism rather than the *saving* messiah of Christian orthodoxy. But why would he find it profitable to maintain this largely non-christological stance? One would think he would want to make James as "Christian" as possible in order to underscore his orthodoxy. What canonical value would there be in his construction of a text that is overtly Jewish and covertly Christian? Why speak of forgiveness of sin (5:15-16, 20) without reference to the cross? Why speak of a "birth by a word" (1:18) without reference to regeneration or the resurrection? Why conceal Jesus' teaching in the guise of OT wisdom? Why valorize the law and not the gospel? Why appeal to OT models of faith and avoid any appeal to the character of Jesus?

The answer can be found if we locate the letter in the context of the controversies of the second century rather than the first. "James" was not writing to Jews of the first-century synagogue; *he was writing to a second-century Christian readership in order to promote the essentially Jewish underpinnings of Christian faith and practice.* The letter was written, that is, in a period that was deeply in need of a proper understanding of the relationship between Israel and the church. James was written to present the church with a more fully Catholic Jewish-Christianity, to remind the church, as Rob Wall has put it, that it "must become more Jewish to become more Christian."[166] Indeed, it is surely because of James' traditional orientation toward the old covenant that he was seen to be the most appropriate apostolic candidate to address those who sought to extract Christianity from its roots in historic Israel, *for in his historicized life and teaching, James himself could be seen as the Christian embodiment of a continuous old and new covenant.* Allison noted that "James' grounding of his moral exhortations in theological rather than christological principles provides a genuine bridge between Christians and Jews who share a belief in the One God, Creator, Lawgiver and Judge."[167] James does indeed seek to provide this bridge, only it is not between Christian and non-Christian Jews of the first century; the Jacobian bridge was designed to help span the gap between the old and new covenants that emerged in association with the second-century Marcionite crisis.

Conclusion

Despite the efforts of those who have sought to establish the authenticity of the letter of James, this chapter has shown that such a position is difficult to maintain. It is true that neither authenticity nor pseudonymity can be proved beyond the shadow of a doubt, but I have tried to show that a pseudonymous origin offers a more plausible account of the letter's provenance. We explored the various scholarly rationalizations set forward to explain the letter's late canonical arrival and found them all to be lacking. We considered the arguments set forward in favor of the letter's authenticity; and when we balanced them against the arguments presented in favor of pseudonymity, the latter arguments were found to be more persuasive. We then asked, in light of the letter's third-century canonical arrival, what grounds existed for securing a first-century provenance. We found that little existed beyond scholarly preconceptions regarding the acceptable range of dating NT texts. From there we isolated particular features of first- and second-century James traditions and found that indeed the letter of James can be seen to betray an awareness of traditions about James that only came to the fore in the second century. We noted,

---

[166] E. E. Lemcio and R. Wall, *The New Testament as Canon: A Reader in Canonical Criticism* (JSNTSup 76; Sheffield: Sheffield Academic, 1992), 265.

[167] M. Hogan, "The Law in the Epistle of James," *SNTSU* A22 (1997): 91; cited by Allison, "Fiction of James," 566.

further, that among all the wide variety of second-century writings related to James, none show any dependence on (or even awareness of) the canonical letter. On these evidentiary bases I concluded that it is quite plausible indeed to assign a second-century *Sitz im Leben* for the letter of James.

Thinking back on the discoveries from canon history presented in my first chapter, it seems that the Catholic Church of the second century was in desperate need of an orthodox letter from James the Just. Despite all the residual evidence of James' role in the earliest church, he was terribly under-represented in the available Catholic literature of the time. It is quite possibly that this reality enabled "Jewish-Christian" and "gnostic" sects to champion James as their particular apostolic hero, placing him in opposition to other apostolic figures and bolstering his authority by means of supposedly authentic documentary witnesses. The Catholic tradition, understanding itself to represent universal Christianity, chose a different route: rather than oppose the earliest apostolic heroes, they focused instead on proclaiming the harmonious unity of the primitive kerygma. They found support for their position in the Acts of the Apostles and the writings of Paul, who affirmed both the unity of the earliest apostles ("James and Cephas and John, who were reputed to be Pillars, gave to me and Barnabas the right hand of fellowship," Gal 2:9) and the essential harmony of their proclamation ("whether then it was I or they, so we preach and so you believed," 1 Cor 15:11).

But there were problems with this harmonious image. First, the overwhelming vigor of the Pauline witness tended to promote readings that were deemed unacceptable among those of the nascent Catholic tradition, most particularly having to do with Christianity's relation to Israel (Marcion) and the nature of Christian freedom (2 Pet 3:15-17). Second, the other available apostolic letters, 1 Peter and 1 John, were honored, but not nearly so much as those of Paul, and therefore failed to offer the kind of unified front required to correct the tendency toward Paulinist heresy. According to my hypothesis, the letter of James was the second-century remedy to this weakness in the Catholic apostolic documentary witness. According to this reconstruction of events, Catholic Christians connected in some way with the traditions of "Jewish Christianity" wrote the letter in the hopes of creating a theologically coherent, fully apostolic letter collection balanced according to the two-sided mission of the earliest church, that of Paul and the Jerusalem Pillars. Not only would such a collection offer a more theologically orthodox representation of the earliest mission to Jews, it would also facilitate a more vigorous defense against the distortions to which the Pauline message proved susceptible.

If the author of James, in fact, had the creation of a Pillars collection in mind, we should expect to find evidence of it in his letter. We should discover attempts on his part to link his thought with that of the two other widely available Pillar letters, 1 Peter and 1 John, in order to create a group of witnesses sufficiently coherent and harmonious to be considered a "collection." We should also anticipate some kind of deliberate engagement with the Pauline witness, one designed to enable a more Catholic-shaped reading of that canonical collection. Further, if my analysis of the function of James is correct, we should also expect to find our author consistently turning the links with these new covenant texts in the direction of the old covenant in order to secure the continuity of the two. My final chapter, then, turns to an exegetical demonstration of the viability of my hypothesis.

CHAPTER THREE

Reading James as a Canon-conscious Pseudepigraph

My second chapter argued that James of Jerusalem did not write the canonical letter of James. Sufficient evidence exists to suggest that the canonical letter might have been composed sometime in the second century, possibly penned by someone who sought to forge together a collection of Pillar letters that would serve as a canonical counterbalance to the Pauline letter collection. My first chapter demonstrated this possibility on the basis of the historical development of the NT canon, a development that revealed how the letter appears to have gone into circulation when the church was in need of a robust apostolic witness in support of a right reading of Paul. My second chapter extended this argument by means of an analysis of traditions about James of Jerusalem, traditions that enabled us to claim that the canonical letter bears witness to the second-century "historicized" James. But it is not enough for us to stop at the level of historical reconstruction, for my introduction insisted that the letter of James was an example of a text composed with its placement within a literary collection in mind. I have provided enough historical background to justify a literary reading of the collection through this particular interpretive lens; what remains, then, is a demonstration of the plausibility of my historical hypothesis on literary grounds. It must be kept in mind that in this chapter I am testing out a hypothesis, based on external evidence, to see if it could make plausible sense of the otherwise rather ambiguous historical and literary data. As we have stated before, the wide variety of scholarly positions on the provenance of James validates such an investigation. When it comes to the letter of James, we are all dependent at some level on hypothetical reconstructions.

I begin with a brief consideration of the dominant scholarly account of the literary parallels between James and the other apostolic letters. Though the majority of contemporary scholars account for these similarities on the basis of their supposed common appeal to hypothetical "traditional source materials," a second-century origin for the letter of James allows for an alternate explanation: our author may have intentionally alluded to and/or echoed these letters in order to enable the acceptance of his own into their increasingly restricted company. But more than that, in agreement with the Eastern tendency to list James first among the CE, my analysis will show that James can be read as a text that was designed to *introduce* the other apostolic letters, in order to orient their subsequent reception according to the particular theological agenda I have been outlining thus far. Throughout my investigation we will note, for example, that the James side of these parallels reveals a consistent effort to downplay sharp distinctions between the "old" and "new" work of God in favor of an emphasis on the continuous singularity of God's actions in history. Further, we will see that our hypothetical author's redactional *shaping* of the apostolic letter collection was concerned to affect the canonical *shape* of two letters in particular. *Within* the CE, our author sought primarily to shape reader reception of 1 Peter. As for the apostolic letter collection as a whole, however, this lead letter of the CE collection can be seen to recurrently engage the letter that came to be placed at the lead of the *other* apostolic letter collection, that is, Paul's letter to the Romans.

The Analysis of Intertextual Affinities
in Modern Biblical Scholarship

Most scholars of the early twentieth century assumed that the similarities between James and other apostolic texts pointed to direct literary dependence, but there was little agreement on the direction of the borrowing. J. B. Mayor, for one, believed that Peter, John, and Paul all borrowed from the older letter of James.[1] In comparing the similar passages, he concluded that 1 Peter and 1 John offered more developed expressions, making James the more likely prototype. The same features led Charles Bigg to the opposite conclusion.[2] For him, the apparent discontinuity of James betrayed a greater dependence on sources than 1 Peter, which presented a far more continuous progression of thought. Not all scholars of the period were arguing for direct borrowing, however. Ropes's commentary on James allowed for its possible dependence on Romans or Galatians, but as for the letter's "striking similarities" with 1 Peter, they were to be explained by each authors' independent appeal to "common religious and literary influences" that "made up a common stock used independently by many writers in widely distant places for a long period."[3]

---

[1] J. B. Mayor, *The Epistle of St. James,* 2nd ed. (London: Macmillan, 1897), xcviii.
[2] C. Bigg, *The Epistles of St. Peter and St. Jude* (ICC; Edinburgh: T&T Clark, 1901), 23.
[3] J. Ropes, *The Epistle of St. James* (ICC; Edinburgh: T&T Clark, 1916), 22–23.

Later form-critical scholars took up similar explanations of the evidence. Dibelius's commentary insisted that the affinities were due to the fact that the author was simply fixing earlier authoritative oral and written sources.[4] E. G. Selwyn claimed to have identified four such sources underlying the text of 1 Peter, but he had this to say about James:

> That St. Peter had read Romans and Ephesians is not antecedently improbable, and the author of James, if it is not in its present form by St. James himself, may have been acquainted with 1 Peter. But there is nothing in the evidence to require such suppositions.[5]

Since he argued that the sources behind the NT letters were current in the middle of the first century, with the corresponding canonical texts written soon thereafter, Selwyn was obliged to remain uncertain about the placement of James within this collective:

> The individuality of this epistle, and the uncertainty as to its date, make the parallels between it and 1 Peter more difficult to account for. . . . If direct dependence exists, then 1 Peter is much more likely to be original than James.[6]

The later James is placed, the more likely it is that it was in some way dependent on available apostolic literature.

Though subsequent scholarship grew to be critical of the confidence with which the pioneers of form criticism established the "sources" behind the texts,[7] a more cautious form-critical account of the parallels has nevertheless come to dominate contemporary biblical scholarship. Indeed, the consensus position sees little need to argue for literary dependence at all between James and any other NT text.[8] It should be clear by now, however, that though form and source-critical insights into early Christian tradition have offered a persuasive means of accounting for the similarities among many apostolic texts, the matter is far from settled when it

[4] M. Dibelius, *James*, ed. H. Greeven, trans. M. Williams (Hermeneia; Philadelphia: Fortress , 1976), 75.

[5] E. G. Selwyn, *The First Epistle of St. Peter* (London: Macmillan, 1947), 19.

[6] Selwyn, 462–63.

[7] See E. Lohse, "Parenesis and Kerygma in 1 Peter," in *Perspectives on First Peter*, ed. Charles Talbert (Macon, Ga.: Mercer University Press, 1986); and J. N. D. Kelly, *Commentary on the Epistles of Peter and Jude* (BNTC; London: A&C Black, 1969), 11f., for early reconsiderations of form studies.

[8] E.g., F. Mussner, *Der Jakobusbrief* (Freiburg: Verlag Herder, 1964), 33–35; L. Goppelt, *A Commentary on 1 Peter*, ed. F. Hahn, trans. J. E. Alsup (Grand Rapids: Eerdmans, 1993), 30f.; R. Brown, *Epistles of John* (ABC 30; New York: Doubleday, 1982), 4; J. R. Michaels, *1 Peter* (WBC 49; Waco, Tex.: Word Books, 1988), xlii–xlv; P. Davids, *The Epistle of James* (NIGTC; Grand Rapids: Eerdmans, 1982), 24–27; idem., *The First Epistle of Peter* (NICNT; Grand Rapids: Eerdmans, 1990), 5–6; C. Burchard, *Der Jakobusbrief* (HNT 15/1; Tübingen: Mohr Siebeck, 2000), 16; and J. H. Elliott, *1 Peter* (ABC 37B; New York: Doubleday, 2000), 29–30.

comes to the letter of James.[9] Simply put, it is obvious that the question of literary dependence is directly related to the relative dating of the texts under exploration. For most commentators, the question is guided by the assumption that the letters in question were written within roughly the same time period, that is, before the end of the first century.

For example, Matthias Konradt has recently agreed with the consensus that neither James nor 1 Peter is directly dependent on the other, but he also (quite rightly) finds the connections between the two far too close to be explained away by general appeals to shared tradition.[10] Instead, according to Konradt's reconstruction, the two letters witness to a specific branch of source material associated with late first-century Syrian Antioch. Konradt's work is insightful, but his argument hangs on the supposition that the composition of James is roughly contemporaneous with that of 1 Peter. My research argues for the possibility that James was written well after 1 Peter and most other apostolic writings had achieved a level of authority. In this case, the author of James would have most certainly appealed to the so-called "common stock of early Christian tradition" in his composition (Sheppard's "canon 1"), but through the course of the second century that body of traditional materials would reflect a "canon-consciousness" increasingly centered on the Synoptic gospels, the letters of Paul, 1 Peter, and 1 John—just as Trobisch and others have argued was the case for the author of 2 Peter, who quite clearly wrote his letter with an existing collection of apostolic texts in mind.[11]

When I argue that the author of James sought to intentionally link his letter with the authoritative apostolic texts of his day, we need not suppose he did so slavishly, with the said texts open before him at his writing table. Noting the numerous and extraordinarily dense intertextual links between James and other early Jewish and Christian authoritative writings, Wiard Popkes has suggested that the pseudonymous author was working with a *Zettelkasten*, a sort of file box containing bits and pieces of traditional material that he reworked to make his own distinctive point.[12]

> Our model of intertextuality would equally explain James's method of incorporating early Christian material. James would have taken notes from various tradi-

---

[9] See F. W. Beare (*The First Epistle of Peter* [Oxford: Basil Blackwell, 1961], 10), R. Bauckham (*James: Wisdom of James, Disciple of Jesus the Sage* [London: Routledge, 1999], 156), and M. Konradt (*Christliche Existenz nach dem Jakobusbrief* [SUNT b.22; Göttingen: Vandenhoeck & Ruprecht, 1998], 328–30) as examples of commentators who reflect discomfort with the "common stock" explanation.

[10] M. Konradt, "Der Jakobusbrief als Brief des Jakobus," in P. von Gemünden, et al., *Der Jakobusbrief: Beiträge zur Aufwertung der „strohernen Epistel,"* (Münster: Lit Verlag, 2003), 16–53; idem., *Christliche Existenz*, 328–30.

[11] See D. Trobisch, *The First Edition of the New Testament* (Oxford: Oxford University Press, 2000), 86–96.

[12] W. Popkes, "James and Scripture: An Exercise in Intertextuality," *NTS* 45 (1999): 213–29.

tions, written or oral, primary or secondary. He would have assembled them in his file. All these notes, excerpts and clippings, as it were, would then be used in generating his own text.[13]

Popkes' suggestion seems quite plausible to me, but it seems just as likely that the author of James was simply working from memory intentionally echoing and alluding to the authoritative texts he and his community knew quite well. As already noted, recent studies in orality and literacy in early Christianity have demonstrated that the interaction between text and speech was far closer in the ancient world than in the modern.[14] Contrary to modern practice, all ancient writing and reading had an oral-aural character about it. Words were written in order to be spoken; even when reading alone, most read audibly.[15] Authors thus wrote according to the conventions of oral rhetoric and made use of stylistic devices in order to signal shifts in thought and to enable memorization. As Risto Uro has put it, "texts in the ancient world functioned rather more like our tape recorders than our books . . . writing tended to be used as an *aid to memory* rather than as an autonomous and independent mode of communication."[16] Within this environment, memory would have played a greater role in communication than it does for modern readers and hearers who are used to having ongoing access to fixed texts. Intentional allusion and echo (and even explicit quotation) would have been far less word-for-word than our modern text-based practices require, relying instead on the "echoing" or "recollection" of key words, memorable phrases, recognizable cadences, and familiar themes.[17] Neither author nor reader would have needed direct access to the text being alluded to for the communicative intent to be received, for both would have had the kind of intimacy with the scriptures that comes from multiple hearings on the part of listeners who were sensitively attuned to aural reception.

Having made this point, it is crucial that the reader carefully distinguish what I present in this chapter from the work of others I have criticized thus far. Mayor and Bigg had the same literary parallels before them but came to opposite conclusions about the direction of dependence involved. Johnson and Laws list a number of parallels between James and *Hermas* and conclude that the latter is dependent on

[13] Popkes, "James and Scripture," 221.

[14] For this information I am indebted to three studies of early Christian reading and writing: Risto Uro, "*Thomas* and the Oral Gospel Tradition," in *Thomas at the Crossroads*, ed. Risto Uro (Edinburgh: T&T Clark, 1998), 8–32; Harry Gamble, *Books and Readers in the Early Church* (New Haven: Yale University Press, 1995); and Paul Achtemeyer, "Omne Verbum Sonat," *JBL* 109 (1990): 3–27.

[15] See the *JBL* discussion emerging from Achtemeier's article: M. Slusser, "Reading Silently in Antiquity," *JBL* 111 (1992): 499; and F. D. Gilliard, "More Silent Reading in Antiquity," *JBL* 112 (1993): 689–94. Despite Gilliard's correction, the basic premise of Achtemeier's thesis stands.

[16] Uro, 16–17.

[17] R. B. Hays, *Echoes of Scripture in the Letters of Paul* (New Haven: Yale University Press, 1989), 20.

the former simply on the presumption that James is the earlier text. Analyses of the same inexact parallels between James and the words of Jesus lead some to presume that James is appealing to oral tradition that predates the canonical gospels, others to think he is dependent on Q, others Matthew, and still others Luke. In the face of this I have come to the conviction that one simply cannot make a strong argument for the dating of texts on the basis of literary parallels. Such evidence can be accounted for in too many different ways. This is why I did not start this book with the in-depth analysis of the intertextual links I am going to explore in this chapter: The literary evidence is hugely significant, and indeed it inspires the *conceptual* basis of the point I am arguing in this book; but the literary evidence alone is slippery and thus cannot be presented as the sole *substantial* basis for my argument. Instead, the evidence from reception and tradition history presented in the first two chapters has been offered first to allow me to move ahead with the hypothesis that James was composed in the second century. On *this* basis I am provided with a warrant for reading the literary parallels according to the terms of the hypothesis being promoted. This chapter is therefore intended to be a "performance" of the historical hypothesis at the literary level, a reading of James as a canon-conscious pseudepigraph.

Because of this, I will not always set complicated redactional schemes before the reader in an attempt to demonstrate the exact mechanics of our author's allusions to the other apostolic letters. On my view, he simply has detailed knowledge of the texts and alludes to them consciously. As we will see, some of his allusions will be more lexical and syntactical (for example, Jas 1:1-4 and 1 Pet 1:1, 6-9), and others more thematic or formal (for example, Jas 2:14-17 and 1 John 3:16-18). Some are so amazingly exact that a conclusion of literary dependence will seem unavoidable, while others are less convincing on their own. But the unevenness of the links need not force us to retreat into the amorphous "common stock of tradition" explanation. If James is indeed a product of the second century, the parallels would point quite plausibly to our author's desire to bind his letter to those of his illustrious apostolic predecessors in order to ensure the reception of his text into their increasingly restricted company.

What follows, then, is neither a full-fledged commentary, nor a thorough study of the "theology" of James; it is a heuristic analysis of its parallels with apostolic letters known to be available and authoritative by the later second century. I will not take the time to entertain every interpretive option for the passages under review, nor will I offer anything more than a peripheral engagement with the many noncanonical and deuterocanonical writings that quite clearly influenced the author of the letter. Instead, I offer an intertextual reading of James and the other apostolic letters designed to test my historical hypothesis on literary grounds.

One final objection to the consensus position must be made. One of the chief supporting arguments against literary dependence among these texts makes much of the fact that the parallel passages use the alleged "traditional material" in different ways.[18] The parallels between James and 1 Peter, 1 John, and Paul's letters that agree in terminology and form often disagree theologically, so a shared source is considered more plausible than direct literary dependence. According to my hypothetical reconstruction, however, a divergent use of shared material by the author of James makes perfect sense. The second-century author sought to link his letter with 1 Peter, 1 John, and the letters of Paul in the hopes of creating a collection of letters from the Pillars of the Jerusalem church. In order to do this, he would need to include numerous echoes of 1 Peter and 1 John in order to achieve a sense of *coherence*, so that the historicized James might be heard to speak in basic agreement with his co-Pillars Peter and John. But in order to ensure the reception of the letter-group as a collection from the mission *to Jews*, he would also need to engage in some level of *correction* in order to shift the reception of all the letters in the direction of his assumptions regarding the theological landscape of that particular mission.

Put another way: if the author was in fact writing against the backdrop of second-century Christianity in order to promote the Jewish roots of Christian faith and practice, would we not expect a consistent effort on his part to turn the linked passages in the direction of his particular theological concern? If he wanted to emphasize the conviction that God's new covenant in Christ is fully consonant with God's former covenant with Israel, would we not expect him to echo the other letters in a manner that would emphasize their continuity and downplay any sense of their historical duality? Further, if this letter were designed to *introduce* the very letters to which it is intentionally linked, as my introduction suggested, would he not offer a redaction that would set the tone for their ensuing reception?

A Redaction Reading of James

Diaspora

I begin with two aspects of the prescripts of James and 1 Peter. First, we note that James is identified as a "servant of God and of the Lord Jesus Christ," while Peter calls himself "apostle of Jesus Christ." Though the latter title is explicitly Christian, the former has deep roots in Jewish literature as a designation for the heroes of Israel's past who functioned as mediators between God and the people of Israel.[19] Certainly an "apostle" can also claim the title "servant of Christ" (Rom 1:1; Gal

---

[18] Cf., e.g., Ropes, 22–23; S. Laws, *The Epistle of James* (BNTC; Peabody, Mass.: Hendrickson, 1980), 18; L. T. Johnson, *The Letter of James* (ABC 37A; New York: Doubleday, 1995), 53–55; Elliott, *1 Peter*, 23; Konradt, *Christliche Existenz*, 328–30.

[19] See p. 153 for relevant citations; cf. Dibelius, *James*, 65–66; Laws, 45; R. P. Martin, *James* (WBC 48; Waco, Tex.: Word Books, 1988), 4, 7; Johnson, *James*, 168; R. Wall, *Community of the Wise: The Letter of James* (Valley Forge, Pa.: Trinity Press International, 1997), 41; K. W. Niebuhr, "Der Jakobusbrief," *NTS* 44 (1998): 422.

1:10; Phil 1:1; 2 Pet 1:1), but only the letter to Titus is written from a "servant of God." Since James lacks the more specifically Christian title "apostle," and includes the rarer "servant of God," it is not illegitimate to assume, as numerous scholars have, that the author of James has the OT precedent in mind and wants his readers to pick up on the allusion.[20]

Second, and far more significantly, both letters are addressed to recipients associated with "the diaspora." The twelve occurrences of the noun διασπορά in the LXX always refer in some way to God's punitive scattering of unfaithful Israel in exile among the nations of the Gentiles.[21] The only other occurrence of this word apart from its use in the prescript of James and 1 Peter is John 7:35, where it is used in the technical, more geographical sense typical of the LXX: "The Jews said to one another, 'Where does this man intend to go that we will not find him? Does he intend to go to the diaspora among the Greeks and teach the Greeks?'" None of the Apostolic Fathers make use of it, and its few occurrences in patristic writings are exclusively in reference to the Jews (*TDNT* 2.104). The fact that James and 1 Peter are the only letters in all canonical and non-canonical Christian writing to use this rare term in their address cannot be coincidental; it is evidence from the very start of a possible formal relationship between the two letters.

1 Peter

It is undeniable 1 Peter has the OT precedent for διασπορά in mind. A surface reading of the letter might lead us to assume that the recipients are themselves ethnically Jewish, as the document is permeated with language and imagery traditionally associated with Israel: There are references to election (1:1; 2:4-10; 5:13), exile (1:1, 17; 2:12; 5:13), the Passover (1:13, 19), and the sacrificial system (1:2); there are appeals to significant figures from OT history (1:10-12; 3:6, 20); most significantly, outsiders are called "Gentiles" (2:12; 4:2-4). At the same time, however, the author addresses the readers in ways that would only make sense if they were Gentiles: they once lived like Gentiles (1:14; 4:2-4) in ignorance of God (1:14); they were "ransomed from the futile ways" of their ancestors (1:18); their faith and hope were in something other than God (1:21); they were called "out of darkness into his marvelous light" (2:9), having formerly been "not God's people" (2:10). The dominant reading, therefore, affirms that the letter addresses Gentiles as though they were Jews. The author has taken up traditional Jewish terminology and imagery in the conviction that Christian believers constitute a new Israel and are therefore the continuation of the OT people of God.[22]

[20] Cf., e.g., Dibelius, *James*, 65–66; Laws, 45; Martin, 4, 7; Johnson, *James*, 168; Wall, *James*, 41; Niebuhr, "Der Jakobusbrief," 422.

[21] Deut 28:25; 30:4; Neh 1:9; Ps 146:2; Isa 49:6; Jer 15:7; 41:17; Dan 12:2; Jdt 5:19; 2 Macc. 1:27; *Pss. Sol.* 8:28; 9:2; cf. W. C. van Unnik, "'Diaspora' and 'Church' in the First Centuries of Christian History," in *Sparsa Collectica III: The Collected Essays of W.C. Unnik* (NovTSup 31; Leiden: Brill, 1983), 95–103.

[22] Martin, lxxix; Michaels, 6; E. Best, *1 Peter* (NCBC; Grand Rapids: Eerdmans, 1971), 69–70.

The recipients are not simply of the dispersion, however; they are also ἐκλεκτός and παρεπίδημος. The three terms radiate a particular theological effect when juxtaposed in this manner. References to the election of Christians come up throughout 1 Peter (1:1; 2:4, 6, 9; 5:13), though most conspicuously at the beginning and the end, forming a kind of *inclusio*.[23] Likewise the identity of the recipients is located deep in the past of Israel's salvation history: they have been elected according to the foreknowledge of God the Father (1:2), and therefore inhabit the privileged space formerly belonging to the people of Israel alone. Παρεπίδημος is translated in a wide variety of ways, though "sojourner,"[24] "exile,"[25] or "stranger"[26] are most common. It is paired in 2:11 with the related term πάροικος (cf. 1:17), a word bearing legal overtones that might be translated "resident aliens."[27] Given the overall emphasis on social persecution in the letter (cf. 2:12, 19–20; 3:9, 14–16; 4:4, 12–16) it seems that ἐκλεκτός and παρεπίδημος are linked intentionally. Both the recipients (members of a worldwide family in exile, 5:9) and the author (writing from "Babylon," the representative location of exile, 5:13) are exiles *because* they are chosen; they struggle as strangers in the world *because* of their particular standing before God. Διασπορά in 1 Peter, therefore, functions as a theologically rich figuration; it is a scriptural image that infuses theological significance into the social persecution experienced by the recipients. Like Diaspora Jews, they live a marginalized existence, scattered as strangers over the earth, committed to the norms of a world far away from the surrounding society. Like diaspora Jews, they live away from their homeland and share the hope of a future ingathering.

A crucial difference between the Jewish and Christian diaspora, however, lies in the location of the "Jerusalem" they seek.[28] As Paul taught, "Hagar is Mount Sinai in Arabia; she corresponds to the present Jerusalem, for she is in slavery with her children. But the Jerusalem above is free, and she is our mother" (Gal 4:25-26). In 1 Peter the earthly Jerusalem has been displaced; in fact it had probably been destroyed, for now God's promised inheritance is not equated with the land, but is instead "imperishable, undefiled, and unfading, kept in heaven for you" (1:4). We return, then, to the issue of the appropriation of Israel's identity in 1 Peter. This tendency occurs in other NT texts, but there we generally find a polemic that develops a corresponding theme of Christianity's displacement of Israel (cf. Matt 21:42-43; Acts 13:46; 18:5-6; 28:28; Phil 3:3).[29] Israel's identity is fully appropriated in 1 Peter, but there is no corresponding theme of displacement: Israel's failure

---

[23] Michaels, 7.

[24] ASV, NAB, Bigg, Selwyn; Beare, *1 Peter*; PDavids, *The First Epistle of Peter*.

[25] RSV, NRSV, ESV, ISV, Best.

[26] KJV, NIV, Elliott, Michaels.

[27] Elliott, *1 Peter*, 312.

[28] Beare, *1 Peter*, 49.

[29] For this I am indebted to the discussion of "Audience and Genre" in Michaels, xlix–lv.

to heed God's call is not discussed, and there is no polemic against the law or the temple. Indeed, Israel *qua* Israel seems to no longer exist, for its past is recast as proto-Christianity: the prophets were not serving themselves but future Christians (1:10-12); God's people are no longer defined by race or homeland but by "obedience to Jesus Christ" (1:2). Similarly, Israel's heroes are adopted as proto-Christians: the OT prophets prophesied about the sufferings and glories of Christ by the Spirit of Christ (1:11); both Sarah and the letter recipients share in the same hope (3:5); Noah's experience of the flood was an anticipation of Christian baptism (3:20-21); even Jews long dead have heard the gospel of Christ proclaimed (4:6).[30] In 1 Peter, then, the Jewish past becomes the property of Gentile Christianity; Israel becomes the "controlling metaphor" for the church.[31] The letter's recurring emphasis on old and new leaves the "old" historic Israel without an ongoing identity. As a people of the past, they are simply absorbed into the Gentile present. 1 Peter therefore reflects the widespread belief that Christians were, in Pauline terms, "the true circumcision" (Rom 2:28-29).

James

The prescript of James plays an important rhetorical role in the proper interpretation of the letter as a whole. Let us take a moment to consider again what James 1:1 communicates about its author and recipients. The name of James attached to a purportedly apostolic letter inevitably calls to mind the most well-known early church leader by that name, James the Just, who was known from the gospels, Acts, and Galatians (and indirectly from Jude) as the brother of the Lord and leader of the church in Jerusalem. However, as I noted toward the end of chapter two, further elements of the letter address suggest that the implied author is the *historicized* James of later church tradition. In the address "to the twelve tribes in the diaspora," readers recall more precisely the later, heightened understanding of James' authority: James was the first bishop of the first gathering of believers in Jerusalem; this letter is therefore to be received as a kind of episcopal encyclical sent from Jerusalem, the geographical center of emergent Christianity.

Further, James is presented as standing in the kind of privileged position that demands an audience with all the people of Israel. In this, one recalls the way that the Pseudo-Clementine *Recognitions* and the memoirs of Hegesippus presented James as a high priestly leader of immense authority who worked tirelessly for the conversion of the Jews. Thus, "diaspora" in James does not function in the figurative sense we find in 1 Peter; in fact it seems to be used primarily in the technical, geographical sense of the LXX and John 7:35 to identify the recipients as literal diaspora Jews. Though our hypothetical second-century author would have intended the Jewish "diaspora" to apply figuratively to his Christian readership (as the author of 1 Peter intended for his), the implied author of the letter intended a very literal designation:

[30] Michaels, l.
[31] P. Achtemeier, *1 Peter* (Hermeneia; Philadelphia: Fortress, 1996), 69–73.

he is James of Jerusalem, the leader of the Christian mission to Jews, addressing an ethnically Jewish audience residing in the diaspora.

It is possible that the author's use of the term reflects his concern over the absorption of Israel's identity found throughout 1 Peter. Where 1 Peter implies that historic Israel has no ongoing significance, the letter of James insists that there are, in fact, literal Jews in the world who are interested in hearing from the Jewish leader James the Just. The letter maintains that the Christian body includes not only Gentile Christians who are "honorary Jews,"[32] but also readers who are actual, ethnic Jews. The address of 1:1 is therefore almost certainly *retrospective*, designed to assert a distinct rhetorical situation: in this new actualization of the historic James, the reader is whisked back into an earlier period in Christian history wherein a vibrant mission to Jews existed in Jerusalem. The force of the letter's presence at the head of the CE collection must be fully felt at this point: this is a collection of letters emerging from the Christian mission *to Jews*. The canonical positioning of James and 1 Peter, then, offers a powerful witness to the continuity of God's covenants with Israel and the church. On the one hand, while the letter of James asserts that Christianity is *from Jews* and *for Jews*, 1 Peter's address to *Gentiles* as the eschatological Israel underwrites the history of earliest Christianity according to the Acts of the Apostles, which insists that the mission to the Gentiles was both born out of and embraced by the Jewish mission, well before Paul officially undertook his own mission (cf. Acts 8:26-40; 10:1–11:26). On the other hand, the sequence underscores the Pauline conviction that the salvation of God is "to the Jew *first* (James), and also to the Greek (1 Peter)" (Rom 1:16; 2:9-10). The sequence challenges Gentile (Marcionite?) readers who may forget that their inclusion in the salvation of God is the result of their being engrafted into the root of Israel (Rom 11:17).[33]

The parallel prescripts also connote a particular view of the relationship between the historicized James and Peter. As I noted in my introduction, Western church fathers of the second-century Catholic tradition understood the earliest apostolic leadership to be constituted by the relationship between Peter and Paul, "the two most glorious apostles," according to Irenaeus of Lyon (*Adv. Haer.* 3.3.1–2 [SC 211.30–32]). When the Eastern author of James imitated 1 Peter in its address to the "diaspora" (and, as we will see, wrote much of his opening chapter in imitation of 1 Peter 1:1–2:3), he may have been attempting to redraw the lines of authority according to a different scheme. Peter and Paul may be connected because of their association with Antioch, Corinth, and Rome, but James and Peter shared an earlier connection to the historic Jesus and the mother church in Jerusalem. In that city James sat on the throne. Though Peter was generally acknowledged to be the first among the twelve, his territory was the mission field. And though he was considered the first bishop of Rome, James was the first bishop of the first church in Jerusalem, *and Peter reported to him*. By addressing his letter "to the diaspora," the author offers

---

[32] K. Stendahl's term, quoted in Michaels, l.

[33] This construal of the Pauline connection is borrowed from Bauckham, *James*, 157.

a dramatic reassertion of James' apostolic authority. James writes "to the diaspora" from the mother church at the center of the Christian mission; Peter writes as a missionary who is a participant in that scattering, addressing his letter to other "exiles of the diaspora" like himself. Put sharply, James 1:1 asserts James' authority over Peter. As we have seen, this was a recurring theme in some strands of the later *Jakobusbild* analyzed in chapter 2.

Finally, with these differing rhetorical situations in mind, what kind of "diaspora" does each letter envision? In the LXX the diaspora was consistently described as a place of trials, difficulties and tribulations that threatened the believer's faithfulness to God (for example, Deut 4:25-31; 28:25f.; 30:3-4; 1 Kgs 22:17; Ps 43:11; 146:2-3; Isa 11:12; 56:8; Jer 13:12f.; 41:17; Tob. 13:5). Likewise, James is written to believers in the diaspora who are susceptible to the temptations (1:13-15) and deceptions (1:16) of the "world" (4:4-10), and may thus be led to "wander" (1:16; 5:19-20) after other gods. It seems safe to say, then, that our hypothetical author (like the author of 1 Peter) was also drawn to the diaspora image because of what it conveys about the experience of believers in the world: the diaspora is a place where God's people encounter various trials. However, as we will see, each letter envisions the "trials" differently. In 1 Peter, the trials have primarily to do with the *affliction* of social persecution; in James, however, the trials have more to do with the *allure* of the surrounding pagan society.

THE JOYFUL ENDURANCE OF TRIALS

The idea that faith is tested through trials is deeply rooted in the scriptures of Judaism. The central positive example was Abraham, who was tested and found faithful (Gen 22:1-18; cf., e.g., Jdt 8:26; Sir 44:19–20; *1 Macc.* 2:52; *4 Macc.* 16:18–20; *Pirke Avot* 5:3; Heb 11:17-19). Correspondingly, the negative example of Israel's failure to be faithful when they tested God in the wilderness (Exod 17:1f.; Num 14:20f.; Deut 9:22; cf., e.g., LXX Ps 77; 94:8f.; 105:14; Isa 7:12; Wis 1:2; Sir 18:23; Heb 3:7-10). Later Jewish wisdom literature associated "the test" with Hellenistic understandings of the probative role of afflictions in the human life (Jdt 8:25-27; Wis 3:5f.; Sir 2:1-6; 4:17-18; 2 Macc. 6:12-17; 4 Macc. 7:18-23; cf. *TDNT* 6.26); *4 Maccabees* in particular developed the theme in relation to Israel's martyrs whose patient endurance of trials rendered them worthy of honor before God. As we will see, our author appears to have had these classical Jewish traditions foremost in his mind when he shaped his account of the endurance of trials theme found in 1 Peter 1:6-9 and Romans 5:3-4.

Though a comparison of the passages shows that all three are structurally and terminologically quite similar, one immediately notes that James and 1 Peter seem closer to one another than either is to Romans:

James 1:2-4		
Joy	various trials	knowing that the
χαράν // πειρασμοῖ . . . ποικίλοις // γινώσκοντες ὅτι τὸ		
testing of your faith	produces endurance	perfection
δοκίμιον ὑμῶν τῆς πίστεως κατεργάζεται ὑπομονήν // τέλειον		

1 Peter 1:6-9		
Rejoice	various trials	that the genuineness of your
ἀγαλλιᾶσθε // ποικίλοις πειρασμοῖς ἵνα τὸ δοκίμιον ὑμῶν τῆς		
faith	result	
πίστεως τέλος		

Romans 5:3-4					
Boast sufferings	knowing that	produces	endurance	character	hope
καυχώμεθα θλίψεσιν εἰδότες ὅτι κατεργάζεται ὑπομονήν δοκιμήν ἐλπίδα					

One might add to this the fact that James and 1 Peter enter into their related discussions of joy in suffering at the beginning of their epistles, just after the parallel diaspora reference—further evidence of design in the relationship between the two letters—while Paul's is found in the midst of a broader discussion of Christian justification. On the terminological and structural bases alone, then, the James passage is closer to 1 Peter than that of Romans, though all three appear related.

1 Peter

The recipients of 1 Peter "have been born anew [ἀναγεννήσας] into a living hope through the resurrection of Jesus Christ from the dead" (1:3b), in order to receive "an inheritance which is imperishable, undefiled, and unfading, kept in heaven" (1:4) for those who "by God's power are guarded through faith for a salvation ready to be revealed in the last time" (1:5). The readers are "born anew into" a hope that has everything to do with what awaits them in the future; thus their existence is entirely reordered according to an eschatological reorientation made possible by Christ's resurrection. "In this" believers rejoice, "though now for a little while it is necessary" [ὀλίγον ἄρτι εἰ δέον]" for them "to be grieved by various trials" [λυπηθέντες ἐν ποικίλοις πειρασμοῖς]. Given that the recipients are abused for their Christian lifestyle (3:14-16; 4:4) and beliefs (3:15; 4:14-16), it seems clear that the unhappy "trials" described are, in fact, experiences of social persecution. They are able to rejoice *in spite of* this suffering-induced grief because the persecution is qualified in two important ways. First, in contrast to the inheritance that is "imperishable" and "unfading," the adversities they experience are "now" (ἄρτι) and "for a little while" (ὀλίγος); thus the pressure of temporal struggles is made relative in relation to the eternal salvation awaiting those who have been "born anew." The same sentiment is reaffirmed at the end of the letter: "After you have suffered a little while [ὀλίγον παθόντας αὐτὸς καταρτίσει], the God of all grace . . . will himself restore, confirm, strengthen and establish you" (5:10).

Second, the suffering is dignified by a theological reconsideration: They are not meaningless miseries but ποικίλοις πειρασμοῖ, the "various trials" of the test of faith tradition. The ἵνα clause (1:7) informs us that these trials are purposeful: they occur "in order that the genuineness of your faith [ἵνα τὸ δοκίμιον ὑμῶν τῆς πίστεῶ] . . . may result in [εὑρεθῆ εἰς[34]] praise and glory and honor at the revelation of Jesus Christ." Δοκίμιον is a neuter noun formed from the adjective δοκίμος ("genuine," "tested"); here it indicates the result of the trials and is therefore translated "genuineness" (*TDNT* 2.259).[35] The presence of the metallurgic metaphor (a regular feature of the "test of faith" tradition [for example, LXX Ps 65:10; Job 23:10; Isa 48:10; Zech 13:9; Mal 3:2-3; Sir 2:1-9]) also helps us to understand the δοκίμιον in context: by the use of extreme heat, the refiner melts away the various contaminants that keep the precious metal from being wholly pure. In the same way, the endurance of persecution has a refining effect on the believer, resulting in the recognition of "genuineness" at the Parousia. The "outcome" (τέλος) of this (1:9) is then found in "obtaining [κομιζόμενοι] the salvation of your souls." The fact that κομίζω is often used to describe the receipt of a reward simply underscores the overwhelmingly eschatological focus of the entire passage (for example, 2 Cor 5:10; Eph 6:8; Heb 11:13; 1 Pet 5:4).[36] Though present persecution causes grief, Christians nevertheless experience joy in the glorious reality of their imminent eternal inheritance.

Romans

Like 1 Peter 1:6-9, the parallel Romans passage on joy in suffering arises amidst comments regarding eschatological hope. After introducing God's gift of righteousness apart from the law (3:21-31), and supporting it by the example of Abraham (4:1-25), Paul turns to the implications for the life of the believer who has been made righteous by faith in Christ (chaps. 5–8). Through Jesus, Paul asserts, believers "have obtained access to this grace in which we stand," and on this basis are able to rejoice in the "hope of sharing the glory of God" (5:2). But here the Romans passage differs from 1 Peter, for in that letter the joyful apprehension of the living hope of the resurrection of Christ was threatened by the grievous reality of trials in the life of the believer. Where 1 Peter suggested Christians rejoice in hope *in spite of* these trials, Paul makes the even more radical claim that Christians rejoice *not only* in hope *but also* in the experience of suffering itself (5:2b-3a).

But why boast in suffering? Paul claims that Christians boast in suffering because of what it accomplishes: "suffering produces endurance [ὑπομονή], and

---

[34] Goppelt (91) notes that the verb is used to express the outcome of a trial (cf. 2 Pet 3:14; Rev 2:2).

[35] Cf. Davids, *James*, 68.

[36] Davids, *1 Peter*, 59.

endurance [produces] a tested character [δοκιμή], and a tested character [produces] hope" (5:3-4). The feminine noun δοκιμή is a rare word not found anywhere before Paul, though it is obviously related to the more common δοκίμιον and its attendant image of a metallurgic process (*TDNT* 2.255). In his use of it elsewhere, it sometimes means "ordeal" (2 Cor 8:2) or "proof" (2 Cor 9:13; 13:3), but in relation to people it seems to describe a "character" that has been tested and proved faithful (2 Cor 2:9; Phil 2:22).[37] This suffering-tested character, we are told, produces hope, presumably the kind referred to in 5:2, the "hope of sharing in the glory of God." Thus Paul asserts that Christians boast in suffering because it is the means by which God generates an eschatologically oriented, hope-filled character in the life of the believer.

This hope is confirmed in the believer's experience; it "does not disappoint [οὐ καταισχύνει] because God's love has been poured into our hearts by the Holy Spirit which he has given to us" (5:5). The verb καταισχύνω is translated "put to shame" (BDAG 517) and as James D. G. Dunn notes, its use here echoes a LXX theme.[38] While it is possible that Paul has Isaiah 28:16 in mind ("he who believes in him will not be put to shame"), as he cites that verse in 9:33 and 10:11, other passages use the verb in specific reference to the hope and trust of the forefathers:

> **Psalm 21:4-6**: In you our fathers hoped; they hoped, and you rescued them. To you they cried out and were saved; in you they hoped and were not put to shame [κατῃσχύνθησαν].

> **Sirach 2:10**: Consider the ancient generations and see: who ever trusted in the Lord and was put to shame [κατῃσχύνθη]?[39]

Indeed, even apart from these examples, it is obvious that Paul has Abraham in mind in this discussion of the purposefulness of suffering: The opening phrase (δικαιωθέντες οὖν ἐκ πίστεως, 5:1a) grounds this discussion in the surrounding context of justification by faith in Christ, and the repetition of key words from the previous section on Abraham (boast, 4:2; grace, 4:4,16; hope, 4:18; glory, 4:20) links the discussion of boasting in suffering with Abraham's hopeful trust in God. In this, Paul was simply following Jewish tradition, which often turned to Abraham as an example of endurance in suffering and faithfulness in testing.

---

[37] "Character" is preferred by C. H. Dodd, *The Epistle of Paul to the Romans* (MNTC; London: Hodder & Stoughton, 1932), 72; J. D. G. Dunn, *Romans 1–8* and *Romans 9–16* (WBC 38A & 38B; Waco, Tex.: Word Books, 1988), 245; RSV; NRSV; NIV, but it seems too generic; C. K. Barrett (*A Commentary on the Epistle to the Romans* [London: A&C Black, 1962], 104) suggests "tried character," and the ASV prefers "approvedness."

[38] Dunn, *Romans*, 252.

[39] Cf. Isa 54:1-4, and the *Prayer of Azariah* 35–42, which refers to Abraham in particular.

James

The parallel "joy in trials" passage in James reveals a good deal about our author's concerns. Initially one is struck by the fact that this passage is found at the very beginning of the letter, with nothing to introduce it apart from the prescript, in contrast with 1 Peter's opening eschatological affirmation to contextualize the theme. A quick glance over the form of the passage reveals a related difference: where the rhetoric of 1 Peter and Romans assumes the readers' basic agreement, the author of James speaks in the imperative in order to present an authoritative instruction.

The passage opens in verse two with a command: "Count it nothing but joy, my brethren, whenever you fall into various trials." The imperative form of the verb ἡγήομαι calls the reader to engage in a kind of reasoning (cf., for example, Wis 7:8; Acts 26:2; Phil 3:7-8; 1 Thess 5:13); thus the trials are to be "reckoned" or "counted" as joy. Indeed, the adjective πᾶσαν tells us they are to be considered "nothing but joy" or "pure joy," that is, joy unmixed with other emotions.[40] While 1 Peter 1:6 candidly admits that rejoicing over the future is intermingled with grief over present persecution, and Romans 5:2-3 calls believers to "boast" in afflictions, James seems to discourage such expressions in favor of a more reasoned attitude. Further, where 1 Peter refers to a specific context ("though now for a little while it is necessary"), James generalizes: One must count trials as joy "whenever" (ὅταν) one might "fall into" (περιπίπτω) them. Thus, what is commanded is a consistent, confident and resolutely positive orientation toward the trials of life.

The phrase τὸ δοκίμιον ὑμῶν τῆς πίστεως in James requires a different translation from its exact counterpart in 1 Peter. Where δοκίμιον indicated the *result* of suffering in that text, here it signifies the *instrument* of the verb κατεργάζεται; thus it is not "the genuineness of your faith" but "the testing of your faith." Further, here tests of faith "produce endurance" (κατεργάζεται ὑπομονήν) as they do in Romans 5. But James has yet another exhortation for his readers: "But let patient endurance have its perfect work [ἔργον τέλειον], in order that you may be perfect and complete [τέλειοι καὶ ὁλόκληροι], lacking in nothing." Several comments must be made about the interpretation of this passage in context. Though it is, of course, the case that the letter is eschatological in outlook,[41] it is noteworthy that this particular exhortation does not find its immediate basis in eschatological fulfillment. According to 1 Peter, believers rejoice in suffering because they know that through trials their faith will be proved genuine at the revelation of Jesus, but James makes no mention of Jesus or his coming revelation; the goal is not genuineness at the

---

[40] Laws, 50.

[41] Argued in T. C. Penner chap. 3: "The Eschatological Framework of the Epistle of James" (*The Epistle of James and Eschatology* [JSNTSup 121; Sheffield: Sheffield Academic, 1996], 121–213). It is true that 1:12 repeats many of the key words in vv. 2-4 (ὑπομένω, πειρασμός, δόκιμος) in describing eschatological reward, and thereby forms an *inclusio* for 1:2-12; but the absence of such a theme in vv. 2-4 places the emphasis on the current moral perfection of the believer.

Parousia per se, but the current moral perfection of the believer. As Laws reminds us, both τέλειος and ὁλόκληρος carry connotations of moral completeness and blamelessness;[42] one finds a parallel in 3:2, where the "perfect man" (τέλειος ἀνήρ) makes no mistakes and controls himself entirely. Thus, where 1 Peter appeals to the test of faith tradition in an overtly eschatological manner to encourage readers to hold out amidst persecutions, James does so in an ethical and probative manner more akin to the tradition's Hellenistic Jewish origins. The orienting goal is not the cessation of suffering at the end of time, but the "perfect work" of a character made whole through the endurance of trials.

What kind of "trials" does our author have in mind? Where 1 Peter is written to provide an enduring word of hope amidst temporary social persecutions, the passage in James is concerned to make the generalized assertion that ongoing "tests of faith" are an appropriate and necessary component of the believer's life. Again, this is the historicized James writing to Jewish believers in the diaspora; whether they "hold the faith of Jesus Christ" (2:1) or not, accommodation to the ways of the foreign culture remained a grave temptation. The letter will go on to make it clear that the believers are to resist this temptation to accommodate, to remain unstained by the world (1:27), unaffected by the world's system of valuing (1:9-11; 2:1-7; 4:13-17), and undivided in their allegiance to God alone (4:4-10). Thus, it seems that the "trials" James the Just has in mind are not the afflictions of persecution, but the seductive allures of the pagan lifestyle.

Considering the three passages in tandem, we note that while James 1:2-4 is terminologically and structurally closer to 1 Peter 1:6-9, it is thematically closer to Romans 5:3-4.[43] Though in context both Romans and 1 Peter are celebrating *hope*, James and Paul ultimately agree in their praise of the virtuous, enduring *character* that results from suffering. What separates the James and Romans passages, of course, is Paul's christology. Like 1 Peter, Paul understands Christian suffering and hope through the interpretive framework of the death and resurrection of Christ (for example, Rom 8:17; 2 Cor 1:3-7; Phil 1:29-30). The author of James, by contrast, grounds his exhortation to faithful endurance in an entirely non-christological manner. Like the James of Hegesippus, so also the piety exhorted in the letter is not patterned after Jesus, but after a kind of heroic image of holiness derived from various traditional Jewish sources. We have already noted how Abraham functioned in this tradition as an exemplar of patience in suffering and faithfulness in testing. Like Paul in Romans 5, James also has Abraham in mind: in its concern to relate faith with its appropriate product by means of ὑπομονή, the opening exhortation of James anticipates the Abraham argument in 2:14-26. Note especially the correspondence between 1:3-4 with 2:22:

---

[42] Laws, 54; cf. Gen 6:9; Deut 18:13; Sir 44:17; Wis 15:3.
[43] Dibelius, *James*, 75–76; Davids, *James*, 66.

1:3-4: ". . . the testing of your faith [πίστεως] produces [κατεργάζεται] stead-fastness. And let steadfastness have its full [τέλειον] effect, that you may be per-fect [τέλειοι] and complete. . . ."

2:22: ". . . faith [πίστις] was active along with [συνήργει] his works [ἔργοις], and by the works faith [πίστις] was perfected [ἐτελειώθη]."[44]

The author of James appears to have taken the Petrine "joy in trials" passage as his model, and shifted it in a more Pauline direction in order to anticipate his more direct interaction with Paul's view of Abraham in 2:14-26.

But Abraham is not the only model behind this text. Later the reader is told, "As an example of suffering and patience [μακροθυμία] . . . take the prophets who spoke in the name of the Lord. Behold we call those blessed who endured [ὑπομείναντας]; you have heard of the endurance [ὑπομονή] of Job, and you have seen the purpose [τέλος] of the Lord, how the Lord is compassionate and merciful." In his non-christological appeal to these themes, it seems that the author of James wanted "to revive again the historic sentiment"[45] of early Judaism for his second century Gentile readers. Hence, while the orienting model for Chris-tian suffering in 1 Peter and Romans is Christ, in James it is Abraham, Job, the prophets, the other faithful characters celebrated in the LXX test of faith tradi-tion—and, of course, the historicized James himself. As we will see, this is but one of the many ways the second century author of the letter reanimated the voice of the historicized James in order to reorient Christian affirmations according to his reconstructed kerygma of the earlier Christian mission to Jews.

THE PROPHETS OF ISRAEL

Early Christians found the prophetic writings of Israel to be a source of invalu-able riches in their reflection on what God had done in Jesus of Nazareth. Among these texts, pride of place belonged to Isaiah, whose words are widely quoted in nearly every NT text and have contributed to almost every area of the church's theology.[46] Its use in 1 Peter is a case in point; the author appeals to the writing of this prophet far more than any other, referring to it on as many as twenty-one occasions.[47] Though much could be said about these passages, the important point to be grasped for our purposes is the way in which 1 Peter consistently interprets the scripture in an overtly Christian and/or christological manner for the benefit of his Gentile audience. I have already demonstrated how Israel's historical identity is understood in 1 Peter to form the prehistory and present identity of the Gentile church. The passage currently under examination (1:23-25) offers us yet another

---

[44] Johnson, *James*, 178; Wall, *James*, 148.

[45] Dibelius, *James*, 72.

[46] See, e.g., J. Sawyer, *The Fifth Gospel: Isaiah in the History of Christianity* (Cambridge: Cambridge University Press, 1996).

[47] Ten of these are direct citations: 1:23-24; 2:6, 8, 9; 2:22, 24, 25; 3:14, 15; 4:14.

instance of this trend. Likewise, the parallel passage in James (1:9-11) will provide another example of our author's concern to reorient Petrine texts in a more traditionally Jewish direction.

1 Peter

As a scriptural substantiation for the claim, "You have been born anew, not of perishable seed but of imperishable, through the living and abiding word of God" (1:23), the author cites Isaiah 40:6-8 (from the LXX[48]). As is clear from its many other appearances in early Christian texts, Isaiah 40 was among the most important prophecies for understanding Christ as the fulfillment of OT prophetic promises (e.g., Matt 3:3; 24:35; Mark 1:2-3; Luke 1:76; 2:30; 3:4-6; 21:33; John 1:23; Rom 11:34; 1 Cor 2:16; Rev 22:7, 12; 1 Clem. 34; Dial. 50). The inaugural prophecy of second Isaiah (chaps. 40–55) conveys God's consolation to the exiled people of Israel. As many commentators have noted, the citation of Isaiah 40:6-8 makes it quite clear that the author of 1 Peter had God's consolation of exiled Israel in mind when he wrote his letter.[49] Like Isaiah 40, 1 Peter is addressed to believers who, despite their divine election, are suffering in exile (1:1, 17; 2:11). The verses prior to both Isaiah 40:6-8 and 1 Peter 1:24-25 call believers to prepare for the immanent revelation of God (Isa 40:3-5; 1 Pet 1:6-8, 13, 20). Most significantly, in the verses following the cited Isaiah text, the addressee is commissioned by God to be "one who preaches good news [εὐαγγελιζόμενος] to Jerusalem" (40:9). In the same way, after quoting "the word of the Lord abides forever," the author of 1 Peter offers this interpretation: "That word is the good news which was preached [εὐαγγελισθέν] to you" (1:25b).

Two points must be articulated concerning this interpretation of the Isaiah passage. First, though the living and abiding "word" of God in 1:23 is λόγος, the "word" of the Lord quoted from Isaiah and the "word" that was preached as good news in 1 Peter 1:25 are both ῥῆμα. Thus the author of 1 Peter is drawing a connection between the verbal "word" spoken by the prophet and the "word" that had been preached to his audience. Second, the author has made a significant alteration to the LXX source: where the LXX has, "the word of our God [θεός] abides forever," 1 Peter 1:25 has "the word of the Lord [κύριος] abides forever." The change enables the implication the author seeks to make: the eternal "word of the Lord" is the same as the preached gospel of Christ that the recipients of the letter have already heard.[50]

Thus, when the author says of God's enduring word, "that word is the good news which was preached to you," he is making two important claims. On the one hand, he is drawing to a conclusion the point he has been making throughout the first chapter: the "good news" preached about Christ is equated with the imperishable seed that gives birth to new life. Just as God once delivered the people of Israel

---

[48] Note that the LXX differs from the NT in its omission of most of v. 7.

[49] Selwyn, 152; Goppelt, 127; and Elliott, 1 Peter, 390.

[50] Kelly, Commentary, 81; Elliott, 1 Peter, 391.

from their temporary exile in Babylon, so now God in Christ has enabled a new birth that will deliver Christians from the sufferings of this temporary existence. On the other hand, the author is making a striking claim about the status of ancient Jewish prophecy. The reference to the Christian proclamation of good news in 1:25 calls to mind an earlier passage in the letter (1:3-9) that addressed the revelation of Jesus Christ and the salvation it will bring. In 1:10-12 the author goes on to claim,

> The prophets who prophesied of the grace that was to be yours searched and inquired about this salvation; they inquired what person or time was indicated by the Spirit of Christ within them when predicting the sufferings of Christ and the subsequent glory. It was revealed to them that they were serving not themselves but you, in the things which have now been announced to you by those who preached the good news to you through the Holy Spirit sent from heaven, things into which angels long to look.

The words of the ancient Jewish prophets are not contextually authenticated, for they were addressing future events. Their focus was Christ, and their true audience was not their Jewish contemporaries but later Gentile Christians; indeed, the author asserts it was "revealed to them" that this was the case. It is therefore not enough to simply say that the Isaianic context of exile and deliverance was *parallel* to that of the letter's recipients; it is more precisely viewed as a *prefiguration* of what God would do later in Christ and among Christians.

This is not the kind of typological prefiguring we find, for example, in 1 Corinthians 10:1-11, where OT figures and events serve as examples or warnings for the Christian church. It more closely approaches the sort of typology of fulfillment we find in the letter to the Hebrews, where what happened in shadowy form *then* is concretely actualized *now*. But the typology in Hebrews involves a denigration of the prototype: the OT priest entered a "copy of the true" sanctuary Christ now inhabits (9:24); Christians now worship in a "greater and more perfect" temple (9:11); Christ's is a "more excellent ministry" as the mediator of a "better covenant" (8:6), one that renders the former obsolete (8:13). Such polemical denigration is not found in 1 Peter, which offers no explicit argument that the church has *displaced* Israel. If anything, the Christianity of 1 Peter has *absorbed* Israel; as Achtemeier puts it, the reality of Israel passes "without remainder" into the reality of the new people of God.[51] Thus 1 Peter might be seen to present an implicit denigration of historic Israel insofar as the latter ceases to exist as an independent entity; it "existed as a chosen people simply to point forward to the people who would be chosen in Christ."[52] There are no Christians, Jews, or Pagans in 1 Peter; there are only Christians, proto-Christians and non-Christian "Gentiles." The word of the Lord that abides forever is the Christian gospel, the ancient Jewish prophets are the servants of later Gentile Christians, and the words of the prophets are properly understood as proto-gospel.

---

[51] Achtemeier, 69.
[52] Achtemeier, 70.

James

The use of Jewish prophetic literature in James could not be more different, for in this letter we do not find a fulfillment-interpretive strategy wherein the prophets point exclusively to Christ and Christianity. Indeed, there is no mention of prophetic fulfillment and Christ is barely named. Instead, it is the *prophets themselves* who serve as examples for James.[53] First, James speaks in imitation of the prophets: He uses imagery found in prophetic literature;[54] calls friends of the world "adulteresses" (μοιχαλίδες), a prominent prophetic description of idolaters (cf. Isa 57:3; Jer 3:8-9; 13:27; Ezek 16:38; 23:45; Hos 3:1); and his condemnation of the rich in 5:1-6 clearly echoes a variety of prophetic texts (for example, Isa 5:8-9; 51:8; Jer 12:3). Second, he assumes a prophetic ethical stance: he identifies pure religion in terms of caring for orphans and widows (1:27; cf. Isa 1:17; Jer 7:6; Zech 7:10), and he sides unequivocally with the poor against the rich (5:1-5; cf. Isa 3:14-15; Amos 2:6-7; 3:10; 4:1; 8:4-6). Finally, as I have already noted, he lists the prophets themselves as examples "of suffering and patience" (5:10) and Elijah as an example of righteousness and fervent prayer (5:16-18). As we have seen, where 1 Peter uses the prophets to point to Christ, James points directly to the prophets themselves. Once again we recall Hegesippus's depiction of James' piety, one shaped entirely according to the ideals of the OT with no indication of anything distinctly "Christian" about it.

This difference between the two letters is borne out in the parallel appeal to Isaiah 40 found in James 1:9-11. The fact that this is the third significant point of connection with 1 Peter in eleven short verses (in sequence, no less) strengthens the supposition that some kind of formal connection exists between the two.

James	1 Peter	Link?
1:1	1:1	Recipients in the διασπορά
1:2-4	1:6-9	Rejoice/be joyful in various trials (ποικίλοις πειρασμοῖς) + the testing/genuineness of your faith (τὸ δοκίμιον ὑμῶν τῆς πίστεως)
1:10-11	1:23-24	Extended allusion to/quotation of Isaiah 40

If this formal connection corresponds to the terms set out by my hypothesis, then the author of James has come to the Isaiah 40 passage *through* his recollection of its use in 1 Peter; therefore we should expect to find a redactional shift that agrees with our author's concern to preach in harmony with Peter, whilst speaking in the distinctive voice of the historicized James of Jerusalem. Accordingly, we note immediately that he does not cite the text as 1 Peter does, but instead blends the Isaianic terminology allusively into a command for believers to be conformed according to

[53] Johnson, *James*, 32.
[54] Compare 1:10-11 with Isa 40:6-7; 2:23 with Isa 41:8; 4:8 with Zech 1:3; 4:14 with Hos 13:3.

the reality of God's eschatological judgment. So while the author of 1 Peter cites Israel's authoritative prophetic texts, the author of James paints James himself in the image of an authoritative prophet of Israel.

A closer examination of the passage will expand this point. Like 1 Peter, our author has also grounded his allusion in the broader literary context of Isaiah 40, but in a strikingly different manner. The Petrine author cited the text as a prophetic *foretelling* of a christological *fulfillment*: "That word [the word of God preached by Isaiah] is [fulfilled in] the good news which was preached to you [the gospel of Christ preached by the apostles]." Significantly, however, the author of James omits Isaiah 40:8 from his allusion. Instead, he has James of Jerusalem follow the text quite literally as a prophecy of God's immanent eschatological judgment. Todd Penner has demonstrated the extent to which this interpretation dominated in second temple Judaism.[55] This more traditional understanding of the text applies equally well to the grass imagery, which was often used not simply as an image of human temporality (as in 1 Peter and elsewhere[56]) but as a cipher for human wickedness: note especially the Targum of Isaiah 40:6-8, which substitutes "all flesh is grass" with "all *the wicked* are as grass . . . the wicked one dies, his plans perish, but the word of our God abides forever."[57]

Three points of contact between Isaiah 40 and James 1:9-11 reveal that our author approached the text in this more traditional manner. First, in lieu of the fact that Israel's "humiliation" had ended (40:2), Isaiah states that every valley "will be filled" (πληρωθήσεται) and every mountain "will be humbled" (ταπεινωθήσεται, 40:4). The author of James takes up these images of reversal and focuses them on the lowly brother (ὁ ταπεινός) who is exhorted to boast in his exaltation (ὑψόω), and the rich person (ὁ πλούσιος) who is called to do likewise in the face of his coming humiliation (ταπεινόω). Second, where the LXX of Isaiah compares "all flesh" to fading grass, our author follows the tradition reflected in the Targum by focusing the image on the "wicked" rich person himself: "Like the flower of the grass *he* will pass away" (Jas 1:10b). Indeed, the author intensifies the eschatological condemnation by the addition of verbs that emphasize the rich person's destruction: he will not simply fall (ἐκπίπτω), he will "pass away" (παρέρχομαι); he does not simply wither (ξηραίνω), he will "die out" (μαραίνω) right in the midst of his busy life. Finally, Isaiah 40:3 calls Jerusalem to "prepare the way [ὁδός] of the Lord" and to "make straight the path [τρίβος] of God." Our author appears to have had this call in mind when he framed his Isaiah 40 allusion with an emphasis on the "ways"

[55] Penner, 204–6; cf. *1 En.* 1.6; 57.3; *Pss. Sol.* 11.4; *T. Mos.* 10:4; 1QS.8.14; *Sib. Or.* 3.680; 8.234.

[56] Job 14:1-2; Ps 37:1-2, 20; 90:5-6; 103:15-18; Isa 37:27; 51:12; *2 Bar* 82.7; 4Q185.1:9-12; *2 Esdr.* 15:50. The wording of the grass imagery in James corresponds most closely to Isaiah 40:7.

[57] See R. Davidson, "The Imagery of Isaiah 40:6-8 in Tradition and Interpretation," in *The Quest for Context and Meaning: Studies in Biblical Intertextuality in Honor of James A. Sanders*, ed. Craig A. Evans and Shemaryahu Talmon (Leiden: Brill, 1997), 37–55.

of the unstable and the rich: The "double-minded man" of James 1:8 does not receive anything from God because he is "unstable in all his ways [ὁδοῖς]"; likewise, the rich person of v. 11 is warned that he will "fade away in the midst of his ways [πορείαις]." Read intertextually, then, the historicized James is asserting in 1:9-11 (and throughout, but especially in passages like 2:1-7, 4:13-16 and 5:1-6) that the arrogant, supposedly exalted "way" of the rich will in fact be humiliated because it fails to prepare the "way" of the Lord's salvation.

It should not be missed that this "preparation for salvation" is precisely the stated purpose of the letter of James: as the reader is told in the final verse, "whoever brings back a sinner from the error of his way [ὁδός] will save his soul from death and will cover a multitude of sins" (5:20; cf. 1:16). In contrast to 1 Peter, the implied James is not interested in comforting his readers; indeed, much of the letter seems designed to increase the level of *discomfort* experienced by believers who have made themselves at home in the diaspora. Likewise, the dominant theme is not christological *fulfillment*, but an exhortation to *prepare* for God's imminent arrival as eschatological judge, as the subsequent verse makes plain: "Blessed is the man who endures trial, for when he has stood the test he will receive the crown of life which God has promised to those who love him" (1:12; cf. 2:12-13; 4:7-10,11-17; 5:1-11). James is here writing as an authoritative leader to Jews in the literal diaspora, whose trials are not associated with oppressive *abuse* per se but with the seductive *allure* of their surrounding pagan culture which constantly entices them to wander away from the narrow paths of God's salvation.

By way of transition to the next section, I conclude with one further contextually significant parallel between James and 1 Peter. Though our author omits the important reference to the "word" of God in his parallel appeal to Isaiah 40, he does go on immediately to speak of a "word" of God in the opening chapter of his letter. In parallel with 1 Peter 1:23, James says in 1:18 that God "gave us birth through a word of truth" (ἀπεκύησεν ἡμᾶς λόγῳ ἀληθείας). Of course, when 1 Peter describes being born anew through the word of God he uses ἀναγεννάω and not ἀποκυέω as James does (he chose that verb in order to parallel his previous use of the same verb in 1:15, where sin gives birth to death). Nevertheless, James' connection of "birth" language with "word of truth" is striking, given that Paul frequently uses "word of truth" as a designation for the gospel (2 Cor 6:7; Eph 1:13; Col 1:5; 2 Tim 2:15). Going on to James 1:21, readers are exhorted to "receive with meekness the implanted word which is able to save your souls" (δέξασθε τὸν ἔμφυτον λόγον τὸν δυνάμενον σῶσαι τὰς ψυχὰς ὑμῶν). For a number of very valid reasons, most interpreters hear in this yet another implicit reference to the gospel. First, though the notion of an ἔμφυτος λόγος derives from Stoic thought[58] and can be translated "innate word" (cf. Wis 12:10), the fact that the λόγος must be "received" points to a word that comes from *outside* the individual, not inside.

_____

[58] M. A. Jackson-McCabe (*Logos and Law in the Letter of James: The Law of Nature, the Law of Moses, and the Law of Freedom* [NovTSup 100] Leiden: Brill, 2001]) offers an extended defense of reading James as a Stoic text.

Further, the verb δέχομαι is often combined with λόγος in Christian exhortations to receive the gospel (Luke 8:13; Acts 8:14; 11:1; 17:11; 1 Thess 1:6; 2:13; cf. 2 Cor 11:4). Third, the idea of an "implanted word" is reminiscent of a number of OT texts that describe God's intention, after the punitive dispersion of the Jews, to place the law within their hearts (for example, Deut 30:1-14; Jer 31:33). Finally, with all this in mind, it is easily assumed that a "word" described in a Christian text as being "able to save your souls" must refer to the Christian gospel. Despite all this, it has to be acknowledged that the connection is never made overtly clear for us. Though the text abounds with suggestions that the author has the gospel in mind, it is the reader who must make this connection on the author's behalf.

Just as the reader is ready to make this connection, however, the author goes on to exhort in 1:22 that the "word" must be "done" and not simply "heard." The phrase is an extremely close echo of Romans 2:13.

> **Romans 2:13**: For it is not the hearers of the law [οὐ γὰρ οἱ ἀκροαταὶ νόμου] who are righteous before God, but the doers of the law [ἀλλ᾽ οἱ ποιηταὶ νόμου] who will be made righteous.

> **James 1:22**: But be doers of the word [γίνεσθε δὲ ποιηταὶ λόγου], and not hearers only [καὶ μὴ ἀκροαταί], deceiving yourselves.

Though our author uses λόγος instead of νόμος, it is clear that he too has the "law" in mind here. The illustrative simile offered in 1:23-25 compares the one who hears but does not "do" with one who looks into a mirror and, going away, immediately forgets what he looked like. "But he who looks into the perfect *law* of liberty [ὁ δὲ παρακύψας τέλειον τὸν τῆς ἐλευθερίας] and perseveres, being no hearer of forgetfulness but a doer of works, he will be blessed in his doing" (1:25). The mirror of v. 24 into which one "observes" one's face is set in parallel with the "perfect law of liberty" which is "looked into"; thus the "word" that is to be "done" is the law, the perfect νόμος of liberty.

Once again, many have heard in this "perfect law of liberty" an indirect reference to the gospel. First, though some Stoically influenced thinkers in early Judaism could associate the observance of the law with freedom (*Prob.* 45; 4 Macc. 5:22-26; *Pirke Avot* 3:5; 6:2), the equation of the two is not found in the LXX and has struck many interpreters as a Christian way of speaking about the law as it has been fulfilled in Christ.[59] Second, in 2:8 our author will refer to Leviticus 19:18 ('You shall love your neighbor as yourself') as the νόμος βασιλικός. Whether this is rendered "the royal law," "the law of the king," or "the law of the kingdom," it brings to mind Jesus' assignment of the love command as a summary of the Torah. Finally, in 2:12 the "royal law" is equated with a "law of liberty" that is presented as the standard by which all believers will be judged. Given all this, many read νόμος in James as a cipher for a "christologically modified" νόμος, that is, the law as it is understood

---

[59] E.g., Davids, *James*, 99–100; Martin, 51.

through the lens of the gospel.[60] But why does James not make this connection explicit for his readers? He speaks repeatedly of the "word," using terminology used elsewhere to describe the gospel, but he never makes the gospel connection overt; and the clarification he does offer thwarts our expectations, because he equates "the word" not with the Christian gospel but with an earlier dispensation of God's word, that of the Jewish law. Once again, it seems that the author is echoing 1 Peter in an intentionally ambiguous fashion in order to plant Christian terminology firmly in Jewish soil. Read in parallel, it seems as though our author is striving to make sure his readers do not dissociate the word of the gospel from God's prior word to Israel.

We turn in the next section to look more closely at the presentation of the law in James as compared to that of Paul in Romans. Before we turn away temporarily from 1 Peter, however, I should take a moment to summarize the opening parallels between James and 1 Peter.

James	1 Peter	Link?
1:1	1:1	Recipients in the διασπορά
1:2-4	1:6-9	Rejoice/be joyful in various trials (ποικίλοις πειρασμοῖς) + the testing/genuineness of your faith (τὸ δοκίμιον ὑμῶν τῆς πίστεως)
1:10-11	1:23-24	Extended allusion to/quotation of Isaiah 40
1:18	1:23	Birth (ἀποκυέω / ἀναγεννάω) by a λόγος
1:21-25	1:23-25	Λόγος as gospel/law

We see that the two letters make contact at five points, in parallel sequence, in their first twenty-five verses. This impressive level of interaction suggests something more than an unintentional, independent appeal to the same "common stock" of traditions. If James is a second-century text, it simply makes more sense to assume that James is literarily dependent on 1 Peter.

The Law

It is clear that the author of our letter wanted to demonstrate that James of Jerusalem shared a broad agreement with the Apostle Paul regarding such centrally Jewish themes as the nature of Torah and God's identity as lawgiver and eschatological judge. This accord is made evident by, among other things, a number of intriguing parallels.

---

[60] Cf. Martin (67) who suggests that νόμος in James means "law," but νόμος with a modifier refers to something different—a new, Christian law.

Romans 2:5-6: But by your hard and impenitent heart you are storing up [ϑησαυ-ρίζεις] wrath for yourself on the day of wrath when God's righteous judgment will be revealed. For he will give to each one according to his works. . . .

James 2:14; 5:3: What does it profit, my brethren, if a man says he has faith but has not works? Can his faith save him? . . . You have stored up [ἐϑησαυρίσατε] treasure for the last days.

Romans 2:11: For God shows no partiality [οὐ γάρ ἐστιν προσωπολημψία παρὰ τῷ ϑεῷ]. All who have sinned without the law will also perish without the law, and all who have sinned under the law will be judged by the law.

James 2:1, 9: My brethren, show no partiality [μὴ ἐν προσωπολημψίαις] as you hold the faith of our Lord Jesus Christ . . . if you show partiality, you commit sin, and are convicted by the law as transgressors.

Romans 2:13: For it is not the hearers of the law [οἱ ἀκροαταὶ νόμου] who are righteous before God, but the doers of the law [οἱ ποιηταὶ νόμου] who will be made righteous.

James 1:22: But be doers of the word [γίνεσϑε δὲ ποιηταὶ λόγου], and not hearers only [καὶ μὴ μόνον ἀκροαταί], deceiving yourselves. . . . But he who looks into the perfect law of liberty and perseveres, being no hearer of forgetfulness but a doer of works, he shall be blessed in his doing.

Romans 13:8-10: Owe no one anything, except to love one another; for he who loves his neighbor has fulfilled [πεπλήρωκεν] the law. The commandments, "You shall not commit adultery, you shall not kill, you shall not steal, you shall not covet," and any other commandment, are summed up [ἀνακεφαλαιοῦται] in the sentence, "You shall love your neighbor as yourself." Love does no wrong to a neighbor; therefore love is the fulfilling of the law [πλήρωμα οὖν νόμου ἡ ἀγάπη].

Galatians 5:3, 14: I testify again to every man who receives circumcision that he is bound to keep the whole law [ὀφειλέτης ἐστὶν ὅλον τὸν νόμον ποιῆσαι]. . . . For the whole law [πᾶς νόμος] is fulfilled [πεπλήρωται] in one word, "You shall love your neighbor as yourself."

James 2:8-11: If you really fulfill [τελεῖτε] the royal law, according to the scripture, "You shall love your neighbor as yourself," you do well. But if you show partiality, you commit sin, and are convicted by the law as transgressors. For whoever keeps the whole law [ὅστις γὰρ ὅλον τὸν νόμον τηρήσῃ] but fails in one point has become guilty of all of it. For he who said "Do not commit adultery," said also "Do not kill." If you do not commit adultery but do kill, you have become a transgressor of the law.

Romans 14:4: Who are you to judge the servant of another [σὺ τίς εἶ ὁ κρίνων ἀλλότριον οἰκέτην]? It is before his own Master that he stands or falls.

James 4:12: There is one lawgiver and judge, he who is able to save and to destroy. But who are you that you judge your neighbor [σὺ δὲ τίς εἶ ὁ κρίνων τὸν πλησίον]?

But despite these and other points of agreement, it is evident that our author sought in his letter to uphold the traditional notion that the two leaders had serious disagreements when it came to the ongoing significance of Torah for the life of the believer.

Does the Law Bring Liberty and Life, or Slavery and Death?

Our author refers to the law as "the perfect law of liberty" (1:25). Paul would have entirely disagreed.[61] For Paul the law was certainly "spiritual" (Rom 7:14) and even "holy and just and good" (7:12), but it was not perfect *precisely because* it could not liberate the believer (8:3) or give life (Gal 3:21). In fact, its advent aroused and increased sin (Rom 5:20; 7:5). Thus, where James says the law brings freedom (ἐλευθερία), Paul insists the law brings slavery (δουλεία). In Romans Paul speaks of the law as that which "held us captive" (7:6); it may be spiritual, but for carnal humans who are "sold under sin" (7:14) it simply "revives" sin and leads to death (7:9-11). Indeed, Paul can say, "the very commandment which promised life proved to be death to me" (7:10). Standing in contrast to this is the "law of the Spirit of life in Christ Jesus" which "has set me free from the law of sin and death" (8:2). While it is quite clear that Paul is actually *defending* the law in Romans 7 by naming sin the real culprit (cf. 7:7, 12-14), the fact remains that he has associated the two so closely in his discussion that it is difficult if not impossible to separate them. Though the law is holy, it had nevertheless become sin's ally and agent in the cultivation of slavery and death.[62] Likewise, in Galatians, Paul can refer to Jewish believers who insist on the circumcision of Gentiles as "false brothers who slipped in to spy out our freedom [ἐλευθερία] which we have in Christ Jesus, that they might bring us into bondage [ἵνα ἡμᾶς καταδουλώσουσιν]" (Gal 2:4). The comparison of the law to slavery continues in chapter four, where the reader is presented with an allegory comparing Hagar and Sarah to the two covenants, one "from Mount Sinai, bearing children for slavery . . . corresponds to the present Jerusalem. But the Jerusalem above is free, and she is our mother" (Gal 2:24-26). To be sure, rather than bring life and freedom, Paul asserts that the law brought slavery, sin, and death.

A closer examination increases the possibility that the author of James might have intended his discussion of sin, freedom, and the law in 1:13-25 to be read

---

[61] Though Jackson-McCabe (249–50) alerted me to the idea that the qualifier "liberty" was motivated by Paul's description of the law as "slavery," the extended comparison that follows is largely my own.

[62] Dunn, *Romans*, 377.

against the Pauline construal of the law as it is presented in Romans 7:7-11. Beyond
the conspicuous fact that one refers to the law as "freedom" and the other as "slavery," readers should take note of how the debate unfolds amidst the following
important parallels:

1) Paul does not call the law "sin" in Romans 7:7, but illustrates his belief that
the law gives knowledge of sin by insisting, "I would not have known desire
[ἐπιθυμία] if the law had not said, 'do not covet' [οὐκ ἐπιθυμήσεις]."
James 1:14, by contrast, insists that the experience of ἐπιθυμία is entirely
one's own.

2) Paul says that sin received (λαμβάνω) opportunity in the law, and through
the law sin was able to work (κατεργάζομαι) all kinds of ἐπιθυμίαν in
him (Rom 7:8a). By contrast, James 1:15 insists the opposite: ἐπιθυμία
"*con*ceived" (συλααμβάνω) sin, and remedy is found in doing works of the
law (1:25).

3) Paul insists, "Apart from the law sin lies dead [νεκρός]. I was once alive
[ζάω] apart from the law, but when the commandment came sin was made
alive again and I died [ἀποθνῄσκω]; and the commandment which was
supposed to lead into life led me into death [θάνατος]" (Rom 7:8b-10).
The law is thus sin's instrument in killing.[63] By contrast, James 1:15 says that
it is sin alone, when fully developed, that gives birth to death (θάνατος),
but one is blessed when the "perfect law" is "done" (1:21-25).

4) Though Paul insists that sin found opportunity through God's law, and
through the law sin "deceived me and by it killed me" (Rom 7:11), the
reader of James 1:13-16 is charged to "not be deceived" into thinking that
God is the cause of the sin that results in death.

Paul claimed that ignorance was bliss before the coming of the law (Rom 7:7),
but the law brought desire and death. The author of James considered this line of
thought a deception that by implication risked making God the ultimate source
of temptation, sin, and death. Though Paul could affirm, "Christ is the end of the
law" (Rom 10:4), "you are severed from Christ, you who would be justified by the
law" (Gal 5:4), and "I died to the law so that I might live to God" (Gal 2:19), our
hypothetical author found in the traditional image of James an early apostolic leader
who maintained a far less oppositional position on the matter. Here was a follower
of Christ who apparently saw no conflict between gospel and law. We should recall
that the second-century historicized James of Jerusalem functioned as a kind of
liminal figure whose life and teaching bridged the two covenants; he was firmly
grounded in the old, yet nevertheless bore witness to the new by means of that very
grounding. Despite Paul's strident differentiation between the two covenants, the
first bishop of the first Christian church (before whom Paul stood as a subordinate)
was one who was famous for both his unqualified observance of the Torah as well

[63] Dunn, *Romans*, 381.

as his ultimate sacrificial witness to Christ. Where the contours of Paul's mission required him to highlight the *difference* between the old and the new covenants, the life and witness of James of Jerusalem was a testimony to their *integrity*; and since this difference was one of the keynotes of the opening letter of the Pauline collection, the opening letter of the Pillars collection would have to strike a canonical balance by accentuating their unity. This concern to protect the ongoing significance of the Jewish law against those inclined to set it aside is evident in a number of passages in James, but most clearly in 2:8-13, to which we now turn.

Leviticus 19:18 as Summary or Fulfillment of the Torah?

Consider the following parallel statements regarding the fulfillment of the law:

Romans 13:8-10: Owe no one anything, except to love one another; for he who loves his neighbor has fulfilled [πεπλήρωκεν] the law. The commandments, "You shall not commit adultery, you shall not kill, you shall not steal, you shall not covet," and any other commandment, are summed up [ἀνακεφαλαιοῦται] in the sentence, "You shall love your neighbor as yourself." Love does no wrong to a neighbor; therefore love is the fulfilling of the law [πλήρωμα οὖν νόμου ἡ ἀγάπη].

Galatians 5:3,14: I testify again to every man who receives circumcision that he is bound to keep the whole law [ὀφειλέτης ἐστὶν ὅλον τὸν νόμον ποιῆσαι]. . . . For the whole law [πᾶς νόμος] is fulfilled [πεπλήρωται] in one word, "You shall love your neighbor as yourself."

James 2:8-11: If you really fulfill [τελεῖτε] the royal law, according to the Scripture, "You shall love your neighbor as yourself," you do well. But if you show partiality, you commit sin, and are convicted by the law as transgressors. For whoever keeps the whole law [ὅστις γὰρ ὅλον τὸν νόμον τηρήσῃ] but fails in one point has become guilty of all of it. For he who said "Do not commit adultery," said also "Do not kill." If you do not commit adultery but do kill, you have become a transgressor of the law.

---

the parallels here are extraordinary. As Popkes points out,[64] James 2:8-11 and Romans 13:8-10 are the only places in the NT where Leviticus 19:18 is listed alone as the "royal" or "fulfilling" law, and placed alongside items from the second table of the Decalogue, under a discussion of what faithful law observance entails. It is likewise noteworthy that the two specific laws referred to in each text—those against adultery and killing—are listed together against their original ordering in Exodus 20 and Deuteronomy 5. Further, James 2:8 cites Leviticus 19:18 and not 19:15, which (as I will show below) is clearly more thematically appropriate to his argument. In my opinion, our author has done this because he desired to take issue with Paul's use of Leviticus 19:18 as a totalizing command which enables the believer to

[64] Popkes, "James and Scripture," 222–24.

claim fulfillment of the whole law. For while the verb ἀνακεφαλαιόω suggests that
Leviticus 19:18 is viewed as a "summary" of the law, the perfect tense of πληρόω
and the noun πλήρωμα suggest something more: Paul is saying that those who love
their neighbors have enacted a complete performance of what the law requires.[65]
While Jesus would have agreed that Leviticus 19:18 could be seen as a kefavlaion
of the law (Mark 12:28f.; Matt 22:34f.; Luke 10:25f.), his statement does not go so
far as to suggest that one could entirely fulfill one's duty to Torah simply by loving
one's neighbor, as Paul appears to insist.

Does the author of James agree with Paul on this matter?[66] Many commentators
believe he does, given the claim of 2:8: "If you really fulfill the royal law, according
to the scripture, 'you shall love your neighbor as yourself,' you do well."[67] According
to this reading, James approaches the law through the lens of Jesus' teaching referred
to above; thus the "royal law" (νόμος βασιλικός) is the "law of the King" (that
is, Jesus), the "law of the kingdom" (of God, as proclaimed by Christians), or the
"kingly law" (that is, the law which rules all others). The first portion of chapter 2
opens by condemning partiality in the community of faith and elaborates by means
of an illustration: when rich and poor persons enter "your synagogue" (2:2) and
more concern is shown for the comfort of the rich person than the poor one, James
asks, "have you not made distinctions among yourselves and become judges with
evil thoughts" (2:4)? Since, as Paul argues, the one who keeps Leviticus 19:18 has
fulfilled the law, the one showing partiality has transgressed the law: thus, "If you
really fulfill the royal law . . . you do well; but if you show partiality, you commit sin,
and are convicted by the law as transgressors" (2:8-9). Those who read the passage
in this way often conflate the "royal law" of 2:8 with the "perfect law of liberty" of
1:25 and the "law of liberty" in 2:12, arguing that the "law" in the letter of James
is really the "new law" as it is reinterpreted by Jesus. Accordingly, it is concluded
that James has here turned to Jesus' teaching as a means of arguing that the one who
shows partiality has broken Jesus' "royal law" of Leviticus 19:18. Conversely, the
one who truly keeps the royal law (which requires impartiality) has, in the Pauline
sense, fulfilled the whole law.

Though this reading has the merit of enabling greater harmony between Paul
and James, it cannot be maintained in its entirety. James does appear to hold Leviticus 19:18 as a summary of the law, but he is not simply insisting that those who
show partiality have broken that law. Indeed, he seems to be arguing (against the
kind of teaching we find in Paul) that those who show partiality are transgressors
even if they can claim to love their neighbor. Several points can be made to draw out
the difference between the two teachings.

First, though the modifier "royal" might justifiably lead Christians to think of
Jesus or the Kingdom of God, the author himself directs our attention not to the

[65] Barrett, *Romans*, 250–51; Dunn, *Romans*, 776–83.
[66] Again, I am indebted to Jackson-McCabe (165–76) for the broad contours of my
reading of 2:8-11.
[67] E.g., Martin, 67; Davids, *James*, 114–17; Johnson, *James*, 61.

teaching of Jesus, but to the *text* of Leviticus itself: the royal law is "according to the scripture" (κατὰ τὴν γραφήν).[68] Further, Jesus' teaching on the "summary of the law" connects Leviticus 19:18 with the *Shema* of Deuteronomy 6:4, but James does not link the two here. Instead, 2:8-11 follows on a prohibition of partiality (2:1-7). This is further indication that Leviticus 19 is in mind and not the teaching of Jesus per se, for three verses prior to the love command in Leviticus we find a prohibition against partiality. Thus his question in 2:4 ("have you not made distinctions among yourselves and become *judges* with evil thoughts?") makes sense in light of Leviticus 19:15: "You shall do no injustice in *judgment*; you shall not be partial to the *poor* or defer to the *great*, but in righteousness shall you *judge* your neighbor" (again, the fact that our author quoted Leviticus 19:18 and *not* the contextually more appropriate 19:15 strongly suggests his intention to interact with Paul's corresponding use in Romans 13:8-10. This prohibition against partiality is presented separately from the love command, which is coupled with hating a neighbor, taking revenge, and bearing grudges (19:17-18a). Thus, while the "Pauline" reading of James 2:8 considers impartiality to be a sub-point of a totalizing command, "love your neighbor as yourself," Leviticus 19 presents them as two separate (albeit intimately related) commands. That is, it is conceivable that someone could avoid revenge and hatred at the personal level while nevertheless participating communally in an unjust system that shows partiality against the poor. This is precisely what the author of James is warning against in 2:1-13.

Second, a consideration of the structure of 2:8-11 supports this reading by showing that James is conceiving of someone who actually thinks they are fulfilling the law even though they participate in an unjust system of communal partiality.

2:8 If you really fulfill the royal law, according to the scripture, you shall love your neighbor as yourself, you do well.	2:10a For whoever keeps the whole law . . .	2:11b If you do not commit adultery . . .
2:9 But if you show partiality, you commit sin, and are convicted by the law as transgressors.	2:10b . . . but fails in one point has become guilty of all of it.	. . . but do kill, you have become a transgressor of the law.

The three columns above[69] present cases where someone falsely thinks they can fulfill the whole law by merely fulfilling a part of it: the upper row presents the believer's claim to qualify as one who has fulfilled the law, and the bottom row indicates their

---

[68] It is sometimes countered (Ropes, 198; Davids, *James*, 114) that νόμος would not be used of a single commandment, for which ἐντολή would be the correct term. Note however that Paul uses the two terms synonymously in Romans 7.

[69] The illustrative separation of 2:8-10 into these columns was borrowed from Jackson-McCabe (171–72).

disqualification. Thus, according to the third column, the fact that a person has *not* committed adultery (qualification) does not allow them on that basis to claim that they have kept the law if they in fact commit murder (disqualification). In the second column: someone may claim on the basis of the "royal law" to have kept the whole law (qualification), but if they fail in one point they nevertheless become guilty of it all (disqualification). Likewise, in the first column, believers may be able to claim that they fulfill the royal law (qualification), but if they have shown partiality, they are considered transgressors just the same (disqualification). The author is presenting his historicized James as arguing *against* the Pauline notion that a single law could function as a covering for all the others, even if that law is widely held to be a "summary" of the Torah. When Paul says, "the whole law [ὁ πᾶς νόμος] is fulfilled in one word, 'You shall love your neighbor as yourself'" (Gal 5:14), James replies, "whoever keeps the whole law [ὅστις γὰρ ὅλον τὸν νόμον τηρήσῃ] but fails in one point has become guilty of all of it" (Jas 2:10).

Finally, consider the author's words to his interlocutor in 2:8: if you fulfill the royal law, "you do well" (καλῶς ποιεῖτε). Those who opt for the "Pauline" reading take this praise quite literally: the author is commending those who "really" (μέντοι) fulfill the royal law. But consider the use of the same phrase in 2:19: "You believe that 'God is one'? You do well [καλῶς ποιεῖς]; even the demons believe, and shudder!" The point there is clear: believing "God is one" is vital, but it is not enough to qualify someone for salvation. In the same way, fulfilling the royal law is good and necessary, but it is not enough to keep one from being disqualified as a transgressor of the law. It should not go unnoticed that the two καλῶς ποιέω claims follow on references to Leviticus 19:18 and Deuteronomy 6:4, the very two commandments Jesus highlighted as the summary of the law. One can easily envisage here a concern to correct those who have come to believe rather blithely that verbal recitation of creeds and expressions of love to self-selected "neighbors" is enough to excuse other infidelities. Given the pervasive condemnation of the rich and championing of the poor in this letter, it seems quite likely that the author of James has directed 2:1-13 (and other passages) against culturally accommodated Christians who "love their neighbors" while residing quite comfortably within a system that mistreats the poor.

But we would miss the point of this section if we only sought to read it from the perspective of our hypothetical actual author. What is the implied author, James the Just, saying about the ongoing significance of the law in this passage? An attempt to answer that question must begin with a reconsideration of the context our author has chosen for his illustration. The instance of partiality is said to take place in a συναγωγή, but the exact referent of the term is rather difficult to determine.[70] The

---

[70] See Dibelius (*James*, 132–34), Johnson (*James*, 221–22), and Martin (57–58, 61) for helpful summaries of the evidence, as well as the influential article by R. Ward ("Partiality in the Assembly," *HTR* 62 [1969]: 87–97), which argues that the situation described is a judicial assembly. It turns out that Ward is not the first to have argued this point. For a very helpful extension of his position by appeal to a number of older commentaries, see D.C. Allison, Jr., "Exegetical Amnesia in James" (*ETL* 86 [2000]: 162–66).

manuscript tradition is divided over whether or not a definite article should precede the noun.[71] With the article, we would think most naturally of a *building*, a *Jewish synagogue*. Without one, the term simply suggests a gathering of people, an *assembly*. If a Christian gathering were intended, one is led to wonder why the author did not use the term ἐκκλησία, as he does later in 5:14. This has led some to conclude that the passage supports an early date for the letter, assuming it suggests a time before Christians separated from the synagogue.[72] But this is a mistaken assumption, for the interchange of the two terms continued well into the second century: though Justin used συναγωγή and ἐκκλησία antithetically to describe Jewish and Christian assemblies (*Dial.* 63.5) other early Christian writers were quite content to use συναγωγή as a description of a Christian gathering.[73]

While evidence can be garnered in support of either position, Johnson is absolutely correct when he notes, "the force of James' example does not derive from its historical referentiality, but from its rhetorical situation."[74] Given the way the language and content of the letter so consistently evokes a Jewish context, the rhetorical situation is unavoidably that of a gathering of *Jewish* believers who "hold the faith of our Lord Jesus Christ" (2:1).[75] In turn, when one recalls the letter's address to Jewish believers residing in the diaspora, the implied context becomes quite clear: the leader of the mother church in Jerusalem is writing to Jewish believers gathered together in *synagogues* throughout the diaspora, exhorting them to observe the injunctions of the law and reminding them that the various commands of Torah are still quite valid even though Jesus taught they were "summed up" by the love command.

Why would our author imagine James needed to remind believers of this? An answer might be found in Acts 21, which tells the story of the final encounter in Jerusalem between James and Paul. After Paul offers a report of his missionary work to James and the elders, they confront him regarding rumors that have been trickling in from Jews in the diaspora.

> **Acts 21:20b-25**: You see, brother, how many thousands there are among the Jews of those who have believed; they are all zealous for the law, and they have been told about you that you teach all the Jews who are among the Gentiles to forsake Moses, telling them not to circumcise their children or observe the customs. . . . Do therefore what we tell you. We have four men who are under a vow; take these men and purify yourself along with them and pay their expenses. . . . Thus all will know that there is nothing in what they have been told about you but that you yourself live

---

[71] The article is included in ℵ² A P 33. 1739 and the majority text; excluded in ℵ* B C Y 630. 1505 *pc.*

[72] E.g., J. B. Adamson, *James: The Man and His Message* (Grand Rapids: Eerdmans, 1989), 105.

[73] Cf. *Herm. Mand.* 11.9,13–14; Ign. *Pol.* 4.2 uses the plural form, urging Polycarp to "let assemblies [συναγωγαί] be held more frequently."

[74] Johnson, *James*, 227.

[75] Johnson (*James,* 228) insists the concept of προσωπολημψία is unintelligible apart from its LXX background.

in observance of the law. But as for the Gentiles who have believed, we have sent a letter with our judgment that they should abstain from what has been sacrificed to idols and from blood and from what is strangled and from unchastity.

A rumor has circulated that Paul teaches diaspora Jews to forsake the law, "telling them not to circumcise their children or observe the customs." The accusation was well grounded: Romans includes the claim, "he is not a real Jew who is one outwardly, nor is true circumcision something external and physical; he is a Jew who is one inwardly, and real circumcision is a matter of the heart, spiritual and not literal" (2:28-29). Later, in an address "to those who know the law" (7:1), he insists that believers "have died to the law" (7:4) and are "discharged from the law," since they "serve not under the old written code but in the new life of the Spirit" (7:6). Paul did indeed appear to be teaching Jews to forsake the Torah. James was therefore concerned that the rumor be squelched; and though Paul had elsewhere condemned those whose zeal for the law led them to compel others to observance in order "to make a good showing in the flesh" (Gal 6:12), James nevertheless commanded him to do just that, so that "all will know that there is nothing in what they have been told about you but that you yourself live in observance of the law" (Acts 21:24b).

Intriguingly, James goes on in this text to immediately refer back to the letter the Jerusalem leadership sent to Gentile believers (Acts 15:22-29). It is possible that herein our hypothetical second-century author discovered a "canonical context" for his letter of James: for just as the apostolic letter to *Gentile* believers was concerned to outline the exact contours of law observance to which they were accountable as non-Jews, so also James' diaspora letter to *Jewish* believers is concerned to uphold an observance of "the whole law" against those who believed the law was abrogated by the gospel and could therefore be fulfilled by the observance of a single totalizing command. Both are occasioned by a crisis having to do with law observance by Jewish and Gentile believers in the diaspora. Put sharply, the canonical letter of James *to Jews* may have been imagined to function as a follow up to the letter of Acts 15 written *to Gentiles*.

All that remains is a reconsideration of what it is our author means by "the law." My analysis has shown that the term connotes something different for our two authors. For the author of the letter of James, the law is associated with liberty and life; for Paul, it is associated with slavery and death. And yet, a careful reading of their respective claims will not allow for an easy polarization of the two positions. For one thing, it is clear that James is not actually thinking of every command when he exhorts the keeping of "the whole law," for as we have noted elsewhere, the "law" in James is consistently associated with the ethical demands of the Torah, and terms associated with the ceremonial aspects of the law are used figuratively. Likewise, it is clear that Paul does not mean to set aside the entire law when he insists that believers are discharged from it! For it is not the law *as such* that Paul condemns, but a fleshly approach toward the law that sought justification through its outward performance; it is by *this* means that the law revives sin and brings death.[76] But

---

[76] Dunn, *Romans*, 373.

God's law is "holy and just and good" (Rom 7:12) and must be fulfilled; and this can only be done, according to Paul, when believers approach it not according to the flesh but according to the Spirit of Christ. It is only in this way that "the just requirement of the law might be fulfilled in us, who walk not according to the flesh but according to the Spirit. . . . For the mind that is set on the flesh is hostile to God; it does not submit to God's law, indeed it cannot" (Rom 8:4-5, 7a). Paul is in no way opposed to "doing the law" (Rom 2:13), but he *is* opposed to the notion that the law can be done apart from the empowering presence of the Spirit.

Viewed in this way, it makes sense to understand "the law" in James as a post-Pauline, Catholic reframing of the Torah designed to help readers avoid heterodox interpretations of the Pauline literature. The occasionally inflammatory language of the Pauline approach to the law threatened the unity of the divine word and provided fuel for the theology of second-century theologians who sought to drive a wedge between the two covenants. The presentation of the law in the letter of James will not allow for such an opposition. Where Paul's letters may lead some to believe that the Torah was entirely abolished in Christ, James the Just was selected to be the one who would inform believers (and Marcionites) everywhere "that there is nothing in what they have been told about" Paul, but that he himself lived "in observance of the law" (Acts 21:24).

1 John

It seems equally possible that our hypothetical author also had certain passages from 1 John in mind here, for the pertinence of keeping God's commands is exhorted throughout that letter (2:3-11; 3:22-24; 4:21; 5:2-3). One specific commandment the author has in mind is the "new commandment" given by Jesus (John 13:34-35): "This is his commandment, that we should believe in the name of his son Jesus Christ and love one another, just as he commanded us" (1 John 3:23). But it may be a mistake to assume that the author is thinking of this commandment alone, for in seven of the fourteen occurrences, ἐντολή is in the plural. There may be a single new commandment of Jesus, but this in no way replaces the numerous "old" commandments of God.[77] Indeed, our author would have surely been in agreement in

---

[77] While it is often argued that the shift from plural to singular "commandment(s)" in 1 John is theologically insignificant (since the plural "commandments" are focused on the one "command" of Jesus; so, e.g., I. H. Marshall, *The Epistles of John* [NICNT; Grand Rapids: Eerdmans, 1978], 128–29; J. Lieu, *The Theology of the Johannine Epistles* [Cambridge: Cambridge University Press, 1991], 52. J. Painter (*1, 2, and 3 John* [SP 18; Collegeville, Minn.: Liturgical Press, 2002], 169) notes that 1 John is (perhaps intentionally) ambiguous as to whether the "commandments" are those of Jesus or God, and Brown (*Epistles of John*, 251–52, 280–81) makes the case that the author of 1 John often uses "word" and "commandment" interchangeably on the basis of prior OT usage. Thus, when 2:7 speaks of the "old commandment which is the *word* you already heard," the "word" here may be understood to refer to the "old" word of God's commandments to Israel (e.g., the "Ten Words," the *decalogue*): ". . . by speaking twice as frequently of the commandment(s) and by always

1 John 5:3: "For this is the love of God, that we keep his commandments. And his commandments are not burdensome." Consider 2:8-9:

> Yet I am writing you a new commandment, which is true in him and in you, because the darkness is passing away and the true light is already shining: He who says he is in the light and hates his brother is in the darkness still.

The point is repeated again later in the letter: "If anyone says, 'I love God' and hates his brother, he is a liar; for he who does not love his brother whom he has seen cannot love God whom he has not seen" (4:20). Some apparently claim to reside in the light, to know and love God, but fail to love their siblings in the faith—a situation quite comparable to that described in the second chapter of the letter of James, where believers claim to love their siblings but simultaneously show partiality against the poor. Both letters are concerned about the division between creed and deed (a subject that will be addressed in greater detail below). This positive attitude toward the keeping of God's commandments is one of the distinctively "Jewish" elements of 1 John, a letter often considered to be among the least "Jewish" in the NT. Indeed, it is precisely this concern for commandment keeping that enables 1 John to be read as an authoritative Pillar-letter from the Jerusalem mission to Jews.

ASKING IN PRAYER

1 John

When speaking of prayer, 1 John focuses on the *confidence* believers can have in making requests to God.

> Little children, let us not love in word or speech but in deed [ἔργῳ] and in truth. By this we will know that we are of the truth, and reassure [πείσομεν] our hearts before him whenever our hearts condemn [καταγινώσκῃ] us; for God is greater than our hearts, and he knows everything. Beloved, if our hearts do not condemn us, we have confidence [παρρησίαν] before God; and we receive from him whatever we ask [αἰτῶμεν], because we keep his commandments and do what is pleasing before him (1 John 3:18-22).

The author describes believers who are uncertain of their standing before God and whose hearts "condemn" them. How might they be reassured that God does not condemn them as well? By keeping the commandment to love one another not "in word or speech" but "in truth" according to the verifiable data of ἔργα. Believers who experience condemnation can nevertheless be confident that they are of the truth when they exhibit obedience to God's will as expressed in the commandments, particularly as they are expressed in *the* commandment to love one another (3:24). Therefore, "we receive from him whatever we ask because we keep his com-

---

referring them to God and never explicitly to Jesus (the opposite of the GJohn practice), he implicitly reminds his readers more vividly of the Ten Commandments" (281).

mandments and do what is pleasing before him" (3:22). It follows that the quality of one's relationship with God is determined in part by the quality of one's relationship with others. Failure to actively love the neighbor results in an uncertain standing before God, and an uncertain standing before God results in condemning hearts, unconfident prayers, and unfulfilled requests.

This notion of "confident" prayer must not be misconstrued as a contractual agreement for mutual reciprocation, for later it says: "And this is the confidence that we have in him, that if we ask anything *according to his will* he hears us; and if we know that he hears us in whatever we ask, we know that we have the requests made of him" (5:14-15). The determinative element, then, is the doing of God's will in commandment keeping *and* request making. Confident prayer is thus conditioned to avoid reduction to self-gratification. Gifts are sought in prayer (αἰτήματα, "askings"), but the gifts one seeks are those that accord with the will of the gift giver. One prays not in order to fulfill one's own desires but to participate in the will of God. An example of just such a prayer is immediately provided:

> If any one sees his brother committing what is not a mortal sin, he will ask, and God will give him life for those whose sin is not unto death. There is sin that is unto death; I do not say that one is to pray for that. All wrongdoing is sin, but there is sin that is not unto death. (1 John 5:16-17)

We cannot enter at this point into the task of identifying the nature of the sin πρὸς θάνατον, but two points should be highlighted. First, determining whether it is God[78] or the praying believer[79] who gives life to the sinner is ultimately less important than the unavoidable conclusion that the praying believer has acted as a mediator in God's will to forgive another's sin.[80] The confident believer receives her request, including even God's provision of "life" for the unstable and unconfident sinning believer. Again we find an emphasis on the communal nature of prayer, that by it those who are confident in the community can restore those who are not. Second, though "all wrongdoing is sin," it is noteworthy that there is a class of sin that is "deadly" which stands outside the purview of the community's intercession. Life cannot be given to such a person whose sin leads to this particular death; whatever it is, it remains unaffected by the confidence building apparatus of the community.

James

The letter of James turns to the subject of prayer almost immediately:

[78] R. Schnackenburg, *The Johannine Epistles: A Commentary*, trans. R. Fuller and I. Fuller (Kent: Burns & Oates, 1992), 249; Marshall, 246; Painter, *Just James*, 316; S. Smalley, *1, 2, 3 John* (WBC 51; Dallas: Word Books, 2002), 300.

[79] R. Bultmann, *A Commentary on the Johannine Epistles*, trans. R. P. O'Hara et al. (Hermeneia; Philadelphia: Fortress, 1973), 87; C. H. Dodd, *The Johannine Epistles* (MNTC; London: Hodder & Stoughton, 1946), 135.

[80] The best option is a conflation of the two: Brown, *Epistles*, 611–12; Lieu, *Theology*, 64.

James 1:5-8: If anyone lacks wisdom, let him ask God who gives to all without hesitation [ἁπλῶς] and without reproaching, and it will be given him. But let him ask in faith, with no doubting [διακρινόμενος], for he who doubts is like a wave of the sea that is driven and tossed by the wind. For that person must not suppose that a double-minded man, unstable [ἀνὴρ δίψυχος ἀκατάστατος] in all his ways, will receive anything from the Lord.

In James, God is "giving" (διδόντος; cf. 1:12, 17, 21; 2:5; 4:6, 10; 5:7, 18; thus "asking" that is directed to this God must be done "in faith" that this God gives without hesitation or condemnation. The adverb ἁπλῶς (meaning "simply" or "openly"; BDAG 104) contrasts God's unhesitating generosity with that of the double-minded asker.[81] Coming as it does just after the discussion of trials, the resulting image is of someone who is uncertain whether to trust that God can save her from the trial.

But such a person must not only be confident that God is indeed giving; she must also consider the condition of her asking if her prayer is to be heard.

James 4:1-3: What causes wars, what causes fightings among you? Is it not your passions [ἡδονή] that are at war in your members? You desire [ἐπιθυμεῖτε] and do not have; so you kill; and you covet and cannot obtain, so you fight and wage war. You do not have, because you do not ask; you ask and do not receive because you ask evilly [κακῶς αἰτεῖσθε] to spend it on your passions.

In contrast to the person who trusts completely in the giving God, we find described here persons whose "passion" (ἡδονή, used synonymously with ἐπιθυμία) leads to wars within and without. After having been told that ἐπιθυμία gives birth to sin and results in death (1:14-15), readers now see the process at work through two examples. The first is described in the parallel statements of verse 2: He desires/covets something and does not have/cannot obtain it, so he kills/fights/wages war in order to get it; he "does not have" because he "does not ask"—a deliberate echo of 1:5, where the one who lacks is directed to ask the giving God. Yet verse 3 describes another person who does indeed ask but still does not receive because she asks for the sake of her passions. She has turned to prayer as a means of achieving the things she could not get through struggle. As Johnson insists, this kind of asking is not simply "wrong,"[82] it is evil (κακός), being not simply an employment of the wrong prayer formula but an attempt to manipulate God.[83] But since God gives only "perfect gifts from above" (1:17) and "cannot be tempted by evil" (1:13), the asking is futile.[84] The asker does not receive because she fails to grasp the nature of God's giving, either because she doubts God's ability or because she manipulates God into giving for evil reasons. Like the unconfident asker of 1 John who does not receive because he fails to ask in confidence, so also the "double-minded, unstable" person

---

[81] Martin, 18.
[82] See Martin, 147, and most English translations.
[83] Johnson, *James*, 278.
[84] Burchard, 168.

struggling with "doubt" (διακρίνω; cf. 2:4) is warned that such an asker should not expect to receive anything from the Lord.

The final prayer passage is particularly significant for the way in which it concretizes the links among the three Pillar letters:

> **James 5:13-20**: Is any one among you suffering? Let him pray. Is any cheerful? Let him sing praise. Is any among you sick? Let him call for the elders of the church, and let them pray over him, anointing him with oil in the name of the Lord; and the prayer of faith will save the sick man, and the Lord will raise him up; and if he has committed sins, he will be forgiven. Therefore confess your sins to one another, and pray for one another, that you may be healed. The prayer of a righteous man has great power in its effects. . . . My brethren, if any one among you wanders from the truth and some one brings him back, let him know that whoever brings back a sinner from the error of his way will save his soul from death and will cover a multitude of sins.

The petitionary nature of the prayer described in this passage (δέησις, "request"), draws readers back to the previously examined passages having to do with "asking," namely, the opening exhortation to "ask in faith" (1:6) and the later condemnation of those who "ask evilly" (4:3). This "prayer of faith" is "effective" (ἐνεργέω), as the subsequent example of Elijah seeks to demonstrate. If my hypothesis is correct, it would seem clear that the historicized James himself also was intended to be drawn to the reader's mind as an example in this regard, especially given the widespread tradition that it was James' beseeching God's forgiveness for the people of Israel that held back the destructive tide of Vespasian's army.[85] Indeed, one of the most frequently recalled characteristics of the historicized James among Catholics was that his knees were as hard as those of a camel from his constant kneeling in petitionary prayer. Since James the Just was especially known for the powerful effect of his supplication, it makes sense that he would champion it in this particularly miraculous fashion.

Despite the many important insights regarding the nature of prayer in this passage, my interest is in highlighting its intersection with 1 Peter and 1 John. Others have considered the parallel endings of James and 1 John, the most well known study being that of F. O. Francis who established that James does, in fact, include various characteristics of a "genuine" ancient letter.[86] Francis showed that both James and 1 John have a "double opening statement," which was then demonstrated to be a recognizable characteristic in numerous ancient Hellenistic letters. Further, he showed that the lack of a letter ending was more common than often thought, which served to render the abrupt endings of James and 1 John less anomalous than they had previously appeared. Indeed, like James and 1 John, Francis shows that Christian letter endings often included summaries signaled by πρὸ πάντων,

---

[85] Hegesippus in Eusebius's *Hist. Eccl.* 2.23.18; Origen, *Comm. Matt.* 10.17 and *Cels.* 1.47; 2.13; Eusebius, *Hist. Eccl.* 3.7.8; Jerome, *Vir. ill.* 2; *1–2 Apoc.*

[86] F. O. Francis, "The Form and Function of the Opening and Closing Paragraphs of James and 1 John," *ZNW* 61 (1970): 110–26.

eschatological injunctions, and a health wish that made reference to prayer. On this basis he argued that James and 1 John are actual letters, the similarities between the two being attributable to a known letterform.

Though I have no significant quarrel with most of the findings of Francis's study, it is noteworthy that most of his work focused on the establishment of the double-opening form and the existence of certain broad ingredients in the letter closing. His analysis of the closing of James and 1 John, however, finds numerous parallels between the two but offers no examples from other letters to support his contention that these follow a known form. While Francis rightly notes that the common reference to prayer at the end of Christian letters usually take the form of "terse notations" (cf. 2 Cor 13:7; Eph 6:18f.; Phil 4:6; Col 4:2-3; 1 Thess 5:17; Phlm 22; Heb 13:18), James and 1 John differ from his hypothesized "form" in their extended discussions of the topic. Further, these extended discussions include a number of parallels that may point more to direct influence than a shared epistolary form:

1) Both are *prayers of request* (προσεύχομαι, εὐχή, δέησις in James; αἰτέω, αἴτημα in 1 John).
2) The prayer spoken of is on behalf of *another believer*.
   a. The repeated τις ἐν ὑμῖν in James 5:13, 14, 19; the repeated ἀλλήλων in 5:16.
   b. "If anyone sees his brother . . ." (1 John 5:16).
3) Both stress the *power* of prayer by calling it confident (παρρησία, 1 John 5:14) or faithful (πίστεως, Jas 5:15).
4) Both stress that such prayer will be *effective*.
   a. "The prayer of faith will save the sick man . . . the prayer of righteousness has great power in its effects" (Jas 5:15).
   b. "This is the confidence which we have . . . that if we ask anything according to his will he hears us . . . we know that we have obtained the requests made of him . . . he will ask, and God will give" (1 John 5:14-15, 16)
(5) The recipient of prayer in both passages is identified as a *sinner* (Jas 5:15, 16, 20; 1 John 5:16-18).
(6) Both describe a *soteriological* restoration of the brother.
   a. "The prayer of faith will save the sick one and the Lord will raise him up, and if he has committed sins, he will be forgiven . . . whoever brings back a sinner . . . will save his soul" (Jas 5:15, 20).
   b. "I write this . . . that you may know you have eternal life . . . he will ask, and God will give him life . . ." (1 John 5:13, 16).[87]

---

[87] John only uses a σώζω cognate in 4:14; his preferred term is "life" or "eternal life" (cf. 1:1, 2; 2:25; 3:14, 15; 5:11, 12, 13, 16, 20).

(7) This salvation is a deliverance from *death* (ἐκ θανάτου, Jas 5:20; πρὸς Θάνατον, 1 John 5:16-17).

(8) Both letters end with a reference to falling away into *error* (Jas 5:20) or, more specifically, *idolatry* (1 John 5:21).

The last point requires a bit of explanation in the case of James. The sinning brother is designated as one who "wanders" (πλανάω, v. 19) into "error" (πλάνη, v. 20); since the use of the word group in the LXX describes those who transgress the law (for example, Deut 11:28; 13:6; Isa 9:15; 30:20-22; Jer 23:17; Ezek 33:19; Prov 14:8; Wis 5:6; 12:24; Sir 11:16), often in the context of being led astray into idolatry, commentators have found it at least possible that the "error" spoken of in James has idolatry imagery hovering in its background (*TDNT* 6.233–36).[88]

Regardless, both letter endings say the same thing, in effect: "The sinning recipient of faithful prayer will be saved from death." There is, however, one way in which the author of James diverged from the parallel text in 1 John. Where both make it clear that believers can affect another's status before God, 1 John draws a limit to the communal concern: "There is a sin which is unto death; I do not say that one is to pray for that" (5:16). He probably has in mind here the "children of the devil" (3:10); since "they are of the world" (4:5) and "the whole world is in the power of the evil one" (5:19), these should not be the focus of communal prayer. The author of James, by contrast, will not allow believers to think that errant siblings are to be left alone. His closing sentence (as well as his entire letter) is an open-ended exhortation to seek and save those in the community who have gone astray.

This also helps to explain his apparent allusion to the proverb found in 1 Peter 4:7-8: "The end of all things is at hand; therefore be sane and sober for your prayers; above all, hold unfailing love for one another, since *love covers a multitude of sins.*" 1 Peter's allusion to Proverbs 10:12 suggests that such community-building practices have the capacity to "cover sin"—a phrase which clearly implies forgiveness (LXX Ps 31:1; 84:3; Dan 4:24; Rom 4:7). It is notoriously difficult to determine whose sins are covered in this proverb, the one who loves[89] or the one who is loved;[90] but given the overtly communal nature of the context it is mistaken to require such an individualistic decision. What is envisioned is the capacity of unfailing love to "cover" sin in its commitment to hospitality and its refusal to hold a grudge, as the subsequent verse suggests.[91] The author of James appears to have alluded to the same proverb found in 1 Peter at the very end of his letter in a similar spirit, asserting that communal concern should be oriented toward the restoration of God's people through the forgiveness of sins.

---

[88] Davids, *James*, 199; Martin, 218.

[89] Beare, *1 Peter*, 159; Kelly, *Commentary*, 178.

[90] Best, 159; Achtemeier, *1 Peter*, 296.

[91] Selwyn, 217; B. Reicke, *The Epistles of James, Peter, and Jude* (ABC 37; New York: Doubleday, 1964), 122; Goppelt, 298; Michaels, 247; Elliott, *1 Peter*, 751.

GOD AND THE WORLD AS INCOMPATIBLE ALLEGIANCES

The notion that believers should be whole and perfect is perhaps *the* overarching theme in James.[92] Here we find τέλειος occurring five out of the nineteen times it appears in the NT (1:4 [2x]; 1:17; 1:25; 3:2). Τελ- words are often connected with other key terms such as ἔργον (1:4; 2:22), σοφίας (1:5, 17), πίστις (2:22), and νόμος (1:25; 2:8, 10). Related words abound: τελέω (2:8), ἀποτελέω (1:15), τελειόω (2:22), τέλος (5:11), ὅλος (2:10; 3:2, 3, 6), and ὁλόκληρος (1:4). This call to wholeness is intensified by recurring references to those who are its opposite: they are "double-minded" (δίψυχος, 1:8; 4:8) and "unstable" (ἀκατάστατος, 1:8; 3:8, 16), with conflicting allegiances (2:1-7; 4:4) and desires (1:14-15; 4:1-2) that leave them doubting (διακρίνω, 1:6; 2:4; διαλογισμός, 2:4), and in communal conflict (2:1-7; 4:1-2). Against this state of personal and social disequilibria, the author insists that believers must choose—between purity and contamination (1:26-27), between the wisdom from above and wisdom that is earthly (3:13-18), between social advancement and social holiness (2:1-7; 5:1-5), and ultimately, between God and the world (4:4).

1 Peter

Τελ- words are used differently in 1 Peter than in James, having less to do with the perfection of the believer and more to do with the eschatological "completion" of all things in Christ (1:9, 13; 4:7, 17; 5:9). Having said that, exemplary Christian conduct in the world is one of the central themes of 1 Peter: we find numerous calls to "do right" (2:14, 15, 20; 3:6, 11, 17; 4:19); obedience and disobedience are notable themes (1:2, 14, 22: 2:8; 3:1, 6, 20; 4:17); indeed, six of the thirteen NT occurrences of the word "conduct" (ἀναστροφή) are found in this letter (1:15, 18; 2:12; 3:1, 2, 16; cf. ἀναστρέφω, 1:17), and in two places this conduct is linked specifically with reference to one's "work" (ἔργον, 1:17; 2:12). Most notable are the numerous calls to be "holy" (1:14-16; 2:5, 9; 3:5), "purified" or "pure" (1:22; 2:2; 3:2), undefiled (1:4), and sanctified (1:2; 3:15). Commentators have long noticed the influence of the Levitical holiness code (Lev 17–26) on this letter, most conspicuously in the "priesthood" language of 2:5 and 9, the "holiness" language of 1:14-16, and the passages that call believers to separate from the practices of the Gentile world (1:14-18; 4:1-4).[93] As exiles in the dispersion, God's people are to live differently than the other peoples of the world.

　　Given the consistent concern for holiness of conduct and the rejection of Gentile lifestyles, it is notable that the letter does not push these themes dualistically.

---

[92] E.g., Bauckham, *James*, 100–101, 177–85; Laws, 29–32; Martin, lxxix–lxxxi; D. J. Moo, *The Letter of James* (PNTC; Grand Rapids: Eerdmans, 2000), 43–46; R. Hoppe, *Der theologische Hintergrund des Jakobusbriefes* (FB 28; Würzburg: Echter Verlag, 1977); W. Popkes, "New Testament Principles of Wholeness," *EvQ* 64.4 (1992): 319–32.

[93] See, e.g., Selwyn, 460; Elliott, *1 Peter*, 360–64, 449–55.

The "world" (κόσμος) is not a theologically loaded term for that which must be excluded. It is simply the physical location of the metaphorical diaspora (5:9). As exiles and aliens in a foreign culture, Christians are urged to live differently, but that difference does not entail a retreat from society (cf. 2:11–3:21). Surely Christians must be vigilant since "the devil prowls about like a roaring lion, seeking whom he may devour" (5:8), but the devil can be resisted (5:9). Indeed, there is a real *openness* to the world in 1 Peter born out of missiological concerns: good Christian conduct has the power to make non-believers ashamed (3:16), to glorify God (2:12), and possibly even convert (3:1); Christians are therefore to witness to God's work (2:9) and offer account to outsiders for the different character of their Christian existence (3:15). As the elect and holy people of God, 1 Peter calls Christians to be different, but the difference balances holiness with cultural engagement. Such a balance is carefully struck in 2:9, where Christians are called to be "a chosen race, a royal priesthood, a holy nation, God's own people" for the specific reason that they might "declare the wonderful deeds of him who called you out of darkness into his marvelous light."

1 John

In 1 John, Christian orientation to the κόσμος could not be described more differently. Certainly God's commitment to saving the world through Christ is undeniable (2:2; 4:9, 14), as is the fact that Christian life is unavoidably lived in the world (4:17). But apart from these few more neutral uses of the term, "the world" in 1 John functions in the letter's dualistic framework as a cipher for everything that is opposed to God: "Do not love the world or the things in the world. If anyone loves the world, love for the Father is not in him. For all that is in the world . . . is not of the Father but is of the world" (2:15-16). The letter polarizes the things of God and the things of the κόσμος, insisting that believers must vigorously exclude the latter if they claim to love God. Indeed the two represent opposing and exclusive realms wherein beings "abide": faithful believers abide in God and the things of God (1 John 2:10, 14, 24-28; 3:6, 9, 24; 4:12-16), but the world is the abode of the antichrists (4:3), false prophets who propagate a heterodox Christology (4:1), and even the devil himself. The author can therefore assert without qualification, "the whole world is in the power of the evil one" (5:19). Likewise, former members of the Christian community who in some way oppose the recipients of the letter belong to the world: "They are of the world, therefore what they say is of the world, and the world listens to them" (4:5).

It must be noted here that the dualism stops short of full extension in this letter. The author reminds the readers of this in a variety of ways: He asserts, "he who is in you is greater than he who is in the world" (4:4); he reminds them that Christ died for the sins of the *whole* world and not theirs only (2:2); that the darkness is passing away and the true light is already shining (2:8); that the world is passing away, but the one who does the will of God lives forever (2:17); that the Son of God destroyed the works of the devil (3:8), and that faith in Christ enables believers to have victory over the world (5:4-5; cf. 2:13-14; 4:4). There is thus an eschatological dimension that overcomes the dualism in 1 John and keeps it in check. Nevertheless, in this letter there is no room for the kind of openness to the world found in 1 Peter. Whether the world is described as a corrupting characteristic (2:15-16), a hateful and deceitful people (3:1,13-15; 4:5), a false teaching (4:1-6), or a malevolent power (5:19), it belongs to a realm that is opposed to God; and those who are born of God must resist affection for it: "If anyone loves the world, love for the Father is not in him."

James

The primary passage for comparison in James is the strongly dualistic 3:13–4:10. There "wisdom from above" is contrasted with wisdom that is "earthly, unspiritual, devilish" (3:15), and the "friend of the world" is revealed to be "the enemy of God" (4:4). Earlier passages of the letter have prepared us for the themes encountered here. After exhorting readers to "be doers of the word, and not hearers only, deceiving yourselves" (1:22), the opening section of the letter concludes at 1:26-27:

> If anyone thinks himself religious [εἴ τις δοκεῖ θρησκὸς εἶναι], and does not bridle his tongue but deceives [ἀπατάω] his heart, this one's piety is worthless. Piety that is pure [καθαρός] and undefiled [ἀμίαντος] before God and the Father is this: To visit orphans and widows in their distress, and to keep oneself unstained [ἄσπιλος] from the world.

The world "stains" the self in such a way that one's religion is defiled and rendered worthless. The diaspora context is again reasserted here; given the overtly cultic roots of the words used figuratively in this context,[94] it is apparent that we are dealing with a notion of purity and cleanliness that has been disassociated from the temple cult in Jerusalem.

It is worth pointing out that εἴ τις δοκεῖ εἶναι (1:26) is a distinctively Pauline phrase (1 Cor 3:18; 8:2; 11:16; 14:37; Gal 6:3; Phil 3:4). Its repeated use in 1 Corinthians forms a rhetorical pattern that underscores the central theme of the letter, with Paul challenging Christians who think they are wise, knowledgeable, and spiritual to reconsider their condition.[95] The use of the phrase is exactly paralleled in James, where those who consider themselves to be religious are also exhorted to reassess their piety. Related to this is the phrase μὴ πλανᾶσθη, which is also a Pauline favorite (1 Cor 6:9; 15:33; Gal 6:7) and is likewise exactly paral-

---

[94] θρησκεία (cf., e.g., Wis 14:18; 4 Macc. 5:7; *Ant.* 1:222), καθαρά (cf., e.g., Lev 4:12; 7:19; Num 8:7; Deut 12:15), and ἀμίαντος (Lev 5:3; Num 5:3; Deut 21:23).

[95] See G. Fee, *The First Epistle to the Corinthians* (NICNT; Grand Rapids: Eerdmans, 1987), 711. Especially noteworthy are those instances where those who "suppose" something about themselves are considered "deceived" (ἐξαπατάω, 1 Cor 3:8; φρεναπατάω, Gal 6:3).

leled in the NT only in James (1:16). Still another related parallel between James and the Corinthian correspondence is found in their shared use of the rare words ἀκατάστατος and ἀκαταστασία (1 Cor 14:33; 2 Cor 12:20; Jas 1:8; 3:8, 16) to describe personal and communal instability.[96] This particularly remarkable cluster of lexical parallels presents us with further compelling evidence of a post-Pauline *Sitz im Leben* for our letter.[97]

The focus of one's piety on care for the economically impoverished is immediately expanded in the next section (2:1-7), where "world" comes up again in relation to the poor: "Has God not chosen those who are poor in the world to be rich in faith and heirs of the kingdom which he has promised to those who love him?" A similar distinction between rich and poor has already been made (1:9-11) and will be reinforced with vigor later (4:13–5:5). While it is clear that the author intended to offer a general contrast between the one who acts in "faith" and the one who hesitates in double-minded instability, by 2:7 it appears that the instability the author has in mind is rooted in "worldly" concerns associated with wealth and communal influence. Such concerns result in mental as well as communal division, double-mindedness within, and discriminatory partiality without.

These themes continue in 3:1-12, where the notion of bridling one's tongue (1:26) is picked up once again:

> If anyone makes no mistakes in speech, he is a perfect man, able to bridle the whole body also. . . . The tongue is an unrighteous world [ὁ κόσμος τῆς ἀδικίας] among our members, staining [σπιλόω] the whole body, setting on fire the cycle of nature and set on fire by hell . . . no human being can tame the tongue—a restless evil [ἀκατάστατος κακός]. . . . With it we bless the Lord and Father, and with it we curse men, who are made in the likeness of God. From the same mouth come blessing and cursing (3:2, 6, 8-10a).

Where 1:27 presented the world as an unrighteous source of stain, here it is asserted that the "tongue" is itself an "unrighteous world" which functions as the conduit through which the stain of the world is made evident. The reference to the "perfect man" (3:2) hearkens back to the earlier exhortation (1:4) for believers to be "perfect and complete," and likewise, the repetition of ἀκατάστατος recalls the mental division described in 1:6-8. Finally, the concern that tongues can be divided, blessing God and cursing humans, recalls the partiality induced communal division of 2:1-7.

These recurring themes of division and wholeness are drawn to fruition in 3:13–4:10. A series of intense rhetorical questions (3:13; 4:1; 4:4; 4:5), culminate

---

[96] The words are found in the NT only here and at Luke 21:9 and 2 Corinthians 6:5, where the meaning is more political (e.g., tumult, revolution).

[97] In an unpublished paper read at the 2005 Annual SBL ("The Letter of James as a Document of Paulinism?"), Margaret Mitchell raised this passage among several others as evidence that the author of James knew 1 Corinthians.

in a scriptural citation (4:6), which produces a stunning barrage of imperative commands: "Submit to God! [7a] Resist the devil! [7b] Draw near to God! [8a] Cleanse your hands! [8b] Purify your hearts! [8c] Be miserable, mournful, and weeping! [9a] Turn laughter and joy into mourning and dejection! [9b] Humble yourselves before the Lord! [10]" Johnson calls this section a "call to conversion,"[98] but it may be more accurately considered a call to *wholeness*. After the theme was established in 1:2-8, every subsequent passage building up to 3:13–4:10 alternates between exhorting wholeness by *inclusion* and wholeness by *exclusion*.[99] Inclusion is exhorted in 1:22-25 (must be hearers *as well as* doers), 2:8-12 (must keep royal law *as well as* other commandments), and 2:14-26 (must have faith *as well as* works). Exclusion is exhorted in 1:13-21 (cannot believe in good God *and* that God sends temptation), 1:26-27 (cannot be religious *and* not bridle tongue), and 2:1-7 (cannot hold faith *and* be partial against the poor).

The call to exclusion is continued in 3:13–4:10. In 3:13-18, "wisdom" is polarized: one is earthly, the other is from above (cf. 1:5,17); one is natural, the other spiritual; one is demonic, the other divine. The wisdom from above is meek, pure, peaceable, gentle, open to reason, full of mercy and good fruits, without uncertainty (ἀδιάκριτος; cf. 1:6; 2:4), and without hypocrisy. The wisdom "from below" is characterized by bitter jealousy, selfish ambition, falseness, disorderliness, and vileness. Then, like a prosecuting attorney, the author presents the damning evidence: there is not peace in the community; indeed there are feuds and conflicts due to the ἐπιθυμία residing deep within them and among them (4:1-3—here again we find another significant link with the early chapters of 1 Corinthians, where Paul condemns that community's divisions as resulting from a similar devotion to worldly σοφία). Thus the wisdom of the community is not "from above" but "from below"; they have been weighed in the scales and found to be on the side of that which is earthly, natural, and demonic. Hence, the prophetic judgment and call to repentance of 4:4-10: "Adulteresses! Friends of the world! Enemies of God! Humble yourselves before the Lord!"

What is of particular interest to us, of course, is the way in which our hypothetical author can be seen to have included a series of overt allusions to 1 Peter, reformatted according to the dualistic logic of 1 John, with further allusions to Romans 7 and 8. The following table is provided to demonstrate the terminological and formal correspondence among these letters.

---

[98] Johnson, *James*, 287.
[99] Cf. Bauckham, *James*, 177–85.

James 3:13–4:10

¹³ Who is wise and understanding among you? *By his good conduct let him show his works* [δειξάτω ἐκ τῆς καλῆς ἀναστροφῆς τὰ ἔργα αὐτοῦ] in the meekness of wisdom.

⁴·¹ What causes wars, and what causes fightings among you? Is it not *your passions that are at war in your members* [ἐκ τῶν ἡδονῶν ὑμῶν τῶν στρατευομένων ἐν τοῖς μέλεσιν ὑμῶν]? ² *You desire* [ἐπιθυμεῖτε] and do not have, so you kill.

⁴ Adulteresses! Do you not know that *friendship with the world* [φιλία τοῦ κόσμου] is *hostility with God* [ἔχθρα τοῦ θεοῦ]? Therefore whoever wishes to be a *friend of the world* [φίλος . . . τοῦ κόσμου] makes himself an *enemy of God* [ἔχθρὸς τοῦ θεοῦ].

⁶ But he gives more grace; therefore it says, "*God opposes the proud, but gives grace to the humble*" [ὁ θεὸς ὑπερηφάνοις ἀντιτάσσεται, ταπεινοῖς δὲ δίδωσιν χάριν].

⁷ᵃ *Submit* [ὑποτάγητε] yourselves therefore to God.

1 Peter 2:11-12

¹² Maintain *good conduct* [ἀναστροφήν . . . καλήν] among the Gentiles, so that . . . *they may see your good works* [ἐποπτεύοντες ἐκ τῶν καλῶν ἔργων] and glorify God on the day of visitation.

¹¹ Beloved, I beseech you as aliens and exiles to abstain from the *passions of the flesh* [τῶν σαρκικῶν ἐπιθυμιῶν] that *wage war against your soul* [στρατεύονται κατὰ τῆς ψυχῆς].

Romans 7:23

I see a different law in my *members* [μέλεσιν], *waging war* [ἀντιστρατευόμενον] against the law of my mind and making me a prisoner of the law of sin which is in my *members*.

1 John 2:15-16

"Do not *love the world* or the things in the world. If anyone *loves the world* [ἀγαπᾷ τὸν κόσμον], love for the Father is not in him. For all that is in the world, the lust [ἐπιθυμία] of the flesh and the lust of the eyes and the pride [ἀλαζονεία] of life, is not of the Father but is of the world.

Romans 8:7

For the mind that is set on the flesh is *hostility to God* [ἔχθρα εἰς θεόν]; it does not *submit* to God's law [τῷ γὰρ νόμῳ τοῦ θεοῦ οὐκ ὑποτάσσεται].

1 Peter 5:5-9

⁵ᵇ Clothe yourselves . . . with humility toward one another, for "*God opposes the proud, but gives grace to the humble*" [ὁ θεὸς ὑπερηφάνοις ἀντιτάσσεται, ταπεινοῖς δὲ δίδωσιν χάριν].

⁵ᵃ Likewise you that are younger *submit* [ὑποτάγητε] to the elders.

^{7b} *Resist the devil* [ἀντίστητε δὲ τῷ διαβόλῳ] and he will flee from you. ⁸ Draw near to God and he will draw near to you. ⁹ Cleanse your hands, you sinners, and purify your hearts, you double-minded. Be wretched and mourn and weep. Let your laughter be turned to mourning and your joy to dejection. ¹⁰ *Humble yourselves before the Lord and he will exalt you* [ταπεινώθητε ἐνώπιον κυρίου καὶ ὑψώσει ὑμᾶς].

⁸ Be sober, be watchful; your adversary *the devil* [διάβολος] prowls around like a roaring lion, seeking some one to devour. ⁽⁹⁾ *Resist him* [ἀντίστητε], firm in your faith.

⁶ *Humble yourselves therefore under* the mighty hand of *God, that* in due time *he may exalt you* [ταπεινώθητε οὖν ὑπὸ . . . θεοῦ ἵνα ὑμᾶς ὑψώσῃ].

The many noteworthy parallels in the James and 1 Peter passages support my conclusions thus far. As expected, we find that James speaks in the same voice as Peter, citing the same scriptural text (Prov 3:34 in Jas 4:6 and 1 Peter, in agreement against the LXX source) and linking it with what is probably an adapted dominical saying (which also agrees against the source; compare Jas 4:10/1 Pet 5:6 with Matt 23:12/Luke 14:11). Further, both passages agree in exhorting "good conduct" and calling for a demonstration of works (Jas 3:13; 1 Pet 2:12).[100] But it is here that the different orientation of the two letters is revealed. Given the communal nature of the virtues and vices in James 3:13–4:3, it is presumable that the demonstration of "good conduct" called for in that letter is for the benefit of the believing community; indeed, the verse seeks specifically to identify the one who is wise and understanding "among you" (3:13). By contrast, the "good works" in 1 Peter are a demonstration for the benefit of those outside the community, "that they may see your good works and glorify God." This demonstration is threatened in both texts by "passions" internal to the believer; but while in James internal passions have a negative, divisive result *within* the community of faith, the central negative result in 1 Peter occurs *outside* the community of faith. In the former, the synagogue of believers is threatened, but in the latter, it is the Christian mission to unbelievers that is at stake. Our hypothetical author seems to have taken the exhortation of 1 Peter and reshaped it according to the rhetorical context of his implied author, James the Just, whose central concern is that the stain of the world might not permeate the community of God's people dispersed away from Jerusalem.

The two bookends of the Petrine exhortation are drawn together in James 4:4 by a prophetic denunciation in language foreign to that of 1 Peter: "Adulteresses! Do you not know that friendship with the world is enmity with God?" In these verses I hear a triple allusion. The first is that of 1 John 2:15-16, where it is made abundantly clear that love for the world and love for God are incompatible. But in 1 John, believers must not love the world because it is the abode of those whose

---

[100] Popkes ("James and Scripture," 226) notes the striking parallels here and likewise asserts the possibility that James is dependent on 1 Peter in this case.

heretical teaching about Jesus leads them into all kinds of unchristian behaviors and attitudes. In James, one must not mix with the world because its passions seduce God's people into the way of infidelity. Again we are struck by the primary difference between James and 1 John: While the latter's view of the world is informed by its christology, the view of the former is shaped according to its diaspora setting.

The second allusion is that of Romans 8:7-8, where we read, "For the mind that is set on the flesh is hostility [ἔχθρα] to God; it does not submit [ὑποτάσσεται] to God's law, indeed it cannot; and those who are in the flesh cannot please God." While ἔχθρος ("enemy" or "hostile") is rather common in the NT, ἔχθρα ("enmity" or "hostility") is less so (Luke 23:12; Rom 8:7; Gal 5:20; Eph 2:14, 16; Jas 4:4). Its use in James and Romans is undeniably similar, and forms a striking point of agreement between the two texts.

This particular Romans reference sensitizes us to hear another allusion from just earlier in Paul's letter: "For I delight in the law of God, in my inmost self; but I see in my members [μέλεσιν] another law warring against [ἀντιστρατεύομαι] the law of my mind and making me captive to the law of sin which dwells in my members" (Rom 7:22-23). Again, there is a good deal of agreement here. A person is described as being divided along similar lines as that found in James: He has two laws working within him, one in his head and the other in his "members," and they are at war with one another. Indeed, Paul and James are in complete agreement in upholding steadfast faith against wavering doubt: Romans 4:20 praises Abraham because "no unfaith made him waver [οὐ διεκρίθη τῇ ἀπιστίᾳ] concerning the promise of God" that he and Sarah would bear a son (cf. Rom 14:23). For Paul, however, the division is not simply psychological (as in James) but soteriological, grounded in the distinction between the old self that is captive to sin and the new self that is liberated by the Spirit. Our author posits no such metaphysical distinction between old and new, for his vision is entirely ethical. To accomplish this difference he appears to have taken the Pauline psychology of salvation and removed the polemical connection between law and sin residing at its core—a redactional agenda we have already witnessed in my analysis of each author's discussion of the law.

The third allusion is that of the OT prophets, whose tone the author inhabits here most graphically in the condemnation of his readers as "adulteresses." The language is vividly reminiscent of the invective of Israel's prophets, who regularly compared God and God's people to a marriage relationship wherein the bride had been unfaithful (for example, Isa 54:5; 57:3; Jer 3:6-10, 20; Ezek 16, esp. v. 32; Hos 3:1; 9:1). Those who "hold the faith" (2:1) are here denounced as being idolatrously unfaithful to God. As such, they have not simply wandered away from God, but they have willed (βούλομαι) to position themselves (καθίστημι) in a way that is hostile to God's ways in the world. In contrast with Abraham, whose status as "friend of God" was made manifest in the works that expressed his faith, the bitter jealousy, selfish ambition, and murderous conflict that characterizes the community of readers establishes their identity as "adulteresses" whose friendship with the world makes them "enemies of God."

Faith Works

1 Peter

Though "good works" are clearly an important aspect of the changed lifestyle that must result from new birth in Christ (2:11), 1 Peter does not contain the kind of anxious exhortation we find in James regarding the necessary integration of πίστις and ἔργον. Though faith (1:5, 7, 9, 21; 5:9) and belief (1:8; 2:6, 7) are surely important concepts, both are subsumed under the broader category of hope that dominates the letter's theological vision for the persecuted Christian. As 1:21 makes plain, faith and hope are basically synonymous for the author,[101] providing the vision and motivation for his ongoing concern with right conduct among non-believers, of which "good works" is a subset.

One important aspect of the right conduct described has to do with the role of speech in the believer's life. After exhorting readers to "not return evil [κακός] for evil or reviling [λοιδορία] for reviling, but on the contrary, bless" (3:9), Psalm 34 is brought in for scriptural support: "He that would love life and see good days, let him keep his tongue from evil and his lips from speaking guile" (3:10). This is not the first time we have heard this "verbal" theme in the letter. After 1:22 called readers to "an unhypocritical [ἀνυπόκριτος] love of the brethren," 2:1 charged readers to "put away all malice [κακία] and all guile [δόλος] and hypocrisy [ὑπόκρισις] and envy and all slander [καταλαλιά]." These terms are soon drawn together in the "pattern" (ὑπογραμμός) of Jesus, who "committed no sin; no guile [δόλος] was found in his mouth; when he was reviled [λοιδορέω], he did not revile in return; when he suffered, he did not threaten [ἀπειλέω], but he trusted to him who judges justly" (2:22-23). Thus an important aspect of right conduct is the role of proper speech in Christian witness: believers are to avoid hypocrisy and falsehood (utilized as a means of avoiding suffering?) or reviling and threatening (as a response to those who cause suffering?), for resorting to either is contrary to the example of Jesus. But this does not mean that believers should not speak at all; indeed, they are called to declare God's virtues (2:9), being ready at all times to offer a defense (ἀπολογία) to anyone enquiring about the hope that motivates their unusual lifestyle as exiles in the dispersion (3:15).

1 John

The author of 1 John is insistent about the need to integrate what one *says* with what one *does*. This is evidenced early in the letter (1:6-2:10; cf. 4:20), where a pattern is developed that contrasts the negative example of one who merely claims something about his relationship with God with the positive example of one whose right action before God makes her relationship self-evident. The congruence of what one says and does is but one of several means by which the author enables the community to "test the spirits" (4:1) in order to differentiate between true and false

---

[101] Kelly, *Commentary*, 78; Davids, *1 Peter*, 75 n. 15.

claims of faithfulness to God.[102] Hence (as in 1 Peter, though here with the added element of the spiritual "test"), we find an emphasis on "doing," e.g., "by this we know that we love the children of God, when we love God and *do* his commandments (5:2; cf. 1:6; 2:17, 29; 3:4, 22).

This particular means of "testing" true and false faith according to what one does comes to focus in 3:7-18, where we find a three-fold repetition of ἔργον (the only occurrences of the word in the letter). After being reminded that "he who does right is righteous" and "he who commits sin is of the devil" (3:7b-8a), the reader is told that Jesus appeared "to destroy the *works* of the devil" (3:8b). Then comes the test: "By this it may be seen who are the children of God and who are the children of the devil: Whoever does not do right is not of God, nor he who does not love his brother" (3:10). A few verses later the example of Cain is presented: he was "of the evil one" and murdered his brother "because his own *works* were evil and his brother's righteous" (3:12). The "evil work" proved Cain's patrilineage, for he recapitulated the deeds of the evil one. The pericope closes with a scenario that again contrasts saying and doing, this time by means of "word" and "work":

> Anyone who hates his brother is a murderer, and you know that no murderer has eternal life abiding in him. By this we know love: that he laid down his life for us, and we ought to lay down our lives for the brethren. But if anyone has the world's goods and sees his brother in need, yet closes his heart against him, how does God's love abide in him? Little children, let us not love in word or tongue but in work and truth (3:15-18).

Regardless of what claims one might make about one's relationship to God, it is one's actions that offer the decisive demonstration of one's faith. Of course, the author of 1 John does not actually use the word "faith" in these instances. He prefers the verbal form πιστεύω (3:23; 4:1, 16; 5:1, 5, 10, 13), which is often linked to confidence-building knowledge (for example, 4:16, "so we know and *believe* the love God has for us"; 5:5, "who is it who overcomes the world but he who *believes* that Jesus is the Son of God?"). Thus, as in 1 Peter, so also in 1 John there is a concern for appropriate verbal witness; but in contrast to 1 Peter, 1 John develops this topic polemically, with speech persistently set in contrast to action.

James

As we have seen, the notion that belief must be manifested in action is a theme in the letter of James not limited to the oft-studied 2:14-26. Already in the first chapter we see that faith should be tested by trials to produce endurance (1:3), that believers should ask in faith without doubting (1:6-8), that believers should be doers of works (1:25), and that authentic religion involves caring for the vulnerable (1:27). Like 1 John, this concern for right action is accompanied by a disdain for speech devoid of action, primarily in the similarly persistent tendency to characterize negatively

[102] On the "test" theme in 1 John, see Lieu, *Theology*, 49–71.

individuals who "say" something (1:13; 2:3,14,16,18; 4:13). Further, believers must be "slow to speak" and "quick to hear" (1:19); truly religious people "bridle their tongue" (1:26); slander and boasting are condemned (4:11-17); plain speech is exhorted (5:12); indeed, an entire section is devoted to the dangers of the tongue (3:1-12). All of our "Pillar" letters address right verbal and non-verbal witness, but James and 1 John stand as parallels apart from 1 Peter in their mutual concern to provide a sharply focused contrast between speaking and doing.

Consider the frequently overlooked parallel with 1 John that is embedded in the James passage.

James 2:14-17	1 John 3:16-18
[14] What use is it, my brethren, if someone says he has faith but he has no works? Can that faith save him? [15] If a brother or sister is without clothing and lacking daily nourishment, [16] and one of you says to them, "Go in peace, be warmed and be filled," and yet you do not give them what is necessary for the body, what use is that? [17] Even so faith, if it has no works, is dead by itself.	[16] By this we know love, that He laid down His life for us, and we ought to lay down our lives for the brethren. [17] But whoever has the world's goods, and sees his brother in need and closes his heart against him, how does the love of God abide in him? [18] Little children, let us not love in word or in speech, but in work and truth.

As we have seen elsewhere in these letters, each passage provides a contrast between saying and doing wherein deeds are presented as being superior to speech without deeds. Most striking, however, is the many formal, thematic, and verbal parallels that exist in the imaginary encounter with a needy sibling in faith:

(a) The scenario in each is described hypothetically by means of three subjunctive verbs (Jas 2:15, ὑπάρχω; 2:16, εἴπῃ; 1 John 3:17, ἔχω, θεωρέω) combined with indefinite or relative pronouns (τις in James; ὅ in 1 John).

(b) The subject encounters a person who is specifically identified as an ἀδελφός (with James inclusively adding ἢ ἀδελφή). Thus the encounter is between two believers.

(c) The faith sibling encountered is poor and in need; likewise the subject believer is described as being in a position of being able to help, but fails to do so.

(d) The failure in each is attributed to an assumption that a verbal expression of love and concern is sufficient (this is implied in 1 John 3:18, and made explicit in Jas 2:16).

(e) The image ends with a rhetorical question to make the reader reconsider his or her status before God. This is explicit in the Johannine question, "How does the love of God abide in him?" The Jacobian question, "What does it profit?" is a repetition of the opening question in 2:14, where the "profit" in mind is overtly soteriological: "Can his faith save him?"

(f) Immediately after the rhetorical question a closing summary statement is provided which repeats the original contrast and emphasizes the superiority of ἔργα.

Though it is my historical reconstruction that allows us to place James in the dependent position here, support is found in the author's apparent extension of the images found in the Johannine letter. James 2:15 expands the description of the poor sibling from the simple "brother in need" in 1 John to a brother or sister who is "naked [γυμνός] and lacking daily nourishment," and James 2:16 adds the speech that is implied in 1 John 2:18 ("Go in peace, be warmed and filled") and an extended description of 1 John's "closing the heart" (that is, they "do not give them what is necessary for the body").

There is one important difference, of course, between these two passages: while 1 John exhorts believers to remember that Christian *love* is manifest "in work and truth" (3:18), James is arguing about *faith* (2:14). Of the fifteen occurrences of ἔργον in this letter, twelve occur in 2:14-26. This recurring word is paired most often with the noun πίστις or the verb πιστεύω, found fourteen of nineteen times in this same passage. As we have already noted, the fact that this topic is addressed by means of πίστις and ἔργον makes best sense against a Pauline backdrop. The supposition that James 2:14-26 was written with Romans 2–4 in mind was sufficiently demonstrated in chapter 2. Recalling the many other links with the letter to the Romans we have discovered in our intertextual reading, the case for reading these two passages in tandem is made all the more legitimate.

Almost certain injury awaits the one who attempts to scale the mountain of secondary literature on the subject of faith and works in James and Paul, and the reader should not expect a thorough survey of the debate here. Our point of inquiry is rather precise: how did our hypothetical author intend to shape the broader apostolic witness by means of this passage? Let us begin with some comments on the structure and rhetoric of the pericope. Several factors stand against the assumption that the author of James intended to level an *attack* on Paul or his justification formula.[103] First, despite a history of interpretation that has focused narrowly on 2:14-26, we must recognize that this passage is a sub-section of a larger unit encompassing the whole of chapter 2.[104] The two halves of the chapter (2:1-13 and 14-26) are connected by a series of verbal links:

---

[103] For James as an attack on Paul, see M. Hengel, "Der Jakobusbrief als antipaulinische Polemik," in *Tradition and Interpretation in the New Testament*, FS E. Earle Ellis, ed. G. F. Hawthorne and O. Betz (Grand Rapids: Eerdmans, 1987), 248–78, 253–55, as well as the relevant sections in Lüdemann, *Opposition to Paul*.

[104] See esp. D. F. Watson, "James 2 in Light of Greco-Roman Schemes of Argumentation." *NTS* 39 (1993): 94–121; and Martin, 78–79.

(a) Both sections open with a vocative ἀδελφοί μου addressed in the context of "faith" (vv. 1, 14).

(b) A hypothetical example of an interaction with a poor person is introduced (vv. 2, 15).

(c) Each section cites one of Jesus' two "summary of the law" commandments, for example, Leviticus 19:18 (v. 8) and Deuteronomy 6:4 (v. 19).

(d) καλῶς ποιέω is repeated in association with each "summary" command (vv. 8, 19).

(e) Each section ends with a reiteration of the concern that speech and deeds correspond rightly in the life of the believer. 2:12 ends the first section with "so speak and so do"; 2:26 summarizes the second with, "So [verbal] faith without works is dead."

Both sections bring to light how deficient faith is made manifest. Thus, 2:14-26 is misread if it is understood to be *primarily* a self-standing attack on Paul's doctrine of justification. It is the continuation of an argument the author has been making from the very beginning of the letter. Having said that, 2:14-26 does read as a separate, theological *Exkurs*;[105] the passage should not be read out of context, but neither can it be read as a discussion of the virtue of generosity with no connection whatsoever to Pauline theology.[106]

Ironically, the rhetoric of the passage is a second factor that keeps us from automatically reading this section as a direct attack on Paul. Most of 2:14-26 is a diatribe, and though it was often assumed that an actual antagonist stood behind this argumentative style, recent studies in Greco-Roman rhetoric have shown otherwise. Diatribes generally presented an imaginary interlocutor toward purely pedagogical or hortative ends and were "motivated by concern rather than contempt."[107] Indeed, the purpose of 2:14-26 is to offer a teaching about what kind of faith "saves." The identities of the interlocutors in 2:14 and 18 are not elaborated; they are hypothetical, presented by means of the indefinite pronoun τις and (in the case of 2:14) a subjunctive verb ("if someone might say . . ."). Compare this, for instance, with 2 John 10, which undoubtedly has an actual situation in mind: "If someone [τις] comes [*indicative*] to you and does not bring [*indicative*] this teaching. . . ." The interlocutors in James are presented far less concretely; they simply provide illustrative backdrop for the theological discussion of 2:20-26.

The third factor is the most obvious, but worth mentioning just the same. Our author does not mention Paul or overtly cite his letters. In fact, the author describes

[105] Burchard, 110.

[106] *Pace* Davids, *James*, 130–32.

[107] S. Stowers, "The Diatribe," in *Greco-Roman Literature and the New Testament: Selected Forms and Genres,* ed. D. Aune (SBLSBS 21; Atlanta: Scholars Press, 1988), 81–82; cf. D. Aune, *The New Testament in its Literary Environment* (Philadelphia: Westminster, 1987), 200–202, 219–20; and the discussions in Dibelius (*James*, 149–51, 156) and Penner (53–55).

a situation entirely dissimilar to the one Paul addresses in Romans and Galatians, where the setting was not poverty and wealth but the possibility of self-justification by the performance of works of the law. Paul grounds the issue in the inclusion of the Gentiles in the eschatological Israel; but as we have seen, the Jew/Gentile conflict that so dominated Paul's ministry is nowhere to be found in the letter of James. Further (as we will see below), it is clear that the two authors present the key terms in the discussion quite differently. Clearly the author of James does not intend to speak *directly* to Paul's teaching in Romans. And yet the language employed in each is so similar! Like the teaching of Jesus, which is glaringly evident in the letter despite the author's failure to attribute the material to Jesus himself, so also the distinctively Pauline teaching on justification floats quite palpably above the surface of 2:14-26 even though Paul himself is not named. This fact has led the majority of scholars to read the passage with Paul in mind. However, given the points of disconnect just articulated, most conclude that if the author of James did have Pauline teaching in view, it must have been based on a misunderstanding of some sort: either the author has himself misunderstood Paul's teaching, or he is opposing individuals who represent a misunderstood, distorted "Paulinism." In either scenario, it is assumed that the author of James does not truly understand Paul's teaching.

My hypothesis that our author is indeed interacting with Pauline texts (namely the letter to the Romans) rules out the possibility that he is merely responding to someone else's misunderstood Paulinism (though I do think a misconstrual of Paul's teaching motivates the section). The possibility that he misunderstood Paul is also unlikely (though having access to texts does not ensure a faithful transmission of the intended message, as the history of Protestantism has made quite clear!). Again, it does not seem that an actual polemic between the two is underway, and the context for the discussion is different in each.

It seems as though the author of James wanted his readers to *hear* Paul somewhere in the background, but did not want to appear to be disagreeing with him. This makes perfect sense according to my hypothesis—for indeed, how could any second-century author seeking the approval of the Catholic community openly critique *The Apostle*? Vasiliki Limberis has suggested that this very reality accounts for the rhetorical style of the passage:

> [T]he genre itself assumes that the opponent is imaginary with whom he can argue sarcastically and even angrily. . . . This is vital for our situation for James. By using diatribe he does not have to attack Paul *ad hominem*. . . . The genre itself generalizes or neutralizes the potentially bitter debate.[108]

By careful use of the indirect, pedagogical rhetoric of the diatribe, our author was able to focus on the *issue* rather than the *person*. Of course, Limberis believes that

---

[108] V. Limberis, "The Provenance of the Caliphate Church: James 2:17-26 and Galatians 3 Reconsidered," in *Early Christian Interpretation of the Scriptures of Israel*, ed. C. A. Evans and J. A. Sanders (JSNTSup 148; Sheffield: Sheffield Academic, 1997), 413.

James himself wrote the letter and did indeed intend to attack Paul's teaching, albeit indirectly. But the mid-first-century context for such a debate was the inclusion of the Gentiles in the eschatological Israel, and given the absence in James of any hint of this situation (as well as many other features of the letter that point to a late date), Limberis's reconstruction seems doubtful. An alternative situation is the one presented earlier in my study: James of Jerusalem is writing to Jewish believers in the diaspora after the scenario described in Acts 21, in order to offer clarification of the apostolic position in response to confusion arising from Paul's teaching. He does not intend to malign Paul in any way; but he is the highest authority among believers, and as such, it falls to him to be the one to set the record straight.

This is the *implied* context of the letter. The *actual* second-century author envisioned in my hypothesis, of course, does not view the situation in precisely these terms. He is well aware of the stories that pit James and Paul against one another, and he has no intention of overemphasizing this traditional animosity. Thus, his own intention is not simply to have James set the record straight against Paul, but to create a canonical collection of letters that would position James and Paul as equal authorities standing in creative, canonical tension with one another. He does not want to banish Paul, but he also knows what sort of distortions can result when believers rely on Paul alone.

But what exactly did he wish to convey? An answer to this question can only be proposed after 2:14-26 has been subjected to closer analysis. First, what exact claims do the interlocutors make? The first (v. 14) is presented as claiming that he has faith, but the author immediately points out that he has no accompanying works and asks, "Can his faith save him?" This primary soteriological question governs the entire discussion: can someone be saved if the faith they claim to possess is not made evident in the works they perform? The author then appeals *to the audience* for an answer by means of the poor sibling scenario already analyzed: if someone is lacking clothes and food, "and one of you" (ἐξ ὑμῶν) offers verbal blessing but no physical help, "what is the profit"? The rhetorical question implies a negative answer, which is assumed in the summary statement of v. 17: "So faith by itself, if it has no works, is dead." This verse is a repetition (a *commoratio* according to Duane Watson) of the primary faith/works terms set forth in v. 14 (the *propositio*).[109] The two verses form by means of *inclusio* the basic claim of the broader passage: Faith and works are necessarily assimilated; one cannot claim to have one without demonstration of the other. The *commoratio* is repeated at regular intervals throughout the passage (vv. 17, 20, 24, 26) in order to keep the basic point constantly in view.

But what of the second τις introduced at verse 18? Dibelius labeled this verse "one of the most difficult New Testament passages" to interpret because of its unclear articulation of the participants in the discussion (who is the σύ, and who is the ἐγώ?), and because of the extent of the quotation (does it include 18a only, all of 18, or all of 18-19?).[110] Burchard has recently offered a thorough excursus on

[109] Watson, "James 2," 108.
[110] Dibelius, *James*, 154.

the matter, identifying seven different primary translations that have resulted in at least thirty-three different interpretive conclusions![111] Given my limited space, I will simply explain my own interpretive choices. First, the τις in verse 18 is not the same τις of verse 14. Our author would not have repeated the indefinite pronoun if the speaker in mind had been previously introduced.[112] Second, the speech of the second τις is limited to verse 18a, "You have faith and I have works." The voice of the author clearly reappears in the *commoratio* of verse 20 ("faith apart from works is useless"), but what of verses 18b-19? The ironic statement—"you believe that God is one; you do well; even the demons believe, and shudder"— is little more than an ironic *commoratio*: "Faith" that amounts to verbal assent to dogma is soteriologically vacant, for even demons make such a confession. It is no different than the dead faith of the one who *says* he has faith but has no corresponding works. Add the fact that the καλῶς ποιέω of 2:8 is repeated, and we are led to the conclusion that verse 19 also represents the voice of the author. Likewise verse 18b ("show me your faith apart from your works and I by my works will show you my faith") restates the author's basic position by way of a sarcastic request, for obviously a faith that has no works cannot be demonstrated. The δεῖξόν μοι ("show me!") is a diatribal imperative that assumes an opposing posture in relation to what precedes it.[113] Thus, the τις is speaking in verses 18a and 18b-19 represents the response of the author.

Third and finally, the τις of verse 18a is neither an ally of the author[114] nor an opponent (the dominant position), but someone attempting a mediating position between the author and the τις of verse 14.[115] The adversative ἀλλά is enough to rule out the possibility that the speaker is an ally. The use of the future indicative verb in place of the earlier present subjunctive ("someone *might* say" followed by "but someone *will* say") suggests that the second τις is making a response of some sort based on what was said in verses 14-17. The fact that this person is also presenting an incorrect position is indicated by the fact that he *says* it, since we have come to see that people who *say* things in James are presented negatively (1:13; 2:3,14,16; 4:13). This second τις appears to be attempting a mediating position between that of the author and the first τις: is it not true that some people have faith and others have works? Are both not independently valid?[116] The author's reply in 18b-19, as we have seen, is a two-pronged response against this position, for it still seeks to argue that faith without works is (at least potentially) salvific.

In sum: both interlocutors represent different ways of claiming that someone can have faith apart from works, the first by asserting that faith alone is sufficient, and the second by suggesting that faith and works are different qualities attributable to

[111] Burchard, 118–21.

[112] Burchard, 120.

[113] Davids, *James*, 124.

[114] See Mayor, Adamson, and Mussner.

[115] See Burchard, 120.

[116] D. J. Verseput, "Reworking the Puzzle of Faith and Deeds in James 2:14-26," *NTS* 43 (1997): 108.

different people. One need not look far for antecedents to such positions. The claim
that one is "justified by faith apart from works" is easily derived from Paul's crucially
nuanced claim that believers are "justified by faith apart from works *of the law*" (Rom
3:28; Gal 2:16). More interesting is the claim of the second τις in v.18a, that faith
and works are independently valid. Many commentators have drawn attention to
how faith is ranked independently in Pauline gift lists:[117]

> **Romans 12:6-8**: Having gifts that differ according to the grace given to us, let
> us use them: if prophecy, in proportion to our faith; if service, in our serving . . .
> he who contributes, in liberality; he who gives aid, with zeal; he who does acts of
> mercy, with cheerfulness.

> **1 Corinthians 12:8-9**: To one is given through the Spirit the utterance of wisdom,
> and to another the utterance of knowledge according to the same Spirit, to another
> faith by the same Spirit, to another gifts of healing by the one Spirit.

With this background in mind, one can easily imagine the very response put forward in v.18a against the claim that faith without works is dead. "But what if I do
not have the gift of service, aid-giving or mercy?" asks the interlocutor. "My gift is
prophecy; my faith is exercised by what I *say* on God's behalf. Others are gifted to
do works of mercy." While Paul obviously affirmed that gifts of the Spirit are various,
he would have heartily disagreed with the idea that differing gifts exempt some from
acting righteously, as any moderately careful reading of Romans makes plain. It is
not inappropriate for us to conclude that our author's correction attempts to present
a more thorough understanding of Pauline teaching against those who misuse it to
support their workless faith.

Given the singular, diatribal *commoratio* of verse 20 ("Do you want to be
shown, O empty man, that faith apart from works is useless?"), it is evident that
the interlocutor of verse 18 is still being addressed when our author turns to the
example of Abraham in 2:21-24. After the repeated *commoratio* condemnation of
the supposed separability of faith and works, verse 21 may come as a surprise: "Was
not Abraham our father justified by works when he offered his son Isaac upon the
altar?" Though the rhetorical question appears to actually commit the crime the
author has been combating all along (apparently elevating "works" to the detriment
of "faith"), Marian Soards and others have shown the extent to which this statement (and indeed all of 2:21-24) rests on an appeal to traditional Jewish exegesis of
Abraham's faith.[118] Numerous examples have been culled to demonstrate how the
exegetical tradition read Genesis 15:6 (Abraham "believed God, and it was reckoned

---

[117] E.g., Ropes, 208; Laws, 123–24; Davids, *James*, 123; Martin, 87.

[118] M. L. Soards, "The Early Christian Interpretation of Abraham and the Place of James
Within That Context," *IBS* 9 (1987): 18–26; cf., e.g., the extensive analysis in Dibelius,
James, 168–74; I. Jacobs, "The Midrashic Background for James 2:21-23," *NTS* 22 (1976):
457–64; R. Ward, "The Works of Abraham: James 2:14-26," *HTR* 61 (1968): 283–90;
Verseput, "Reworking," 111–15.

to him as righteousness") in light of Abraham's obedience, focusing particularly on the story of the offering of Isaac in Genesis 22 as the culminating demonstration of Abraham's faith; for example, 1 Maccabees 2:52, "Was not Abraham found faithful *when tested*, and it was reckoned to him as righteousness?" (for example, *Jub.* 17:15–18; 18:15–16; Sir 44:19–22; 1 Macc. 2:52; *m. Kidd* 4:14; *Abr.* 167; *Deus.* 1.4; *Ant.* 1.223, 233–34). Our author is therefore appealing here to an entirely well known line of thought among Jewish believers: the *faith* of Abraham was shown in his radical *obedience* to God. As we have seen so often before, so also here the author of James is reaching back into pre-Christian Judaism in order to realign a particularly Christian claim in light of Jewish tradition.

It is at this point that verses 22-24, in particular, become most interesting. First, we note in verse 22 the second person singular form of the verb βλέπω, indicating that the interlocutor of verse 18a is still being addressed; hence the subject under review remains our author's thesis regarding the assimilation of faith and works. The other two verbs in the sentence articulate the particular co-agency our author has in mind. In Abraham's case, faith worked with (συνηργέω) works. Faith and works are *synergistic*, each requiring the other in order to function properly. The second verb states that faith "was completed" (ἐτελειώθη) by works. Despite the fact that "faith" is the subject of both clauses,[119] one must not conclude that Abraham had "faith" first and "works" later, for that would support the possible separation of the two. Note the subtle interplay of the active and passive voice in this sentence: "Faith was working together with his works, and from the works, faith was completed." Faith actively enabled the work, but faith was, in turn, passively completed by the works. The two entities do not exist in a causal relationship: it would be mistaken to elevate the role of faith in our author's presentation by arguing that the faith described here is "the unfinished state of faith" waiting to be "brought to maturity" by works.[120] The relationship between the two constitutes a synergistic and reciprocal whole. The author is not describing mature "working" faith and immature "non-working" faith, but *true and false faith*. Having said that, one must also resist the reverse claim that the author knows only "works" and denigrates "faith," for the investigation of saving *faith* is the focus of his inquiry (v. 14). The issue is neither "faith first and works later," nor "works are superior to faith," but *"the faith that saves is a faith that works."*

The language of verse 23 extends this logic. Just as faith *was completed* by works, so also in the act of offering Isaac in Genesis 22, "the scripture *was fulfilled* which says, 'Abraham believed God, and it was reckoned to him as righteousness.'" This is the only use of fulfillment language in James, language that is used throughout the NT to describe later (Christian) fulfillment of earlier (Jewish) prophesy. This is not the intention here; the author is not necessarily saying that God somehow *prophesied* Abraham's faith, which was then *fulfilled* later in the offering of Isaac,[121]

---

[119] Johnson, *James*, 243.
[120] Davids, *James*, 128.
[121] See Mayor, 100; and Ropes, 221.

for again, this would allow for the very separation of faith and works our author rejects. As above, in citing the scripture the author is standing on traditional ground whereby the righteousness of Abraham reckoned in Genesis 15:6 was understood in light of the work of offering Isaac in Genesis 22. In James the two passages are drawn together by the crucial verse 22, which makes it clear that this particular scriptural pairing is not simply traditional but is a response to the interlocutor of verse 18a, a response intended to defend a properly synergistic understanding of faith and works against those who argue that one can exist without the other.

Paul was of course the principal proponent of this very position:

> **Romans 4:2-5**: If Abraham was justified by works, he has something to boast about, but not before God. For what does the scripture say? "Abraham believed God, and it was reckoned to him as righteousness." Now to one who works, his wages are not reckoned as a gift but as his due. And to one who does not work but trusts him who justifies the ungodly, his faith is reckoned as righteousness.

In arguing that Abraham was considered righteous apart from anything he had done, Paul has wrenched apart the traditional wholeness of Abraham's life of obedient faith. In a dramatic reassertion of the traditional understanding, the author of James states what appears to be the exact reverse in 2:24: turning away from the imaginary interlocutor and back to his audience, he concludes his presentation of the example of Abraham by means of his third *commoratio*, "You see that a person is justified by works and not by faith alone."

This final clause requires comment. As before, the phrase "justified by works" is not meant to imply a separation of faith and works. By "works" our author means the synergistic "faith works" that he has been describing all along, that is, faith working with works, and works completing faith. The difficult phrase, of course, is "not by faith alone." Does the author of James intend to contradict Pauline teaching on this point? Not at all; again, the "faith" he condemns is the caricatured "faith" of the interlocutors. But there remains a Pauline referent behind this text, for the interlocutors rely on Pauline theology for their understanding of justification. In his defense, Paul *never* used the phrase "by faith alone." But he did speak of "faith *apart from* works" (Rom 3:28) and paired "faith" with "not by works" (Gal 2:16). He also claimed that the people of Israel failed to be righteous "because they did not pursue it through faith, but as if it were based on works" (Rom 9:32). Paul separated faith and works, and the author of James was troubled by this separation. Likewise, Paul would have *never* reduced faith to the articulation of pious words and intellectual assent to doctrine, as in the negative example of "faith" in the James passage. But he did say, "if you confess with your mouth and believe in your heart, you will be saved; for a person believes with his heart and is justified; and he confesses with his lips and is saved" (Rom 10:9-10). "Faith alone" is never claimed in such passages, but it is easily (mis-)inferred by those who claim "Paul alone"—especially in a context wherein the major debates regarding the ongoing validity of the law were basically settled. In such a context Paul's crucially qualified "works *of the law*" would be easily overlooked.

Again in Paul's defense, it is worthwhile considering his own use of the term ἔργον.[122] Of the sixty-eight times it appears in the Pauline writings, nine are "works of the law" (Rom 2:15; 3:20, 28; Gal 2:16 (x3); 3:2, 5, 10), eight clearly imply "works of the law" (Rom 3:27; 4:2, 6; 9:12, 32; 11:6; Eph 2:9; 2 Tim 1:9), and ten use the term pejoratively, as in the contrast between "fruit of the Spirit" and "works of the flesh" in Galatians 5:19-23 (Rom 13:12; 1 Cor 5:2; 2 Cor 11:15; Gal 5:19; Eph 5:11; Col 1:21; 4:14, 18; Tit 1:16; 3:5). The remaining forty-one occasions finds Paul using the term in a positive sense exactly akin to its use in James and the Jewish tradition, that is, to describe faithful effort. The Pauline canon uses ἔργον in a "Jacobian," positive sense on forty-one occasions and negatively on twenty-seven; bracket out the disputed letters and the total makes twenty-one positive, nineteen negative. Thus, half to two-thirds of the Pauline uses of ἔργον imply a basic agreement with the attitude expressed in James that "works" are a necessary aspect of the believer's life. Augustine was keenly aware of this, and constantly repeated Galatians 5:6 in his *De fide et operibus* for this very reason: "For in Christ Jesus neither circumcision nor uncircumcision is of any avail, but faith working through love." Clearly, though in the relevant passages our authors are using this key term differently, a broader view helps us to see the more widespread agreement between the two.

But there are other ways in which these two clearly disagree. Paul and the author of James mean something different by the verb δικαιόω. Where Paul understands the term in a forensic sense (before his works, Abraham was *declared to be righteous* by God), for the author of James, it is a demonstrative term (because of his works, Abraham is *demonstrated to be righteous*). For Paul, righteousness in Christ is a two-stage process involving God's primary gift of justification by faith and humanity's secondary response of faithful, spirit-empowered works. The author of James, however, refuses to accept the possible existence of a metaphysical state of "faith" that cannot be demonstrated by deeds: "Show me your faith apart from your works, and I by my works will show you my faith" (2:18). From his perspective, a real, *whole* faith is one that is performed by the *whole* person, verbally and actively, with head, heart, mouth, and hands working in complete union. Paul would, of course, agree, but while he grounds this holistic view of human righteousness in an initial gift of God in Christ, the author of James offers no overt sign that human righteousness is derived christologically. Read on its own terms, the letter's representation of human righteousness is of a moral act of the will, one that requires strenuous effort and endurance.

Of course, none of us actually reads the letter of James on its own terms. Indeed, if my hypothesis is correct, *no one was ever intended to read the letter on its own terms,* for it was written to be read in canonical conversation with the letters of Peter, John, and Paul. Hence, 2:14-26 *must* be read in conversation with Romans 2–4 in order to be rightly understood. Returning then to the question posed at the beginning of this section: how did our hypothetical author intend to shape the broader apostolic witness by means of this passage? Clearly he was concerned to offer a strenuous defense of the traditional conceptualization of faith against those who would affirm

[122] Cf. Johnson, *James*, 60.

a false, truncated "faith" of intellectual assent evidenced only by means of ecclesial association and pious speech. Given the broader context of the second chapter, it seems that the particular focus of concern had to do with believers whose thin, verbal affirmation of faith allowed for an easy accommodation to the unrighteous practices of their surrounding society. They believed they could be friends of God while remaining friends with the world.

This "thin" faith appears to have been justified on the basis of Pauline teaching. James of Jerusalem's defense against this falsehood was grounded in the traditions of Judaism, which reached its zenith in the example of Father Abraham, whose trust in God was shown through his righteous life. This was, of course, also the teaching tradition of Jesus, which consistently married hearing, speaking, and doing in the life of the believer. In this way James functions as a kind of bridge text, enabling a reconciliation of the "justification by faith" passages in Paul with the ethical injunctions of the gospels, as Origen (the earliest Jacobian tradent) rightly recognized.

> [T]he one who does not have faith would be uncircumcised in the heart and the one who does not have works would be uncircumcised in the flesh. For one without the other is condemned, seeing that also faith without works is called "dead" [Jas 2:17, 26], and that no one is justified before God by works without faith [Rom 3:20; Gal 2:16]. Thus, I am convinced that the prophetic word shall be properly applied to that people which is made up of believers, to whom it is being said, "No foreigner who is among you in the midst of the house of Israel, who is uncircumcised in heart and uncircumcised in flesh, shall enter my sanctuary" [Ezek 44:9]. Doubtless this is what the Lord also says in the Gospel, "He who believes in me keeps my commands" [John 14:15, 21, 23]; and again, "he who hears these words of mine and does them" [Matt 7:24]; and likewise, "why do you say to me, 'Lord, Lord,' and do not do what I say?" [Luke 6:46]. You see, then, that everywhere faith is joined with works and works are united with faith. (*Comm. Rom.* 2.9.396–408 [*VL* 16.165.396–166.408; FC 103.156])

Against those who would use Pauline writings to isolate the *proclamation* of faith in a way that marginalized the *performance* of faith as demanded in the teaching of Jesus, James leads the Pillars of Jerusalem in the insistence that authentic, soteriologically profitable faith is evidenced in the life of the whole person, and never by the tongue alone.

Conclusion

Throughout this chapter we have noted a series of parallels between James, 1 Peter, 1 John, and the letters of Paul. Even apart from my historical reconstruction, a number of these connections are strong enough to warrant an affirmation of literary dependence. When considered in light of the historical evidence, the broader hypothesis is justified: the author of this second-century letter can be shown to have intentionally linked his letter with the authoritative apostolic letters of his day in order to create a literarily coherent and theologically robust Pillars collection to shape a fully orthodox reception of the Pauline collection. To conclude this chapter, I briefly reconsider the numerous points of contact just examined in order to entertain a few thoughts regarding the specific nature of our author's utilization of these particular texts.

JAMES AND 1 PETER

It is quite apparent that the first letter of Peter is the authoritative model to which our author sought most vigorously to bind his own. This is the case not only because of the sheer weight of parallels between the two, but most strikingly, by the way in which all but the last two parallels are presented *in consecutive order*.

James	1 Peter	Link?
1:1	1:1	Recipients in the διασπορά
1:2-4	1:6-9	Rejoice/be joyful in various trials (ποικίλοις πειρασμοῖς) + the testing/genuineness of your faith (τὸ δοκίμιον ὑμῶν τῆς πίστεως)
1:10-11	1:23-24	Extended allusion to/quotation of Isaiah 40
1:18	1:23	Birth (ἀποκυέω/ἀναγεννάω) by a λόγος
1:21-25	1:23-25	Λόγος as gospel/law
3:13; 4:1	2:11-12	Good conduct (καλὴ ἀναστροφή) + works (ἔργα) + passions (ἐπιθυμία/ἐπιθυμέω)
4:6-10	5:5-9	Quotation of Prov 3:34 + call to submit (ὑποτάσσω) + resist the devil (ἀντίστητε τῷ διαβόλῳ) + call to humble self (ταπεινώθητε) before God/Lord that he may exalt (ὑψόω)
5:20	4:8	Allusion to Prov 10:12 (καλύψει/καλύπτει πλῆθος ἁμαρτιῶν)

As a correction to those who looked to Peter and Paul as the primary leaders of the ancient Christian church, our hypothetical author needed to reaffirm the traditional authority of James of Jerusalem. James sat on the first episcopal throne, James was the earliest leader of the earliest Christian church, and though second-century heterodox Christians championed him, his stature was such that Catholic Christianity could not afford to set him aside. But establishing lines of authority was not all our author was interested in accomplishing, for James had a theological perspective of his own to contribute to the apostolic kerygma. For this reason our author was not interested in merely echoing 1 Peter, but sought through his echoes to shift the thought of the latter text in order to ensure a particular reception of its teaching. The parallel passages reflect a persistent concern on the part of the author to reassert the essentially Jewish underpinnings of Christianity: 1 Peter uses "diaspora" figuratively, but James intends it quite literally; 1 Peter describes its Gentile readership in terms previously associated with Israel as though Israel has ceased to exist, but the implied readership of James is ethnic Israel itself; 1 Peter looks to the prophets as witnesses to the gospel of Christ, but James looks to the prophets themselves as models of faith; indeed, in 1 Peter the primary faith exemplar is Christ, but in James it is Abraham, Rahab, Job, the prophets, and Elijah; furthermore, in 1 Peter the "word" is the Christian gospel, but in James it is overtly associated with the word of the Torah.

Read in conjunction, these two letters together offer a powerful witness to the continuity of God's covenants with Israel and the church. While the letter of James asserts that Christianity is *from Jews* and *for Jews*, 1 Peter's address to *Gentiles* as the eschatological Israel underwrites the history of earliest Christianity according to the Acts of the Apostles, where the mission to the Gentiles was born out of and embraced by those involved with the mission to the Jews (cf. Acts 8:26-40; 10:1–11:26) well before Paul's mission got underway. The letters present an image of these two early Christians standing back to back, with James expressing Christian identity *retrospectively* within the thought world of Israel, and Peter expressing Israelite identity *prospectively* within the mission to the Gentiles. Together the letters attributed to them form the foundation of the NT literary deposit of the apostolic mission they represented.

James and 1 John

The parallels with the first letter of John are far less persistent and striking than those of 1 Peter, but those that have presented themselves are just as conspicuous.

James	1 John	Link?
1:13; 2:14; 4:13	2:4-9; 3:18	Faithless saying contrasted with faithful doing
2:14-17	3:16-18	Hypothetical encounter with poor sibling (ἀδελφός) to illustrate superiority of works (ἔργα) over words
4:4	2:15-16	Friendship/love of the world (φιλία τοῦ κόσμου/ἀγαπᾷ τὸν κόσμον) incompatible with devotion to God
5:13-20	5:14-17	Prayer for another is effective for restoring the sinner and delivering from death (ἐκ θανάτου/πρὸς θάνατον)

Our author was concerned to link his text with 1 John so that the Jerusalem Pillars could be heard to speak in unison, but his approach to this letter had more to do with *coherence* than *correction*. Between the two, 1 Peter was in need of greater "canonical shaping" than 1 John.

Our hypothetical author found much in 1 John with which to echo in agreement. Clearly he was drawn to the ethical dualism in the letter more than anything else. All three letters place great emphasis on the conduct of the believer, but James follows 1 John in its elevated assertion that conduct is the ultimate determinant of one's status before God. Along the way, both letters notably and repeatedly contrast those whose belief is made manifest in action with those whose belief is merely a matter of the head and the tongue. The result is a heightened sensitivity to a theme shared by all three letters: *the separation of the believer from the seductive practices of the surrounding culture.* Both James and 1 John loudly proclaim that believers cannot claim to be "of God" and simultaneously maintain allegiance to that which is ungodly. 1 Peter addresses its beleaguered, suffering audience as "aliens and exiles" in order to provide the kind of conceptual framework that might strengthen them "for a little while" (1:6; 5:10) to resist accommodation until the return of Christ. When it is read in conjunction with James and 1 John, however, this message of temporary resistance to accommodation becomes a strident exhortation to *always* remain different, separate, holy, and unstained from the world. The result is a Pillars collection with an overarching sectarian ecclesiology to balance the missiological ecclesiology of the Pauline collection.123 In the Pillars, contact with the world is primarily corruptive; in the Paulines it is primarily evangelistic. In the Pillars, believers are pilgrims in a foreign land; in the Paulines, they are missionaries sent out to proclaim the new creation. The two theological emphases exist in creative tension as part of a canonical whole, and it is ultimately the combined, parallel witness of James and 1 John that anchors the sectarian pole.

JAMES AND PAUL

For too many commentators, the relation between the canonical James and Paul has been skewed by an imbalanced isolation of James 2:14-26 from the rest of the letter. Not only has this made them less attentive to the other important parallels between the two, it has also led too often to the conclusion that their respective theologies are entirely at odds with one another. As we have seen, however, there are quite a number of agreements and disagreements between the two authors, creating a complex interaction that calls for a far more nuanced assessment.

---

123 See R. Wall, "Ecumenicity and Ecclesiology: The Promise of the Multiple Letter Canon of the New Testament," in *The New Testament as Canon: A Reader in Canonical Criticism*, ed. E. E. Lemcio and Wall (JSNTS 76; Sheffield: Sheffield Academic, 1992), 184–207.

Jas	Rom	1 Cor	2 Cor	Gal	Link?
1:2-4	5:3-4				Boast/be joyful about trials/afflictions which produce endurance (κατεργάζεται ὑπομονήν)
1:6; 2:4	4:20; 14:23				Condemnation of doubting (διακρίνω)
1:8; 3:8, 16		14:33	6:5; 12:20		ἀκατάστατος/ἀκαταστασία
1:13-25	7:7-12			4:21-31	Law of liberty or slavery?
1:16		6:9; 15:33		6:7	Do not be deceived (μὴ πλανᾶσθη)
1:22	2:13				On being not hearers (ἀκροαταί) but doers (ποιηταί) of the word/law
1:26		3:18; 8:2; 11:16; 14:37		6:3	If anyone thinks himself to be (εἴ τις δοκεῖ . . . εἶναι)
2:1, 8-11	2:1, 11				Partiality (προσωπολημψία) forbidden
2:8-11	2:21-23				Condemnation of partial law keeping
2:8-11	13:8-10			5:14	Fulfilling the law + Lev 19:18
2:14, 17	2:6-10			5:6	Works (ἔργα) as criterion of judgment/ salvation
2:18	12:6-8	12:4-10			Can faith and works be separated?
2:14-24	3:27-4:25			2:16	Faith (πίστις) + works (ἔργα) + justification (δικαιόω) + Abraham + quotation of Gen 15:6
4:4	8:7-8				Enmity with God (ἔχθρα τοῦ θεοῦ / εἰς θεόν)
4:12	14:4				Who are you to judge? (σὺ τίς εἶ ὁ κρίνων)
5:3	2:5				Storing up (θησαυρίζω) for the day (ἡμέρα) of judgment

As we have seen throughout, the vast majority of intertextual linkages between the letters of James and Paul are found in the letter to the Romans. One cannot surmise on this basis that our hypothetical author knew *only* Paul's letter to the Romans, of course, since we have found impressive parallels with other Pauline letters as well. It is impossible to make any confident claims about the extent of our author's working Pauline letter collection, but the fact that he knew of Paul's teaching as it appears in several of his extant letters seems plain. The letter to the Romans is our author's primary dialogue partner. On the face of it this is not all that surprising, for Romans is the longest of Paul's writings, and further, its subject matter (namely the role of Torah in salvation history) makes it a natural conversation partner for the letter of James. The fact that most of the links between Paul and James occur in this letter, however, makes good sense canonically, for the two letters function as the orienting texts for their respective letter collections. Each one in its own way sets the tone for the reception of the remaining letters in their epistolary sub-group: Romans as the opening *tour de force* of Pauline theology and James as the unequivocally Jewish witness to the earliest Christian mission in Jerusalem.

As we have seen, there is widespread agreement between the authors. Both are working out of the same Torah traditions, and further, the hypothesized author of James is a Catholic Christian committed to an orthodox view of an apostolic kerygma fundamentally informed by Pauline thought. The letter of James is therefore most certainly not an "antipaulinische Polemik."[124] As for 2:14-26, the "Paulinism" condemned is indeed based on a misunderstanding of Paul, but the misunderstanding is not that of our author. The "faith" he condemns is not Pauline "faith" per se, but the caricatured "faith" of his interlocutors that was supported by a particular understanding of Pauline theology. As I have shown, the "correction" James offers is not really all that far from Paul's own attitudes. But we have also discovered some crucial differences. Though they agreed that fulfilling God's law was fundamental, Paul's conviction that ongoing "fleshly" adherence to the law was a kind of slavery from which Christ came to set God's people free would not have allowed him to agree with James' view of the Torah as the "perfect law of liberty." Though they agreed in looking to Abraham as the paragon of righteousness, Paul believed Abraham was *declared* to be righteous before his works, while James refused to accept the notion that real faith could exist without being *demonstrated*. Hence we cannot say that the two are perfectly complementary as they stand. But they are not incompatible either. How then ought their relationship be understood?

Was our hypothetical second-century author a "Paulinist" who was trying to defend Paul?[125] Not exactly: what he wanted to defend was the developing Catholic tradition of Christian thought, most particularly its insistence on continuity with Jewish tradition and the essential harmony of the apostolic kerygma. Willi Marxsen

---

[124] *Pace* Hengel.
[125] This is the position promoted by W. Marxsen (*Introduction to the New Testament: An Approach to its Problems* [Oxford: Basil Blackwell, 1968], 231) and Mitchell.

is, of course, not incorrect when he states that our author wanted "to bring back a Paulinism that had been misinterpreted and distorted to the truly Pauline position,"[126] yet more must be said than that. Like most of his contemporaries, our author revered Paul, yet he was quite aware that Paul's teaching was being used to support opinions deemed unorthodox by nascent Catholic theology; indeed, Augustine's "perplexing problem in the writings of the Apostle Paul" was a subject of regular discussion among later second- and early third-century Catholics, as the survey in chapter one revealed. A correction was needed.

Everyone knew the stories of disagreements between James and Paul, and our author felt no real need to pretend they did not exist; but he also could not present his epistolary James in direct conflict with "the Apostle," for that would only serve to underwrite the notion that the leaders of the Jerusalem mission did not share the same theological message as Paul. As Tertullian insisted on behalf of the Catholics against Marcion, the division between Paul and the Jerusalem Pillars was not a division of *kerygma* but a division of *labor*, not a different gospel, but the same gospel preached to different audiences. Against Marcion's fundamentalism it was affirmed that apostolic unity did not require rigid uniformity. Our author took full advantage of this particularly Catholic vision of the diversity of the earliest Christian mission, for it enabled a situation wherein Paul and James could speak in rather different, mutually corrective tones without implying that they were inharmonious. Our author used their traditional "difference" to his advantage, creating a text that would ensure the proper reception of the Pauline message when the two were read in canonical conversation. The result is not a perfect agreement, but neither do they inhabit completely opposing positions. They exist in creative, canonical tension with one another. As Wall explains it, "the 'canonical' result" of their union "is that two different kerygmata form two discrete yet integral parts of a biblical whole."[127] The two apostles are to be read as mutually interpreting. This is precisely what Irenaeus and Tertullian did when they interpreted Paul's letters through the Catholic lens afforded by the Acts of the Apostles, and what Origen did when he used passages from James to enable a more fully Catholic interpretation of Paul's letter to the Romans. The composition of a letter from James of Jerusalem is the logical extension of this catholicizing trend, for it enabled the creation of a two-sided letter collection to correspond with the vision of the earliest apostolic mission presented in the Lukan narrative.

In this regard, John Reumann is exactly correct: The author of James was working "to defend what Paul took to be central, righteousness-justification involving faith—a faith that is expressed obediently to God in service . . . James protects the Pauline view at a point where it has seemed vulnerable in application, as the history of theology demonstrates."[128] But Martin is also right to recognize that in this "rehabilitation" of Paul we also find a "rehabilitation" of James; for just as Paul

[126] Marxsen, 231.
[127] Wall, *James*, 151.
[128] J. Reumann, *Righteousness in the New Testament* (Philadelphia: Fortress, 1982), 158.

needed to be propped up at his weak point, James also needed to be reclaimed from the heterodox who championed him as their supreme authority.[129] The result is a theologically circumscribed Paul, a fully Catholic James, and a NT canon informed by the entire apostolic witness and not by Paul alone.

---

[129] Martin, 83–84; I am indebted to him for alerting me to the comments of Reumann and Marxsen.

CHAPTER FOUR

CONCLUSION

This study bears a number of possible implications for contemporary New Testament research. Methodologically, my goal has been to offer a canonical reading justified on historical grounds, or put another way, a historical hypothesis demonstrated to be plausible by a combination of literary and canonical evidence. It is up to others to determine whether or not I have been successful in this endeavor. Regardless, it is offered in the hope that it might contribute to a movement away from the occasionally rancorous and simplistic state of affairs wherein "modern" historical critics caricature literary readings as exercises in historical imagination, and "postmodern" literary critics condemn historical investigation as a philosophically dubious endeavor. What we need is more critical interplay to demonstrate how the historical and literary characteristics of the Bible can be mutually informing. This book has tried to do just that.

I have also sought to offer a substantial contribution to contemporary research on the letter of James. Like the methodological state of affairs just described, current James research appears to be similarly polarized between those who insist on its early authenticity and those who take its late pseudepigraphy simply for granted. Rather than present a mediating position, however, I have chosen a side. Against those who argue for authenticity, I have tried to present a compelling alternative account for the letter's origin as a second-century pseudepigraph. My hypothesis offers a single explanation for a number of confusing features of the letter that have had to be explained away by interpreters seeking to establish its authenticity. In the past we have been offered thin explanations for the letter's late canonicity; the literary parallels between it and other apostolic letters have been too easily explained away by appeal to amorphous categories like "the common stock of early tradition"; the letter's confusing lack of overt christological reflection has been obscured by readings that fill in the gaps to show that its Christology is quite high; and its engagement with Pauline thought is often either denied outright or too easily harmonized. My hypothesis, by contrast, seeks to offer a credible explanation for all these obscurities, one that puts forward an account of exactly why it was that someone might have found it necessary to pen the letter in the name of James of Jerusalem. There is more to do, of course. I have focused exclusively on the intertextual links that enabled the creation of the CE collection, but further work should be done to work the hypothesis out in relation to the rest of the canon, especially the gospels and the Acts of the Apostles. I do not assume that everyone will accept what has been presented here, but it is hoped, at the very least, that this new hypothesis for the letter's origin will open new, heretofore unconsidered lines of inquiry.

Finally, I have offered an account of the formation of the CE collection that has implications for how we understand the historical development of the NT canon, so the remainder of my closing comments will focus here. Disagreement over the question of exactly when the NT came into being dominated much of twentieth-century scholarship on the "canonization process," and the major positions on the issue are now well known.[1] At the beginning of the century, Theodor Zahn noted the widespread early use of many proto-NT texts and concluded that a "canon" of scripture was in existence (in concept if not in form) by the end of the first century, being the spontaneous and unselfconscious product of early Christian devotion. There is much to support such a view, assuming we emphasize *concept* over *form*— that is, that we understand "canon" to refer to an *authoritative standard* (Sheppard's canon 1) rather than a closed, *authoritative list* of books (canon 2)—for as I have shown, there was no CE collection in existence until sometime in the third century. Zahn's *proto*-NT may very well have existed by the end of the first century, and likewise Trobisch's very Western "first edition of the NT" may have been published in the mid-second century as he has supposed; but the very earliest instantiation of the NT *final form* cannot have emerged much before Origen's work in the first half of the third century. It quite likely emerged in the period after Origen.

In sharp contrast to Zahn stands the position of Albert Sundberg.[2] Sundberg argued that we must distinguish between the authoritative *use* of texts considered "scripture" and the listing of a closed *collection* of texts comprising a "canon." Since

---

[1] This account follows the recent treatments of the subject by J. Barton (*Holy Writings, Sacred Text: The Canon in Early Christianity* [Louisville: Westminster John Knox, 1997], 1–34) and H. Gamble ("The New Testament Canon: Recent Research and the *Status Quaestionis*," in *The Canon Debate*, ed. L .M. McDonald and J. A. Sanders [Peabody, Mass.: Hendrickson, 2002], 267–94).

[2] His agenda is set out in two articles in particular: "Towards a Revised History of the New Testament Canon," *SE* 4 [= *TU* 102] (1968): 452–61; and "Canon Muratori: A Fourth-Century List," *HTR* 66.1 (1973): 1–41.

such lists do not appear until the fourth and fifth centuries, Sundberg insisted that one cannot speak of a NT canon in existence before that time. Sundberg's position has enjoyed widespread acceptance, but it is not without serious problems. For one thing, his sharp distinction between "scripture" and "canon" is unsound, for its understanding of canon is overly literary; it emphasizes its reference to an *authoritative list* (canon 2) to the neglect of its connotation of an *authoritative standard* (canon 1).[3] As my study of the traditions surrounding James of Jerusalem has shown, we should be able to speak of traditions being *canonical* long before they took their final literary form. Indeed, Meade's notion of "canon-consciousness" requires a more fluid sense of the term, for as I have argued, the author of James created his letter in engagement with a particular canon of apostolic tradition and literature. Further, Sundberg's focus on the variety of fourth- and fifth-century canon lists obscures the distinction between the *earliest instantiation* of a complete NT and its *universal acceptance*. The Western church did not officially recognize all seven CE until the beginning of the fifth century, but this fact should not lead us to ignore the fact that *some* churches in the East were quite likely working with the final form of the NT as much as two hundred years earlier.

Between these two major options—the "early" emergence of a proto-NT that developed naturally, and the "late" universal acceptance of a final form imposed by ecclesiastical authority—stands Adolf von Harnack. Against Zahn, Harnack insisted that the evidence only showed that the proto-NT texts were known and used early on, not that they were "scriptural" per se.[4] Such texts were not considered "scripture" until the end of the second century, for it was then that Catholic Christians sought to define themselves against the numerous heterodox movements of the period, most notably that of Marcion who, Harnack believed, was the one responsible for publishing the first Christian canon. Though Harnack's famous claim that the NT was "an anti-Marcionite creation on a Marcionite basis"[5] held sway for much of the twentieth century, most contemporary scholars would rightly consider this an exaggeration: The processes that would result in the NT were already underway by the end of the first century, the "gospel + apostle" framework Harnack attributed to Marcion was widespread long before his day,[6] and the final form of the NT has been shown to contain a number of features that Marcion did not anticipate.[7]

---

[3] Cf. the critiques in D. Meade, *Pseudonymity and Canon* (WUNT 39; Tübingen: J. C. B. Mohr, 1986), 24; B. Childs, *The New Testament as Canon: An Introduction* (Valley Forge, Pa.: Trinity Press International, 1985), 238.

[4] See the sixth appendix of Adolf von Harnack, *The Origin of the New Testament and the Most Important Consequences of the New Creation*, trans. J. R. Wilkinson (New York: Macmillan, 1925).

[5] A. von Harnack, *Marcion: The Gospel of the Alien God*, trans. J. E. Steely and L. D. Bierma (Durham, N.C.: The Labyrinth Press, 1990).

[6] F. Bovon, "The Canonical Structure of Gospel and Apostle," in *Canon Debate*, 516–27.

[7] E.g., D. Balás, "Marcion Revisited: A 'Post-Harnack' Perspective," in *Texts and Testaments: Critical Essays on the Bible and Early Church Fathers*, ed. W. E. March (San Antonio:

Instead, Marcion's NT is now best viewed as a case of "arrested development,"[8] one that "forced more orthodox Christians to examine their own presuppositions and to state more clearly what they already believed."[9] Against Harnack, then, the majority of interpreters now do not believe that Marcion was the central figure in the formation of the NT canon.

It seems that all of the aforementioned scholars have erred in that they have sought to fix a particular "moment" wherein canonization can be said to have occurred.[10] Zahn was correct in that the concept of a Christian canon seems to have developed organically very early on. But Sundberg is also correct, for we cannot speak of a closed canon until the fifth century. Between the two positions one finds localized development and definition; but what must be pressed is the fact that the focus of this development and definition had primarily to do with the CE collection. The post-second-century "closing of the canon" had little to do with the Gospel and Pauline collections and everything to do with the final shape of the CE. Scholarly discussions of canon formation must therefore take the development of this collection much more seriously than they have in the past.

With this in mind, therefore, we must join Trobisch and others in reemphasizing the role of Marcion in the development of the final form of the NT. Harnack was, of course, wrong to assign such a central, creative role to Marcion, for as I have already noted, the NT itself did not come into being as a direct response to his truncated canon. The CE, however, did come into being during a season of church history characterized by ongoing response to the Marcionite threat, and as I have argued, the collection itself reflects a set of concerns attributable (at least in part) to anti-Marcionite polemics.

My study has tried to show that the two letters to arrive latest on the canonical scene—James and 2 Peter—reflect these proto-catholic anti-Marcionite polemics in their content, primarily in their authorizing of the Jewish scriptures, and their particular vision of apostolic harmony. Further, they perform a vital "linking" role in the apostolic letter collection as a whole. Again, without these two letters the second-century apostolic letter collection included a Pauline collection, a letter from Peter, three letters from John, a letter from Jude, *Barnabas*, and *1 Clement*. Add 2 Peter to the group, and 1 Peter, Jude, and the Pauline collection are forged into a kind of anti-Marcionite Peter-Paul letter collection. But this configuration left the Johannine letters, *Barnabas* and *1 Clement* unaccounted for. Add the letter of James to the broader collection, and a "logic" is created that infuses it with a particular interpretive strategy. As I have shown, James includes a series of parallels that link

---

Trinity University Press, 1980), 95–108; and Barton, chap. 2, "Marcion Revisited," in *Holy Writings*, 35–62.

[8] Gamble, "*Status Quaestionis*," 292.

[9] R. M. Grant, *The Formation of the New Testament* (New York: Harper & Row, 1965), 126.

[10] For an extremely helpful rethinking of these scholars' views, see Barton, *Holy Writings*, 1–34.

it with 1 Peter and 1 John; on this basis the Petrine and Johannine collections are merged under a "Pillars of Jerusalem" rubric. Jude would quite naturally be included in this group, because (a) it would have already traveled about with 1–2 Peter (witness P72), (b) it allows the Pillars collection to achieve the magic "seven-letter" status of wholeness and completion, and (c) its authorial identification as "the brother of James" enables the creation a collection of letters embraced by the brothers of Jesus. *1 Clement* was already widely considered to be sub-apostolic, so it need not be included in a collection of letters from the earliest apostles. *Barnabas* also did not fit in this Pillars collection, in part because Barnabas himself was historically associated with Paul, but also because the content of the letter attributed to him did not fit the collection theologically. Indeed, I have suggested that one of the key points of the collection was its assertion of an appropriate understanding of Christianity's *continuity* with Jewish tradition. A letter insisting that the people of Israel "lost" the covenant (4.7) and "were thus abandoned" (4.14), being "unworthy to receive it because of their sins" (14.1), simply could not be included. Thus we arrive at a seven-letter collection of non-Pauline letters organized around the interpretive rubric of the Jerusalem Pillars.

If my hypothesis is correct, it means that the addition of the letter of James was the ultimate step in the achievement of the final Eastern form for the NT canon. Throughout my study I have avoided assigning a place and date for the writing of the letter, preferring instead a general assignment of "the second-century East." My hypothesis that anti-Marcionite polemics played a role in the composition of this letter need not oblige us to fix a particular decade and locale for its arrival, but perhaps a more concrete proposal for the letter's provenance can be offered. Though more investigation is required for greater certainty, it might make sense to assume that the Eastern addition of James took place *after* the Western addition of 2 Peter and its attendant "Peter-Paul" anti-Marcionite letter collection, since the addition of James can be seen to resolve the tensions created by that premature solution. Thus it would suggest that the letter is later than 2 Peter. That would, in turn, suggest that the parallels between James and other second-century literature, particularly the *Shepherd of Hermas*, represent their common appeal to available λόγοι σοφῶν,[11] as Ropes, Dibelius, and others have insisted[12]—though it seems to me that we should not rule out the possibility that James is dependent on *Hermas*. Either is possible depending on when it was that the letter was actually written, but the assumption that it is later than 2 Peter pushes us in the direction of the mid-second century. Having said that, Marcion's excommunication is dated to 144 C.E.; if James was penned as a reaction against the rise of Marcionism, does that not require us to place the letter in the latter half of that century? Not really; William Farmer has argued

---

[11] So S. R. Llewelyn, "The Prescript of James," *NovT* 39 (1997): 385–93, 393.

[12] J. Ropes, *The Epistle of St. James* (ICC; Edinburgh: T&T Clark, 1916), 88–89; M. Dibelius, *James*, ed. H. Greeven, trans. M. Williams (Hermeneia; Philadelphia: Fortress, 1976), 32.

that it is a mistake to date Marcion's activity too narrowly.[13] Marcion's trial in Rome in 144 must have been necessary because of concerns created by his teaching, but there is no reason to assume that his *Antitheses* was published after his trial. Harnack guessed that Marcion was born around 85 C.E.; if that is correct, Farmer suggests the temporal scope of his influence should be stretched back to as early as 110 C.E. Indeed, given Marcion's popularity, it is clear that he was a spokesman for a set of widely held assumptions among Greco-Roman Christians. In this way Marcion functioned more as a "type" in early Christianity; he was a specter whose teaching undoubtedly haunted the church before his historical person and continued to preoccupy long after his death. My point is simply to say that associating James with Marcionism does not help us fix the date of the letter with any certainty.

We cannot place the letter too early, for we have insisted that its terminus ad quem must account for its late canonicity. Irenaeus and Tertullian did not know it, and my study suggests that they would have happily received it were it available to them. Given the range of possibilities, and the uncertainty of the data, it would be foolhardy to make a firm stand on the letter's provenance. Nevertheless, for the sake of closure, I conclude with a concrete statement of the results of my tested hypothesis, with apologies to those who think it too far outside the acceptable range of dating for NT texts: the letter of James was probably written sometime in the middle of the second century, possibly by someone associated with the church in Jerusalem, given that church's keen interest in maintaining James' authority (one might recall Eusebius's claim that the Jerusalem church of his day continued to venerate James and had, in fact, preserved his original episcopal throne; *Hist. Eccl.* 7.19). The letter was born out of the same broader anti-Marcionite logic that fueled the composition of 2 Peter and the writings of Irenaeus and Tertullian. It was written to forge together a Jerusalem Pillars letter collection to balance the emphases of the Pauline collection, defend the authority of the Jewish scriptures, and uphold the continuity of the covenants—in short, to protect against the theological distortions that tended to arise whenever readers championed Paul alone. Origen first advocated the letter in the early third century. By the time of Eusebius's writing, that is, by the year 300, the CE collection was a known canonical quantity in the Eastern churches, and for some Christians at least, the NT had reached its final form.

---

[13] W. Farmer, "Some Critical Reflections on Second Peter: A Response to a Paper on Second Peter by Denis Farkasfalvy," *SecCent* 5 (1985): 30–46.

SELECT BIBLIOGRAPHY

I. PRIMARY SOURCES: TEXTS, TRANSLATIONS, AND COMMENTARIES

Amphilochius of Iconium
—*Iambi ad seleucum*—
Text:
Oberg, E. *Iambi ad seleucum*. PTS 9. Berlin: Walter de Gruyter, 1969.
1–2 Apocalypse of James
Text:
Veilleux, A. *La Première Apocalypse de Jacques et la Seconde Apocalypse de Jacques*. BCNH 17. Québec: Les Presses de l'Université Laval, 1986.
Translation:
Robinson, J. M. *The Nag Hammadi Library in English*. Leiden: Brill, 1977. 242–48.
Apocryphon of James
Text:
Kirchner, D. *Epistula Jacobi Apocrypha: Die zweite Schrift aus Nag-Hammadi-Codex I*. Berlin: Academie-Verlag, 1989.
Translations:
Cameron, R. *Sayings Traditions in the Apocryphon of James*. Philadelphia: Fortress, 1984.
Robinson, J. M. *The Nag Hammadi Library in English*. Leiden: Brill, 1977. 29–36.

Athanasius of Alexandria
—*Epistula 39*—
Text:
    Patrologia graeca. Edited by J.-P. Migne. 25:1435ff.
Translations:
    Brakke, D. *Athanasius and the Politics of Asceticism*. Oxford: Clarendon, 1995. 326–32.
    Metzger, B. *The Canon of the New Testament*. Oxford: Clarendon, 1987. 312–13.
Augustine of Hippo
—*De fide et operibus*—
Text:
    Zycha, J. CSEL 41:33–97. Vienna: F. Tempsky, 1900.
Translation:
    Ligouri, M. *Saint Augustine, Treatises on Marriage and Other Subjects*. Vol. 27 of *The Fathers of the Church*. Edited by R. J. Deferrari. Washington, D.C.: Catholic University of America Press, 1955. 213–82.
—*In epistulam Iohannis ad Parthos tractatus*—
Text:
    Agaësse, P. SC 75. Paris: Cerf, 1961.
Translation:
    Leinenweber, J. *Love One Another, My Friends: Saint Augustine's Homilies on the First Letter of John*. San Francisco: Harper & Row, 1989.
Cassiodorus
—*Institutiones divinarum et saecularium litterarum*—
Text:
    Mynors, R. A. B. *Cassiodori Senatoris Institutiones*. Oxford: Clarendon, 1937.
Clement of Alexandria
—*Adumbrationes Clementis Alexandrini in epistolas canonicas (Cassiodorus)*—
Text:
    Stählin, O., and L. Früchtel. *Clemens Alexandrinus III*. GCS 3. Berlin: Academie-Verlag, 1970. 203–15.
Translation:
    Donaldson, J., and A. Roberts, eds. *ANF* 2.567–77.
—*Paedagogus*—
Texts:
    Marrou, H.-I. *Clément d'Alexandrie, Le Pédagogue Livre I*. SC 70. Translated by M. Harl. Paris: Cerf, 1960.
    Marrou, H.-I. *Clément d'Alexandrie, Le Pédagogue Livre II*. SC 108. Translated by C. Mondésert. Paris: Cerf, 1965.
    Marrou, H.-I. *Clément d'Alexandrie, Le Pédagogue Livre III*. SC 158. Translated by C. Mondésert and C. Matray. Paris: Cerf, 1970.
Translations:
    Donaldson, J., and A. Roberts, eds. *ANF* 2.206–96.
    Wood, S. P. *Clement of Alexandria: Christ the Educator*. FC 23. New York: Fathers of the Church, 1954.

—*Quis dives salvetur*—
Text:
> Stählin, O. *Clemens Alexandrinus III*. GCS 3. Leipzig: Hinrichs'sche, 1909.
> 157–91.

Translations:
> Butterworth, G. W. *Clement of Alexandria*. LCL 92. London: Heinemann,
> 1919.
> Donaldson, J., and A. Roberts, eds. *ANF* 2.586–604.

—*Stromata*—
Texts:
> Le Boulluec, A. *Clément D'Alexandrie Les Stromates, Stromate VII*. SC 428.
> Paris: Cerf, 1997.
> Stählin, O., and L. Früchtel. *Clemens Alexandrinus II: Stromata Buch I–VI*.
> GCS 2. Berlin: Academie-Verlag, 1985.

Translations:
> Chadwick, H., and J. E. L. Oulton. *Alexandrian Christianity: Selected Transla-*
> *tions of Clement and Origen*. LCC 2. Philadelphia: Westminster, 1954.
> Donaldson, J., and A. Roberts, eds. *ANF* 2.299–567.
> Ferguson, J. *Clement of Alexandria: Stromateis Books One to Three*. FC 85.
> Washington, D.C.: Catholic University of America Press, 1991.

Cyprian of Carthage
—*Opera*—
Text:
> Bénevot, M., et al. *Sancti Cypriani episcopi opera*. CCSL 3, 3A, 3B, 3C, 3D,
> 3E. Turnhout: Brepols, 1972–2004.

—*Treatises*—
Translation:
> Deferrari, R. J. *Saint Cyprian: Treatises*. FC 36. Washington, D.C.: Catholic
> University of America Press, 1958.

—*Epistulae*—
Translation:
> Clarke, G. W. *The Letters of St. Cyprian of Carthage*. ACW 44–47. New York:
> Newman Press, 1984 (vols. 44–45), 1986 (vol. 46), and 1989 (vol.
> 47).

Cyril of Jerusalem
—*Catecheses*—
Text:
> Reischl, W. C., and J. Rupp. *Cyrilli Hierosolymarum archiepiscopi opera quae*
> *superunt omnia I*. Hildesheim: Georg Olms Verlagsbuchhandlung,
> 1967.

Translations:
> McCauley, L. P., and A. A. Stephenson. *The Works of Saint Cyril of Jerusalem*.
> Vol. 1. FC 61. Washington, D.C.: The Catholic University of America
> Press, 1969.
> Schaff, P. *NPNF*² 7.27–28.

Eusebius of Caesarea
 —*Historia Ecclesiastica*—
 Text:
  Schwartz, E., and T. Mommsen. *Eusebius Werke*. GCSNF 6.1–2. Berlin: Akademie Verlag, 1999.
 Texts with English Translations:
  Lake, K. *Eusebius I: The Ecclesiastical History, Books I–V*. LCL 153. Cambridge, Mass.: Harvard University Press, 1926.
  Oulton, J. E. L. *Eusebius II: The Ecclesiastical History, Books IV–X*. LCL 265. Cambridge, Mass.: Harvard University Press, 1932.
 Translations:
  Lawlor, H. J., and J. E. L. Oulton. *Eusebius, Bishop of Caesarea: The Ecclesiastical History and the Martyrs of Palestine*. London: SPCK, 1927.
  Schaff, P., trans. *NPNF*² 1.80–387.
  Williamson, G. A. *Eusebius: The History of the Church From Christ to Constantine*. New York: Penguin Books, 1989.
Gospel of Thomas
 Text and Translation:
  Layton, B., ed. *Nag Hammadi Codex II, 2–7*. Vol. 1. NHS 20. Translated by T. Lambdin. Leiden: Brill, 1989.
 Translations:
  Cameron, R., ed. *The Other Gospels: Non-Canonical Gospel Texts*. Philadelphia: Westminster, 1982. 23–37.
  Layton, B. *The Gnostic Scriptures*. ABRL. New York: Doubleday, 1987. 376–99.
  Robinson, J. M. *The Nag Hammadi Library in English*. Leiden: Brill, 1977. 117–30.
  Wilson, R. McL., trans. *Gospels and Related Writings*. Vol. 1 of *New Testament Apocrypha*. Edited by E. Hennecke and W. Schneemelcher. Philadelphia: Westminster, 1963. 511–22.
Hippolytus
 —*Refutatio omnium haeresium*—
 Text:
  Marcovich, M., ed. *Hippolytus Refutatio Omnium Haeresium*. PTS 25. Berlin: Walter de Gruyter, 1986.
Ignatius of Antioch
 —*Epistolai*—
 Texts and Translations:
  Ehrman, B. *The Apostolic Fathers*. 2 vols. LCL 24 & 25. Cambridge, Mass.: Harvard University Press, 2003.
  Holmes, M. W. *The Apostolic Fathers: Greek Texts and English Translations*. Rev. ed. Grand Rapids: Baker Books, 1999.
Irenaeus of Lyon
 —*Adversus haeresis*—
 Text:
  Rousseau, A., et al. *Irénée de Lyon, Contre Les Hérésies, Livres I–V*. SC 263, 264 (vol. 1); 293–94 (vol. 2); 210, 211 (vol. 3); 100 (vol. 4); 152, 153 (vol. 5). Paris: Cerf, 1965–1982.

Translations:
Donaldson, J., and Roberts, A., eds. *ANF* 1.315–567.
Grant, R. M. *Irenaeus of Lyons.* London: Routledge, 1997.
Unger, D. J., ed. *St. Irenaeus of Lyon Against the Heresies.* ANC 55. New York: Paulist Press, 1992.

Jerome
—*Epistulae*—
Text:
LaBourt, J. *Saint Jérome Lettres.* 8 vols. Paris: Socíeté d'Édition, 1949–1963.
Translations:
Schaff, P. *NPNF²* 6.
Wright, F. *Select Letters of Saint Jerome.* LCL 262. Cambridge, Mass.: Harvard University Press, 1933.
—*De viris illustribus*—
Text:
Patrologia latina. Edited by J.-P. Migne. 23.607ff.
Translations:
Halton, T. P. *On Illustrious Men.* FC 100. Washington, D.C.: Catholic University of America Press, 1999.
Schaff, P. *NPNF²* 3.353–402.
Vielhauer, P. *Gospels and Related Writings.* Vol. 1 of *New Testament Apocrypha.* Edited by E. Hennecke and W. Schneemelcher. Philadelphia: Westminster, 1963. 163.

Josephus
—*Antiquitates judaicae*—
Text:
Niese, B. *Flavii Iosephi opera.* Berlin: Weidmann, 1892.
Text and Translation:
Feldman, L. H. *Jewish Antiquities, Books 18–20.* Vol. 9 of *Josephus.* LCL 433. Cambridge, Mass.: Harvard University Press, 1969.
Translations:
Mason, S. *Josephus and the New Testament.* 2nd ed. Peabody, Mass.: Hendrickson, 2003.
Whiston, W. *The Works of Josephus: Complete and Unabridged.* Peabody, Mass.: Hendrickson, 1987.

Muratorian Fragment
Text, Translation, and Commentary:
Hahnemann, G. *The Muratorian Fragment and the Development of the Canon.* Oxford: Clarendon, 1992.
Translation:
Metzger, B. *The Canon of the New Testament: Its Origin, Development, and Significance.* Oxford: Clarendon, 1987. 306–7.

Origen of Alexandria
—*Contra Celsum*—
Text:
Borret, M. *Contre Celse 1–5.* SC 132 (Livres 1–2), 136 (Livres 3–4), 147 (Livres 5–6), 150 (Livres 7–8), 227 (Introduction générale–tables et index). Paris: Cerf, 1967–1976.

Translations:

Chadwick, H., and J. E. L. Oulton. *Alexandrian Christianity: Selected Transla-tions of Clement and Origen.* LCC 2. Philadelphia: Westminster, 1954.

Donaldson, J., and A. Roberts, eds. *ANF* 4.395–669.

—*De principiis*—

Text:

Crouzel, H., and M. Simonetti. *Traité des Principes 1–5.* SC 252 (Livres 1–2), 253 (Livres 1–2 frags.), 268 (Livres 3–4), 269 (Livres 3–4 frags.), 312 (Compléments et index). Paris: Cerf, 1978–1984.

Translations:

Butterworth, G. W. *Origen On First Principles.* London: SPCK, 1936.

Donaldson, J., and A. Roberts, eds. *ANF* 4.239–394.

—*Comentarii in evangelium Joannis*—

Text:

Blanc, C. *Commentaire sur S. Jean.* SC 120 (Livres 1–5), 157 (Livres 6 and 10), 222 (Livre 13), 290 (Livres 19–20), 385 (Livres 28 and 32). Paris: Cerf, 1966–1992.

Translations:

Donaldson, J., and A. Roberts, eds. *ANF* 10.297–408.

Heine, R. E. *Origen's Commentary on the Gospel According to John, Books 1–10* (FC 80) and *Books 13–32* (FC 89). Washington, D.C.: Catholic University of America Press, 1989, 1993.

—*Commentarium in evangelium Matthaei*—

Texts:

Benz, E., and E. Klostermann. *Origenes Matthäuserklärung I–III.* GCS 10–12.2. Leipzig: J. C. Hinrichs, 1935–1968.

Girod, R. *Commentaire sur L'Évangile selon Matthieu.* SC 162 (Livres 10–11). Paris: Cerf, 1970.

Translation:

Donaldson, J., and A. Roberts, eds. *ANF* 10.411–512.

—*Commentarii in Romanos*—

Text:

Bammel, C. P., et al. *Römerbriefkommentar des Origines.* VL 16 (Buch 1–3), 33 (Buch 4–6), 34 (Buch 7–10). Freiburg: Verlag Herder, 1990–1998.

Translations:

Scheck, T. P. *Origen, Commentary on the Epistle to the Romans Books 1–5* (FC 103) and *Books 6–10* (FC 104) Washington D.C.: Catholic University of America Press, 2001, 2002.

Photius of Constantinople

—*Bibliotheca*—

Text:

Patrologia graeca. Edited by J.-P. Migne. 103.384ff.

Translation:

Wilson, N. G. *Photius: The Bibliotheca.* London: Duckworth, 1994.

Protevangelium of James

Text and Translation:

Hock, R. *The Infancy Gospels of James and Thomas.* Scholar's Bible, vol. 2. Santa Rosa, Calif.: Polebridge Press, 1995.

Translations:

> Cameron, R. *The Other Gospels: Non-Canonical Gospel Texts.* Philadelphia: Westminster, 1982. 107–21.
>
> Cullmann, O. "Infancy Gospels." Pages 363–401 in *Gospels and Related Writings.* Vol. 1 of *New Testament Apocrypha.* Edited by E. Hennecke and W. Schneemelcher. Philadelphia: Westminster, 1963.

Pseudo-Clementine Recognitions

Text:

> Rehm, B., and F. Paschke. *Rekognitionen.* Vol. 2 of *Die Pseudoklementinen.* GCS 51. Berlin: Akademie-Verlag, 1965.

Translation and Commentary:

> Jones, F. S. *An Ancient Jewish Christian Source on the History of Christianity: Pseudo-Clementine Recognitions 1.27–71.* Atlanta: Scholars Press, 1995.

Rufinus of Aquileia

—Commentarius in symbolum apostolorum—

Text:

> Simonetti, M. *Tyrannii Rufini Opera.* CCSL 20. Turnholt: Brepols, 1961.

Tertullian of Carthage

—Opera—

Text:

> Dekkers, E., et al. *Tertullian: Opera pars 1 & 2.* CCSL 1–2. Turnholt: Brepols, 1954.

Translation:

> Donaldson, J., and A. Roberts, eds. *ANF* 3–4.165.

Text and Translation:

> Evans, E. B. *Tertullian Adversus Marcionem.* Oxford: Clarendon, 1972.

—De praescriptione adversus haereticorum—

Translation:

> Greenslade, S. L. *Early Latin Theology: Selections from Tertullian, Cyprian, Ambrose, and Jerome.* Philadelphia: Westminster, 1956. 25–64.

—De pudicitia—

Translation:

> Le Saint, W. P. *Tertullian: Treatises on Penance. ACW* 28. New York: Newman Press, 1959. 40–125.

—Scorpiace—

Translation:

> Dunn, G. *Tertullian.* New York: Routledge, 2004. 105–34.

Victorinus of Pettau

—Commentarius in apocalypsin—

Text:

> Haussleiter, I. CSEL 49. Vienna: F. Tempsky, 1916.

Translation:

> Donaldson, J., and A. Roberts, eds. *ANF* 7.345–46.

2. Collections of Texts and Translations

Aland, B., K. Aland, M. Black, C. M. Martini, B. M. Metzger, and A. Wikgren. *The Greek New Testament*. 4th ed. Federal Republic of Germany: United Bible Societies, 1993.

———. *Novum Testamentum Graece*, 27th ed. Stuttgart: Deutsche Bibelgesellschaft, 1993.

Charlesworth, J. H. *The Old Testament Pseudepigrapha*. 2 vols. London: Darton, Longman & Todd, 1983, 1985.

Donaldson, J. and A. Roberts, eds. *The Ante-Nicene Fathers: Translations of the Writings of the Fathers Down to A.D. 325*. Electronic edition of American Reprint of the Edinburgh edition. Oak Harbor: Logos Research Systems, 1997.

Ehrman, B. *The Apostolic Fathers*. 2 vols. LCL 24 & 25. Cambridge, Mass.: Harvard University Press, 2003.

Holmes, M. W. *The Apostolic Fathers: Greek Texts and English Translations*. Rev. ed. Grand Rapids: Baker Books, 1999.

Lake, K. *The Apostolic Fathers*. 2 vols. London: William Heinemann, 1914.

Layton, B. *The Gnostic Scriptures*. ABRL. New York: Doubleday, 1987.

Lightfoot, J. B. *The Apostolic Fathers*. 5 vols. London: Macmillan, 1890. Repr., Grand Rapids: Baker, 1981.

Neusner, J. *The Mishnah: A New Translation*. New Haven: Yale University Press, 1996.

Rahlfs, A., ed. *Septuaginta*. 8th ed. Stuttgart: Deutsche Bibelgesellschaft, 1996.

Robinson, J. M. *The Nag Hammadi Library in English*. Leiden: Brill, 1977.

Schaff, P. *The Nicene and Post-Nicene Fathers of the Christian Church*. Electronic edition of the American reprint of the Edinburgh edition. Oak Harbor: Logos Research Systems, 1997.

Wise, M., M. Abegg, and E. Cook. *The Dead Sea Scrolls: A New Translation*. San Francisco: Harper San Francisco, 1996.

Yonge, C. D. *The Works of Philo: Complete and Unabridged*. Peabody, Mass.: Hendrickson, 1996.

3. General Bibliography

Achtemeier, P. *1 Peter*. Hermeneia. Philadelphia: Fortress Press, 1996.

Adamson, J. B. *The Epistle of James*. NICNT. Grand Rapids: Eerdmans, 1976.

———. *James: The Man and His Message*. Grand Rapids: Eerdmans, 1989.

Adna, J. "James' Position at the Summit Meeting of the Apostles and the Elders in Jerusalem (Acts 15)." Pages 125–61 in *The Mission of the Early Church to Jews and Gentiles*. Edited by J. Adna and H. Kvalbein. Tübingen: Mohr Siebeck, 2000.

Aland, B. *Die Grossen Katholischen Briefe*. Vol. 1 of *Das Neue Testament in Syrischer Überlieferung*. *ANTF* 7. Berlin: Walter de Gruyter, 1986.

Aland, B., and K. Aland. *The Text of the New Testament*. Grand Rapids: Eerdmans, 1987.

Aland, K. *Kurzgefasste Liste der griechischen Handschriften des Neuen Testaments*. Berlin: Walter de Gruyter, 1963.

———. *The Problem of the New Testament Canon*. London: Mowbray, 1962.

Allison, D. C. ,Jr. "Exegetical Amnesia in James." *ETL* 86 (2000): 162–66.

———. "The Fiction of James and its *Sitz im Leben*." *RB* 4 (2001): 529–70.

Aune, D. *The New Testament in its Literary Environment*. Philadelphia: Westminster, 1987.

Baasland, E. "Literarische Form, Thematik und geschichtliche Einordnung des Jakobusbriefes." *ANRW* II.25.5, 3646–84. Berlin: De Gruyter, 1988.

Balás, D. "Marcion Revisited: A 'Post-Harnack' Perspective." Pages 95–108 in *Texts and Testaments: Critical Essays on the Bible and Early Church Fathers.* Edited by W. E. March. San Antonio: Trinity University Press, 1980.

Balz, H., and W. Schrage. *Die katholischen Briefe.* NTD 10. Göttingen: Vandenhoeck & Ruprecht, 1973.

Barnes, T. D. *Constantine and Eusebius.* Cambridge, Mass.: Harvard University Press, 1981.

———. *Tertullian: A Historical and Literary Study.* Oxford: Oxford University Press, 1971.

Barrett, C. K. *A Commentary on the Epistle to the Romans.* London: A&C Black, 1962.

———. *A Commentary on the First Epistle to the Corinthians.* A&C Black, 1971.

———. "Paul and the 'Pillar' Apostles." Pages 1–19 in *Studia Paulina.* Edited by J. N. Sevenster and W. C. van Unnik. Haarlem: De Erven F. Bohn N.V., 1953.

Barton, J. *The Cambridge Companion to Biblical Interpretation.* Cambridge: Cambridge University Press, 1998.

———, ed. *Holy Writings, Sacred Text: The Canon in Early Christianity.* Louisville: Westminster John Knox, 1997.

Bauckham, R. "James and Jesus." Pages 100–137 in Chilton and Neusner, *The Brother of Jesus.*

———. "James and the Jerusalem Church." Pages 415–80 in *The Book of Acts in its First Century Setting.* Edited by R. Bauckham. Grand Rapids: Eerdmans, 1995.

———. "James and the Gentiles (Acts 15:13-21)." Pages 154–84 in *History, Literature, and Society in the Book of Acts.* Edited by B. Witherington. Cambridge: Cambridge University Press, 1995.

———. *James: Wisdom of James, Disciple of Jesus the Sage.* London: Routledge, 1999.

———. *Jude, 2 Peter.* WBC 50. Waco, Tex.: Word Books, 1983.

———. *Jude and the Relatives of Jesus in the Early Church.* Edinburgh: T&T Clark, 1990.

———. "Pseudo-Apostolic Letters." *JBL* 107 (1988): 469–94.

———. "2 Peter: An Account of Research." *ANRW* II.25.5, 3713–52. Berlin: Walter de Gruyter, 1988.

Bauer, W. *Orthodoxy and Heresy in Earliest Christianity.* London: SCM Press, 1971. Eng. trans. of *Rechtgläubigkeit und Ketzerei im ältesten Christentum,* 1934. Edited by R. Kraft and G. Krodel.

Beare, F. W. *The First Epistle of Peter.* Oxford: Basil Blackwell, 1961.

———. "Some Remarks on the Text of 1 Peter in the Bodmer Papyrus (P^{72})." *SE* 3 [= *TU* 88] (1964): 263–65.

Best, E. *1 Peter.* NCBC. Grand Rapids: Eerdmans, 1971.

Bethge, H. G. "Der Text des ersten Petrusbriefes im Crosby-Schøyen-Codex (Ms. 193 Schøyen Collection)." *ZNW* 84 (1993): 255–67.

Bigg, C. *The Epistles of St. Peter and St. Jude.* ICC. Edinburgh: T&T Clark, 1901.

Bindemann, W. "Weisheit versus Weisheit: Der Jakobusbrief als innerkirchlicher Diskurs." *ZNW* 86 (1995): 189–217.

Blackman, E. C. *The Epistle of James.* London: SCM Press, 1957.

Boobyer, G. H. "The Indebtedness of 2 Peter to 1 Peter." Pages 34–53 in *New Testament Essays: Studies in Memory of T. W. Manson.* Edited by A. Higgins. Manchester: Manchester University Press, 1959.

Bovon, F. "The Canonical Structure of Gospel and Apostle." Pages 516–27 in McDonald and Sanders, *Canon Debate.*

Brakke, D. *Athanasius and the Politics of Asceticism*. Oxford: Clarendon, 1995.

Brewer, J. A. "The History of the New Testament Canon in the Syrian Church II: The Acts of the Apostles and the Epistles." *AJT* 4 (1900): 345–63.

Brooks, J. A. "The Place of James in the New Testament Canon." *SJT* 12 (1969): 41–51.

———. "Clement of Alexandria as a Witness to the Development of the New Testament Canon." *SecCent* 9.1 (1992): 41–51.

Brown, R. *The Epistles of John*. ABC 30. New York: Doubleday, 1982.

———. "Not Jewish Christianity and Gentile Christianity but Types of Jewish/Gentile Christianity." *CBQ* 45.1 (1983): 74–79.

———. *An Introduction to the New Testament*. ABRL. New York: Doubleday, 1997.

Brown, S. K. "Jewish and Gnostic Elements in the Second Apocalypse of James." *NovT* 17.3 (1975): 225–37.

Bruce, F. F. *The Canon of Scripture*. Downers Grove, Ill.: InterVarsity, 1988.

Bultmann, R. *A Commentary on the Johannine Epistles*. Translated by R. P. O'Hara et al. Hermeneia. Philadelphia: Fortress, 1973.

Burchard, C. *Der Jakobusbrief*. HNT 15/1. Tübingen: Mohr Siebeck, 2000.

Cameron, R., ed. *The Other Gospels: Non-Canonical Gospel Texts*. Philadelphia: Westminster, 1982.

———. *Sayings Traditions in the Apocryphon of James*. Philadelphia: Fortress, 1984.

von Campenhausen, H. *Ecclesiastical Authority and Spiritual Power*. London: A&C Black, 1969.

———. *The Formation of the Christian Bible*. Translated by J. A. Baker. Philadelphia: Fortress, 1972.

Cantinat, J. C. M. *Les Épîtres de Saint Jacques et de Saint Jude*. SB. Paris: J. Gabalda, 1973.

Carrington, P. *The Primitive Christian Catechism: A Study in the Epistles*. Cambridge: Cambridge University Press, 1940.

Carroll, K. L. "Toward a Commonly Received New Testament." *BJRL* 44 (1962): 327–49.

Chapman, J. "The Original Contents of Codex Bezae." *Exp* 6 (1905): 46–53.

Chester, A., and R. P. Martin. *The Theology of the Letters of James, Peter, and Jude*. Cambridge: Cambridge University Press, 1994.

Childs, B. *Introduction to the Old Testament as Scripture*. Philadelphia: Fortress. 1979.

———. *The New Testament as Canon: An Introduction*. Valley Forge, Pa.: Trinity Press International, 1985.

———. *Biblical Theology of the Old and New Testaments*. Minneapolis: Fortress, 1993.

Chilton, B. "James in Relation to Peter, Paul, and the Remembrance of Jesus." Pages 138–59 in Chilton and Neusner, *The Brother of Jesus*.

Chilton, B., and C. A. Evans, eds. *James the Just and Christian Origins*. Leiden: Brill, 1999.

Chilton, B., and J. Neusner, eds. *The Brother of Jesus: James the Just and His Mission*. Louisville: Westminster John Knox, 2001.

Conzelmann, H. *The Acts of the Apostles*. Hermeneia. Philadelphia: Fortress, 1987.

———. *History of Primitive Christianity*. Translated by John E. Steely. London: Darton, Longman & Todd, 1973.

Cranfield, C. E. B. *The First Epistle of Peter*. London: SCM Press, 1954.

Crossan, J. D. *The Birth of Christianity: Discovering What Happened in the Years Immediately After the Execution of Jesus*. San Francisco: Harper San Francisco, 1998.

———. *The Historical Jesus: The Life of a Mediterranean Jewish Peasant*. Edinburgh: T&T Clark, 1991.

Crouzel, H. *Origen*. Edinburgh: T&T Clark, 1989.

Dalton, W. J. *Christ's Proclamation to the Spirits: A Study of 1 Peter 3:18–4:6*. AnBib. 23. Rome: Pontifical Biblical Institute, 1989.

Danielou, J. *The Theology of Jewish Christianity*. London: Darton, Longman & Todd, 1964.

Davids, P. *The Epistle of James*. NIGTC. Grand Rapids: Eerdmans, 1982.

―――. "The Epistle of James in Modern Discussion." *ANRW* II.25.5, 3621–45. Berlin: Walter de Gruyter, 1988.

―――. *The First Epistle of Peter*. NICNT. Grand Rapids: Eerdmans, 1990.

―――. "James's Message: The Literary Record." Pages ᴧᴠ–ᴧᴧ in Chilton and Neusner, *The Brother of Jesus*.

―――. "Palestinian Traditions in the Epistle of James." Pages 33–57 in Chilton and Evans, *James the Just*.

Davidson, R. "The Imagery of Isaiah 40:6-8 in Tradition and Interpretation." Pages 37–55 in *The Quest for Context and Meaning: Studies in Biblical Intertextuality in Honor of James A. Sanders*. Edited by Craig A. Evans and Shemaryahu Talmon. Leiden: Brill, 1997.

Deissmann, A. *Light from the Ancient East*. Grand Rapids: Baker, 1980.

Dibelius, M. *James*. Hermeneia. Edited by H. Greeven. Translated by M. Williams. Philadelphia: Fortress, 1976.

―――. *Studies in the Acts of the Apostles*. London: SCM Press, 1956.

Di Berardino, A., ed. *The Golden Age of Latin Patristic Literature From the Council of Nicea to the Council of Chalcedon*. Vol. 4 of *Patrology*. Westminster, Md: Christian Classics, 1986.

Dobschutz, E. "The Abandonment of the Canonical Idea." *AJT* 19 (1915): 416–29.

Dodd, C. H. *The Epistle of Paul to the Romans*. MNTC. London: Hodder & Stoughton, 1932.

―――. *The Johannine Epistles*. MNTC. London: Hodder & Stoughton, 1946.

Donelson, L. *From Hebrews to Revelation*. Louisville: Westminster John Knox, 2001.

Döpp, S., and W. Geerlings, eds. *Dictionary of Early Christian Literature*. Translated by M. O'Connell. New York: Crossroad, 2000.

Drummond, J. *The New Testament in the Apostolic Fathers*. Oxford: Oxford University Press, 1905.

Dunn, J. D. G. *The Epistle to the Galatians*. BNTC. Peabody, Mass.: Hendrickson, 1993.

―――. *The Parting of the Ways: Between Christianity and Judaism and their Significance for the Character of Christianity*. London: SCM Press, 1991.

―――. *Romans 1–8* and *Romans 9–16*. WBC 38A & 38B. Waco, Tex.: Word Books, 1988.

―――. *Unity and Diversity in the New Testament*. London: SCM Press, 1977.

du Preez, J. "'Sperma autou' in 1 John 3:9." *Neot* 9 (1975): 105–12.

Ehrman, B. "The New Testament Canon of Didymus the Blind." *VC* 37 (1983): 1–21.

―――. *The Orthodox Corruption of Scripture*. New York: Oxford University Press, 1993.

Elliott, J. H. *1 Peter*. ABC 37B. New York: Doubleday, 2000.

Elliott, J. K. Review of D. Trobisch, *The First Edition of the New Testament*. *ExpT* 112.12 (2001): 422–23.

Elliott-Binns, L. E. *Galilean Christianity*. London: SCM Press, 1956.

―――. "James 1:18: Creation or Redemption?" *NTS* 3 (1956): 148–61.

Epp, E. J. "Issues in the Interrelation of New Testament Textual Criticism and Canon." Pages 485–515 in McDonald and Sanders, *Canon Debate*.

Evans, C., R. Webb, and R. Wiebe. *Nag Hammadi Texts and the Bible: A Synopsis and Index.* Leiden: Brill, 1993.

Evans, C. A. "From Gospel to Gospel: The Function of Isaiah in the New Testament." Pages 651–91 in *Writing and Reading the Scroll of Isaiah: Studies of an Interpretive Tradition.* Vol. 2. Edited by C. C. Broyles and C. A. Evans. Leiden: Brill, 1997.

Fahey, M. *Cyprian and the Bible: A Study in Third-Century Exegesis.* Tübingen: J. C. B. Mohr, 1971.

Farkasfalvy, D. M. "The Ecclesial Setting of Pseudepigraphy in Second Peter and its Role in the Formation of the Canon." *SecCent* 5 (1985): 3–29.

Farmer, W. R. "Some Critical Reflections on Second Peter: A Response to a Paper on Second Peter by Dennis Farkasfalvy." *SecCent* 5 (1985): 30–46.

Farmer, W. R., and D. M. Farkasfalvy. *The Formation of the New Testament Canon.* New York: Paulist Press, 1983.

Ferguson, E. "Catholic Church." *Encyclopedia of Early Christianity.* 2nd ed. New York: Garland, 1998.

———. "Factors Leading to the Selection and Closure of the New Testament Canon." Pages 295–320 in McDonald and Sanders, *Canon Debate.*

Fee, G. *The First Epistle to the Corinthians.* NICNT. Grand Rapids: Eerdmans, 1987.

Fischer, B. *Beiträge zur Geschichte der Lateinischen Bibeltexte.* VL 12. Freiburg: Verlag Herder, 1986.

Francis, F. O. "The Form and Function of the Opening and Closing Paragraphs of James and 1 John." *ZNW* 61 (1970): 110–26.

Francis, J. "'Like Newborn Babes'—The Image of the Child in 1 Peter 2:2-3." *StudBib* 3 (1978): 111–17.

Franzmann, M. *Jesus in the Nag Hammadi Writings.* Edinburgh: T&T Clark, 1996.

Gaertner, B. *The Theology of the Gospel of Thomas.* London: Collins, 1961.

Gamble, H. *Books and Readers in the Early Church: A History of Early Christian Texts.* New Haven: Yale University Press, 1995.

———. *The New Testament Canon: Its Making and Meaning.* Philadelphia: Fortress, 1985.

———. "The New Testament Canon: Recent Research and the *Status Quaestionis.*" Pages 267–94 in McDonald and Sanders, *Canon Debate.*

Goehring, J. E. *The Crosby-Schøyen Codex, MS 193.* CSCO 521. Louvain: Peeters, 1990.

Goodspeed, E. *A History of Early Christian Literature* (Revised and enlarged by Robert M. Grant). Chicago: University of Chicago Press, 1966.

Goppelt, L. *A Commentary on 1 Peter.* Edited by F. Hahn. Translated by J. E. Alsup. Grand Rapids: Eerdmans, 1993.

Grant, R. M. *The Formation of the New Testament.* New York: Harper & Row, 1965.

———. "Early Alexandrian Christianity." *CH* 40 (1970): 133–44.

———. *A Historical Introduction to the New Testament.* London: William Collins & Sons, 1971.

———. *Eusebius as Church Historian.* Oxford: Clarendon, 1980.

———. *Irenaeus of Lyons.* London: Routledge, 1997.

Green, G. L. "The Use of the Old Testament for Christian Ethics in 1 Peter." *TynB* 41.2 (1990): 276–89.

Gregory, A. *The Reception of Luke and Acts in the Period Before Irenaeus: Looking for Luke in the Second Century.* Tübingen: Mohr Siebeck, 2003.

Gustafsson, B. "Eusebius' Principles In Handling His Sources As Found In His Church History, Books I–VII." *TU* 79 (1961): 429–41.

Guthrie, D. *New Testament Introduction: Hebrews to Revelation*. 4th ed. Downers Grove, Ill.: InterVarsity, 1990.

Haas, C. "Job's Perseverance in the Testament of Job." Pages 117–54 in *Studies on the Testament of Job*. SNTSMS 66. Edited by M. Knibb and P. van der Horst. Cambridge: Cambridge University Press, 1989.

Haenchen, E. *The Acts of the Apostles: A Commentary*. Philadelphia: Westminster, 1971.

Hagner, D. *The Use of the Old and New Testaments in Clement of Rome*. NovTSup 34. Leiden: Brill, 1973.

Hahneman, G. *The Muratorian Fragment and the Development of the Canon*. Oxford: Clarendon, 1992.

Hanson, R. P. C. *Allegory and Event*. London: SCM Press, 1959.

———. *Tradition in the Early Church*. London: SCM Press, 1962.

Harnack, A. *Geschichte der altchristlichen Literatur bis Eusebius, II: Die Chronologie*. Vol. 1. Leipzig: Hinrichs'sche Buchhandlung, 1897.

———. *Marcion: The Gospel of the Alien God*. Translated by J. E. Steely and L. D. Bierma. Durham, N.C.: The Labyrinth Press, 1990.

———. *The Origin of the New Testament and the Most Important Consequences of the New Creation*. Translated by J. R. Wilkinson. New York: Macmillan, 1925.

Hartin, P. J. *James and the 'Q' Sayings of Jesus*. JSNTSup 47. Sheffield: Sheffield Academic, 1991.

———. *James*. SP 14. Collegeville, Minn.: Liturgical Press, 2003.

———. *James of Jerusalem: Heir to Jesus of Nazareth*. Collegeville, Minn.: Liturgical Press, 2004.

Hays, R. B. *Echoes of Scripture in the Letters of Paul*. New Haven: Yale University Press, 1989.

Helderman, J. "ANAPAUSIS in the Epistula Jacobi Apocrypha." Pages 34–43 in *Nag Hammadi and Gnosis*. Edited by R. Mcl. Wilson. Leiden: Brill, 1978.

Hengel, M. "Der Jakobusbrief als antipaulinische Polemik." Pages 248–78 in *Tradition and Interpretation in the New Testament*. FS E. Earle Ellis. Edited by G. F. Hawthorne and O. Betz. Grand Rapids: Eerdmans, 1987.

———. *Judaism and Hellenism*. Vol. 1. Translated by J. Bowdon. London: SCM Press, 1974.

Henige, D. *Historical Evidence and Argument*. Madison: University of Wisconsin Press, 2005.

Hennecke, E. and W. Schneemelcher, eds. *New Testament Apocrypha*. 2 vols. Translated by R. McL. Wilson. Philadelphia: Westminster, 1963.

Hiebert, D. E. "Designation of Readers in 1 Peter 1:1-2." *BibSac* 137 (1980): 64–75.

Hill, C. E. *The Johannine Corpus in the Early Church*. Oxford: Oxford University Press, 2004.

Hills, J. "Little children, keep yourselves from idols: 1 John 5:21 Reconsidered." *CBQ* 51.2 (1989): 285–310.

Hogan, M. "The Law in the Epistle of James," *SNTSU* A22 (1997).

Hoppe, R. *Der theologische Hintergrund des Jakobusbriefes*. FB 28. Würzburg: Echter Verlag, 1977.

Ingrams, L. et al. *The Oxyrhynchus Papyri*. Vol. 34. Egypt Exploration Society, 1968.

Jackson-McCabe, M. A. *Logos and Law in the Letter of James: The Law of Nature, the Law of Moses, and the Law of Freedom*. NovTSup 100. Leiden: Brill, 2001.

Jacobs, I. "The Midrashic Background for James 2:21-23." *NTS* 22 (1976): 457–64.

Jeremias, J. "Paul and James." *ExpT* 66 (1954–1955): 368–71.

Johnson, L. T. *Brother of Jesus, Friend of God: Studies in the Letter of James*. Grand Rapids: Eerdmans, 2004.

———. *The Letter of James*. ABC 37A. New York: Doubleday, 1995.

———. "The Use of Leviticus 19 in the Letter of James." *JBL* 101 (1982): 391–401.

———. *The Writings of the New Testament: An Interpretation*. Philadelphia: Fortress, 1986.

Kalin, E. "Re-Examining New Testament Canon History: 1) The Canon of Origen." *CurTM* 17 (1990): 274–82.

———. "The New Testament Canon of Eusebius." Pages 386–404 in McDonald and Sanders, *Canon Debate*.

Katz, P. "The Johannine Epistles in the Muratorian Canon." *JTS* 8 (1957): 273–74.

Kelly, J. N. D. *A Commentary on the Epistles of Peter and Jude*. BNTC. London: A&C Black, 1969.

———. *Jerome: His Life, Writings, and Controversies*. London: Duckworth, 1975.

Kenyon, F. *Our Bible and the Ancient Manuscripts*. London: Eyre & Spottiswoode, 1958.

Klein, M. *Ein vollkommenes Werk: Vollkommenheit, Gesetz und Gericht als theologische Themen des Jakobusbriefes*. BWANT 139. Stuttgart: W. Kohlhammer, 1995.

Klijn, A. F. J. "The Study of Jewish Christianity." *NTS* 20 (1973–1974): 419–31.

Kloppenborg, J. S. "The Reception of the Jesus Tradition in James." Pages 93–141 in Schlosser, *Catholic Epistles*.

Knox, W. L. "The Epistle of James." *JTS* 46 (1945): 10–17.

Koester, H. *History and Literature of Early Christianity*. Vol. 2 of *Introduction to the New Testament*. 2nd ed. New York: Walter de Gruyter, 2000.

Konradt, M. *Christliche Existenz nach dem Jakobusbrief*. SUNT 22. Göttingen: Vandenhoeck & Ruprecht, 1998.

———. "Der Jakobusbrief als Brief des Jakobus: Erwägungen zum historischen Kontext des Jakobusbriefes im Licht der traditionsgeschichtlichen Beziehungen zum 1 Petrusbrief und zum Hintergrund der Autorfiktion." Pages 16–53 in *Der Jakobusbrief: Beiträge zur Aufwertung der „strohernen Epistel.“* Edited by P. von Gemünden, et al. Münster: Lit Verlag, 2003.

Kummel, W. G. *Introduction to the New Testament*. London: SCM Press, 1975.

Lake, K. "The Sinaitic and Vatican Manuscripts and the Copies sent by Eusebius to Constantinople." *HTR* 11 (1918): 32–35.

Lampe, G. W. H. *A Patristic Greek Lexicon*. Oxford: Clarendon, 1961.

Lapham, F. *Peter: The Myth, the Man and the Writings*. JSNTSup 239. Sheffield: Sheffield Academic, 2003.

Laws, S. *The Epistle of James*. BNTC. Peabody, Mass.: Hendrickson, 1980.

Lemcio, E. E., and R. W. Wall, eds. *The New Testament as Canon: A Reader in Canonical Criticism*. JSNTS 76. Sheffield: Sheffield Academic, 1992.

Lieu, J. *Neither Jew Nor Greek? Constructing Early Christianity*. New York: T&T Clark, 2002.

———. *The 2nd and 3rd Epistles of John: History and Background*. Edinburgh: T&T Clark, 1986.

———. *The Theology of the Johannine Epistles*. Cambridge: Cambridge University Press, 1991.

Limberis, V. "The Provenance of the Caliphate Church: James 2:17-26 and Galatians 3 Reconsidered." Pages 397–420 in *Early Christian Interpretation of the Scriptures of Israel*.

JSNTSup 148. Edited by C. A. Evans and J. A. Sanders. Sheffield: Sheffield Academic, 1997.

Llewelyn, S. R. "The Prescript of James." *NovT* 39 (1997): 385–93.

Lodge, J. G. "James and Paul at Cross-Purposes? James 2:22." *Bib* 62 (1981): 195–213.

Lohse, E. *The Formation of the New Testament*. Translated by M. E. Boring. Nashville: Abingdon, 1981.

———. "Parenesis and Kerygma in 1 Peter." Pages 37–59 in *Perspectives on First Peter*. Edited by C. Talbert. Macon, Ga.: Mercer University Press, 1986. Eng. translation by John Steely of original German article (*ZNW* 45 [1954]: 68–89).

Longenecker, R. N. *Galatians*. WBC 41. Dallas: Word Books, 1990.

Luedemann, G. *Heretics: The Other Side of Christianity*. London: SCM Press, 1996.

———. *Opposition to Paul in Jewish Christianity*. Translated by M. E. Boring. Minneapolis: Fortress, 1989.

Luhrmann, D. "Gal. 2:9 und die katholischen Briefe." *ZNW* 72 (1981): 65–87.

Mack, B. *The Lost Gospel: The Book of Q and Christian Origins*. San Francisco: Harper, 1993.

Marshall, I. H. *The Epistles of John*. NICNT. Grand Rapids: Eerdmans, 1978.

Martin, R. P. *James*. WBC 48. Waco, Tex.: Word Books, 1988.

Marxsen, W. *Introduction to the New Testament: An Approach to its Problems*. Oxford: Basil Blackwell, 1968.

Mason, S. *Josephus and the New Testament*. 2nd ed. Peabody, Mass.: Hendrickson, 2003.

Massebieau, L. "L'epitre de Jacques: est-elle l'oeuvre d'un chretien?" *RHR* 31–32 (1895).

Mayor, J. B. *The Epistle of St. James*. 2nd ed. London: Macmillan, 1897.

McDonald, L. M. *The Formation of the Christian Biblical Canon*. Rev. ed. Peabody, Mass.: Hendrickson, 1995.

McDonald, L. M. and J. A. Sanders, eds. *The Canon Debate: On the Origins and Formation of the Bible*. Peabody, Mass.: Hendrickson, 2002.

McNeile, A. H. *An Introduction to the Study of the New Testament*. 2nd ed. Oxford: Clarendon, 1953.

Meade, D. *Pseudonymity and Canon*. WUNT 39. Tübingen: J. C. B. Mohr, 1986.

Meier, J. P. "The Testimonium: Evidence for Jesus Outside the Bible." *BRev* 7.3 (1991): 20–25.

Metzger, B. *The Canon of the New Testament: Its Origin, Development, and Significance*. Oxford: Clarendon, 1987.

———. *The Early Versions of the New Testament*. Oxford: Clarendon, 1977.

———. *Text of the New Testament*. Oxford: Clarendon, 1992.

Meyer, A. *Das Raetsel des Jakobusbriefes*. Giessen: Töpelmann, 1930.

Michaels, J. R. *1 Peter*. WBC 49. Waco, Tex.: Word Books, 1988.

Mitchell, M. "The Letter of James as a Document of Paulinism?" Unpublished paper presented at the 2005 SBL Annual Meeting.

Mitton, C. L. *The Epistle of James*. London: Marshall, Morgan & Scott, 1966.

Moffatt, J. *The General Epistles of James, Peter and Jude*. MNTC. London: Hodder & Stoughton, 1928.

———. *An Introduction to the Literature of the New Testament*. Edinburgh: T&T Clark, 1918.

Mommsen, T. "Zur Lateinischen Stichometrie." *Hermes* 21 (1886): 142–56.

Moo, D. J. *The Letter of James*. PNTC. Grand Rapids: Eerdmans, 2000.

Moroziuk, R. P. "The Meaning of ΚΑΘΟΛΙΚΟΣ in the Greek Fathers and Its Implications for Ecclesiology and Ecumenism." *PBR* 4 (1985): 90–104.

Moulton, J. H. "Synoptic Studies II: The Epistle of James and the Sayings of Jesus." *Exp* 7.4 (1907): 45–55.

Munck, J. *The Acts of the Apostles.* ABC 31. New York: Doubleday, 1967.

Mussner, F. *Der Jakobusbrief.* Freiburg: Verlag Herder, 1964.

———. "Die ethische Motivation im Jakobusbrief." Pages 416–23 in *Neues Testament und Ethik: Für Rudolf Schnackenburg.* Edited by Helmut Merklein. Freiburg: Herder, 1989.

Niebuhr, K. W. "Der Jakobusbrief im Licht fruehjudischer Diasporabriefe." *NTS* 44 (1998): 420–43.

———. "A New Perspective on James? Neuere Forschungen zum Jakobusbrief." *TLZ* 129 (2004): 1019–44.

Obermüller, R. "Hermeneutische Themen im Jakobusbrief." *Bib* 53.2 (1972): 234–44.

Oulton, J. E. L. "Rufinus's Translation of the Church History of Eusebius." *JTS* 30 (1928–1929): 150–74.

Painter, J. *Just James: The Brother of Jesus in History and Tradition.* Edinburgh: T&T Clark, 1999.

———. *1, 2, and 3 John.* SP 18. Collegeville, Minn.: Liturgical Press, 2002.

Parker, D. C. *Codex Bezae: An Early Christian Manuscript and its Text.* Cambridge: Cambridge University Press, 1992.

Parker, D. C., and C.-B. Amphoux. *Codex Bezae: Studies from the Lunel Colloquium, June 1994.* Leiden: Brill, 1996.

Penner, T. C. *The Epistle of James and Eschatology.* JSNTSup 121. Sheffield: Sheffield Academic, 1996.

Perdue, L. G. "Paraenesis and the Epistle of James." *ZNW* 72 (1981): 241–56.

Perkins, P. *First and Second Peter, James, and Jude.* Interpretation. Louisville: John Knox, 1995.

Popkes, W. "James and Paraenesis, Reconsidered." Pages 535–61 in *Texts and Contexts: Biblical Texts in Their Textual and Situational Contexts.* Edited by T. Fornberg and D. Hellholm. Oslo: Scandinavian University Press, 1995.

———. "James and Scripture: An Exercise in Intertextuality." *NTS* 45 (1999): 213–29.

———. "The Mission of James in his Time." Pages 88–99 in Chilton and Neusner, *Brother of Jesus.*

———. "New Testament Principles of Wholeness." *EvQ* 64.4 (1992): 319–32.

Pratscher, W. *Der Herrenbruder Jakobus und die Jakobustradition.* FRLANT 139. Göttingen: Vandenhoeck & Ruprecht, 1987.

Puech, H.-Ch. "Gnostic Gospels and Related Documents." Pages 1:231–362 in Hennecke and Schneemelcher, *New Testament Apocrypha.*

Quasten, J. *The Beginnings of Patristic Literature.* Vol. 1 of *Patrology.* Antwerp: Spectum Publishers, 1986.

Quinn, J. D. "Notes on the Text of the P⁷²." *CBQ* 27 (1965): 241–49.

Reicke, B. *The Epistles of James, Peter, and Jude.* ABC 37. New York: Doubleday, 1964.

Reumann, J. *Righteousness in the New Testament.* Philadelphia: Fortress, 1982.

Ropes, J. *The Epistle of St. James.* ICC. Edinburgh: T&T Clark, 1916.

Rusch, W. G. *The Later Latin Fathers.* London: Duckworth, 1977.

Sanders, J. A. "Adaptable for Life: the Nature and Function of Canon." Pages 531–60 in *Magnolia Dei—The Mighty Acts of God: Essays on the Bible and Archaeology in Memory of G. Ernst Wright.* Edited by F. M. J. Cross, et al. Garden City: Doubleday, 1976.

————. *Canon and Community: A Guide to Canonical Criticism*. Philadelphia: Fortress, 1984.

————. *Torah and Canon*. Philadelphia: Fortress, 1972.

Sanders, J. T. *Ethics in the New Testament: Change and Development*. London: SCM Press, 1975.

Sawyer, J. F. *The Fifth Gospel: Isaiah in the History of Christianity*. Cambridge: Cambridge University Press, 1996.

Schlosser, J., ed. *The Catholic Epistles and the Tradition*. BETL 176. Leuven: Leuven University Press, 2004.

Schlosser, J. "Le Corpus Épîtres des Catholiques." Pages 3–41 in Schlosser, *Catholic Epistles*.

Schmithals, W. *The Office of an Apostle*. Nashville: Abingdon, 1965.

Schnackenburg, R. *The Johannine Epistles: A Commentary*. Translated by R. Fuller and I. Fuller. Kent: Burns & Oates, 1992.

Schoedel, W. R. "Scripture and the Seventy-Two Heavens of the First Apocalypse of James." *NovT* 12 (1970): 118–29.

Scrivener, F. H. *Bezae Codex Cantabrigiensis: being an exact Copy, in ordinary Type, of the celebrated Uncial Graeco-Latin Manuscript of the Four Gospels and Acts of the Apostles, written early in the Sixth Century, and presented to the University of Cambridge by Theodore Beza A.D. 1581. Edited, with a critical Introduction, Annotations, and Facsimiles*. Cambridge: Cambridge University Press, 1864.

Scott, J. J. "James the Relative of Jesus and the Expectation of an Eschatological Priest." *JETS* 25.3 (1982): 323–31.

Seitz, O. J. F. "The Relationship of the Shepherd of Hermas to the Epistle of James." *JBL* 63 (1944): 131–40.

Selwyn, E. G. *The First Epistle of St. Peter*. London: MacMillan, 1947.

Sevenster, J. N. *Do You Know Greek? How Much Greek Could the First Jewish Christians Have Known?* NovTSup 19. Leiden: Brill, 1968.

Shepherd, M. H. "The Epistle of James and the Gospel of Matthew." *JBL* 75 (1956): 40–51.

Sheppard, G. T. "Canon." Entry in *Encyclopedia of Religion*, 3.62–69. Edited by M. Eliade. New York: Macmillan, 1987.

————. "Canonical Criticism." In *ABD* 1.861–66. Edited by D. N. Freedman. New York: Doubleday, 1992.

Sidebottom, E. M. *James, Jude and 2 Peter*. CBC. London: Thomas Nelson & Sons, 1967.

Siker, J. "The Canonical Status of the Catholic Epistles in the Syriac New Testament." *JTS* 38 (1987): 311–40.

Skeat, T. C. "The Codex Sinaiticus, the Codex Vaticanus, and Constantine." *JTS* 50 (1999): 583–625.

Smalley, S. *1, 2, 3 John*. WBC 51. Dallas: Word Books, 2002.

Smith, M. *Clement of Alexandria and a Secret Gospel of Mark*. Cambridge, Mass.: Harvard University Press, 1973.

Soards, M. L. "The Early Christian Interpretation of Abraham and the Place of James within That Context." *IBS* 9 (1987): 18–26.

————. "1 Peter, 2 Peter, and Jude as Evidence for a Petrine School." *ANRW* II.25.5, 3827–49. Berlin: Walter de Gruyter, 1988.

Souter, A. *The Text and Canon of the New Testament*. London: Duckworth, 1913.

Spina, F. "Canonical Criticism: Childs Versus Sanders." Pages 165–94 in *Interpreting God's Word for Today: An Inquiry Into Hermeneutics From a Biblical Theological Perspective*. Edited by W. McCown and J. E. Massey. Anderson, Ind.: Warner Press, 1982.

Spitta, F. *Der Brief des Jakobus untersucht*. Göttingen: Vandenhoek & Ruprecht, 1896.

Spittler, R. P. "Job, Testament of." In *ABD* 3.869–71. Edited by D. N. Freedman. New York: Doubleday, 1992.

Stowers, S. "The Diatribe." Pages 71–83 in *Greco-Roman Literature and the New Testament: Selected Forms and Genres*. SBLSBS 21. Edited by D. Aune. Atlanta: Scholars Press, 1988.

Strecker, G. "On the Problem of Jewish Christianity." Pages 241–85 in *Orthodoxy and Heresy in Earliest Christianity*. Edited by W. Bauer. London: SCM Press, 1971.

Sundberg, A. C. "Canon Muratori: A Fourth-Century List." *HTR* 66.1 (1973): 1–41.

———. "Dependent Canonicity in Irenaeus and Tertullian." *SE* 3.2 (1964): 403–9.

———. "The Making of the New Testament Canon." Pages 1216–24 in *Interpreter's One Volume Commentary on the Bible*. Edited by C. M. Laymon. London: Wm. Collins Sons, 1971.

———. "Towards a Revised History of the New Testament Canon." *SE* 4 [= *TU* 102] (1968): 452–61.

Tasker, R. *The General Epistle of James*. London: Tyndale Press, 1956.

Telfer, W., ed. *Cyril of Jerusalem and Nemesius of Emesa*. LCC 4. London: SCM, 1955.

Theissen, G. *The New Testament*. London: T&T Clark, 2003.

Thiele, W. "Probleme der Versio Latina in den Katholischen Briefen." Pages 93–94 in *Die Alten Übersetzungen des Neuen Testaments, Die Kirchenväterzitate und lektionare*. ANTF 5. Edited by K. Aland. Berlin: Walter de Gruyter, 1972.

Thompson, M. *Clothed with Christ: The Example and Teaching of Jesus in Romans 12.1–15.13*. JSNTSup 59. Sheffield: JSOT Press, 1991.

Townsend, M. J. *The Epistle of James*. London: Epworth, 1994.

Trigg, J. *Origen: The Bible and Philosophy in the Third-Century Church*. Atlanta: John Knox, 1983.

Trobisch, D. *The First Edition of the New Testament*. Oxford: Oxford University Press, 2000.

Trudinger, L. P. "ETEPON ΔΕ ΤΩΝ ΑΠΟΣΤΟΛΩΝ ΟΥΚ ΕΙΔΟΝ, ΕΙ ΜΗ ΙΑΚΩΒΟΝ: A Note on Galatians i.19." *NovT* 17.3 (1975): 200–202.

Turner, N. *Style*. Vol. 4 of *A Grammar of New Testament Greek*. Edinburgh: T&T Clark, 1976.

Ulrich, E. "The Notion and Definition of Canon," in *Canon Debate*, 21–35.

Uro, R. "*Thomas* and the Oral Gospel Tradition." Pages 8–32 in *Thomas at the Crossroads: Essays on the Gospel of Thomas*. Edited by Risto Uro. Edinburgh: T&T Clark, 1998.

van Unnik, W. C. "'Diaspora' and 'Church' in the First Centuries of Christian History." Pages 95–103 in *Sparsa Collectica III: The Collected Essays of W. C. Unnik*. NovTSup 31. Leiden: Brill, 1983.

———. "Solitude and Community in the New Testament." Pages 241–47 in *Sparsa Collectica II: The Collected Essays of W. C. Unnik*. NovTSup 30. Leiden: Brill, 1980.

Vielhauer, P. "Jewish-Christian Gospels." Pages 1:117–65 in Hennecke and Schneemelcher, *New Testament Apocrypha*.

Verseput, D. J. "James 1:17 and the Jewish Morning Prayers." *NovT* 39.2 (1997): 177–91.

———. "Genre and Story: The Community Setting of the Epistle of James." *CBQ* 62.1 (2000): 96–110.

———. "Reworking the Puzzle of Faith and Deeds in James 2:14-26." *NTS* 43 (1997): 97–115.

Via, D. "The Right Strawy Epistle Reconsidered: A Study in Biblical Ethics and Hermeutic." *JR* 49 (1969): 253–67.

Wachob, W. H. *The Voice of Jesus in the Social Rhetoric of James.* SNTSMS 106. Cambridge: Cambridge University Press, 2000.

Wall, R. *Community of the Wise: The Letter of James.* Valley Forge, Pa.: Trinity Press International, 1997.

———. "The Canonical Function of 2 Peter." *BibInt.* 9.1 (2001): 64–81.

———. "Ecumenicity and Ecclesiology: The Promise of the Multiple Letter Canon of the New Testament." Pages 184–207 in Lemcio and Wall, *New Testament as Canon.*

———. "The Function of the Pastoral Letters Within the Pauline Canon of the New Testament: A Canonical Approach." Pages 35–36 in *The Pauline Canon.* Edited by Stanley E. Porter. Leiden: Brill, 2004.

———. "Introduction to Epistolary Literature." Pages 369–91 in *NIB* 10. Nashville: Abingdon, 2002.

———. "The Problem of the Multiple Letter Canon of the New Testament." Pages 161–83 in Lemcio and Wall, *New Testament as Canon.*

———. "A Unifying Theology of the Catholic Epistles: A Canonical Approach." Pages 43–71 in Schlosser, *Catholic Epistles.*

Wallace-Hadrill, D. S. *Eusebius of Caesarea.* London: Mowbray, 1960.

Walton, D. "Nonfallacious Arguments from Ignorance." *APQ* 29.4 (1992): 381–87.

———. "The Appeal to Ignorance, or *Argumentum ad Ignorantiam.*" *Argumentation* 13 (1999): 367–77.

———. "Informal Fallacy." Pages 431–35 in *The Cambridge Dictionary of Philosophy.* 2nd ed. Edited by R. Audi. Cambridge: Cambridge University Press, 1999.

Ward, R. "James of Jerusalem in the First Two Centuries." *ANRW* II.26.1, 779–812. Berlin: Walter de Gruyter, 1988.

———. "The Works of Abraham: James 2:14-26." *HTR* 61 (1968): 283–90.

Watson, D. F. "James 2 in Light of Greco-Roman Schemes of Argumentation." *NTS* 39 (1993): 94–121.

———. "A Reassessment of the Rhetoric of the Epistle of James and its Implications for Christian Origins." Unpublished essay, read at the 2005 Annual Meeting of the Society of Biblical Literature.

Webb, R. "Catholic Epistles." *ABD* 2.569–70. Edited by D. N. Freedman. New York: Doubleday, 1992.

Westcott, B. F. *A General Survey of the History of the Canon of the New Testament.* 6th ed. Grand Rapids: Baker Books, 1980.

Wilkins, M. J. "Prayer." Pages 941–48 in *Dictionary of the Later New Testament and its Developments.* Edited by R. P. Martin and P. Davids. Downers Grove: InterVarsity, 1997.

Williams, M. A. *Rethinking "Gnosticism": An Argument for Dismantling a Dubious Category.* Princeton: Princeton University Press, 1996.

Williams, R. R. *The Letters of John and James.* CBC. Cambridge: Cambridge University Press, 1965.

Windisch, H. *Die katholischen Briefe.* HNT 15. Edited by H. Preisker. Tübingen: Mohr, 1951.

Witherington, B. *Jesus the Sage: The Pilgrimage of Wisdom.* Edinburgh: T&T Clark, 1994.

Yates, J. P. "The Reception of the Epistle of James in the Latin West: Did Athanasius Play a Role?" Pages 273–88 in Schlosser, *Catholic Epistles.*

Young, F. "The Non-Pauline Epistles." Pages 290–304 in *The Cambridge Companion to Biblical Interpretation*. Cambridge: Cambridge University Press, 1998.

Zahn, T. *Geschichte des neutestamentlichen Kanons*. 2 vols. Leipzig: Erlangen, 1888–1892.

INDEX OF SELECTED ANCIENT PERSONS, AUTHORS AND TEXTS

Hermas, Shepherd of, 30–31, 41, 46, 72, 75, 104, 115, 118–20, 167, 237, 255

Hilary of Poitiers, 82, 97, 120

Hippolytus of Rome, 45, 97, 242

Ignatius of Antioch, 10–11, 20, 27, 37, 69, 242

Irenaeus of Lyon, 11, 16, 19–20, 24–25, 27, 30–45, 47, 64, 81, 88–89, 94, 97, 105, 132, 136, 173, 230, 238, 242–43, 250, 256; *Adversus haereses/Against Heresies,* 20, 27, 34–38, 78, 88, 105, 132, 136, 173, 242

Isidore of Seville, 85

Jerome, 10, 46, 53, 82–87, 95, 97, 99–100, 117, 130, 132, 201, 243, 245, 252

John Chrysostom, 81, 91

Josephus, 56, 111, 121–22, 126–28, 134, 145, 148–49, 243, 253

Junilius Africanus, 84, 95

Justin Martyr, 27, 195

Marcion, 16–17, 20, 25, 35, 37–40, 42–44, 59–60, 62, 89, 159–60, 173, 197, 230, 235–38, 245, 247, 251

Muratorian Fragment, 9, 46, 76, 86, 97, 243, 251–52

Origen of Alexandria, 10, 19, 24–26, 30, 33–34, 52–64, 67–70, 78, 85–89, 96, 99, 101–102, 104–5, 118, 129, 132–33, 201, 224, 230, 234, 238, 241, 243–44, 249, 252, 256

Philo of Alexandria, 51, 114, 246

Philoxenus of Mabbug, 80, 91

Photius of Constantinople, 49, 244

Protevangelium of James, 129, 137–38, 148, 151, 244

Pseudo-Ambrose, 82, 95, 97

Pseudo-Clementine, *Recognitions,* 132, 140, 146, 172, 245

Rufinus of Aquileia, 50, 53, 58, 61–62, 82, 84, 86–87, 95, 245, 254

Tatian, 80–81

Tertullian of Carthage, 16, 19–20, 24–25, 32, 39–44, 47, 51–52, 64, 88–89, 94, 97, 103, 105, 230, 238, 245, 247, 256; *Adversus Marcionem/Against Marcion,* 20, 40, 42–43, 88, 105, 245

Theodore of Mopsuestia, 81, 91

Theodoret of Cyrus, 81, 91

Thomas, Gospel of, 103, 108, 129, 139–42, 167, 242, 244, 250, 256

Victorinus of Pettau, 10, 245

Index of Selected Modern Authors